ENGAGING AFRICA

Washington and the Fall of Portugal's Colonial Empire

Witney W. Schneidman

with a Foreword by Frank C. Carlucci, III

University Press of America,® Inc.
Dallas · Lanham · Boulder · New York · Oxford

University Press of America,® Inc.
4501 Forbes Boulevard
Suite 200
Lanham, Maryland 20706
UPA Acquisitions Department (301) 459-3366

PO Box 317
Oxford
OX2 9RU, UK

Printed in the United States of America
British Library Cataloging in Publication Information Available

Library of Congress Control Number: 2003114775
ISBN 0-7618-2812-5 (paperback : alk. ppr.)

The paper used in this publication meets the minimum requirements of American National Standard for Information Sciences—Permanence of Paper for Printed Library Materials, ANSI Z39.48—1984

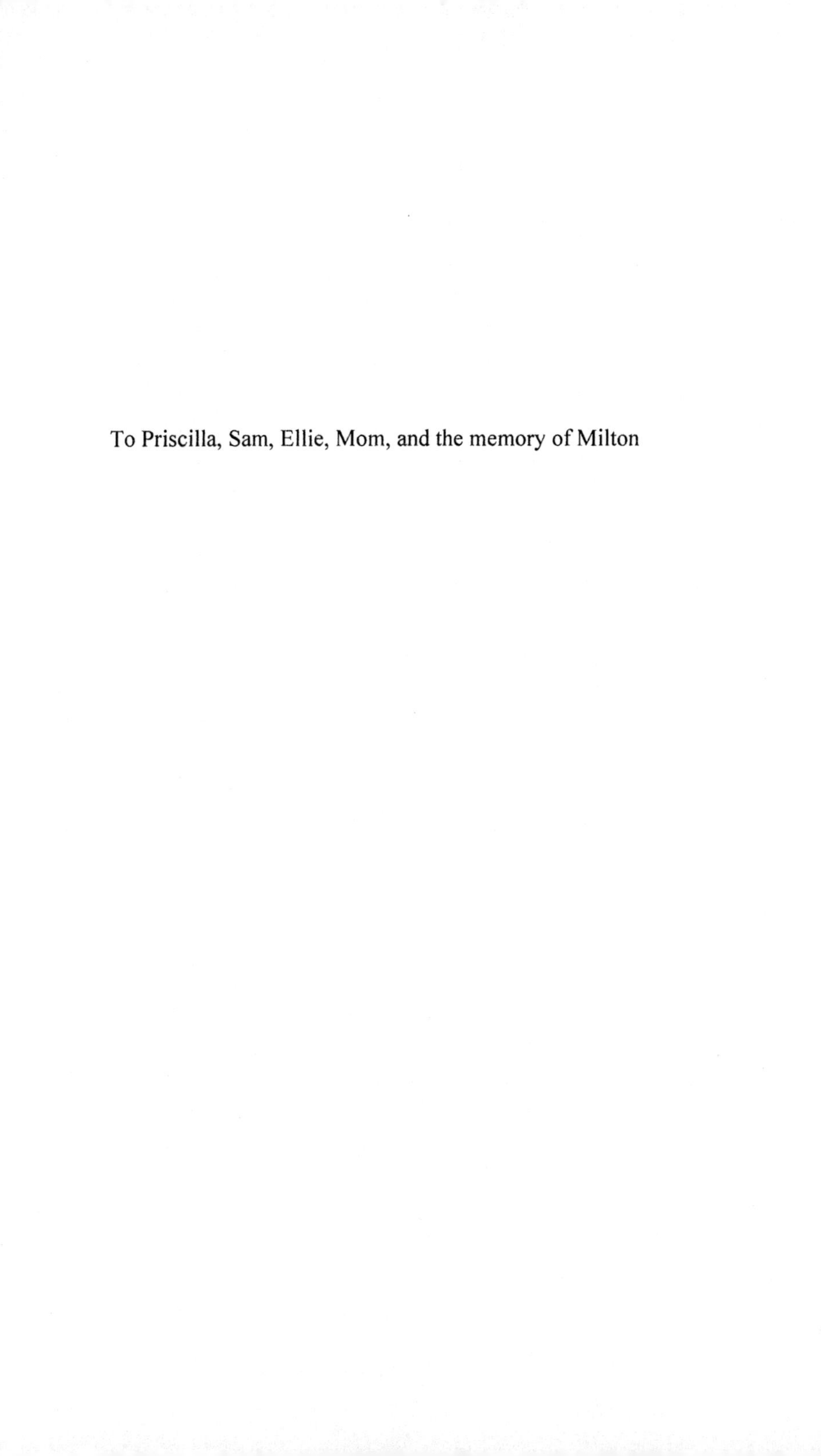

To Priscilla, Sam, Ellie, Mom, and the memory of Milton

Not the least of the acts of statesmanship is gracefully to grant what eventually cannot be withheld.

Edmund Burke

Contents

Chapter 3:
Nixon, Caetano, and Spínola: Partners in Uncertainty

Chapter 4:
Kissinger, Carlucci, and Portugal's Revolution

Foreword

By Frank C. Carlucci, III

The wave of anticolonialism that swept Africa in the early 1960s caught the West by surprise, although the warning signs had been there prior to that time. The wonder is not that Portugal succumbed but that it was able to delay the inevitable as long as it did. Ultimately Portugal was surprised by the strength of the anticolonial movement that started in the colonies and led to the toppling of a dictatorship and the liberation of the colonies.

United States government policy-makers were not unaware of the danger to a NATO ally, but they were torn between supporting African aspirations and protecting our strategic military equities in the Azores. In the end we did nothing, and the communists occupied the vacuum.

Our policy in Africa was largely driven by Cold War considerations although democratic values and human rights did play a role. Would Africa have developed differently had it been otherwise? I doubt it. New leaders were all too willing to sacrifice Africa's competitive advantage in agriculture to buy urban peace, and the resources that poured in from East and West were in large measure squandered. Africa can blame many of its problems on colonialism and rightly so—but that doesn't excuse a lack of leadership in many countries in the post-independence period.

While the Africa tragedy continues, the Portuguese story has a happy ending. A small country, it divested a vast empire, overthrew one dictatorship and went to the brink of another, drew back from civil war and installed a fully functioning democracy that flourishes today. All this happened in two years with very little bloodshed. Arguably, Portugal was the model for the emergence of democracy in Spain and the model for the spread of democracy in Latin America.

Witney Schneidman puts these events into perspective. His work is methodically researched and his conclusions carefully drawn. The description of postrevolutionary Portugal is as accurate as any I have seen. The policy options were clear: isolate Portugal as a lesson to others or work from within to promote democratic evolution. Since the odds were against democracy, the choice the West made to support the democratic forces was not easy, but it worked.

Portuguese Africa and Portugal is a dramatic story, unique in the annals of history. Witney Schneidman has rendered a great service by taking on a neglected tale and telling it extremely well.

Preface

United States policy toward Portugal and its African colonies, Angola, Mozambique, and Guinea-Bissau, defined the contours of American engagement toward Sub-Saharan Africa during the Cold War. Whether it was American policy toward colonial rule in the Portuguese colonies, white minority rule in Rhodesia, or apartheid in South Africa, a constantly vexing issue for policy-makers was how to integrate the twin imperatives of America's historic commitment to self-determination and its geostrategic preoccupation with containing the expansion of Communist influence in Africa. In the case of Portugal and its African colonies, the issue initially played out as a contest between maintaining access to the Azores, the strategically located and Portuguese-controlled military bases in the mid-Atlantic, and pressuring Lisbon to decolonize. It culminated in Portugal's politically tense transition from dictatorship to democracy and a deadly military test of wills between the United States and the Soviet Union in Angola, with the involvement of a host of other nations, including South Africa and Cuba.

The Kennedy administration viewed African nationalism, especially in Portugal's African colonies, as a political reality and inevitable. President John F. Kennedy and his advisers in the White House and the State Department felt that African aspirations for independence deserved American support, as opposed to indifference or opposition. Moreover, working to engage the newly independent nations of Africa and facilitating the transition to independence in Portugal's colonies was seen as an effective preemptive strategy for containing the expansion of Communist influence in Africa. Other advisers in the State Department and the Pentagon thought that such an approach would weaken Portugal, undermine NATO, and open the door to Soviet and Chinese expansion in the region. Efforts to devise a strategy that incorporated these divergent views characterized the Kennedy approach toward Portugal, Angola, and Mozambique and resulted, ultimately, in an ineffective policy.

When Lyndon Johnson succeeded Kennedy as president, the new administration acknowledged that Africa was an important issue, but the urgency for engagement had dissipated. Portugal's prime minister, António Salazar, was unwilling to allow the colonies in Africa any autonomy, let alone independence. His skilled and combative foreign minister, Franco Nogueira, was adept at deflecting all international pressure on Portugal to decolonize. In relations with Washington, Nogueira outlasted all of those who advocated independence for Angola, Mozambique, and Guinea-Bissau. Moreover, the lack of Soviet and Chinese activity in Africa in the latter part of the Johnson administration was a further rationale for Washington's limited attention to the region, and Portugal's colonies in particular.

Nevertheless, in a speech to the African diplomatic corps on 26 May 1966, Lyndon Johnson tried to use American policy toward the region to demonstrate that his administration's foreign policy was not consumed with the war in Vietnam. The lack of follow-up to his speech and the lack of implementation of the imaginative development strategy that he announced on the occasion consigned American policy to Africa to the realm of an afterthought.

The dilemma over "Africa versus the Azores," quiescent in the Johnson administration, ceased to exist completely when the Nixon administration embraced Lisbon and the white minority governments of Rhodesia and South Africa as an element of its strategy of détente and containment. For Lisbon, however, the relaxation of the arms embargo was insufficient for a regime that desperately needed armaments to shore up its faltering military position in Africa. In fact, in the small West African colony of Guinea-Bissau, to which no American administration paid any attention even when Africa was a priority for Washington, the Portuguese government had essentially lost the war against the Partido Africano para a Independência da Guiné e Cabo Verde (PAIGC). The situation became a crisis when Salazar's successor, Marcello Cateano, rebuffed General Spínola, commander of Portugal's military in Guinea-Bissau, who wanted to negotiate an end to the conflict with the PAIGC guerrillas. Spínola's troops were exhausted and demoralized by the decade-old war. The popular general also wanted to facilitate a peaceful transition to independence that would salvage some influence for Portugal in the postcolonial era. When Caetano refused Spínola's overtures and reaffirmed his commitment to Portugal's colonial presence in Africa, the seeds were planted for the demise of the Portuguese dictatorship by radicalized factions of the armed forces.

Oblivious to the fact that the Portuguese regime was about to crumble, the American secretary of state, Henry Kissinger, sought to strengthen Portugal militarily as a way to express appreciation to the Caetano government for allowing the U.S. to use the Azores as a refueling location during the 1973 Arab-Israeli war. When the State Department received a cable from the American embassy in Lisbon on the morning of 25 April 1974 stating that the city was "tense but calm" following a coup d'etat, Washington showed little concern. In fact, one of the most confrontational chapters of the Cold War was about to begin. Initially, Washington said that the coup leaders were "well-known" and "very pro-Western." Over the next eighteen months, Portugal became the first Western government to have communist members in its leadership and Washington sought to isolate Portugal within NATO. In Angola, the Ford Administration initiated a covert military war that ultimately failed for its lack of understanding of the African political environment as well as for the policy's lack of support in the U.S. Congress.

The narrative in this story, based on nearly one hundred interviews, hundreds of declassified policy documents, and many secondary sources, is shaped by an effort to understand the how successive administrations conducted policy toward Portugal, Angola, and Mozambique. More specifically, it addresses the degree to which the United States anticipated the prospects for, and the imminence of, a coup d'etat in Portugal and considers the questions, why did the Kennedy and Ford administrations pay significant attention to the problems presented by Portugal, Angola, and Mozambique whereas the Johnson and Nixon administrations virtually ignored these issues? To what degree did government officials reach out to opposition figures in Portugal, Angola, and Mozambique in anticipation that one day they might be in power? And finally, how much influence was the Africa Bureau in the State Department able to exercise when it came to U.S. policy toward Portugal and Mozambique, and under what circumstances did U.S. in Portugal and Europe determine the American approach to this enduring policy conundrum?

At its heart *Engaging Africa: Washington and the Fall of Portugal's Colonial Empire* is a largely untold story about how the United States engaged in one of the most important episodes in Africa's decolonization experience. It is also the story of how Washington responded to efforts by the Portuguese Communist Party and its radical allies in the Armed Forces Movement to seize control of the government following the coup of 25 April. Finally, *Engaging Africa* is a story about how Africa policy was made during the Cold War as well as the individuals who left their indelible mark on this process.

It is important to note that Portugal's colonial possessions in Africa also included Cape Verde and São Tomé and Principe and, in Asia, East Timor. Their decolonization experience falls outside the scope of this study.

Witney W. Schneidman
Alexandria, Virginia
7 August 2003

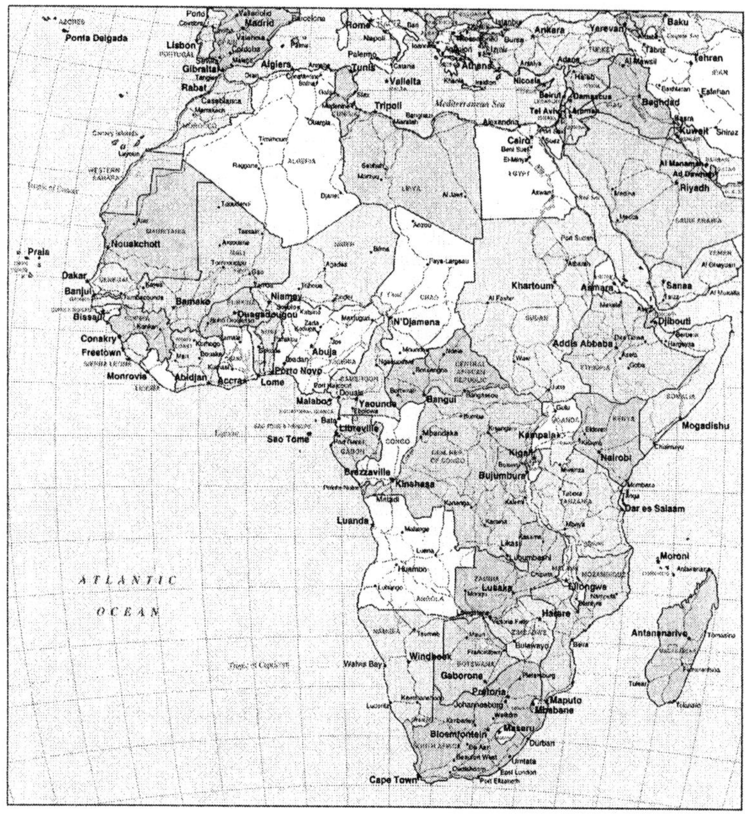

Note. From A. Smith (Ed.), *Facts on File* (New York: Winston, 1999). Used with permission.

Chapter 1

Kennedy and Salazar: Africa versus the Azores

New Strains on American Foreign Policy

The fifteenth session of the United Nations General Assembly marked the time of the Africans. In 1960, the UN admitted fifteen African nations, which signaled the onset of the era of African independence and decolonization. The African nations were young, inexperienced, poor, and unpredictable. More than their flowing robes and grave dignity differentiated the leaders of these nations from their European counterparts. The African leaders each echoed in their way the words of Togo's President Sylvanus Olympio, "Our purpose is not to be drawn into the conflict between the great powers." The African countries were avowedly neutralist but were limited in their ability to conduct that kind of diplomacy. At the same time, the twenty-two African members of the UN garnered influence from the fact that together with the Asian states, the "Afro-Asian bloc," as it was known, constituted the largest in the UN, comprising forty-four of the organization's ninety-eight members.[1]

The Soviet premier, Nikita Khrushchev, was confrontational, blunt, and tireless in his effort to establish the Soviet Union as a protector of the newly independent states. At the UN, he wanted to replace the office of Secretary-General with a three-headed executive composed of one Western, one Communist, and a Third World official. This scheme constituted an attempt to take revenge on Secretary General Dag Hammorskjold for supporting Western proposals to send troops to the Congo[2] to calm a nationalist rebellion following that country's independence in July 1960. The proposal was also calculated to play to neutralist vanities.

President Dwight D. Eisenhower was equally determined to impress upon the African leaders the benefits of American friendship and largesse. In his speech to the General Assembly in September 1960, Eisenhower outlined an elaborate aid program for Africa, signaled American support for UN policies in Africa, and declared American backing for the UN Secretary-General. The day after Eisenhower's speech, the American secretary of state, Christian Herter, handed Dag Hammarskjold a check for five million dollars as advance payment for the UN peacekeeping mission in the Congo.

The Soviet leader was not to be outdone. In a less dramatic but equally purposeful move, Khrushchev proposed that the General Assembly adopt a declaration on the right of all remaining colonies to independence. He wanted to test publicly the American willingness to declare its unequivocal support for the elimination of colonialism and African self-determination.

Throughout the final months of 1960, the American delegation at the UN worked feverishly and successfully to soften the anti-Western language in Khrushchev's proposed resolution. The delegates had been told by the White House and the State Department that they would vote for the resolution if it did not isolate those American allies who still had colonies in Africa.

As the resolution was being presented for a vote in the General Assembly, President Eisenhower deferred to a last minute appeal from British Prime Minister Harold Macmillan not to vote in favor of it; Eisenhower sent instructions to New York to abstain. The American delegation at the UN was furious and protested its voting instructions to the White House—but to no avail.

Khrushchev's proposal, which called for "a speedy and unconditional end to colonialism in all its forms and manifestations," was adopted by the General Assembly on 14 December 1960 by a unanimous vote of eighty-nine to zero, with nine abstentions including the US, Great Britain, France, Portugal, and South Africa. In a burst of defiance, Zelma Watson George, a member of the US delegation at the UN, impulsively stood at her chair on the Assembly floor to join the Third World and Eastern Bloc delegates in applause.[3]

With the abstention, the United States "failed dismally" a crucial test of great power attitudes on decolonization. Deference to European sensitivities would constrain many American actions and attitudes toward events on the continent. Indeed, Washington and its European allies practiced an "unspoken" division of labor in the Third World, especially in Africa, where the US would play a secondary role. Washington also would consistently calibrate its moves toward Africa as if the Soviet Union were the most important state in the region. In addition, the bureaucratic scrap between the American delegation at the UN and senior officials in Washington over how to vote on the resolution would be repeated numerous times as "Africanists" and "Europeanists" in the administration grappled for influence over US policy toward Africa.[4]

Nevertheless, the dominant contours of American policy on African self-determination had been drawn: an abiding concern for European and Soviet interests in Africa and tepid support for African aspirations for self-determination.

Not content with his role in the nonbinding UN resolution, Khrushchev made an even bolder effort to portray the Soviet Union as the champion of the Third World independence movement. In a speech in early January 1961 at the Academy of Social Sciences in Moscow, the Soviet leader reaffirmed the Soviet pledge of peaceful coexistence with the United States. At the same time, Khrushchev made a distinction between world wars and wars of national liberation, which he characterized as "just," "sacred," and "inevitable." The Soviet Premier proclaimed that in circumstances in which Third World people were fighting for the end of colonial rule, they would receive full support from all Communist states.[5]

Khrushchev's speech made a "conspicuous impression" on the US President-elect, John F. Kennedy.[6] In his inaugural address several weeks later, Kennedy responded directly to Khrushchev's challenge, which he interpreted as evidence of the Soviet Union's "ambitions for world domination—ambitions which [the Soviet leadership] fully restated only a short time ago." Kennedy warned the Soviet Premier and other Communist leaders that the US was prepared to "pay any price, bear any burden, meet any hardship, support any friend, oppose any foe to assure the survival and success of liberty." He also cautioned those newly independent nations "who foolishly sought power by riding the back of the tiger" that they would end up under Communist control.[7]

Kennedy's view of the American role in the Third World was predicated on preventing the expansion and dominance of Communist—particularly Soviet—influence. The specter of fragile governments in Africa, Asia, and Latin America collapsing under the governments in Africa, Asia, and Latin America collapsing under the weight of Communist insurgents was at the heart of the Kennedy administration's concern for the Third World in January 1961. At the same time, Kennedy was determined to win the support of the newly independent nations—and assist those that were struggling for self-determination. In Kennedy's view, this strategy was consistent with the historical experience of the United States. It also enabled his administration to gain bipartisan support for containing the spread of Soviet influence in places such as Africa.

Kennedy galvanized his advisers to develop a new dimension of American foreign policy, the counterinsurgency program, to shepherd the process of change and independence in the Third World by both political and military means. In the eyes of two of Kennedy's principal counterinsurgency advisers, Roger Hilsman, director of the Bureau of Intelligence and Research, and Walt Rostow, director of the policy planning staff at the State Department, the primary political forces in the Third World originated in the "stresses and strains" inherent in the revolutionary break with the colonialism. Communism was "best understood as a disease in the transition to modernization."[8] Counterinsurgency programs, therefore, were designed to enhance the ability of newly independent nations to defend themselves during this transition, thereby denying the Soviet Union and the People's Republic of China and their allies, the "Sino-Soviet bloc," opportunities to exploit and influence these states.[9]

At his first National Security Council (NSC) Meeting on 1 February 1961, Kennedy instructed Secretary of Defense Robert McNamara to emphasize counterinsurgency doctrine in the Pentagon's Third World programs. A new NSC committee, the Special Group (C.I.), was formed with Maxwell Taylor, Chairman of the Joint Chiefs of Staff, as chairman and Attorney General Robert F. Kennedy as an enthusiastic member. Taylor's group created the Green Berets, an elite fighting force of twelve thousand, that came to symbolize the counterinsurgency effort. More than one hundred thousand American military officers received specialized training in counterinsurgency, as would nearly seven thousand from foreign countries. Ambassadors and foreign service officers as well were compelled to attend counterinsurgency seminars before assuming their posts in Third World countries.[10] The President's objective was explicit: to beat the Soviets at their own game, to challenge them for the "hearts and minds" of the citizens of the newly independent nations.

An unresolvable dilemma in Kennedy's policy toward the Third World was how to maneuver between the pace at which the European powers were prepared to decolonize and the pressures exerted by local leaders for more rapid progress. Rostow defined the problem as one "of developing rapport and understanding with the next government while dealing effectively with the current one." Rostow concluded that in situations in which a transfer of political power was likely to occur over a relatively short period of time, as in many African colonies, American interests were more likely to be protected "by accepting the risks of leaning forward towards the more modern groups than the risks of clinging to familiar friends rooted in the past."[11]

Nowhere was this dilemma as stark as in Portugal and its African territories. Portugal was a valued member of the NATO alliance that permitted the United States to utilize a strategically situated air base in the Azores islands, in the mid-Atlantic. In a 1961 article in the *Yale Law Review*, Dean Acheson characterized the Azores as "perhaps the single most important (set of bases) we have anywhere." The mid-Atlantic base served as the primary refueling stage for American planes on their way to military and political crises in Europe, the mid-East, and Africa.

Portugal, however, was a determined colonial power that regarded its colonies in Africa as juridically equal to the provinces on the Portuguese mainland—they were an integral part of its national territory and character. The government in Lisbon steadfastly refused to accommodate American urgings and nationalist demands for self-determination in Africa. Lisbon utilized the military bases on the Azores as a trump card to resist American pressure to decolonize. Succinctly spelled out in a State Department study, the United States was faced throughout the 1960s and early 1970s, with an "embarrassing choice between security requirements and basic political principle."[12]

The Problem of Portugal

In 1961, Portugal was a weak but resilient colonial power on the eve of an imperiled era. As John Kenneth Galbraith, then American ambassador in India, observed, "The Portuguese empire has survived not by peculiar merit but for a combination of reasons remarkably related to backwardness, tenacity and pure accident."[13]

Portugal's Prime Minister, Antonio Oliveira Salazar, embodied both the backwardness and the tenacity; to many he was also the cause of imminent peril.

Born to humble origins in 1889, Salazar came of age during a chaotic and tumultuous period in Portugal's history. Between 1910 and 1926, during the democratic First Republic, there were forty-five governments, four of which were toppled by military coups. The Republic "was a kind of interrupted civil war" in which there were incessant bombings, coups and coup attempts, labyrinthine plotting, military mutinies, riots, strikes, and lockouts. The illiteracy rate was seventy-eight percent and, between 1919 and 1924, the worst period economically, there were more than twenty currency devaluations. The period would serve as a bitter prologue to Western Europe's longest surviving dictatorship.[14] It would also leave Salazar with an unvarnished antipathy toward democratic institutions and a total, often brutal, absorption with law and order.

Trained in seminaries as a student, in the small town of Viseu in the hills of central Portugal, Salazar was as gifted and serious a student as he was withdrawn and austere. Earning a law degree and a doctorate in economics at Coimbra University, Portugal's oldest and most prestigious university, the young scholar was also a devout Catholic. Salazar's complex personality blended religious and national fervor with a lucid, intelligent, and rational mentality. He perceived the major dilemma of the modern state as having to maintain political control independent of public opinion and popular passions. Salazar held that social and civil liberties limited the power of the state. Recognizing that the first responsibility of a government is to defend its own existence, Salazar nevertheless believed that political power could be enveloped in Christian values so as to serve the highest interests of society: God, the homeland, and the family.[15] In the words of one UN diplomat, Salazar's style of governing was more applicable to the "timelessness of [the] Church rather than the evolution of [the] state."[16]

In 1928, Salazar, then a thirty-nine-year-old professor of economics at Coimbra, was asked to assume the position of finance minister in the chaotic military-run government that succeeded the First Republic. A frugal, diligent, and stern individual of modest means, Salazar elevated these values to high social virtue. Within two years, he erased the budget deficit. In the process, Salazar began to exert an influence throughout the government far beyond the scope of his portfolio. On 5 July 1932, Portugal's President General Antonio de

Fragoso Carmona appointed Salazar prime minister. Aided by the imposition of a new corporative constitution, which was approved in a national plebescite ten months after Salazar took office, he easily asserted his control over every aspect of Portugal's daily life until he collapsed in ill health in 1968.

Known as the *Estado Novo* (New State), Salazar's government consisted essentially of him governing by decree. In theory he was advised by the Council of Ministers, of which he was the President; in practice Salazar was responsible only to a narrow oligarchy of the most important industrialists, bankers, landowners, generals, and high church officials. Even though there were elections every four years for the National Assembly, and presidential elections every seven years, they were of little importance. Salazar was head of the only legal political party, the *União Nacional* (National Union), and only a small percentage of the population had the right to vote (less than ten percent between 1934 and 1945). Illiterates and women were restricted from voting until 1968, unless they could prove that they were heads of families or that they paid a certain amount of real estate tax.[17]

Except for the controversial 1958 presidential election, a vast system of ruthless political repression prevented any serious opposition from mounting against the government by democratic means. Opponents of the regime, including the Monarchists as well as members of the Communist Party, were harassed constantly and doggedly by the security police, the International Police for State Defense (PIDE). Modeled on the Spanish secret police under General Francisco Franco, PIDE operated a nationwide network of spies and informers that blanketed the country.[18]

Political control was exerted through other means as well. The *Mocidade Portuguesa*, the official Portuguese youth organization, indoctrinated its student members with Salazarist philosophy and values. A network of guilds called *gremios* and employer associations called *sindicatos* tightly controlled labor. Rural laborers and fishermen fell under the dominance of *Casas dos Povos* and *Casas dos Pescadores* (fisherman's guilds or syndicates) that were established in every village and locality throughout the country. Each of these labor structures was supervised by the National Labor Institute and became centers of government propaganda and vigilance.[19]

Strict censorship was also a fact of life in Salazar's Portugal. As all information entering and leaving the country and colonies was stringently monitored, the Portuguese empire came to be known as the "kingdom of silence."

Portugal's backwardness was perpetuated by the dominance of a small, inward-looking elite of landowners, entrepreneurs, and privileged officials. Their primary economic policies revolved around "economic integration" between the colonies and the metropole. This allowed Portugal monopoly control over the colonies' raw materials, principally agricultural products, which Lisbon purchased at artificially low prices and resold on the international market for lucrative profits. Whatever impetus there was toward modernization, it was stifled by a government that "had learned to live off the proceeds of overseas conquests and the riches of other peoples' land and labor."[20]

During his initial years in power, Salazar sought to supplement Portugal's lack of material prosperity by reawakening the nation's imperial pride. Using Portugal's former colony of Brazil as the example, Lisbon's ruling elite developed an ideology that portrayed the Portuguese not as colonizers but as a people possessed with a unique ability to adapt to tropical lands and peoples. As the Portuguese were poor and humble, the defenders of colonialism reasoned, they lacked the exploitative motivations of their European counterparts that, they believed, enabled them to establish multiracial societies wherever they settled.

In 1952, Gilberto Freyre, one of Brazil's most influential authors, codified the myth of "lusotropicalism" in a book he wrote following a government-sponsored tour of Portugal's territories in Africa and Asia. He wrote effusively of "a world that the Portuguese had created," as distinct from other areas controlled by Europeans. According to Freyre, discrimination did not exist between the indigenous populations and colonial administrators and settlers. Not only were the Portuguese "pioneers of modern tropical civilizations," but they also had an appreciation for the values of tropical peoples.[21] Freyre's theory of lusotropicalism became one of Portugal's strongest rationales for why it should maintain its presence in Africa.

This national pride was artificially manufactured, however. As the American scholar, Gerald J. Bender, concluded, "Words were cheap and authors abundant and the country was soon inundated with books, pamphlets, journals and speeches and conferences which glorified the imperial past and Portugal's . . . 'mission' in Africa."[22]

Salazar conducted Portuguese policy against this background and locked into Portugal's heroic past, in the words of the American diplomat, George Ball, "as if Prince Henry the Navigator, Vasco da Gama, and Magellan were his closest advisers." No outside power was going to deter Portugal from carrying out its self-appointed "civilizing mission" in Portuguese-controlled Africa. Salazar's resolve was fortified by an unyielding paranoia about larger powers taking over Portuguese territory. It also reflected Portugal's pride in having been a world power in the fifteenth century and the humiliation of having been occupied by Spain for sixty years during the late sixteenth and early seventeenth century.[23]

Despite Salazar's phobia of external dominance, or perhaps because of it, he performed masterfully as Minister of Foreign Affairs in addition to his other responsibilities from 1936 to 1945. Portugal remained neutral during World War II and influenced General Franco in Spain to do the same. An irritant to the Allies during the war, Portugal was nevertheless able simultaneously to retain its alliance with Britain (which dated back to 1386) and to cooperate with the US while maintaining active relations with Germany, Italy, and Japan.

This maneuvering paid off for Portugal, especially in its relationship with the United States. In return for being able to use the Azores during the World War, in 1943 the US signed a diplomatic note pledging "to respect Portuguese sovereignty in all Portuguese colonies."[24] Largely because of its control over this valuable base, Portugal was asked to become a charter member of the North Atlantic Treaty Organization (NATO).

In 1951, Portugal and the United States signed a defense agreement that provided the United States with base rights in the Azores for a five-year period during peacetime and war. Instead of paying rent, the US agreed to underwrite much of Portugal's involvement in NATO. At the same time the agreement was signed, a secret exchange of notes between the two governments stipulated that American permission would "no doubt . . . be promptly forthcoming" for Portugal to use NATO equipment in any Portuguese colony should it be necessary.[25]

By the late 1950s, however, President Eisenhower was aware of disturbing problems in Portugal's colonies in Africa. Clarence B. Randall, a conservative American steel magnate who had just returned from a visit to sub-Saharan Africa, briefed the president at a 1958 NSC meeting. Randall told Eisenhower:

> The Portuguese colonies of Angola and Mozambique were very badly governed and administered. The Portuguese authorities exploit the resources of these areas mercilessly, and put very little back for

> future development. They believe that the best way to manage the natives is to avoid educating them. Forced labor was very common.[26]

Eisenhower was moved by Randall's report and recommended its written version to all the members of the NSC as "interesting, intriguing and valuable." Yet Portuguese colonialism would not become an issue in Portuguese-American relations during the Eisenhower administration. During a visit to Lisbon in May 1959, he characterized Portugal as a "tremendous friend and ally." A year later in a conversation about Salazar with the American ambassador to Portugal, C. Burke Elbrick, the President commented that "dictatorships of this type are sometimes necessary in countries whose political institutions are not so advanced as ours."[27]

Although it maintained close relations with the US during the 1950s, Portugal was held at arm's length by the rest of the international community. Portugal was unable to join the UN because it refused to recognize, much less comply with, Article 73 of Chapter XI of the UN Charter. This obliged member nations with "non-self-governing territories" to prepare them for self-government and regularly transmit to the Secretary-General information relating to economic, social, and educational conditions. Portugal argued that it had no colonies, only provinces that were an integral part of Portugal, an extension of Portuguese soil.[28] Thus the matter was an internal one for Portugal. In 1955, however, Portugal was admitted into the UN with fifteen other nations as part of an arrangement between the Soviet Union and the Western powers. Salazar would later comment that Portugal's admission was "small change" in a larger political deal.

In spite of Portugal's ties with the West, Salazar remained deeply suspicious of the United States. He saw the US as a society that had its "values wrong," and Americans "as a barbaric people illuminated not by God but by electric light."[29] In his view, the United States was intent on supplanting Portugal's presence in Africa so as to dominate the region economically. Salazar's fear of America's economic strength was at the heart of his refusal to accept aid from the Marshall Plan. In the eyes of the prime minister, the United States was unable to comprehend the importance of Africa to Western Europe. The United States, in its unbounded liberalism, was pushing the Europeans out of Africa and opening the continent to communist penetration and Soviet domination. For this reason, Salazar predicted that the US would ultimately "end up without a friend in the world."[30] More immediately, however, with the inauguration of President John F. Kennedy, Portugal found itself without a friend in the White House.

Snapping Impatient Fingers

The new president saw the world as a battleground between extremes of the right and left, between democracy and totalitarianism, extinction and survival. For him, the battle was most acute in the Third World where nationalism, which he recognized as an opportunity for democracy, was being threatened by the prospect of communist subversion. Following a trip through strife-torn Asia in 1951, Kennedy remarked that nationalism "is the most important international fact of life in the second half of the twentieth century."[31] Therefore, Kennedy concluded, the United States could no longer afford to buttress the "inequitable status quo" of colonialism. The nationalist era had to be acknowledged and accommodated.

Kennedy made his sentiments known most forcefully in a dramatic speech in the Senate on 2 July 1957. Attacking the "paralysis" in Eisenhower's foreign policy, the Senator criticized the administration's silence on France's bloody and tortuous colonial war in Algeria. He condemned the administration for its "cautious neutrality" in an era when the tide of nationalism was "irresistible" throughout the Third World. Calling for a negotiated solution leading to self-determination in Algeria, Kennedy argued that "We have deceived ourselves into believing that we have . . . pleased both sides and displeased no one . . . when, in truth, we have earned the suspicion of all."[32]

Kennedy's speech, "Facing Facts on Algeria," sparked an outpouring of criticism. *The New York Times* condemned as rash his "smashing public attack from the floor of the United States Senate." Former secretary of state John Foster Dulles rebuked him for not condemning Soviet-style imperialism instead. Another former secretary of state, Dean Acheson, chastised Kennedy for his "supreme touch of naïveté," adding that "it will not help us to snap impatient fingers . . . ." In France, *Le Figaro* complained, "It is shameful that our business is so badly directed that we are forced to endure such idiocy."[33]

Such pronouncements and controversy helped to give Kennedy the public stature that he previously did not have. His Senate office came to be frequented by prominent African nationalists such as the Kenyan labor leader Tom Mboya; Holden Roberto, the Angolan nationalist; and A. K. Chanderli, who represented the Provisional Government of the

Algerian Revolution (GPRA) and would later be Algeria's foreign minister. Kennedy was selected to head the subcommittee on Africa that was established by the Senate Foreign Relations Committee in May 1959. With his increasingly frequent absences from Congress to campaign for the Democratic presidential nomination, however, Kennedy held only one brief session of hearings. Chairman Richard M. Nixon would use this against Kennedy during the 1960 campaign, charging that the doors of the subcommittee on Africa closed before they were ever opened.[34]

In spite of Nixon's accusations, Kennedy's stand on self-determination and African independence played a crucial role in his battle with Nixon for the presidency. The candidate's weak Congressional voting record on liberal issues, particularly civil rights, had cost him support among blacks and the liberal wing of the Democratic Party. The alienation of these two constituencies was heightened not only by his defeat of Hubert Humphrey and Adlai Stevenson for the Democratic nomination but by the selection of Lyndon Johnson as vice presidential running mate. Though he was viewed with suspicion by a large group of traditional Democrats, Kennedy's strongly worded speeches on African self-determination and Third World nationalism bolstered the claim that his candidacy represented a new era in American politics and foreign policy.

Kennedy's use of Africa was "a minor classic in political exploitation of foreign policy." During the summer of 1960, he met publicly with Guinean President Sekou Toure in Disneyland and requested Averell Harriman, who had twice been ambassador to the Soviet Union and a former governor of New York, to make a fact-finding tour of the continent. The presidential candidate also made one hundred thousand dollars available to Tom Mboya, the Kenyan labor leader, from the Joseph P. Kennedy Foundation. The grant enabled 250 scholarship students to fly to the United States. The State Department had earlier turned down Mboya's request.[35]

Kennedy mentioned Africa an unprecedented 479 times in his campaign speeches, partially in an effort to strengthen his standing within the liberal wing of the Democratic Party. He essentially was making a pitch for civil rights overseas—and not in the US—and, as a result, the issue did not threaten the segregated South, a bloc of states for which Lyndon Johnson's place on the ticket had been considered a necessary concession.

Kennedy and his advisers perceived 1960 as the "hinge year" during which the doors of colonialism swung open on the era of independence in Africa; it was the New Frontier. Kennedy's identification with Africa personified his political and moral commitment to align the United States with the new and emergent forces in the world.[36]

The Empire Falters

On the first day of his presidency, Kennedy was confronted by an issue in Portuguese-American relations that pitted the "old" against the "new." Early on 22 January, Portuguese dissident Henrique Galvão led a ragtag revolutionary brigade, the Iberian Revolutionary Directorate (DRIL), in the hijacking of the Portuguese luxury liner *Santa Maria* off the coast of Venezuela. Galvão's demands for self-determination in Portugal's African colonies focused worldwide media attention on Portugal's harsh colonial policies and, for the first time, pierced the wall of silence that Salazar had imposed on the colonies. Galvão and his coconspirator, Humberto Delgado, had timed the seizure to coincide with Kennedy's inauguration and the accession to power of Brazilian President Julio Quadros. Galvão and Delgado considered both leaders to be sympathetic to the Portuguese opposition.[37]

Galvão, a former colonial official and deputy in the National Assembly for Angola, first gained notoriety in Portugal in 1947 when he wrote a highly critical report of the corruption, mismanagement, and labor conditions in Angola. He concluded his report with the comment that "only the dead are exempt from forced labor."[38]

In contrast with Galvão, Humberto Delgado was an immensely popular and respected figure in Portugal. A former general in the Portuguese army, Salazar rigged the vigorously contested 1958 election to deny Delgado the presidency.

Questioned about the hijacking at his first presidential news conference, Kennedy tried to adopt a neutral position. He said the United States government was concerned about the lives of the Americans on the *Santa Maria* as well as the ship that "belongs to a country with which the United States has friendly relations." He also commented that he had not ordered the US Navy to board the *Santa Maria*.[39]

The response was an affront to Salazar. The Portuguese prime minister was outraged that the American president did not treat the hijacking as an act of piracy. The American ambassador in Lisbon, C. Burke Elbrick, was called to the Portuguese foreign ministry so that Lisbon could express its "most vehement protest" against the American "neglect" of the 370 Portuguese crew members and the ship's safety. Portuguese officials bluntly reminded Elbrick that the Azores agreement was coming up for renewal in 1962.[40]

Ultimately, the US Navy was instrumental in negotiating a release for the ship, passengers, and crew, as well as sanctuary for Galvão and his accomplices in Brazil. The damage was done, however, as the incident demonstrated to Salazar Kennedy's reluctance to stand by Portugal.

Within days, the tempest over Galvão's hijacking was eclipsed by the brutal reality of violent rebellion in Angola. Before dawn on February 4, a crowd of several hundred Africans armed with machetes and clubs attacked Luanda's main prison and two police barracks. The next day at a state funeral for seven policemen slain in the violence, a group of Europeans, who were leaving the services, turned on a group of African bystanders and killed them in retaliation. In the ensuing daylong riots, Portuguese security forces killed twenty-four Africans and arrested a hundred others. Another raid on a Luanda prison five days later left seven more dead and seventeen wounded. The violence spread east to Malange where security forces killed several hundred Africans were killed while demonstrating against colonial rule.

Portuguese retribution was nearly uncontrolled. Civilian vigilante groups aided by security forces ruthlessly combed the slums of Luanda, shooting suspects on the spot. This massacre of hundreds of Angolans signaled the beginning of a war that undermined the myth of Portugal's "civilizing mission" and, ultimately, its empire in Africa.[41]

To senior officials in the Kennedy administration, Angola was threatening to be a repeat of the political chaos, racial violence, and Soviet-American tension that had accompanied the Congo's independence in 1960. The sudden withdrawal of the Belgians from the Congo had produced a harrowing and catastrophic situation in that country, which the Kennedy administration wanted to avoid at all costs in Angola. At the same time, President Kennedy was increasingly disquieted by instability in the Third World. "Each day the crises multiply," he told the nation in his first State of the Union address, "and the hour of maximum danger is approaching." Soviet and Chinese support for "wars of liberation" made the resolution of these conflicts increasingly complicated.[42]

At the United Nations, George Padmore, Liberia's Ambassador, requested an urgent meeting of the Security Council "to deal with the crisis in Angola." Determined to make a stand, Kennedy responded affirmatively to Adlai Stevenson's request that the US support the inscription of the Angolan issue on the Security Council agenda. Stevenson, the American ambassador to the UN, also asked Kennedy for permission to vote for an expected Afro-Asian resolution calling for self-determination in Angola. Kennedy demurred, saying he would wait until he saw the text before making a decision.[43]

A week later Secretary of State Dean Rusk sent a cable, cleared by the President, to Elbrick in Lisbon instructing him to inform the Portuguese not to expect US support in Security Council or General Assembly debates on Angola. Elbrick was also instructed to issue a *demarche* to Salazar relaying the "serious and sober" American conviction that further violence was likely in Angola unless the Portuguese began "step by step actions . . . towards full self-determination within a realistic timetable." In order not to "be remiss in its duties as [a] fellow NATO member," the United States was informing Portugal that it was "increasingly difficult and disadvantageous to Western interests . . . to support or remain silent on Portuguese African policies."[44] In short, the United States was distancing itself from Portugal to avoid criticism from Afro-Asian countries that, "rightly or wrongly" as one American official wrote, held the US responsible for Portuguese actions.

Salazar greeted the American *demarche* with a cold silence. He thanked Elbrick for coming, sent his regards to President Kennedy, and wished the Ambassador a good afternoon. The most troubling aspect of the American proposal, Salazar would later confide to one of his generals, was the concept of "self-determination." It could only mean one thing—independence—and this was unacceptable.

While Elbrick was delivering his message to Salazar, Rusk called in the Portuguese Ambassador, Luis Esteves Fernandes, and delivered the same message to him. At the same time, the State Department tried to persuade the British and French to apply similar pressure. Balking at the idea of public censure, they agreed to undertake a "quiet diplomatic approach."[45]

On the afternoon of 15 March, Stevenson made good on Kennedy's 1956 pledge that a Democratic administration would "no longer abstain in the United Nations from voting on colonial issues." Speaking to the resolution on Angola, sponsored by Liberia, Ceylon, and the United

Arab Republic, Stevenson said that the guiding principle of American foreign policy was the Declaration of Independence that asserted that governments derived "their just powers" from the consent of the governed. Calling on Portugal to begin "advancement" toward full self-determination so as to avoid "another Congo" and "disastrous consequences," Stevenson voted in favor of the resolution along with the three sponsors and the Soviet Union. Six nations abstained, including Britain and France, and the resolution did not pass.[46]

The American vote was a stark and total reversal of the existing position toward decolonization in Africa. Walter Lippmann applauded Kennedy on his boldness and the *New York Times* called it a "new declaration of independence." As Kennedy would soon learn, however, one vote at the United Nations would not in itself entrench a new direction in American foreign policy.

On 20 April, Stevenson voted again in favor of a General Assembly resolution calling on Portugal to move toward self-determination. Although the resolution passed, this second effort to signal American support for African self-determination was overshadowed by the crushing defeat by Cuban forces of CIA-sponsored insurgents at the Bay of Pigs, which occurred on the same day.[47]

Abetting the Conspiracy in Lisbon

The February uprising in Angola, attributed to the Luanda-based Popular Movement for the Liberation of Angola (MPLA), was followed by an even more dramatic and violent rebellion a month later. Synchronized with the deliberations on Angola in New York at the United Nations, the United Peoples of Angola (UPA) initiated an attack on 15 March on Portuguese settlers at a farm called Primavera in the northern province of Uige, sixty-five miles from the Congo-Angola border. UPA's leader, Holden Roberto, had planned only a limited attack to demonstrate to the world the depth of African frustration with Portuguese colonialism. Contrary to plan, the attack was like "a match to dry kindling." Within ten days the northern part of the country was engulfed in violence and chaos. Caught off guard, the Portuguese responded indiscriminately. Six months after their "comfortable slumber" was "rudely jarred," there were more than one thousand European and twenty thousand African casualties, as well as a state of war in Portugal's most valued colony.[48]

In Lisbon, Salazar's decision to defend Angola "at once and on the largest scale" had divisive repercussions within the military. Publicly, senior army officials supported Salazar's position; privately, there was widespread concern over the army's lack of preparation and inability to engage in extended hostilities.[49]

The United States moved swiftly to exploit the dissension in hopes of influencing Portugal's policies in Africa toward a more acceptable—and supportable—posture.

While Angola was making its way onto the agenda at the UN, Ambassador Elbrick met for lunch in Lisbon with the Portuguese Minister of Defense, General Julio Botelho Moniz. Elbrick briefed Moniz on the upcoming debate and told him of the United States' desire to see Portugal announce in the UN its intention to prepare its colonies for self-determination in the "indeterminate future"—ten, twenty, thirty years. The United States would stand-by Portugal in this difficult task and help with generous economic assistance.[50]

At their second meeting, a three-hour luncheon on 6 March, Elbrick told Moniz it was "becoming increasingly difficult for friends and allies" to support Portugal's colonial policies. He called for "urgent and drastic liberalization."[51] Moniz agreed. He told Elbrick that he favored reforms that would lead to the establishment of autonomous provinces that would be linked to Portugal through a commonwealth relationship, such as Britain had with India. Within Portugal, Moniz felt it was necessary to liberalize the government to include all noncommunist opposition.[52]

On March 28, Elbrick learned that Moniz and three others, including his personal assistant, Major Viana de Lemos, and the commander of the Air Force, Albuquerque de Freitas, had drafted "an extremely strong letter to Salazar urging prompt internal reforms." The letter reflected Moniz's belief that the crisis in Portuguese Africa could not be resolved militarily and that the Armed Forces were faced with a "suicidal mission." A political solution, through constitutional means, was the only way Portugal could sustain its economic and cultural presence in Africa. Portugal, therefore, would need international support to undertake a program of administrative decentralization and progressive political autonomy. As Elbrick had made clear to the dissenting general, Portugal did not have this support.[53]

On the day that the American ambassador learned of the letter to Salazar, Moniz met with the Supreme Military Council, a group of eighteen senior officials, who—except for one—supported the letter.

Army Chief of Staff, General Camara Pina, a staunch Salazar loyalist, was the only person at the meeting to oppose it. They all agreed, however, on the need to maintain the cohesiveness of the Armed Forces. Moniz then met twice with Salazar, that afternoon and the next morning, to discuss the letter. At the conclusion of the second meeting, Moniz realized he had failed to influence the thinking of the seventy-one-year-old dictator.[54]

Following Moniz's failure to persuade Salazar to institute reforms, Supreme Military Council convened for another meeting. The council passed a vote of no confidence in Salazar and reached agreement on the need to exert pressure on the government to bring about the necessary reforms. Mistakenly, Moniz interpreted this agreement as a pledge of allegiance from the key military leaders. On 5 April, a delegation, led by Moniz, met with the elderly, conservative, and ever-cautious President of Portugal, Americo Tomaz. The conspirators asked Tomaz to remove Salazar as prime minister, which only he had the power to do. Ominously for the plotting reformers, Tomaz responded with a ringing declaration of support for Salazar. Frustrated at the turn of events, Moniz communicated to Elbrick that the time for action had arrived or he would become "another revolutionary-minded general without portfolio."[55]

While Moniz continued to confer with his advisers, Colonel Kaulza de Arriaga, the under-secretary of the Air Force, kept the regime informed of the burgeoning conspiracy. After receiving Moniz and his group, President Tomaz immediately informed Salazar that a delegation from the Supreme Council of Defence had requested his dismissal. To the further detriment of the conspirators and their backers, word began to circulate in Lisbon that the American embassy was maintaining "unconventional contacts" with the military. Catching wind of this, Elbrick sent word to Moniz that it would be "very unwise" to meet at this time.[56]

The Defense Minister then flashed Elbrick a message that he was prepared to take action "within a day or two." On the afternoon of 12 April, Moniz activated his plan to depose Salazar. The prime minister was forced to flee from his official residence at São Bento. Taking refuge at the headquarters of the Republican National Guard, Salazar found an unexpected ally in former Defense Minister Santos Costa. Costa mobilized some loyal troops and cut off the Defense Ministry's communications.

The next morning the conspirators met in the Ministry of Defense to oversee the capture of key installations in Lisbon. At noon, however, Salazar dismissed Moniz and his associates, assumed the defense portfolio for himself, and announced sweeping changes in his cabinet. Because Moniz was no longer "authorized" to initiate military commands—and the conspirators remained subservient to Salazar's authority—the coup attempt floundered. Not only did the CIA conclude that Moniz failed because of "a lack of nerve," but his planning was hardly secretive, much less effective. Moniz was also unprepared for opposition from loyalist soldiers in the National Republican Guard (GNR) and the Portuguese Legion rallied by Santos Costa.[57]

Salazar worked the failed coup attempt to his advantage. He purged those in the high military command who opposed him and redoubled his military efforts to combat the uprising in Angola. By portraying the United States as the "agent provocateur" and responsible for the nation's "angry mood," he enhanced his standing in Portugal and among the Portuguese in the colonies. A PIDE-inspired crowd of 20,000, shouting *fora, fora, fora* (out, out, out), marched from Rossio, in the center of Lisbon, to the American embassy; in Luanda another group of protestors pushed the American Consul General's car into the bay. Reflecting Salazar's sentiments, the government-controlled *Diário de Notícias* described the American collusion with Moniz as "ipso facto, the dismemberment of the Western alliance."[58]

Privately, Salazar was incensed over the apparent American role in the conspiracy. It confirmed his worst suspicions about the new American president. He criticized Kennedy's "brusque and cavalier tactics" and canceled emerging plans for social and economic reforms in the colonies.[59] Portugal would not buckle to foreign pressures. Washington would have to recast its tactics or its goals.

Washington: The Battle in the Bureaucracy

On the afternoon that Adlai Stevenson cast his first vote on Portugal at the United Nations, former secretary of state Dean Acheson told the President in a National Security Council meeting that his rebuff to Portugal was "no way to run an alliance." He specifically referred to the vote in the Security Council as "mischief." Pressuring the Portuguese to introduce reforms in Angola, he warned, could only strain relations between the two countries. Another administration official added, "We should have given the quiet approach a try before kicking a friendly government in public."[60]

Acheson's point of view was countered by a group of individuals that Kennedy had brought into government who were decidedly sympathetic to the President's desire to support African aspirations for independence. One of the president-elect's first appointments was Michigan Governor G. Mennen Williams as assistant secretary of state for African affairs. Kennedy described the appointment as "a position of responsibility second to none . . ." in an effort to appease the liberal wing of the Democratic party that was angry at the selection of Lyndon Johnson as vice president.[61] Though Williams' exposure to African issues was limited, he had been a vigorous proponent of civil rights in the US. Williams selected J. Wayne Fredericks, a Michigan businessman, as his deputy, who would come to be regarded within the administration as "the brains of the (Africa) bureau." Fredericks brought into government an intimate knowledge of Africa and impressive bureaucratic skills. He had first gone to Africa in 1948 when his employer at the time, the Kellogg Company, had asked him to open a plant in South Africa. From this experience, Fredericks developed an abhorrence of apartheid and a lifelong commitment to political justice and economic development in Africa.

The Africa Bureau was buttressed by others in the administration who wanted to recast America's relations with Africa. This group of "Africanists" included Robert Kennedy and Chester Bowles, the Under Secretary of State, Adlai Stevenson at the UN, and Harlan Cleveland, Assistant Secretary for International Organization Affairs.

Initially, they had an important ally in Secretary of State Dean Rusk. Early in his career, Rusk had been director of the Office of Special Affairs at State that handled all UN matters. The experience left Rusk with an abiding philosophical commitment to the United Nations and a sensitivity to the aspirations of colonial people. So, in 1961, Rusk was quite prepared to work closely with Stevenson—whom he had supported in his bid for the Democratic Party's presidential nomination—and Cleveland to use the UN as a forum to support African independence and to battle communism in the Third World. Rusk also was willing to tackle the more complicated and subtle problems, which Portugal represented. In one of his first appearances before the Senate Foreign Relations Committee as secretary of state, Rusk ruminated about why the United States frequently found itself tied to weak allies, or the *ancien* regime. Rhetorically, he asked the committee, "Can you or should you invest in a regime when you know in your heart that regime is not viable?"[62]

The infusion of new talent into the Africa Bureau represented a turning point in the way in which Africa was perceived by American decision-makers and the manner in which Africa policy was formulated and implemented. Before the Africa Bureau was established in 1957, it had been part of the Bureau of Near Eastern South Asian and African Affairs. At that time, Africa was considered a "soft assignment" by career diplomats, and a tour in Africa was perceived to be a detriment to career advancement. Thus Africa policy was in large part left to those whose professional experience was primarily in the Middle East or who were sympathetic to European colonial thinking.

The Eisenhower administration made an effort to ensure that this tradition continued. One of Robert Kennedy and Chester Bowles' first tasks after taking office, therefore, was to block the effort of the outgoing administration to reward senior foreign service officers with ambassadorial posts in Africa. Instead, Williams, in consultation with Rusk and Bowles, chose a new set of ambassadors who shared an inclination to support, if not expedite, the transition to independence. Among them were journalist William Attwood (Guinea), Arizona civil rights lawyer William Mahoney (Ghana), and a "forward-thinking" career officer, Edward Gullion (Congo), who had been in disfavor during the Eisenhower administration.[63]

The Africanists in the administration moved quickly to seize the policy initiative. In June 1961, in response to the rebellion in Angola, Dean Rusk created a task force on the Portuguese territories. G. Mennen (Soapy) Williams chaired the task force, which consisted of representatives from seven branches of the government [State, Defense, CIA, the White House, Treasury, Bureau of the Budget, and the United States Information Agency (USIA)]. Rusk instructed the task force to devise a course of action towards Portugal, its African territories, and African states in general.

Within a month the task force produced several policy recommendations but, in the process, revealed deep divisions within the administration over how to respond to demands for decolonization in Portuguese Africa. In grandiloquent prose, the Africa Bureau argued that Angola, like Berlin, was "an important part in the global struggle between freedom and communism for the hearts and minds of men." The Africanists also asserted that the administration come out "unequivocally in opposition to Portugal's policy."[64]

The only point of consensus among the task force members was over the need for private initiatives through diplomatic channels—perhaps a special envoy to talk to Salazar or an attempt to deliberate the issue within NATO instead of in the General Assembly. Should these tactics fail, the Africanists argued, the US ought to be prepared to pressure Portugal in the Security Council, without delay, for reforms leading to self-determination. They also suggested that the US should consider recognizing, "at the appropriate time," a provisional Angolan government if one were to be established.

The Pentagon adamantly opposed these recommendations and submitted its own report, the Military Annex. The Pentagon representatives on the task force opined that a "precipitous and overly aggressive implementation" of such a policy would produce repercussions in Portugal, and possibly in Spain, that could undermine the American strategic capability to respond to crises in Berlin, the Middle East, and Africa. The Defense Department was not prepared to sacrifice access to the Azores under any circumstance—particularly for what it perceived as ambiguous political gains in Africa. As Paul Nitze, Assistant Secretary of Defense, made clear to Kennedy's National Security Adviser, McGeorge Bundy, and G. Mennen Williams at a task force meeting, the US had taken a strong position on Angolan independence with the two votes at the United Nations and therefore could afford to abstain in the future. Williams responded that such an action would be tantamount to a retreat from existing policy.[65]

Kennedy's position on the debate over American policy toward Portugal and Angola was ambivalent and pragmatic. In a July 1961 note to Acheson, the President wrote, "It would be easy to serve one of these interests by neglecting the other. Our object must be to serve them both."[66] But as Kennedy would discover, there was little room for ambiguity in this policy debate. The bureaucratic skirmishing, which pitted the Europeanists, who wanted the US to support Portugal, against the Africanists, who maintained that American security interests were best safeguarded by taking a strong position on African independence, demanded resolution.

Leaning Toward the More Modern Groups

One of the most contentious aspects of this issue—particularly between the United States and Portugal but also within the administration—was American support for the nationalists who were fighting the Portuguese. There was general agreement within the administration that Africa was a "strategic cockpit" in the international arena. As the State Department *Guidelines for Policy and Operations* in Africa concluded, Africa was ". . . the greatest open field of maneuver in the world-wide competition between the [Communist] Bloc and the non-communist world."[67] In the view of State Department strategists, this competition required a political and diplomatic response that ensured that the United States would win this "long-range struggle." The administration decided, therefore, to place a large portion of its resources into "nation-building" and the training of political leaders in Africa. In the Portuguese territories, educational programs and support for nationalist leaders became the administration's link to the future. Nation-building was also consistent with the administration's goals of counterinsurgency and containing the expansion of Soviet influence in Africa.

In 1961, on the recommendation of the Angola task force, Kennedy approved the creation of an educational program at Lincoln University in Pennsylvania for students who had fled Angola, Mozambique, and Guinea-Bissau. One rationale for the program was to keep the students "out of the clutches of the Soviet Union" and to develop a crop of competent young leaders for eventual service in the independent counties. Furthermore, officials such as Williams and Fredericks believed that "continued contact with American ways and American education (would) have a beneficial moderating effect" on the students' "total outlook."[68] In practice, the program was primarily an English language training course that prepared students for education at other universities.

Whatever goodwill was intended, it was lost on both the Portuguese ambassador in Washington and the American ambassador in Lisbon. Their suspicion of the program was heightened by the choice of director, Dr. John Marcum, who along with George Houser, director of the pronationalist American Committee on Africa in New York City, had made a two-week journey in 1961 through the UPA-held territory of northern Angola. In fact, the new Portuguese ambassador in Washington, Vasco Garin, protested to Wayne Fredericks (also a member of the Board of Trustees at Lincoln University) his contacts "with all those African revolutionaries." In an effort to mute Garin's protestations, Fredericks invited him to meet and talk with the "revolutionaries" in the Lincoln program. Garin refused.[69]

From Lisbon, Elbrick cabled that the Portuguese viewed such programs with "extreme bitterness, suspicion, and general lack of confidence . . ."[70] A government that exercised absolute control over its African subjects, naturally considered education overseas, especially in Western countries, "virtual treason." Kennedy nevertheless gave instructions to renew the funding for the program. By 1963, there were twenty-four students from Portuguese Africa studying at Lincoln (nine from Angola, fourteen from Mozambique, and one from Guinea-Bissau). The administration also approved a one million dollar emergency medical and nutrition relief program for the 125,000 Angolan refugees who had fled Portuguese retribution to the neighboring Congo.

Spurred on by reports that four hundred Angolan students had left Kinshasa (then known as Leopoldville) to study in the Soviet Union, the administration was determined to "prevent their going behind the 'Iron Curtain.'" Maxwell Taylor, the President's military advisor, was dispatched to Europe to examine the situation of sixty-one Angolan students who had escaped Portugal to study in France and Switzerland. He wrote the President that it would be "impolitic" to fund the students as the Portuguese would blame the US for their illegal departure from Portugal. An alternative would be "some indirect method of assistance," such as through the CIA, should the administration decide to give the students scholarships. The administration responded positively to this recommendation.[71]

Rusk—under pressure from the Bureau of European Affairs—and Elbrick, however, initially prevailed in having Mozambican students barred from participating in a second program, sponsored by the Agency for International Development (AID) and the CIA. This education program was administered in Dar es Salaam by the African-American Institute program for students from southern Africa who had fled colonial rule. After vigorous protestations from Williams, however, Rusk relented and permitted the Institute to train "three or four especially well-qualified Mozambican students each year." Although it was no threat to Mozambique's ninety-nine percent illiteracy rate, Williams was compelled to write the American ambassador in Tanzania, William Leonhart, and warn him that "no publicity should be given to AID financing of the training of the Mozambicans and that this training should appear as a private effort."[72]

The controversy created over educational support for refugees paled in comparison to the fury created by American assistance to the

Angolan nationalist leader, Holden Roberto. Kennedy met Roberto for the first time in 1959. He subsequently impressed other senior American officials such as Dean Rusk, Robert Kennedy, and Adlai Stevenson as "the most promising leader" among the different Angolan nationalist movements. When asked by these officials whether he was pro-Western or pro-Communist, Roberto won everyone's heart by saying he was "neither . . . only pro-Angola." He won financial and political support, however, with his firm assurances that the UPA was an anticommunist movement threatened by communist-oriented movements in Angola—principally the Movement for the Popular Liberation of Angola (MPLA).[73]

Roberto was an anomaly in American foreign policy. Not only did he have strong support from the Congolese President Cyrile Adoula, an American protegé, but from such prominent radical African leaders as Kwame Nkrumah of Ghana, Sekou Toure of Guinea, and Ben Bella of Algeria. The slender nationalist was a person who "could be impressive if you did not know him well," and became a *cause celebre* within the administration—a product of the idealism and enthusiasm of the era.

In April 1961 Roberto began receiving an annual CIA retainer of six thousand dollars, which was channeled through the CIA Station in Kinshasa (at that time called Leopoldville). The amount was subsequently increased to ten thousand dollars a year.[74] Despite the Africa Bureau's warning to embassies in Africa "not to choose between" the MPLA and UPA,[75] the United States would remain tied to Roberto for the next fourteen years until the UPA, which subsequently became the Front for National Liberation of Angola (FNLA), disintegrated in the violent aftermath of Angola's independence.

Within a month, the Portuguese were aware of the "closer association" between Roberto and the United States. Elbrick cabled Washington that such support was "a delicate and highly dangerous matter . . . . The spectacle of our supporting an ally's enemy can have lasting repercussions among our friends and give exceptional aid and comfort to our own enemies." Elbrick's concerns were supported by the Pentagon and the European Bureau at State. George Ball, who replaced Chester Bowles as undersecretary of state ten months into the administration, took the complaint to Rusk, telling the secretary that it was wrong to try to talk with the Portuguese while "arming the insurrection."[76]

Rusk subsequently instructed Elbrick to tell Portugal's foreign minister that the United States "has not repeat not provided support or aid to Angolan 'terrorists.'" The American ambassador in Portugal was informed that the US was educating the future leaders of that country. As for the financial support to Roberto, Rusk viewed this strictly as an intelligence operation—payment for information about developments in Angola—which was therefore above the reproach of the Portuguese foreign minister.[77]

Portugal's new forty-three-year-old foreign minister, Franco Nogueira, was unconvinced, however, and raised the matter in his initial meeting with Elbrick. Hinting that he would supply evidence at the appropriate time and place, Nogueira was certain that the United States was "responsible for organizing and leading the (military) attacks on Portugal."[78] In an effort to apply pressure of his own, Nogueira called Elbrick to the Foreign Ministry on the evening of 10 February 1962. The young, intense foreign minister presented Elbrick with a document that had allegedly originated in the American embassy in Kinshasa, which proved that a "political accord" existed between the US and Roberto.

Shocked by the insinuation, Elbrick responded that the document was a forgery. Six months before, PIDE officials had broken into consular offices in Luanda and Maputo (then known as Lourenço Marques) and had stolen documents and official stationery. The courtly ambassador raised the possibility that the document was a Soviet maneuver to jeopardize US-Portuguese relations. He pointed out that there was no "Counselor for African Affairs" in the embassy in Kinshasa, which was under the signature on the letter. He promised, nevertheless, the matter would be thoroughly investigated.[79] Before leaving, Elbrick asked for a copy of the document. Flashing a cold smile, Nogueira told the American ambassador the original could be found in Washington. Reflecting on the event, Elbrick concluded that the Portuguese were on an "emotional binge . . . seizing upon every ounce [of] evidence to prove to themselves [that the] US is out to destroy [the] Portuguese role in Africa."[80]

Portuguese War—American Arms

Salazar rushed twenty-five thousand young conscripts (constituting two of Portugal's three NATO divisions) to Angola's defense after the March rebellion, in part equipped with American military materials, including jet aircraft, automatic weapons, napalm bombs, and vehicles. When Kennedy read in a London newspaper article, however, that a bomb fragment with the markings "made in America" had been found in an Angolan village following a Portuguese attack, he instructed Rusk to cease immediately all American military assistance for the Portuguese NATO division. In addition to reprimanding the Portuguese for unauthorized use of American materials, the action was also intended to exploit persistent divisions with Portugal's ruling hierarchy over its involvement in Africa. By denying arms to the Portuguese military, the Americans hoped to catalyze reluctant officers into pressuring the political leadership to normalize relations with the US by adopting a more reformist colonial policy. The administration also thought such pressure would lead to an early renewal of the Azores agreement, which was due to expire at the end of 1962.[81]

The American position was firm. The State Department instructed Elbrick to tell Nogueira that the Portuguese use of American arms in Angola was "contrary" to the 1951 Mutual Defense Treaty. Should Nogueira raise the question of consent in the supplemental secret exchange of letters, Elbrick was to inform him that the United States was "unable [to] give such consent," and that all equipment was to be returned to Portugal as soon as possible.[82]

Before delivering the *demarche* to Nogueira, an agitated Elbrick cabled Rusk that he was "greatly concerned" that it would appear as if the US were "writing off" Portugal. Nevertheless, Embassy officials were aware that the Portuguese were indeed sending American-supplied equipment to Africa along with the NATO units that they were redeploying there.[83]

Nogueira's reaction, as Elbrick expected, was bitter and derisive. Defiantly, the foreign minister asked the American ambassador if the US had the same concern over discovering American arms in the hands of "Angolan terrorists" as it did in finding them in the hands of the Portuguese. Given the crisis over Berlin, he found it extraordinary that the United States would threaten allied unity at such a critical moment. The angry foreign minister stated bluntly that Portugal would never return any equipment so long as it was fighting a war in Angola.

A gloomy Elbrick reported to Washington that "this latest nail in [the] coffin of US-Portuguese relations can only result in a further deterioration in those relations."[84]

This latest *demarche* was underscored by the imposition of a restrictive arms policy, which the State Department would misleadingly refer to as a "complete arms embargo." In August 1961, the decision was made, as recommended by the Angola task force, that the

Portuguese be required to give assurances that American arms furnished through commercially licensed transactions or military assistance programs were used solely for NATO purposes and not in Angola or any other territory. Although the administration controlled the licensing of commercial sales, the onus of the policy rested more on Portuguese promises than American actions. As events would prove, Portugal was not seriously constrained in its use of American weapons in Africa. Furthermore, Rusk and Secretary of Defense McNamara—who was determined to avoid jeopardizing the use of the Azores—persuaded Kennedy, over Williams' objections, to implement the policy privately instead of making a public announcement.[85] The restrictive arms policy would earn the administration some diplomatic leverage at the UN, but it did little to curtail the Portuguese use of American materials in Angola or perceptions among Africans that the United States was supporting Portugal's war effort.

Portugal's Countermoves

Toward the end of 1961 it became apparent to Washington that the Portuguese intended "to pull out all the stops" to force a change in American policies. Salazar was determined to pursue every available means—diplomacy, public opinion and, most critically, the Azores negotiations—to thwart American pressures for self-determination in Angola, Mozambique, and Guinea-Bissau.

The reclusive dictator dispatched Theotonio Pedro Pereira, Salazar's confidante and prospective successor, to become the new ambassador in Washington. A lucid and impressive individual, he expounded forcefully Salazar's dogma equating Communism and African nationalism.

A group of Portuguese businessmen who called themselves "The Overseas Companies of Portugal" had been organized to counter the administration's "propaganda" and actively aided Pereira. Shortly after Stevenson's vote at the United Nations, Lisbon awarded a one million dollar contract to the American public relations firm of Selvage and Lee "to place the affairs of Portugal and Angola in a true and proper perspective."[86] Nogueira instructed the lobbyists to utilize all available channels.

Selvage and Lee sponsored the creation of "The Portuguese-American Committee of Foreign Affairs," which was headed by Dr. Luis Camacho, a Boston born Portuguese-American, to send letters to newspapers, give speeches, and lobby sympathetic congressmen. It also attacked supporters of nationalism in Angola, labeling the American Committee on Africa as "communist-infiltrated" and Holden Roberto as procommunist. Selvage and Lee exerted pressure on the National Broadcasting Corporation (NBC) in the fall of 1961 not to show a documentary on Angola that contained footage of Portuguese atrocities. In a memorandum to NBC, Jim Selvage, president of Selvage and Lee, suggested that "a provocative White Paper at this time . . . could only help recreate a new trouble spot for the United States Government while the Kremlin rejoices—and benefits."[87]

Preying on American cold war fears and racial sensitivities, the lobbying firm working on behalf of the Portuguese placed articles in smaller American newspapers extolling the Portuguese role in Africa and vilifying troublesome Africans as savages or communists. In January 1963, Selvage and Lee organized a tour of Angola for the Newspapers Editors Association whose members worked on small daily and weekly papers. The trip impressed the majority of the group. One editor, Wayne Sellers, from the Rock Hills, South Carolina *Evening Herald* was pointedly unimpressed, however. He wrote home, "I have never seen such blatant brainwashing . . . . I am disturbed that many of our group may have fallen for it."[88]

Simultaneously, the Portuguese government undertook a different tack to counter international criticism. After months of hinting to Western journalists and diplomats, the able and ambitious Minister of Overseas, Adriano Moreira, on 28 August 1961 announced "revolutionary" reforms in the overseas provinces. The centerpiece of the reforms was the repeal of the Native Statute Act of 1954, known as the "indigenato" system, which had previously classified Africans as "indigenas" or "assimilados." (No more than two percent of the Africans in Portuguese Africa qualified as "assimilados" as such status was primarily dependent on levels of income, education, and literacy.) The reforms also included changes in municipal administration and a restructuring of the provisional organs of government. Shortly after Moreira's announcement, Elbrick notified the State Department that the "Embassy believes . . . [the] reforms offer considerable hope for (the) future."[89] More significantly, it provided ammunition for those in the Kennedy administration—such as Elbrick—who wanted to soften American pressures on Lisbon. In essence, Salazar's countermoves were working.

The Dilemma of the Azores

American-Portuguese relations hit their lowest point on 18 December 1961, when the Indian army occupied Goa, a key colonial possession of Portugal's. To many in Lisbon, Goa was a sapphire among diamonds in its collection of colonial territories. The loss of Goa was a tremendous psychological blow to the Portuguese and the government placed the blame on the ineffectiveness and incompetence of its Armed Forces.

In an effort to redirect the government's bitterness and frustration, Salazar and Nogueira condemned the United States' response to the Indian takeover as a "glaring example" of American hypocrisy. Nogueira asked, how could the United States only condemn India through Security Council resolutions for annexing another country's territory, while imposing sanctions against Portugal for defending itself in Angola?[90]

Salazar retaliated quickly against the US. A week after the Indian occupation of Goa, Salazar instructed PIDE to obtain the names and addresses of all Americans living off limits of the Lajes base in the Azores and to monitor their movements. A month later, in January 1962, Salazar made an even less oblique threat when he denied the right of any aircraft bearing United Nations' insignia or in its service to land or refuel in the Azores. Salazar had already denied UN aircraft permission to fly over Angolan territory. As if the messages were not clear enough, the CIA station in Lisbon, which cooperated closely with PIDE even during the most difficult times, reported that renewal of the Azores agreement would be most difficult due to Salazar's "almost psychopathic" dislike for the United States.[91]

The value of the Azores to the United States was immeasurable. It had been used as a refueling station during the shipment of marines to Lebanon in 1958, UN troops to the Congo in 1960 and 1961, and American troops to Berlin in autumn 1961. In the early 1960s, approximately seventy-five percent of all American military air traffic to Europe and the Middle East stopped at the Lajes base. Kennedy and his closest advisers believed that there was a very real possibility that the United States, like the United Nations, would be denied access to the Azores. Even so, Kennedy was not prepared to have his Africa policy held hostage to Salazar's sixteenth century world view.[92]

Kennedy began to search for options on the base negotiations in the spring of 1962. It was not a propitious time for the two allies. "Suspicion and fear [had] induced an exceedingly frosty atmosphere" for the Americans in Lisbon and, contrary to Elbrick's optimistic report five months earlier, there was little hope that relations would improve in the near future.[93] Furthermore, there was no consensus in the American government on how to proceed—at least "three sides of the Pentagon and four sides of the [State] Department" were expected to make recommendations on the best strategy to pursue.[94]

Kennedy had not budged in his determination to retain access to the Azores while maintaining support for self-determination in Angola. While preparing for the Azores negotiations, he told Williams that if "we lose the Azores we will lose support for the UN" in Congress. Congress was in the process of debating the purchase of a one hundred million dollar bond to keep the bankrupt United Nations solvent. Without it the UN peacekeeping force in the Congo would be terminated and this would undermine the administration's entire Africa policy. As one official in the Africa Bureau said, "The awful, baleful influence of the Congo permeated everything."[95]

On 18 April 1962 the President asked Adlai Stevenson to submit his views on the Azores dilemma. A week later, Dean Acheson, at the request of Secretary Rusk, submitted a memo of his own. The skirmishing between the Europeanists and the Africanists within the State Department was approaching a crescendo. It pitted Acheson, Ball, and Miles Kohler, Assistant Secretary for European Affairs, against Stevenson, Williams, and Fredericks, the "hardnosed" Eastern establishment against the "do-gooder" mid-Western liberals.

Throughout his presidency, Kennedy skillfully straddled these two camps. His style, presence, and sympathy for African nationalism appealed to the Stevenson group; his shrewdness, caution, and pragmatism earned the respect of the Acheson camp. Yet between the two groups—particularly between Stevenson and Acheson—little friendship was lost. Acheson was the leader and spokesman of that "nebulous but very real conglomerate of businessmen, lawyers and financiers" who had been so influential in American foreign policy throughout the twentieth century. They were realistic, comfortable with power and determined anticommunists. Acheson also retained the strong, positive impression of Salazar that he had formed at their first meeting in 1952. Stevenson, on the other hand, was the spokesperson for the Roosevelt-Stevenson-Humphrey coalition which, during the 1950s, lobbied for disarmament, decolonization, and normalization of relations with "Red China."[96] It was no surprise that their counsel to Kennedy on the Azores was as dissonant as their personalities and outlooks.

Acheson suggested to Rusk on 25 April that the United States "make a little mood music" to improve relations before opening negotiations with the Portuguese. Rusk could accomplish this in private conversations with Nogueira at the upcoming NATO meeting in Athens and by issuing a public statement of support for newly instituted reforms in Angola and Mozambique. Meanwhile, Acheson also recommended that an effort should be made to persuade the President to direct the Executive Branch (i.e., Stevenson) to refrain from participating in debates or drafting resolutions on Angola at the forthcoming UN General Assembly. By altering its approach, but not its principles, Acheson reasoned, the US would be able, at minimum, to arrange for an extension of the Azores agreement while negotiations were ongoing.[97]

The following day, Stevenson submitted his recommendations. He argued that Angola and the Azores were "two essentially separate issues" and that the United States should resist Portuguese efforts to link them. The Azores should be viewed in an "anti-communist context involving all of NATO." Portugal, on the other hand, could not expect American support for its problems in the colonies until Lisbon changed its policies. To act otherwise would be to confirm Soviet claims that the United States could not "be counted on . . . to support the ultimate freedom for colored peoples." Stevenson also pointed out that Selvage and Lee had to be prevented from framing the issue in terms of "Angola versus the Azores," or "Angola versus communism" so as to avoid creating political problems for the administration in Congress.[98]

The two statesmen agreed, however, that proffering economic inducements to the Portuguese and persuading other countries such as Brazil to take up the cause with Salazar were also necessary for resolving the issue. Kennedy subsequently adopted this approach during conversations with Brazilian President João Goulart and Foreign Minister San Tiago Dantas, who made an official visit to Washington in April 1962. Dantas said that an opportunity to obtain Angolan independence should not be allowed to "slip by in a desultory fashion." Rusk pledged American support and resources if they would be useful. When Dantas discussed the matter with Nogueira a short time later, it was perceived in Lisbon as yet another unsuccessful American attempt to turn Portugal's friends into enemies.[99]

In the meantime, the intragovernment debate on the Azores question was broadening. Sorenson reminded the President that "NATO's stake in this base, and Portugal's stake in NATO were too great to permit the agreement to end." He concluded that concessions and a defensive attitude would only strengthen Portugal's hand and do little to demonstrate the importance of the Azores to Portuguese security.[100]

Chester Bowles, echoing Stevenson's sentiments, suggested to the President that the base be placed under NATO's control. Not only would this shift the burden from the US but it would "challenge the assumption that our European allies are doing us a favor whenever they provide us with the necessary facilities from which to defend their own continent."[101]

Paul Nitze, Assistant Secretary of Defense, countered this argument several days later. In a memo to Kennedy's National Security Adviser, McGeorge Bundy, Nitze outlined a series of critical defense maintenance and communications operations that would cease should the treaty expire. Furthermore, contingency operations outside the NATO framework would be jeopardized as consent to use the facility would be dependent on overall US-Portuguese relations. Though the Pentagon had developed alternatives in case the US lost the Azores, Nitze underscored how expensive and unsatisfactory it would ultimately would be to use these alternatives.[102]

The tide was beginning to turn against the Africanists. Rusk wrote the President that "one of our first tasks is . . . to dispel the exaggerated Portuguese suspicions regarding our involvement with the Angolan dissidents." Williams was barely able to persuade Rusk not to forbid members of the UN mission and the State Department from meeting with Roberto. In return, Williams agreed to make an effort to convince Roberto not to come to the United States.[103]

Playing to Portugal

By mid-1962, Rusk was making a strong bid to defuse tensions between Lisbon and Washington. At a NATO meeting in Athens in early May, he told Nogueira that he had been encouraged by the reference Pereira had made to "internal self-determination" during a speech on the African territories at the Overseas Press Club. Could the Portuguese government elaborate on this and give it more publicity?

The foreign minister became testy and told Rusk that the "point of saturation" had been reached and Portugal was tired of being pressured to change its colonial policies. Nogueira then began to criticize activities of the American Committee on Africa. Rusk replied that it was a private organization over which the government had no power but that he would investigate the organization's anti-Portuguese actions. When Nogueira criticized a recent speech by Adlai Stevenson in which he compared

Portugal's role in Angola to the Soviets in Hungary, Rusk confided that all of Stevenson's future speeches were to be submitted for approval when making specific references to any country. When the Foreign Minister brought up American support for UPA, Rusk admitted that the US was buying information from the group.

After lodging other complaints, Nogueira told Rusk that the government of Portugal had lost all faith in the US and was convinced that the US was trying to expel Portugal from Africa "as soon as possible." Salazar, Nogueira said, was uncertain whether the friendship that existed when Portugal had given the US permission to use the Azores was still in tact. Given the Portuguese distrust, Nogueira rebuffed Rusk when the secretary of state tried to discuss the opening of the base negotiations.[104]

By June 1962, Kennedy was insistent that the Azores issue be resolved. Soviet pressure was beginning to mount in Berlin again and the CIA was reporting unusual Soviet activity in Cuba. He could not afford to risk access to the bases. Therefore, in an effort to soothe the Portuguese and initiate negotiations over the Azores lease, Rusk decided to stop in Lisbon at the end of the month following a tour of west European capitals.

Rusk's objective was to reassure Salazar about its loyalty as an ally. This would be no easy task despite Rusk's reputation for always being effective when "soothing suspicious Congressmen and angry allies." The Portuguese were still offended by the "feeble" and "half-hearted" American rebuke of India after the invasion of Goa. Moreover, on 10 June in Madrid, Overseas Minister Adriano Moreira attacked Kennedy's approach to international affairs as "neutrality toward enemies, hostility toward friends and friendship toward neutrals." In an interview in *US News and World Report* given before Rusk's arrival in Lisbon and published after his departure, Salazar echoed Moreira's charge, describing American policy as being "less favorable to an ally than a neutral . . . ."[105]

In what Rusk would later describe as a "spooky occasion," he paid a courtesy call on Salazar on 28 June and gave him a full review of some of the "innermost and most sensitive problems" of the Atlantic Alliance. It did little to restore Portugal's faith in the United States, and the Secretary of State "failed utterly" to convince the Portuguese leader that colonialism was a thing of the past. Rusk made illusory progress with Nogueira, as the two officials agreed to a "method" in which the United States and Portugal would identify the problems between them and arrive at a solution for resolving them. The American request to extend the Azores

Base Agreement beyond December 31 was to be included in this process.[106]

Rusk's visit to Lisbon did little to resolve the impasse. In fact, Nogueira utilized the agreed upon "method" to wear Washington down. In the middle of August, Nogueira gave Elbrick a "Bill of Complaints" that was intended to serve as an agenda for talks between the two governments. This "agenda" listed sixty-seven items categorized according to past, present, and future. The last of these was the "eventual renewal of Lajes Base (Azores) agreement—financial arrangements." (The meeting between Salazar and Rusk produced a rumor in Lisbon that Portugal would ask the United States for eighty million dollars to renew the Azores agreement.)[107]

By October, Rusk had prepared a response to Nogueira's "agenda" that was little more than a defense of the administration's position. Rusk instructed Elbrick to tell Nogueira that the US Government had no control over the American Committee on Africa, and that the US did not monitor the unfriendly statements of Portuguese officials (such as Moreira's) and neither should the Portuguese. Furthermore, Elbrick reminded Nogueira that "alliances between free nations must have within themselves some latitude for differences of views and for independence of action." Rusk nevertheless made a concession to Portugal by issuing instructions that Roberto was not to be received at the US Mission in New York. Rusk's efforts, however, failed to placate the contentious foreign minister.[108]

The tensions between Lisbon and Washington reached an unexpected turning point during the Cuban missile crisis. Kennedy had agreed to receive Nogueira on 24 October—the day on which the president imposed the naval blockade on Cuba—in part to emphasize the value that the US attached to Portugal as an ally and a member of NATO. Rusk counseled Kennedy to combine "conciliation with firmness" in his talks with Nogueira. The conciliation was aimed at assuring Portugal that the United States was still a friend and not an enemy. The firmness was intended "to dissipate the illusion that the US is now beginning to see the error of its recent policies toward Portugal . . . . We should not permit the Foreign Minister to enjoy the luxury of self-deception" on this matter.[109]

Before going to the White House, Nogueira met with Rusk in his office on the seventh floor of the State Department. Rusk gave Nogueira a full briefing on the crisis between the United States and the Soviet Union in Cuba. He told Nogueira "anything could happen." Rusk then asked Nogueira to tell the President that the United States could have unrestricted access to the Azores should the crisis in Cuba precipitate an outbreak of war between the United States and the Soviet Union. Nogueira replied he could not grant this request without consulting Lisbon. The rarely impassioned Rusk pressed Nogueira harder. He warned him against "illusions" and said, "the situation is extremely grave."

Nogueira looked at the Secretary and paused for a moment. In his imperious and impassive manner, Portugal's foreign minister replied, "It is more than two years that we, the Portuguese, are living in [a] permanent [state of] emergency, and it does not seem to me that any of our allies are much disturbed by this fact."[110]

Nogueira was equally unforthcoming later in the day with the President. An exasperated Kennedy asked Nogueira whether Portugal "could not see its way to proclaiming publicly its acceptance of the principle of self-determination." Nogueira replied that this would be impossible. Once such a statement was made, even a vague one, the Afro-Asian nations would immediately press for more precise and definite commitments. The conversation concluded without any mention of the Azores.[111]

On 31 December 1962 the agreement formally expired. Although the Portuguese allowed the United States to use the base on a "day-to-day" basis for the next nine years, it was a setback for the United States. American security and political interests vis-à-vis the Azores and the newly independent African states were no more protected than they had been the year before. Furthermore, Salazar had done nothing to relieve the crisis in Angola. Instead, the specter of protracted, anticolonial war was looming ever larger not only in Angola, but also in Mozambique and Guinea-Bissau.

Retreat at the United Nations

Although the Portuguese refused to negotiate on the Azores, they cooperated with American diplomatic efforts at the UN during most of 1962. Nevertheless, by the end of the year, the bold move the US had made in the Security Council on 15 March 1961, increasingly appeared more as an anomaly than as a point of departure for a new policy on decolonization and Third World issues in general.

Angola was the first issue to be considered in the General Assembly when it convened on 15 January 1962. In response to an extremely anti-Portuguese resolution introduced by Poland and Bulgaria, forty-five Afro-Asian states introduced a mild resolution that urged Portugal to undertake extensive reforms in the territory. The ensuing debate was long and bitter, and the Portuguese delegation stalked from the hall in protest. Stevenson argued before the Assembly that the solution to the problem in Angola must be based on self-determination for the Angolan people. He was successful in persuading the Afro-Asian states not to condemn Portugal and to substitute "self-determination" for "independence" in the resolution. Both Rusk and Stevenson felt that this substitution would avoid reinforcing Lisbon's fear that the United States was trying to drive Portugal from Africa.[112]

Stevenson urged Washington to vote affirmatively on the resolution. He was supported by Rusk, who cautioned the President that "an abstention on the resolution would be widely regarded as a retreat from the position adopted by your administration last spring." Furthermore, the Afro-Asian states had been conciliatory toward the United States and this ought to be encouraged, if not rewarded. Stevenson's opinion prevailed and the resolution passed overwhelmingly with American support. Within the State Department, the most senior officials in the State Department praised Stevenson's handling of the measure as "brilliant."[113]

In spite of Stevenson's success in New York, his relationship with Kennedy and the administration's outspoken stance at the United Nations were coming under increasing pressure. Part of Stevenson's problem stemmed from the recurrent differences in personality and outlook with Kennedy and many senior administration officials. Stevenson was further disaffected to find himself continually on the outside of policymaking instead of at the center. The former two-time Democratic presidential candidate was, increasingly, a conveyor to the world of what was decided in Washington and not a force in the decision-making process itself. As Stevenson's biographer, John Bartlow Martin concluded, the Ambassador was more effective as the unofficial ambassador from the UN to the United States than vice versa, which, perhaps, was to Stevenson's dismay.[114]

As Stevenson's influence began to wane within the administration (especially after the Cuban missile crisis), Kennedy's overall UN policy came under attack within the US. A March 1962 article in *Harper's*, written by Dean Acheson's friend, William S. White, criticized the Africanists in the administration as lacking "the sophistication to see that the United Nations cannot any longer be allowed to dominate American policy . . . ."[115]

Powerful Democratic senators lodged stronger condemnations. Henry M. (Scoop) Jackson, the influential senator from Washington, speaking before the National Press Club on 20 March, criticized the fact that issues such as Angola commanded a "disproportionate amount of energy from the President and the Secretary of State." Furthermore, it was "unfortunate" that Eisenhower and Kennedy had given the Ambassador to the United Nations cabinet rank. Finally, Jackson asked whether the position was really more important than other ambassadorial posts.[116]

Kennedy moved to play down the criticism as it came at a time when Congress was debating funding for the United Nations. Kennedy wanted the funding measure to pass, which it subsequently did. To get the support of these important senators, however, and to avoid transforming the issue into a confrontation between the White House and Congress, Kennedy did not protest these charges. As a result, the implied criticisms of Stevenson went publicly unanswered, leaving the sensitive ambassador feeling abandoned by the administration.

The Democrats in the Senate were not the only ones creating trouble for Kennedy's Africa policy. Porter Hardy, a combative Democratic Congressman from Virginia, launched an investigation into the administration's Angola policy. He demanded access to classified documents surrounding the *demarche* of March 7. Williams, supported by State Department Legal Adviser Abraham Chayes, told Rusk that "never, to my knowledge, did even the Eisenhower administration permit internal Department policy documents to be scrutinized by Joe McCarthy or his agents." When the documents were not immediately forthcoming, an incensed Porter Hardy threatened to Ball to "blow it up as best I can . . . [and] to do my damnest to see that he [Chayes] gets fired." The White House sided with Williams and Chayes, and instructed Rusk and Ball to tactfully disregard Hardy's requests.[117]

In spite of these Congressional critics, the administration continued to stress the importance of the United Nations in its foreign policy. The United States needed African and Asian support to maintain the peace-keeping operation in the Congo, to keep the People's Republic of China from displacing Taiwan as the representative of China, and to prevent the Soviet Union from gaining more influence at the UN. Furthermore, the United Nations was a valuable venue for an administration intent on disassociating itself from the colonial era and colonial powers. Therefore the United States would continue its efforts to mediate the demands of the General Assembly and the objections of the Portuguese. Clearly, however, Washington was no longer prepared to lead the attack against Portugal in the manner it once had.

In the resolution that passed the General Assembly on 20 April 1961, a special subcommittee was established to visit the Portuguese territories in Africa and to report on conditions. To the Portuguese, such a visit was "out of the question."[118] Rusk worked to resolve this impasse during his visit to Lisbon in June. Based on an idea first put forward by Stevenson, he suggested to Salazar and Nogueira that an independent rapporteur—and an internationally recognized individual—be appointed by the General Assembly to investigate conditions in Angola. Following their positive response, Rusk cabled Elbrick in August 1962 to tell Nogueira that the United States was prepared to make a major diplomatic effort at the UN to have a resolution passed in the General Assembly that would provide for the appointment of a rapporteur. The American objective was to place the Angola issue on a "new and positive basis," and to establish a dialogue between Lisbon and the United Nations.[119]

The response of the African states and other Third World states to the American proposal, however, was not encouraging. In September, the Bolivian diplomat Carlos Salamanca, chairman of the subcommittee appointed to report on Angola, returned to New York from a trip to the Congo to investigate the conditions of Angolan refugees, having been denied permission to enter Angola. The Bolivian official had been very discouraged by what he had seen, especially the large refugee population in the Congo who feared Portuguese reprisals in returning to Angola. He warned Jonathan Bingham, the American representative on the Trusteeship Council, that unless the Portuguese undertook serious reforms, there would be little recourse but to issue a final ultimatum to Portugal, followed by the imposition of coercive measures such as sanctions.[120]

Stevenson had also been informed by the Ethiopian delegates to the UN that if Holden Roberto opposed the rapporteur idea, all the African states would vote against the resolution. Roberto was in no position to be favorably disposed to the United States. His "on again-off again" relationship with the State Department and the stigma of CIA support had cost him the backing of Ghana, Guinea, Mali, the UAR, Morocco, and the Algerian Provisional Government, a group of states known as the Casablanca Group. When Roberto turned to Ghana's Kwame Nkrumah for help, he was told, "The Government of Ghana has given orders that we must not help you because you are in the pay of America." Ghana's denial of assistance to Roberto (in favor of the MPLA) also stemmed from his unwillingness to form a common-front with the MPLA.[121]

As the reaction of the African and Asian states to the American resolution shifted from "luke-warm" to "chilly" during the fall of 1962, the Portuguese seemed increasingly flexible even though they would not support the US during the Cuban missile crisis. Nogueira, perhaps sensing the limits to American patience, agreed to a change in the proposed resolution insisted on by the "Afro-Asian" bloc. This change called for two rapporteurs to be appointed—one for Angola and one for Mozambique. Portugal had been encouraged by an American vote against a strongly-worded anti-Portuguese resolution adopted by the Committee of 17, the General Assembly body that monitored the decolonization process. Lisbon had also benefited at the UN by an International Labor Organization (ILO) report that generally absolved Portugal of practicing forced labor in Angola. Nogueira, ever the diplomatic gamesman, concluded it was worth the risk to overlook reports that members of the US mission to the UN were again "in contact with Holden Roberto," in spite of American pledges to the contrary.[122]

Roberto's disaffection with the United States spread to the African states at the UN who, on 18 December 1962, threatened to amend drastically the proposed American resolution. Stevenson was forced to withdraw the American proposal for the appointment of two rapporteurs to visit Angola and Mozambique. Instead, the Afro-Asian group passed a strongly anti-Portuguese resolution that called for the imposition of sanctions and condemned "the mass extermination of the indigenous population of Angola."[123] The United States cast a negative vote against the resolution along with Portugal, South Africa, and its closest European allies. The failure of the American initiative was another turning point in relations between Lisbon and Washington. It demonstrated to Lisbon the limited extent of American influence in the Security Council as well as the inability of the United Nations to impose sanctions on Portugal. For the United States, the failed resolution was a sharp defeat for an American policy aimed at straddling the breach between the implacable Portuguese and the increasingly impatient African states.

The day after the vote at the UN, a frustrated Holden Roberto wrote President Kennedy from New York. He applauded the earlier American stand at the UN "as an indication of your country's willingness to cleave morality and justice at the risk of severe criticism . . . . Today, on the other hand, purely humanitarian needs of our refugees and students must be left unattended, help cut off because of pressure from the Department of State . . . ." Roberto asked to meet with a White House representative to discuss support for Angola—"a struggle to which you must certainly still subscribe." In one more affront to the Angolan nationalist, the State Department tersely recommended to the White House that "no reply should be made" to Roberto's letter.[124]

The Portuguese Façade

Part of the reason that the administration allowed the issue of Portuguese colonialism to diminish on the American foreign policy agenda stemmed from the Salazar regime's new measure of apparent stability in Portugal and its colonies. Salazar was no longer being faced with conspirators in his own ranks, and the conflict in Angola had abated. In fact, Lisbon was developing other ties that would act as a buffer against American efforts to exert pressure on Portugal. In an obvious attempt to pique the United States, Portugal concluded a trade agreement with Cuba that Nogueira glibly referred to as "mutually advantageous." In Africa, Portugal was materially supporting Moises Tshombe, leader of the secessionist movement in Katanga, a mineral-rich province in the south of the Congo. An independent Katanga allied with Portugal would deny both the MPLA and UPA an important sanctuary from which to attack Angola. An independent Katanga also ran counter to American objectives and the goal of the UN peace-keeping force.

In the face of American pressures and Third World criticism, Portugal grew closer to France and Germany. The French attitude toward Portugal was influenced by its cultural and political interests in Portugal and by France's desire to keep Africa connected to Europe and to limit American political and economic penetration of the continent. Germany shared Portugal's arguments about the threat posed by the Communist bloc. Furthermore, as Germany was not a member of the United Nations, it was not pressured or influenced by the "psychological terrorism" aimed at Portugal from the member states.[125]

While Portugal maneuvered through its international isolation, the regime was having more difficulty in maintaining order within Portugal. A military coup at the Beja garrison in the south of Portugal on New Years day 1962 was disastrously managed and thus easily quelled. General Delgado, who had hijacked the *Santa Maria* in an unprecedented challenge against Salazar's rule, had slipped back into Portugal, via Morocco and Spain, to lead the attack. Instead of mobilizing numerous junior officers who were dissatisfied with Salazar's policies, the attackers were confronted and defeated by loyalist troops who did not remain "neutral" as expected.[126]

The CIA gave credit to the Portuguese Communist Party (PCP) for having "manned and directed" the abortive coup. The PCP, led by the Stalinist lawyer Alvaro Cunhal, was the regime's primary enemy. Its approximately eight thousand members were highly disciplined and organized. Despite PIDE's oppressive vigilance, the PCP had effectively infiltrated student, labor, and intellectual groups. The other anti-Salazar groups—the socialists, various Catholics, and Republicans—did not have the stature nor the organization of the Communist Party, nor were they as effective in opposing the Salazar regime. As a result, these groups did not have strong convictions against collaborating with the Communists. This would have an immense impact on events and alliances in the period after the fall of the Salazar-Caetano dictatorship.

The bungled Beja coup was followed several months later by a student strike at the University of Lisbon. The Salazar regime moved instantly to squash it, occupying the campus with police. This heavy-handed action led to the resignation of the politically influential rector of the University, Marcello Caetano, formerly minister of the presidency, who felt that his authority had been undermined. Caetano's resignation, amidst challenges that he could not control the students on his campus, was an embarrassment and another potential threat for Salazar. Three months after his resignation from the University, the CIA station in Lisbon reported that Caetano had joined a "moderate opposition group," along with former President of Portugal, Craveiro Lopes, and the ousted Minister of Defense, Botelho Moniz. According to the CIA, the group had already decided on a "shadow cabinet" in which Caetano would be prime minister once it had successfully carried out a "rapid bloodless coup." Yet this plot never materialized nor did one that was reportedly being led by Overseas Minister, Adriano Moreira. Those opposed to the Salazar regime were encouraged by the belief that Washington welcomed "a stable but less reactionary Portuguese government." Naturally, they expected immediate American diplomatic recognition once they seized power.[127]

Whatever the truth to the various coup reports, Salazar strengthened his own position in December 1962 by making sweeping changes in his cabinet and other senior governmental positions. Among the changes, Salazar replaced Minister of Education Lopes de Almeido and the Minister for Overseas Adriano Moreira, who many in the regime had regarded "as too ambitious and opportunistic, and suspiciously independent . . . ." In an assessment of the bureaucratic shake-up, Roger Hilsman, director of the Bureau of Intelligence and Research, concluded that "Salazar may well be mustering what he regards as the strongest and most reliable defense-overseas team in anticipation of a worsening situation in Angola and Mozambique."[128]

Hilsman's analysis was prescient. In 1961, Salazar had told Elbrick that with the forthcoming independence of Tanzania (then called Tanganyika), he expected an outbreak of violence in Mozambique, similar to what had occurred in Angola. In fact, in June 1962, the Front for the Liberation of Mozambique (FRELIMO) had been formed in Dar es Salaam, Tanzania's capital. Under the leadership of Eduardo Mondlane, who had attended university in the United States and was on leave from his position as a professor of sociology at Syracuse, FRELIMO was preparing to wage war against the Portuguese in Mozambique. In Angola, the military situation had reached a stalemate. To the State Department, it seemed "unlikely that either the Angolan insurgents or the Portuguese [could] bring about a decisive military settlement of the insurrections in the near future." In both territories, as well as in Guinea-Bissau, Portugal was facing a bleak future in spite of the positive picture portrayed by its official propaganda. Within the administration, however, there was little incentive remaining to be actively concerned with these trends.[129]

The Kennedys and Mondlane

Despite the difficulties encountered at the United Nations and in Lisbon, the Africanists in the administration continued their efforts to strengthen the American position with the nationalist cause in Portuguese Africa. They gained an ally in W. Averell Harriman, who was appointed Under Secretary of State for political affairs in April 1963. Harriman, a shrewd diplomat and bureaucrat, shared the President's concern over Africa and was familiar with the personalities and issues on the continent.

Shortly after becoming Under Secretary, Williams proposed to Harriman a revitalized program for the mounting crisis in Portuguese Africa. Williams pointed out that the "softened approach" that the US had adopted toward Portugal during 1962 had not led to a renewal of the Azores agreement nor to an improved situation in Portuguese Africa. Williams told Harriman that Lisbon interpreted the policy as a "weakening" of the American position that only encouraged them to become more inflexible. In the eyes of the African states, the US had reversed its policy altogether, in favor of Portugal. The Africa Bureau suggested that the US should, in a "discreet fashion," expand contacts with the nationalists, increase educational and refugee assistance, and continue to promote dialogue between the nationalists and the Portuguese at the UN. Harriman approved the recommendations with Rusk's reluctant acquiescence.[130]

Harriman's support came at a propitious time. Earlier in the year, in February 1963, Williams's deputy, Wayne Fredericks, suggested to Attorney General Robert F. Kennedy that he might like to meet Eduardo Mondlane, the newly elected president of FRELIMO. Fredericks suggested a "neutral" place, such as the Metropolitan Club or perhaps Hickory Hill, Kennedy's residence. When Kennedy responded positively to the idea, Fredericks reminded the Attorney General that Rusk had prohibited senior officials from receiving nationalist leaders. Kennedy gave Fredericks a fierce look and said, "I will see him in the office of the Attorney General of the United States. Bring him here. He will sit where you are sitting."[131]

To avoid openly antagonizing Rusk, Ball, and others, Fredericks arranged for Fritz Rarig, a Philadelphia businessman who knew both Mondlane and Kennedy, to accompany the Mozambican nationalist to the meeting with the Attorney General. Once in Kennedy's office, the large and voluble Mondlane began to criticize the growing American role in Vietnam. Robert Kennedy interrupted him, and said he was more interested in hearing about Mozambique's problems. The president of FRELIMO then spoke at length about the situation in Mozambique and FRELIMO's programs for educating Mozambican refugees. Mondlane referred to the "inevitable collapse of Portuguese rule" and said that it would be "tragic" if "indifference and ignorance" coupled with an assumed need "to placate Portugal" prevented the United States from moving "to the forefront in the struggle for freedom."[132]

By the end of the hour-long meeting, Mondlane and Kennedy had established a strong rapport based on a shared vision of the future in Africa and Mozambique. Although the Attorney General remained noncommittal about official American support, he told Mondlane that he personally wanted to help him and his family. Kennedy then proceeded to sign over to the nationalist leader from Mozambique a five hundred dollar check he had received from a previous speaking engagement.[133]

Several days later, Fredericks arranged a meeting for Mondlane with Averell Harriman at Harriman's elegant Georgetown home. The two men emerged from the two hours of conversation with a deep and mutual respect for each other. For Mondlane, his relations with Kennedy and

Harriman were an invaluable opportunity to gain a broader and higher level view of the dynamics of American foreign policy with respect to Europe, the Soviet Union, and Africa. For the American officials, it was an opportunity to interact with an individual whom they thought would become one of Africa's most important leaders.[134]

Following the meeting with Harriman, Fredericks asked Rusk and Ball whether they would be interested in meeting Mondlane. In deference to Portuguese sensitivities, they both refused. Rusk had reservations about Mondlane's "performance" and remarked that Mondlane was an unknown entity. To Ball, such a meeting made little sense.[135]

Robert Kennedy thought otherwise, however. In his opinion, the only correct approach to a colonial issue was to be on the side of the anticolonialist. Covert assistance was required when it was necessary to maintain one kind of relationship, as with Portugal, while forging new ties with future leaders. Furthermore, there was a belief in Washington that warfare could be avoided in the colonies if the nationalist movements could develop strong political, organizational, and educational structures. This would enable the movements to become legitimate alternatives to the colonial government and a force that the Portuguese would have to accommodate.[136]

Several days after their meeting, the Attorney General dropped a note to Mennen Williams and told him he had been "very much impressed" with Mondlane. His education program seemed to merit American attention and help "where feasible." Carl Kaysen, McGeorge Bundy's assistant, also met with Mondlane and found him "very impressive, straightforward, intelligent," and "easy to talk to." Mondlane won respect not only for his leadership abilities but also for the fact that he was leaving a safe life at Syracuse University for a very uncertain future. By April 1963, covert American assistance was being considered for Mondlane: "fifty grand to keep the lid on his people and also stay on top." Harriman lobbied within the administration for this support while Kaysen reassured a skeptical Ball that "the Agency people are absolutely confident that they can do it quietly."[137] In a confidential letter to Robert Kennedy, Rarig urged covert support for Mondlane. In retrospect, his insight is more interesting than whatever influence he may have had:

> The money should not be given on the assumption that we can control Mondlane. In fact, it would be rather foolish to attempt to control him because the attempt would impair his usefulness to us. The truth of the matter is that we cannot control him; we can only trust him . . . . Support for Mondlane would be a good investment for

> us because his program represents the best and only hope of a relatively peaceful solution of the Mozambican problem.[138]

Late that spring, the CIA extended a sixty thousand dollar CIA subsidy to Mondlane, channeled through the African-American Institute in New York.[139] On 10 June 1963, the Ford Foundation extended a $99,700 grant to the African-American Institute to assist the training of Mozambican refugees at the Mozambique Institute in Dar es Salaam.[140] Mondlane's American wife, Janet, directed The Mozambique Institute.

This American financial support did assist Mondlane in consolidating his leadership in FRELIMO, though he was not overly dependent on it. FRELIMO also received material and political support from the Soviet Union and China as well as countries in Western and Eastern Europe. During the 1960s, FRELIMO was the only liberation movement in Africa to receive support simultaneously from the United States, the Soviet Union, and China.[141] The Africa Bureau in the State Department, with the vital support of Averell Harriman, Robert Kennedy, and individuals at the NSC, nevertheless, were a shrinking minority within the administration prepared to accept the risks of aligning with groups of the future as opposed to "clinging to the familiar friends of the past."

The Stalemate in Africa

More conventional strategies for inducing Portugal to grant self-determination in Africa were also being considered in Washington. In January 1962, Paul Sakwa, assistant to the deputy director of plans at CIA, conceived of a "Commonwealth Plan" that he thought the Portuguese might be persuaded to accept. It was based, correctly, on the premise that the Portuguese did not have the economic strength nor military capability to defeat the guerrilla forces in Africa. "A Portuguese military defeat is a foregone conclusion if the revolt in Angola is allowed to acquire momentum and continuity." The plan envisioned Portugal granting Angola and Mozambique self-government within eight years. A referendum would also be held in the colonies to determine the type of relationship that would be maintained. During this period, Roberto and Mondlane would be given "a salaried consultative status" and groomed for the premiership of their respective colonies. To help Salazar swallow the bitter pill of decolonization, Sakwa proposed that NATO offer Portugal five hundred million dollars to modernize its economy.[142]

In developing the proposal, Sakwa identified the issue of central importance to American foreign policy: Should the US allow a friend and ally, such as Portugal, "to commit suicide, perhaps dragging its friends along the same path?" Sakwa realized the odds against his plan when he concluded that Salazar would not accept such a proposal "without the benefit of a frontal lobotomy."

A year later, Chester Bowles, then the President's troubleshooter on Third World affairs, put forward a similar proposal, except that he upped the ante. The objective of Bowles's plan was to "nurture and preserve" the moderate leadership in the nationalist movements and "to produce a basic change of attitude among the Portuguese themselves." Like Sakwa, Bowles proposed that the United States be prepared to match a NATO contribution of five hundred million dollars. Reinforcing a reputation for "spacious" analyses, Bowles reasoned that it would be a "diplomatic bargain" if American efforts could resolve Portugal's "ugly dilemma" at a cost of one hundred million dollars a year for five years.[143]

When George Ball presented Bowles's plan to Salazar in August 1963, the Prime Minister gave a curt reply: "Portugal is not for sale." To Nogueira, the Americans were foolish to think that they could determine, much less guarantee, events over a ten-year period. Such a plan would be the first step down the "slippery slope" to chaos and dislocation of the Portuguese in Africa.[144]

While American overtures proved ineffective, the crisis in Portuguese Africa continued to grow. Elbrick's sympathy for the Portuguese did not obscure from his view the difficulties the country was facing. As he reported to Washington, Portugal's "sword of Damocles" was the growing strength of the anticolonial movement in Portuguese Africa. Portugal was "neither large enough nor affluent enough" to fight guerilla wars on three fronts. His conclusion was ominous: this disturbing trend of events may signal "the demise of the Lusitanian empire," and the Salazar regime. Any new ruling group would quite possibly be "considerably more leftist and or neutralist."[145]

Between 1960 and 1963, Lisbon's military expenditures doubled to forty percent of its annual budget and eight percent of its GNP for the defense of its territories. Forty-five thousand troops were stationed in Angola while in Mozambique there was a force of twenty thousand soldiers to guard against an insurgency that had not yet begun. The war was already underway in Guinea-Bissau, which would become the most critical theater of operations for Lisbon.[146]

In Mozambique, the crisis had created a police state atmosphere and funds were diverted from public works projects to the military. As the American Consul General in Maputo, Mozambique, Thomas K. Wright, observed, "Four and one-half centuries of Portuguese repression has built up a volcano of resentment in Mozambique which under present day conditions is certain to erupt in the not too distant future."[147]

The CIA's analysis of events in Angola was hardly any more encouraging. "While Portuguese troops are able to contain the feuding nationalist forces for the present, the long-run economic drain on Portugal and the rising discontent among Angola's whites seem likely to force Lisbon eventually to grant autonomy to Angola." The discontent among the twenty thousand Portuguese in Angola was heightened by the dismissal of the popular Governor-General, Venancio Deslandes. The removal of Deslandes represented a shift in Portuguese policy and Lisbon announced it would no longer fund the Angolan development plan because of its increased military costs.[148] The higher costs stemmed as much from the collapse of Tshombe's secessionist movement in Katanga—which meant Portugal had to defend another one thousand miles of Angolan border—as from the looming threat in the other territories.

The apparent stalemate between the aims of American diplomacy and Portugal's resolve was prolonged by the nationalists' lack of military success, particularly in Angola. A relatively small group of UPA guerrillas (between five and seven thousand; Roberto claimed to have twenty-five thousand troops under arms) had prevented the Portuguese from completely controlling the northwest section of Angola. Yet the UPA was hardly in a position to defeat the Portuguese militarily. In an effort to strengthen its position, the UPA went through a series of organizational permutations that ultimately diffused, instead of consolidated, the anticolonial aspirations among Angolan nationalists. On 29 March 1962, the UPA formed a common front with the Democratic Party of Angola (PDA), becoming the National Front for the Liberation of Angola (FNLA). Nine days later, Roberto announced the formation of the Revolutionary Government of Angola in Exile (GRAE).[149]

Unrecognized by any government for sixteen months, GRAE benefited directly from the formation of the Organization of African Unity (OAU) in Addis Ababa in May 1963. In the OAU charter, it was enshrined that all free African states would be "dedicated" to the liberation of all African territories still under foreign rule. Ben Bella of Algeria announced that ten thousand Algerian volunteers were ready to join the struggle in Angola. Milton Obote, Prime Minister of Uganda, offered his country as a "training ground" for freedom fighters, and President Sekou Toure of Guinea asked every independent African state to contribute one percent of its national budget to the newly established African Liberation Committee (ALC). Furthermore, the OAU declared that all African states should cut diplomatic ties with Portugal and work to expel Lisbon from all international organizations.[150]

A month after the first OAU meeting, the Congolese government extended formal recognition to GRAE. Prime Minister Cyrile Adoula's announcement on 30 June 1963 was a Congolese attempt to assert its leadership in the growing pan-Africa movement. It was also aimed at pre-empting the influence of the more radical African states that were becoming increasingly frustrated by the persistent divisions within the MPLA. For Holden Roberto, it was a diplomatic coup.

Adoula's announcement came several days after Assistant Secretary G. Mennen Williams was in Kinshasa for conversations with the Congolese Prime Minister. The State Department was highly sensitive to the impression that the US had played a role in the Congo's recognition of GRAE. It immediately sent out a cable to the main embassies in Europe and the forty-five posts in Africa denying that Williams had played a role in Adoula's announcement or that the US was trying to increase its prestige in Southern Africa at the expense of its European allies. The cable asserted that, in fact, Williams had "endeavored (to) dissuade . . . [Adoula] from proceeding on this course," even though the Angola Task Force had made the same recommendation in 1961.[151]

Roberto interpreted this as one more instance of the Kennedy administration trying to undermine him politically. Americans, he charged, pay "lip service to self-determination" while supplying Portugal "with the arms that are used to kill us."[152] Salazar also voiced his suspicions over a possible American role in the recognition of GRAE. Given the "very special relations," he said in a speech in Lisbon, between the United States and the Congo, it was "no surprise" that the Adoula government "recognized *de jure* a kind of terrorist association set up at Kinshasa for the purpose of operating in Angola and avowedly supported by funds from Americans."[153]

Rusk's principal concern was that recognition of GRAE would lead to a rupture of diplomatic relations between Lisbon and Kinshasa and, indeed, Lisbon recalled its *chargé d'affaires*. A formal break in ties would have damaged the efforts the Americans were making at the UN to promote "meaningful talks" between Portugal and African leaders. The

State Department viewed such talks as "inevitably" leading to a dialogue over self-determination. Furthermore, Rusk was concerned that Adoula's move would undermine contacts with the West as well as what he saw as the organization's attempt to change its Marxist orientation. Rusk feared that the result could only lead to "an increasingly complex factional struggle" in Angola.[154] Nevertheless, by the end of the year, GRAE had been recognized by twelve African states.

Factional struggle, or, more appropriately, fratricidal strife, between the FNLA and MPLA was becoming a primary obstacle to the quest for independence in Angola. The tensions were unending between the two movements. Personality was one reason; Roberto was an "obsessive separatist," unsophisticated and deeply suspicious of the MPLA. Agostinho Neto, who became president of the MPLA after wresting the leadership away from the "extremist" Mario de Andrade in December 1962, was the opposite. He was an internationally recognized poet, a trained physician, and a respected leader.

Race and ethnicity were other points of friction between the two organizations. Roberto was a Bakongo nationalist who drew his backing exclusively from the Bakongo in northern Angola. This ethnic identity enabled Roberto to operate effectively in Kinshasa, and led to close relations with Adoula and his associates, especially General Joseph Mobutu. Yet GRAE as an organization won little respect from analysts in the State Department. One study commented that GRAE's leadership "lacks depth and perspective" and another referred to the organization as "essentially parochial." Roberto, thought by Washington to be the most promising nationalist leader in Angola in 1961, was characterized in 1963 as "rigidly uncompromising," "unable to delegate authority," and holding long-range views that were "fuzzy and incomplete." At heart, GRAE was a two-man operation led by Holden Roberto and Jonas Savimbi, GRAE's foreign minister and Roberto's "heir apparent."[155]

The MPLA, on the other hand, was supported by the Kimbundu ethnic group in central Angola and the mulatto intelligentsia in Launda, which imbued the movement with multiracialism in doctrine and membership. Analysts in the American intelligence community thought the MPLA was a better organized movement with leaders who were better trained than those in Roberto's organization. The MPLA's primary weakness was its lack of a broad popular following in Angola. This was exacerbated by the FNLA and the Congolese army that had effectively cut off the MPLA troops from Angola. The MPLA had its strongest supporters in the urban areas, especially Luanda, but it encountered difficulty in overcoming its exile status. The organization was also hindered by its nearly singular reliance on Soviet bloc support and its early identification with the Portuguese Communist Party.

In December 1962, Neto made a trip to the United States in an effort "to remove pro-Communist coloring" from his movement's image.[156] Yet Neto would not succeed in this, nor would the MPLA ever overcome its internal divisions. The MPLA leader encountered other problems as well, such as internal dissension and a lack of military success in the first two years of the revolution. These were the main reasons that the OAU recognized the FNLA/GRAE over the MPLA. As Basil Davidson, the influential journalist, noted in December 1963, "Initially the more influential of the two big nationalist movements, the MPLA has fractured, split, and reduced itself to a nullity. With Roberto Holden's [as he was sometimes referred to] UPA steadily gathering strength and allies, the MPLA has ceased to count."[157]

"Seeking the Best of Both Worlds"

Rebounding from its diplomatic defeat at the UN in December 1962, the Kennedy administration renewed its efforts to break the "dangerous deadlock" between the Portuguese and the African states at the UN. During the spring of 1963, the administration tried to revive the dialogue initiated over the rapporteur proposal. This time the plan was to establish direct talks between the Portuguese and "at least the most constructive African states" that could act as a channel to the nationalist movements. The task was complicated during the spring by the Portuguese conviction that they were winning the war in Angola. At the same time, African rhetoric had become more impassioned. The OAU had threatened "the allies of Portugal that they must choose between their friendship for the African peoples and their support of powers that oppress African peoples." Any hope for a conciliatory environment in the Security Council was further spoiled by accusations from Senegal of Portuguese attacks against its territory.

In early June, the thirty-two members of the OAU announced that they would seek a "full-dress" Security Council debate on the twin issues of apartheid in South Africa and the repression of independence movements in the Portuguese-controlled territories in Africa.[158] Stevenson wrote the President that the United States was facing "a decision situation" and would be under "direct fire" during the Security Council deliberations. Stevenson recommended to Kennedy that the US try to moderate the language of the resolutions, perhaps revive the idea of the rapporteur, and call on the Portuguese to begin talks with "its own *nationalist* leaders on the application of self-determination."[159]

It was evident to the White House that the United States would have to initiate some kind of action to maintain credibility with the African states and to pre-empt resolutions calling for more extreme actions. Kennedy, however, was of a different mind on the issue of Portuguese Africa. This had become evident in May 1963 when he appointed Admiral George W. Anderson as the new American ambassador to Portugal. Anderson had been dropped as Chief of Naval Operations following differences with McNamara and Navy Secretary Fred Korth during the Cuban missile crisis. In spite of protests from the Africa Bureau, Kennedy wanted the contentious Anderson out of Washington. Furthermore, he figured that Anderson and the Portuguese "deserved each other."

At the same time, the President tried a more conciliatory approach toward Nogueira. In a meeting in the Oval Office on 29 May 1963, Kennedy told the Portuguese foreign minister that his decisions of 1961 had been "precipitous."[160]

Kennedy was also smarting from the report of the Clay Committee that was issued on 20 March 1963. Created to defend the administration's foreign aid program, the committee instead issued a report that attacked the very premise of the program. It reasoned that because the African countries were not contiguous to the Communist bloc, they were not part of the "frontier of freedom." Therefore, the new African nations ought to look to their former colonial masters for development assistance; the United States had been "trying to do too much for too many too soon." It recommended that the US grant programs already in operation in Africa should be reduced and new grants be discouraged. New loan requests were to be severely screened.[161]

During a meeting in the Cabinet room on 18 July with Rusk, Harlan Cleveland, Ball, Stevenson and others, Kennedy made it clear that his main priority was Senate ratification of the Test Ban Treaty that was being negotiated with the Soviet Union. Furthermore, sharp disagreement existed in the Western alliance over the Multi-lateral Force and the European Common Market. Kennedy wanted no trouble over the Azores. To lose access to the base would jeopardize Senate ratification of the Treaty and create an even deeper split in NATO. In fact, he asked, why should we take the initiative in pressing for a resolution on Portugal? What if we hung back, did nothing and let nature take its course? Let the

Portuguese Foreign Minister find out for himself how bad things are. The President suggested that the United States should not take the lead nor give the impression that Washington could do much for him—or would do much against him. The President asked Stevenson what position the French would take during the debate. Stevenson replied that, as usual, the French would seek the best of both worlds. "Well, let us try that this time," Kennedy responded.[162]

Kennedy decided on a strategy in which the United States would adopt a firm, hard stand against South Africa and a relatively mild position toward Portugal. The administration felt that pressure on South Africa would "do something in African eyes to make up for restraint in the case of Portugal."[163]

Following the meeting on 18 July, Stevenson returned to New York. As expected, a resolution was submitted to the Security Council, sponsored by Morocco, Ghana, and the Philippines, calling for an arms embargo and labeling Portugal a "threat to international peace" (which created the possibility of further Security Council action under Chapter VII of the UN charter). Working feverishly behind the scenes, Stevenson produced a compromise resolution that he thought would be acceptable to the US, the Afro-Asian nations, and Portugal.

Stevenson's compromise resolution, however, was still stronger than any to which Kennedy and Rusk would agree. Its fate was virtually sealed when the British registered their concern. On 26 July, David Ormsby-Gore, Great Britain's ambassador in Washington and one of Kennedy's closest friends, called George Ball with a message from Prime Minister Alec Douglas-Home. Home wanted Rusk to "keep his eye on the precise terms" of any resolution adopted on the Portuguese territories as it could create an "extremely difficult" precedent for the British in Rhodesia and British Guiana.[164]

When the resolution came up for a vote on 31 July, Kennedy, at the last minute, instructed Stevenson to abstain. Kennedy was determined to avoid further flare-ups with the Portuguese. He told Bundy that "we should bend over backwards" to avoid harassing them. Yet, in preparation for the worst, he sent a memo to Secretary of Defense McNamara requesting his thoughts on contingencies should the US lose access to the Azores.[165]

In the Security Council, an angry and frustrated Adlai Stevenson affirmed that the United States did agree with the substance of the resolution but differed over the tactics to be employed to bring about self-determination in the Portuguese territories. As a sop to the African states, he announced that the United States, "for a number of years," had "followed a policy of providing no arms or military equipment to Portugal for use in these territories . . . . We trust that other states will exercise similar restraint . . . ."

Privately, Stevenson was "disgusted" with Kennedy's decision to abstain. He compared it to Eisenhower's last minute decision in December 1960 to abstain on the resolution condemning colonialism. Stevenson suspected, correctly, that, as in December 1960, the British had unduly influenced the American position. Also, Kennedy did not want anything to jeopardize American access to the Azores.[166]

Following his restrained but terse speech, an agitated Stevenson left the Security Council chamber. He ran into Franco Nogueira in the corridor and the two diplomats exchanged bitter words. This spat came on the heels on two other heated encounters between Portuguese and American diplomats. On 9 July, the Portuguese Naval Chief of Staff, Vice Admiral Roboredo, called in the US Naval attaché in Lisbon to protest the difficulty he was having in purchasing routine equipment from the US. Unable to contain his frustration, Roboredo threw a sheaf of unanswered messages in the attaché's lap and exclaimed that the United States's "absurd conduct of saying one thing and then doing another was no longer acceptable to the Portuguese."

Two weeks later, while Nogueira was in New York preparing for the Security Council debate, José Manuel Fragoso, Nogueira's assistant and director of political affairs, called Elbrick to the Ministry of Foreign Affairs. Fragoso accused the United States of being duplicitous, of saying it was sympathetic to Portugal's situation when in fact the United States was supporting the African position. An indignant Elbrick said he would report these allegations to his government and left Fragoso's office. When he heard about the incident, Kennedy was "highly irritated" and sent a cable to the Portuguese protesting the accusations and Elbrick's treatment. The White House abruptly canceled a meeting that Nogueira was to have had with Kennedy. Thus when Bundy reported the Nogueira-Stevenson encounter to Kennedy, the President "went through the roof."[167]

For all of Kennedy's efforts to placate the Portuguese, there was little that the United States received in return. As Harriman said to Ball, "I think we're jeopardizing the [support of all the] nations of Africa by trying to appease them."[168]

Following the United States's abstention in the Security Council, Salazar picked up the cudgels and attacked Kennedy's foreign policy during a speech in front of 250,000 people at the Cais das Colunas in the center of Lisbon. Salazar equated US support for self-determination in Africa with the aims of the Soviet Union: both states sought "to capture and control markets." Furthermore, the Soviet Union's approach was "coherent and logical." The United States, on the other hand, pursued an irrational policy that reduced the "potential" of European allies "in favor of the . . . enemy, which is Communism." Despite Salazar's criticism of the United States, the Portuguese were sanguine about the future. It appeared to Lisbon that Washington had, "without a doubt, abandoned the idea of managing a rapid collapse of Portuguese policy in Africa." As the Prime Minister commented following a meeting of the Council of Ministers in Lisbon on 6 August 1963, "we hit them well."[169]

Four days later, Rusk responded to Salazar's charges at a news conference in Washington. In his typically understated manner, he said, "We cannot be expected to like" Salazar's allegations. Addressing the most sensitive aspect of the problem, he continued, "It's a very practical notion in the modern world" that the most stable and productive relations are those which "rest upon the consent of those directly involved . . . . We would hope . . . the Portuguese presence in Africa could be sustained by the demonstrated consent of the people," but, softening his tone, this is "for the people themselves to clarify."[170]

With the crossfire between Lisbon and Washington intensifying every week, Kennedy let it be known to his advisers that he wanted it to stop. In an effort to calm the Portuguese, the White House decided to send a personal representative of the president's to Lisbon for consultations with the Portuguese government. Ball suggested to Bundy that Stevenson, who was about to depart for a vacation in Europe, be the one to pay a visit on Salazar. Ball reasoned that "Salazar is a pretty lonely man and may respond to a personal touch of this kind, and Stevenson has a considerable reputation in Europe." In his icy, dry manner, Bundy replied, "In Portugal, Stevenson doesn't have a reputation at all."[171]

In August, Kennedy instructed Ball to stop in Lisbon for a talk with Salazar. The objective of the visit was to reconcile the differences between Lisbon and Washington and to explain to the Portuguese the consequences of their refusal to make "adjustments" in their African policies.

Ball found Salazar to be articulate, thoughtful, and well-read though "absorbed by a time dimension quite different from ours." Sitting in a crimson velvet Louis XIV chair, with his high buttoned shoes and his lap blanket, he appeared more as a "museum-piece" than an iron-fisted dictator. Ball tried to persuade Salazar of the "necessity to establish immediately the *right* of self-determination—not its *implementation* which could come only after a gradual process of preparation." Pointing to the OAU meeting in Addis Ababa as one reason for "the tremendous build up of pressure in Africa," Ball suggested a plan for self-determination based on Bowles's proposals. The Under Secretary asked whether there was any way that Portugal could adopt a position that the US could support. Ball volunteered that the "US would be prepared to absorb some damage to our other interests [in Africa] in order to be helpful." Salazar was unresponsive to this offer and replied that he did not understand why the United States wanted to "interfere" with Portugal's civilizing mission.[172]

Ball concluded his talks with Salazar and Nogueira fearing that "their two points of view were farther apart than he had hoped." He left thinking that Salazar and the Portuguese were living in more than one century. As for Nogueira, Ball quipped to an embassy official, "That chap could be minister of Czechoslovakia tomorrow." Despite Ball's visit and another stop on the way back from Pakistan a week later, and a subsequent exchange of lengthy letters, the cloistered dictator did not change his belief that the US was "plain wrong" in its "evangelical view" of the need to grant independence in Africa.[173]

The Time Factor

Unable to move Portugal as he had wanted, Kennedy had been forced to retreat from his original policy of direct confrontation and pressure. As Assistant Secretary Williams said in his end-of-the-year letter to all American ambassadors in Africa, Washington's support for self-determination "appeared less sure, less clear. While we did what we could vis-à-vis Angola, Mozambique, and South Africa, the limiting conditions became stronger and more patent."[174]

The emergence of other issues were in part responsible for this. Fifteen thousand American "advisers" had been sent to Vietnam, the crisis in Berlin was still simmering, and De Gaulle was becoming increasingly obdurate. With the collapse of the secessionist movement in Katanga and the independence of Algeria, the State Department was eager to claim a victory for its Africa policy and cut its losses. Indeed, as Dean Rusk put it, "I just felt that the informal division of labor we had with our Western European allies was the right way to proceed in

Africa . . . . Africa was not high on my list of priorities." [175] In Congress, Kennedy's domestic programs—on civil rights, tax reform, federal aid to education—were stalled by a coalition of Republicans and anti-administration southern Democrats.[176] Kennedy was unable, and had little incentive, to give the problems of Portugal and Portuguese Africa the same energy and attention he once had.

Even though Kennedy's strategy had changed, the administration continued its efforts to initiate a dialogue between Portugal and the African states at the UN in hopes of producing some kind of breakthrough. While in Lisbon, Ball had persuaded Nogueira to participate in direct talks under the sponsorship of the Secretary General.

On the surface, it appeared that Portugal was in a more conciliatory mood toward its African critics. Salazar had written Congo (Brazzaville) president Filbert Youlou in July to announce that there would be elections in Angola before the end of the year. Nogueira had given Rusk the same message on 2 August. Salazar had also sent a message to the pro-Western Emperor of Ethiopia, Haile Selassie, inviting him to send an observer to Angola and Mozambique "to verify the true situation."[177] Given these signals of cooperation, the Americans were hopeful that, if nothing else, it might be possible to create a meaningful dialogue between Portugal and the Africans. The Portuguese utilized the opportunity to negotiate a nonaggression pact with those African governments that bordered Portuguese territories. Only Malawi consented to signing such a treaty with Lisbon.

On 18 October, a delegation of Portuguese officials led by Franco Nogueira opened talks with representatives from nine African states. From the outset, the prospects for success were dubious. Holden Roberto disclaimed any connection with the talks. Nogueira further muddied the waters by telling the African delegates that he had documentation to prove that Roberto was on the American payroll. Within two weeks, the discussions broke down. The Africa group regretted that there had been no indication of a "fundamental change" in Portugal's position. Nogueira blamed the failure on the inability to agree on a concept of self-determination.[178]

On 7 November, Nogueira met with Kennedy for the last time. Kennedy had been told that the Portuguese had been stalling at the talks in New York. He was advised to urge Nogueira to adopt publicly a more forthcoming position on self-determination. Portuguese cooperation on this point was essential if the US was going to be able to moderate the debate in the UN and influence the Africans.[179]

In their meeting, Kennedy asked Nogueira about the progress of the talks with the Africans. The Portuguese Foreign Minister complained that separately each African diplomat seemed reasonable but together each tried to be more extremist than the other. Toward the end of the discussion, George Ball entered the Oval Office. Kennedy asked him what he thought was the primary point of divergence between Portugal and the United States. Unequivocally, Ball responded, "The time factor." Time was not working to the favor of the Portuguese, and there was no more than a decade to prepare for self-determination in Africa. As the Under Secretary had written Salazar, the American position was not based on "narrow self-interest but on an anxiety to preserve the values of our civilization."[180] Because of Portuguese stalling and the press of other issues, however, American anxiety over the future of Portugal and its colonies in Africa was rapidly diminishing.

Although the Kennedy policy did "lean," or tilt, toward the nationalist organizations in Angola and Mozambique, the effort to have the "best of both worlds" ensured a policy defined by ambiguity. Access to the Azores was an enduring national security interest for the Kennedy Administration, as was identifying with self-determination in Africa. Both interests were served imperfectly, however. Nevertheless, it was important to the American position in Africa that the administration did not altogether abandon its goal of trying to encourage self-determination in Portuguese Africa. It was equally important that the administration did not lose access to the bases on the Azores.

Chapter 2

Lyndon Johnson and Africa: The Right Policy for the Wrong Reasons

---

The Chinese Discover Africa

Africa was thrust onto the Kennedy administration's foreign policy agenda by the emergence of more than thirty new nations on the continent. African issues also intruded early into the Johnson presidency. Policymakers in Washington, however, were not interested in nurturing nationalist passions in Africa. They were transfixed by the notion that Africa, more than ever, was an arena for superpower competition. The unprecedented ten-nation African tour made by China's Prime Minister Chou En-Lai in December 1963 and January 1964 was an undeniable signal that Africa was a prize in the struggle for influence among the great powers. The trip constituted China's most open challenge to the Soviet Union, and it awoke the West to China's emerging interest in the continent. As Dean Rusk acknowledged in February 1964, "The Communist world is no longer a single flock of sheep following blindly behind one leader."[1] Unknown and isolated from the Western world, Beijing's brand of Communism appeared to Washington to be more sinister and subversive than Moscow's. The concern increased in September 1965 when Chinese Defense Minister Lin Piao threatened the West with a series of revolutions throughout the Third World that would "encircle" the industrialized countries.

By the middle of 1964, sixteen African nations had formal ties with Beijing. Twenty-five countries had established relations with the Soviet Union and sixteen had recognized Cuba. Some analysts in the American government downplayed the significance of this, arguing that "Africa is too immense and diverse to be 'taken over' by anyone."[2] Others felt that an increase of Soviet or Chinese influence in the region represented a serious threat to American national security.

Chou En-Lai's proclamation that Africa was "ripe for revolution" seemed to come alarmingly true on 12 January 1964 when a revolt turned the young nation of Zanzibar into a "people's republic" on its thirty-fourth day of independence from the United Kingdom. The new regime was quickly recognized by North Korea, Cuba, China, East Germany, and the Soviet Union. Western observers feared that in the spiraling competition between pro-Moscow and pro-Chinese factions on Zanzibar, "the Chinese branch of communism could gain a foothold" on the Indian Ocean island.[3] From the American point of view, the superpower scramble for influence in Africa was more acute than it had ever been before.

The NSC advisor on Africa, William Brubeck, spelled out American concerns over China's political offensive in Africa in a memo to the President. Brubeck warned Johnson that China's practice of subverting moderate African regimes presented a threat to the strategic position of the United States in Africa. More immediate, Brubeck warned, was the possibility that Beijing might successfully persuade a majority of African governments to vote for their entry into the United Nations.[4]

Although Washington recognized the "revolutionary" government on Zanzibar, the already tense relations suffered further when the thirty-three-year-old chargé d'affaires in the consulate, Frank Carlucci, was expelled for "subversive activities." In a conversation on an open telephone line with Robert Gordon, a diplomat in the American embassy in Dar es Salaam, Carlucci learned that Washington needed more "ammunition" as it concerned a policy initiative. To the nervous Zanzibarians listening in on the conversation, this was grounds to declare Carlucci and Gordon persona non grata. Washington subsequently concluded that there was no basis for the charges.[5]

As China was making diplomatic inroads in Africa, Nikita Khrushchev tried to remind African leaders that the Soviet Union was the true champion of Africa's aspirations. In a New Year's message that Khrushchev sent to heads of government throughout the world, he reaffirmed once again that it was the "sacred right" of those under colonialism to take up arms in an effort to end colonialism. "The quicker and fuller [*sic*] it is done, the better the cause for world peace."[6]

This type of pronouncement had had a chilling effect on the Kennedy administration, newly arrived in office in 1961, and helped to provide the rationale for a significant departure from traditional policy in the case of Portugal and its African territories. The same message in 1964, however, was barely noticed by President Johnson, who was groping to establish his own presidential identity. Administration energies were then focused on creating a Great Society at home and not on taming new frontiers in Africa.

Playing the China Card

The political crisis on Zanzibar reverberated throughout the State Department and helped to undermine the influence of the Assistant Secretary of State for Africa, G. Mennen Williams. Lyndon Johnson had not forgotten that Williams's appointment had been a concession to liberal Democrats angry at Kennedy for his selection as running mate on the ticket. The wariness between Johnson and Williams was exacerbated by the reputation that Williams had earned in some quarters as an inefficient administrator whose view of Africa was sentimental and out of step with the thrust of American foreign policy. As a bureaucrat, Williams "swung an effective broadsword in the arena of general salesmanship and political speech-making, but had neither the taste nor the talent for the fine epée work required in internal staff debate." Williams also had a reputation for being an "activist" assistant secretary who continually tried to bring the "difficult" issues to the attention of the most senior officials. This further eroded Williams's influence, especially with Lyndon Johnson, who "was perfectly happy to have as little to do with Africa as required."[7]

In the wake of the Zanzibar crisis, Averell Harriman was appointed "coordinator" of African issues. Johnson told Rusk and Ball that he wanted "somebody on the seventh floor (where the secretary of state and his top advisers had their offices) to be responsible" for dealing with African problems. As Harriman said in an interview at the time, ". . . everything having to do with Africa . . . will be my responsibility to see that it is tended to right away."[8] Harriman was expected to handle policy issues that could not be settled at the assistant secretary level, and, particularly, "to keep them away from the Secretary."[9]

Harriman's appointment was a slap at Williams, though this bureaucratic shuffle in fact became an asset to the Africa Bureau. Harriman shared a similar outlook with Williams and his principal deputy, Wayne Fredericks, and he also had significant credibility with Johnson, Rusk, and Ball. Nonetheless, the President decided in early

1964 to curtail Williams's ability to define his administration's Africa policy. The message became indelibly clear in March as Williams was preparing to deliver a blistering attack on South Africa's policy of apartheid at the Harvard Law School. Hours before the speech, which had been advertised as a major policy address, the text of Williams' remarks were sharply redrafted by Rusk and Ball, who insisted that he give a noncontroversial assessment of present policy.[10]

Lyndon Johnson was not the only politician who tried to draw some benefit from the upheaval on Zanzibar. Both of Washington's disenchanted allies, Franco Nogueira and Holden Roberto, made an effort to parlay American concern over China into political advantages. In January 1964, Nogueira told the *New York Times* correspondent in Madrid, Paul Hofmann, that the Portuguese were considering opening relations with China.[11] Even though it came on the heels of the French recognition of the People's Republic of China, the American embassy in Lisbon speculated that Nogueira was not seriously considering an exchange of ambassadors with Beijing but was "again engaged in gamesmanship."[12] In fact, according to Nogueira, Salazar vetoed this initiative over concern about the American response.[13]

An embittered Holden Roberto did not hesitate to employ the tactics of his adversary. At the same time that Nogueira leaked his intentions to the *New York Times*, Roberto signaled that he too was going to China for badly needed military and political support. Following a meeting with Chinese Foreign Minister Chen Yi during Kenya's independence celebrations, the CIA reported that Roberto had been promised "large-scale military aid" by the Chinese. Frustrated by Washington, Roberto let it be known that he was considering going to China and Cuba to broaden his base of support.

Cyrile Adoula, Roberto's host in the Congo, who maintained relations with Taiwan and not Beijing, was very concerned about Roberto's "radical change." On 26 March, he told Harriman, who was visiting key African leaders to assure them of President Johnson's interest in Africa, that Holden "was slipping," and this might lead to a leftist takeover of GRAE. According to Adoula, Roberto was moving too slowly against the Portuguese and was under attack for being an "agent of imperialism." Furthermore, a tie between Roberto and China could enable the Chinese, having established political relations across the river in Brazzaville, to penetrate GRAE and, ultimately, the Congo.[14]

At a dinner party the following evening, Adoula asked Harriman to meet quietly with Roberto and to assure the Angolan leader that the United States was not against him or his movement. Refusing this request, Harriman told Adoula that if such a meeting were known to the Portuguese "it would completely destroy our usefulness vis-à-vis Salazar." He added that the United States could contribute most to resolving Roberto's problems by maintaining relations with Portugal and encouraging Lisbon to decolonize. Harriman reminded the Congolese president of the pressures that the United States had been exerting on Portugal. The veteran American diplomat also told Adoula that Mac Godley, the American ambassador in the Congo, was authorized to meet with Roberto anytime Roberto wished. Adoula said he would pass along Harriman's assurances to Roberto.[15]

Roberto's problems became more acute several months later when Cyrile Adoula was toppled in a July 1964 coup, led by the Katangan separatist Moises Tshombe. Tshombe, who had received support from Portugal and South Africa in a bid to challenge the Soviet backing of Patrice Lumumba in the Congo, dismissed Roberto as an "ambitious fraud." As Tshombe was confronted by an insurgency in eastern Congo, aided in part by the Chinese and Soviet Union, he was hardly prepared to allow Roberto to forge new military ties with China and Cuba. As a result, Roberto's diplomatic initiatives stalled leaving GRAE an "organizational fiasco."[16]

At a press conference during this period, McGeorge Bundy noted that it was "absolutely standard practice" for a friendly country irritated with the US to threaten to turn to the Sino-Soviet bloc. He also commented wryly that the United States "should not invariably assume that such a threat requires us to fall over ourselves trying to meet the demands of the man who poses it . . . ."[17]

Anderson Prods Portugal

The responsibility for encouraging Portugal to adopt a position in Portuguese Africa that would be consonant with American objectives fell largely to the pugnacious American ambassador, Admiral George W. Anderson. When Kennedy assigned Anderson to the post in Lisbon, it was originally thought that his military demeanor and combative style would be at home in the drawing rooms of the regal, if worn, Portuguese foreign ministry at the Palacio de Necessidades. Contrary to

Kennedy's expectations, however, Anderson's admiration for Portugal's "reformist" colonial policies characterized his tenure as ambassador.

In his first six months in Portugal, Anderson had no more success than did his predecessor, C. Burke Elbrick, in inducing Portugal to resume discussions over the Azores. Anderson's task was complicated in late 1963 when the State Department instructed him to request permission from Lisbon to open a second consulate in Beira, Mozambique. The State Department also wanted permission to install LORAN-C navigational equipment on Portuguese territory to facilitate trans-Atlantic navigation by American ships and aircraft.

In his first meeting with Nogueira, the Portuguese foreign minister said he was tired of Washington's incessant requests for favors that did not take into account Portugal's interests. To Anderson, this was a signal that a major diplomatic effort would be necessary to obtain Portuguese acquiescence for the consulate in Beira and the placement of the LORAN-C equipment. In an effort to make the requests more palatable to Portugal, the State Department approved Anderson's suggestion that Washington approve the request from Lisbon to purchase six small caliber machine guns for use on their frigates.[18] Anderson was also able to convince Rusk, over the protests of the Consul General in Maputo, Thomas K. Wright, that American information needs in northern Mozambique could be met by an occasional visit of an officer from the Consulate in Maputo, six hundred miles to the south.[19]

The Admiral, however, was not content with Washington's willingness, however modest, to be more forthcoming with the Salazar regime. As the American ambassador saw it, his job was overly complicated by the variety of tasks that he was forced to assume. He was trying simultaneously to persuade the Portuguese to be more forthcoming on self-determination, to improve their image internationally, not to recognize the People's Republic of China, to allow the installation of LORAN-C, and to renew the Azores agreement.[20] To improve his chances of achieving his objectives, therefore, Anderson suggested to Rusk that the United States resume the Military Assistance Program to Portugal, which had been suspended in 1961. He reasoned that as a tactic to persuade Portugal to renew the Azores treaty, the arms embargo had failed and, as a result, had outlived its purpose. Furthermore, it had had an "adverse impact" on relations between the Pentagon and Portuguese military officials.[21]

Rusk expressed sympathy for Anderson's difficulties, but told the Ambassador that the Military Assistance Program could not be renewed. Indeed, in Rusk's view, no military relationship between Portugal and the US could be reestablished until Portugal withdrew the remaining American aircraft from Guinea-Bissau and established a compliance mechanism to ensure that American military equipment furnished to Lisbon in a NATO context would remain in Portugal. Rusk instructed Anderson to tell Nogueira that funds could be released to help the Portuguese purchase LORAN-C receivers if Lisbon responded positively to Washington's original request.[22]

Although Rusk apparently was comfortable with Anderson's approach to the Portuguese, the Africa Bureau was decidedly uneasy. Indeed, Rusk gave Anderson permission to visit Portugal's colonies "and Kenya for contrast," in spite of opposition from G. Mennen Williams.

Following his return to Lisbon, Anderson briefed Salazar on the two-month journey. Anderson told the Portuguese Prime Minister that he had he had been "very favorably impressed" by the economic and social developments in the overseas territories. Nevertheless, he allowed, much remained to be done in Mozambique and Angola before the territories could "mature" politically and economically. The Ambassador asked Salazar whether the Portuguese were not underestimating "the force and drive" of African nationalism. Anderson nonetheless agreed with Salazar's response that, indeed, the source of nationalism was located outside Portuguese Africa. The sly autocrat then used this admission to rebuff Anderson's request for a public statement by Portugal associating itself with "a reasonable concept of self-determination." After all, Salazar replied, "If each dockworker, stevedore, and typist . . . saw ahead of him the prospect of becoming a cabinet member or prime minister, how much attention would he pay to his present duties and function?" Therefore, if Portugal were to accede to American pressures, the problem of nationalism would immediately become a raging *internal* one where none had existed. In the view of the septuagenarian leader, the United States should oppose, "morally and realistically," those states and political movements that practiced "trans-border terrorism," and not Portugal, which was trying to move forward in a peaceful and legal fashion.[23]

Trying to Maintain Portugal's Confidence

Anderson's admiration for Portugal's colonial policies did not obscure the American intelligence community's growing view that Lisbon was beginning to experience significant strains in trying to maintain a war fighting capability in Angola, Mozambique, and Guinea-Bissau. The CIA noted that the Portuguese military, which had expanded from a garrison force of a few thousand in 1961 to 125,000 in 1964,[24] was experiencing serious morale problems. Students, whose academic careers had been interrupted to fight in harsh African terrain, accounted for a large segment of these new recruits. Morale was also affected by the physical and emotional demands of waging a guerrilla war in Africa against an enemy they rarely saw and in support of a cause that they increasingly opposed. The CIA concluded that if these trends continued, "the rising dissatisfaction might . . . convince the military of the need to remove Salazar."[25]

Awareness of these ominous trends did not reach the upper levels of the Johnson administration. With the influence of the Africa Bureau eclipsed, a consensus had emerged among senior officials in the State Department that any new American pressures would seriously aggravate US-Portuguese relations and erode further the minimal influence that Washington had in Lisbon. American policymakers were also concerned that new pressures would further jeopardize American tenancy of the Azores and undermine efforts to obtain sites for the LORAN-C navigational equipment. Nevertheless, the National Security Council concluded that Portugal's prospects in Africa were grim:

> It is no longer a question of whether or not Angola will become independent, the only question is when and how, as was the case with Algeria. By the same token, it is certain that the longer the struggle goes on, the more violent, racist, and Communist infiltrated it may become, the more serious will be the final crisis confronting the U.S. and the more chaotic, radical and anti-Western an emerging independent Angola will be.[26]

Whereas the "Europeanists" were content to relax the pressures on Portugal, the "Africanists" utilized this bleak view of Angola's future to shore up bureaucratic support for strengthening ties to the nationalist movements, GRAE and FRELIMO. G. Mennen Williams proposed to the Special Group, a subcommittee of the NSC that approved all covert operations, a political action program to make FRELIMO and GRAE more credible alternatives to the Portuguese by reducing "the growing influence of radical and communist forces" in the organizations. The program was based on the premise that the struggle for self-determination could not be won militarily. Therefore, the Africa Bureau reasoned, "The nationalists should alter their present tactics [from guerilla warfare] and concentrate their energies, with our clandestine assistance, in setting up extensive political organizations within and outside the territories." Covert American support would go for a number of activities including an aggressive international public relations program, clandestine printing presses and radio stations, the development of nationalist cells in every village, industry and large farm, the organization of peaceful demonstrations and strikes, and the penetration of the Portuguese police by FRELIMO and GRAE partisans and supporters.[27]

To the Special Group, the political action program was a "saleable policy," and it was promptly approved. Yet it never approached its intended level of activity and resulted primarily in a modest increase in the disbursements to the nationalist leaders. In fact, the program essentially served to protect the existing ties with the nationalist movements from those in the foreign policy bureaucracy who wanted to terminate them.[28]

As Johnson campaigned for reelection in the fall of 1964, he sent word to his closest advisers that "foreigners and foreign affairs were to do nothing except, where possible, advance the Johnson electoral cause." The Departments of State and Defense were mobilized to respond to each of Barry Goldwater's campaign charges, and Johnson abandoned his regular Tuesday luncheons with his key foreign policy advisers, including Rusk, McNamara, and Bundy. The White House focused on only a select number of national security problems: Vietnam, policy toward Western Europe, Cuba, nuclear proliferation, blocking China's accession to the United Nations, and foreign aid. Political instability in the Congo was the sole African issue that was even of "marginal" importance to a president that was "about to have the biggest victory of the century." The administration viewed Portuguese territories as a "long-term" problem and one that could not be allowed to jeopardize immediate US foreign policy interests or Johnson's reelection.[29]

Offering "Carrots" to Portugal

Despite the President's lack of interest in Portugal and its faltering colonial empire in Africa, there was still a consensus within the administration over the importance of getting Lisbon to soften its position on self-determination in Africa, LORAN-C, and the Azores. The United States, however, was no longer willing to exert direct pressure on Lisbon to achieve any of these goals. As Dean Rusk put it, "We stopped battering our heads against the wall for the fun of it."[30]

The American retreat from earlier pressures was in part due to Nogueira's determined obstinacy and skill at transforming American protests and requests into pressure on American diplomats. In February 1964, for example, when Anderson asked Nogueira about installing LORAN-C equipment, the Foreign Minister said that such a move would constitute an important form of cooperation with a country that was pursuing a policy hostile to Portugal's interests. Therefore, why should the Portuguese accede to American requests? When Anderson refuted this by saying that the navigational equipment was in the common interests of Western security, Nogueira asked why, if the United States was so concerned about Western security, did the American ambassador in Kinshasa tell the Portuguese chargé d'affairs that it was time for Lisbon to begin negotiating with Holden Roberto? Furthermore, Nogueira continued, why did G. Mennen Williams claim in a recent speech in Canada that communism "has no foothold in Africa?" This particular meeting ended, like many others, in a desultory fashion for the Admiral as Nogueira reminded him that Portugal was just trying to eliminate the risks of losing its position in Africa.[31]

Rusk had no more success than did Anderson in trying to persuade Nogueira to be more conciliatory to American overtures. When he asked his Portuguese counterpart at a NATO meeting in Paris whether Portugal was contemplating a change in its Africa policy, Nogueira replied simply that the recent wave of instability in the Congo and throughout the continent underscored the importance of Portugal maintaining its present course. Rusk and Nogueira, who had developed a close personal rapport in spite of their differences on policy matters, agreed only that Britain and France seemed to be taking less interest in African problems at a time when they should have been more engaged.[32] The effect of such maneuvering by the unyielding foreign minister put the United States in the unenviable position of having publicly moderated its stance on Portuguese colonialism without having achieved any change in Portugal's policies in Africa.

Admiral Anderson, for one, remained hopeful that the Portuguese might "come around." When he returned to Washington for consultations with the State Department in the spring of 1964, the Admiral suggested to Rusk that a presidential emissary be sent on a tour of the Portuguese colonies. Anderson reasoned that this might generate new recommendations that could lead to a breakthrough in US-Portuguese relations. In August 1964, Roswell Gilpatrick, who had just resigned as deputy secretary of defense, was sent to the colonies to personally assess American policy to Portugal, Angola, and Mozambique.

The report from Anderson's African tour had been positive, but Gilpatrick's was glowing. To his eye, the Portuguese had made great advances in housing, education, employment, and public health. Given this favorable situation and the hostile neighbors on the borders of Angola and Mozambique, he felt that there was no alternative to continued Portuguese administration of the colonies. His subsequent policy recommendations were pitched directly at the heart of the difficulties between the US and Portugal. He suggested that the two allies should pursue a policy of "mutual example" in which each side would make a concession to the other. The United States would remove restrictions on the purchase of military spare parts and equipment by Portugal, while Portugal would grant the US continued access to the Azores and allow LORAN-C sites to be established. The US would also refrain from actions at the UN that were inimical to Portugal, if Lisbon continued to try to develop a substantive dialogue with the African states.[33]

Washington followed Gilpatrick's suggestions by setting an example that Lisbon relished. In early 1965, the administration decided to sell Portugal twenty B-26 aircraft. The planes, used as bombers during World War II, were intended for deployment in the colonies. Yet the sale, known as "Operation Sparrow," was "uncovered" several months later by the Treasury Department after only seven of the planes had been delivered to Portugal—without the required export licenses or political assurances from Lisbon.

In the ensuing trial, Lawrence Houston, CIA general counsel, denied charges that the CIA had instigated and organized the illegal sale. In fact, Houston claimed, the CIA was aware of the deal only five days before the first plane was delivered and, at that point, had promptly informed the State Department, Customs, and eleven other agencies.[34]

The illegal sale of the B-26 aircraft to Portugal, engineered by the White House, the Pentagon, and the "Europeanists" at the State Department, was a deliberate attempt to induce the Portuguese to renew the agreement on the Azores. The administration did not see the action as "decisive" in any respect. To the contrary, the planes were the "lowest common denominator," given Lisbon's requests for jet aircraft, napalm, and other materials.[35] In an ultimately futile gesture, Mennen Williams protested the sale to Jeffery Kitchen in the Bureau of Politico–Military Affairs arguing that the sale of military aircraft to Portugal could jeopardize the "entire diplomatic position" of the United States in Africa.[36]

The immediate political repercussions of the initiative were minimal. Arthur Goldberg, who had replaced Adlai Stevenson as ambassador to the UN, was accused by Soviet Ambassador Nikolai Fedorenko at the Security Council in the fall of 1965 of supplying Portugal with planes to suppress the black rebellion in Angola and Mozambique. Goldberg denied it, and recited the American policy that prohibited Portugal from receiving arms from public or private American sources "without specific assurances that they will not be used in the overseas territories." The Hungarian delegate, Ambassador Zoltan Szilagyi, was more specific. In addition to the seven B-26 fighter aircraft, he charged that other NATO armaments and spare parts had been sent to Portugal for use in Africa "on instructions from the competent US authorities." An American delegate to the UN, Eugenie Anderson, conceded that the seven aircraft had been sold to Portugal, but "by private persons . . . without the United States authorities having the slightest knowledge of the operation."[37]

Although the sale of the aircraft may not have undermined the American position in Africa, it crystallized the very different approach that the Johnson administration was using to address the problems in Portuguese Africa. The sale also was tantamount to a death knell for the innovative policies that the Africa Bureau at the State Department had been pursuing under President Kennedy and the influence that G. Mennen Williams had been able to exert.

Admiral Anderson, however, moved quickly to exploit the sale of the war materials to the Salazar regime to his diplomatic advantage. During the spring and summer of 1965, the embassy in Lisbon, in consultation with Washington, finalized the details of yet another diplomatic strategy, the so-called "Anderson Plan." Like previous strategies, this was aimed at persuading the Portuguese to grant self-determination to their colonies. This plan included a plebiscite under UN and OAU supervision, at a specific date to be determined; Portuguese acceptance of free political activity in the territories with full amnesty for refugees; a suspension by African nationalists of anti-Portuguese activities in the UN; and a US commitment to support the Portuguese at the UN and through arms sales if the Africans violated the agreement. If Portugal agreed, the US would also take the initiative in presenting the program to the Africans.[38]

Rusk and Ball met with Nogueira in Washington on 18 June 1965, as Anderson's proposals were being considered in the State Department. Shortly after the meeting began, Nogueira began his wearying tactic of complaining about American pressures on Portugal. He criticized Williams's "anti-Portuguese speeches," the failure of the US to sell Lisbon sixty mortars and some military vehicles, and pressure that Washington exerted on Italy and Canada not to sell military aircraft to Portugal. Nogueira also expressed agitation over financial support that the Ford Foundation had given to anti-Portuguese "terrorist groups"[39] and American assistance to Angolan refugees.

In an effort to assuage the foreign minister, George Ball assured him that the differences between the two countries did not concern principles but tactics. Defensively, Nogueira reminded the sympathetic Ball that no external power could break the ties between Portugal and its African colonies. After Ball replied that the US did not wish these ties to be destroyed, Rusk raised Anderson's idea for a plebiscite. Without hesitation, Nogueira said that Portugal "could never consent to United Nations' participation." Ball and Rusk said that it was vital for Lisbon to demonstrate to the international community that the local populations supported Portugal's policies. Rusk inquired whether there was not a moderate African chief willing to come forward and with whom the Portuguese could work to break the political deadlock. The secretary of state added that a plebiscite would have saved Goa. Nogueira snapped to Rusk that the invasion of Goa came only after the United States gave India the "green light." On that note, the meeting ended.[40]

Anderson presented the American proposals aimed at encouraging Portugal to move toward self-determination in its colonies to Salazar on 22 October 1965 at São Bento, the Prime Minister's residence. Anderson reminded Salazar of Rusk's 18 June suggestion to Nogueira that Portugal "hoist a flag" for its friends to rally around. When Anderson completed his briefing on the initiatives, Salazar said that the Government of Portugal would give them "serious consideration." Before their conversation ended, Salazar said he did not believe African nationalism was invincible or that the Africans could handle independence on their own. He observed with some irritation that these were the same issues with which Washington had been confronting him since Kennedy's inauguration.

As the proposals were being considered in Lisbon, the State Department instructed Arthur Goldberg to consult privately with Nogueira and the African representatives at the UN in an effort to restart the discussion between Portugal and the African states. Having felt deceived by the Portuguese faint-hearted efforts to initiate talks in the latter part of 1963, the African representatives were wary of Goldberg's approaches. On 22 November 1965, Mongi Slim, the Tunisian representative at the UN, informed Goldberg that discussions could only begin if Portugal accepted the following conditions: that self-determination would include all possible choices ranging from immediate independence to remaining provinces of Portugal; that the discussions be held with the representatives of the various nationalist organizations; and that the discussions relate not only to the scope of the principle of self-determination but to the method, the means, and the modalities of the process.[41]

To the Americans, this was a discouraging development; Washington concluded that neither the Africans nor the Portuguese were willing to compromise to resolve their differences. Nevertheless, in explaining the American abstention on an October 1965 Security Council resolution calling for an arms embargo against Portugal, Goldberg said that the most practical possibility for self-determination would be further American discussion between representatives of Portugal and the African nations as called for by the Security Council in December 1963.[42]

On 28 January 1966, American diplomacy reached another dead end in its effort to move the Portuguese toward some form of self-determination in their colonies. Franco Nogueira informed Anderson that if Portugal accepted the US proposals, there would be chaos in the colonies within six months. Therefore, Lisbon could not accept the plan.

There was little American reaction. Nogueira's account of a December 1965 meeting with Rusk in Paris indicates that the American Secretary of State did nothing to underscore active high-level American interest in the plan. Rather, Rusk informed Nogueira that Anderson was going to be replaced.[43]

The failure of the Anderson plan would be the last American effort to induce the Portuguese to move toward some concept of self-determination in its colonies. In fact, for the next eight years, American policy toward Portugal, Angola, and Mozambique would follow the course etched out by Admiral Anderson in his departing cable to the State Department. The Admiral conveyed to Rusk the opinion that "there is absolutely no change likely in the immediate future in the attitude and determination of the Portuguese Government with respect to their African provinces . . . . It is my recommendation that we let this pot simmer on the back burner until some significant event makes a new approach advisable . . . . I see no purpose gained by *unnecessarily* precipitating irritations in Portuguese-United States relations."[44]

Various reasons explain why the issue of Portuguese Africa slipped from the top of the American foreign policy agenda in 1961 to the virtual bottom in 1966. For one, Portugal successfully resisted six years of American pressure to grant some form of self-determination to their African colonies. Second, Salazar seemed to be in a stronger position than at any time since the outbreak of rebellion in Angola in 1961. Portugal had contained the crisis in Angola, its isolation from Europe had been eased through increased trade ties, and the country's economy was strong. Furthermore, the upheavals in East Africa and the Congo had justified the Prime Minister's belief that the Portuguese territories were an "enclave of stability" amidst "a black sea of communism." Sooner or later, he felt, this would become evident to the United States.[45]

The Johnson administration did seem to accept this view, in spite of the decline of morale within the Portuguese military. There were few senior administration officials who were inclined to pay close attention to African issues, particularly in the Portuguese territories. Finally, for most of 1964 and 1965, the Johnson administration was absorbed with gaining passage of its legislative agenda in Congress. Moreover, Johnson was spending little time on foreign affairs—to the President "civil rights [was] everything." Even with foreign aid, which Johnson previously had wanted to "revolutionize" into a massive worldwide plan for uplifting the less-developed nations, the administration submitted a "bare-bones" budget to Congress.[46] In each of his first two years as president, Johnson sent foreign aid requests to Congress that were the smallest in a decade. Johnson was not prepared to complicate or sacrifice Congressional support for his Great Society programs for development assistance to Third World countries.

Perhaps more fundamentally, the Johnson Administration, much like the Kennedy Administration before it, had concluded that the price of inducing Lisbon to grant self-determination in Africa was not worth the costs of a breakdown in the bilateral relationship. The departure from government of a number of policymakers who had been concerned with this issue at the outset of the Kennedy administration facilitated this conclusion. Furthermore, the Africanists in the bureaucracy had been isolated from involvement with this issue, and those in more senior positions, frustrated in their efforts to pressure or bargain with the Portuguese, had their attention seized by other matters, especially Vietnam.

Preempting Racial Lobbies

Lyndon Johnson's lack of general interest in international affairs was another reason why the issue of Portugal and its refusal to grant self-determination to its colonies slipped on the American foreign policy agenda. It was for this reason that Walter Lippman had dismissed Johnson's bid for the presidency in 1960: "For all his shrewdness and skill as a legislative manager, [he] is not a genuine alternative to Kennedy. For Johnson knows little of the outside world."[47] According to one official who worked on Johnson's NSC staff, the President's view of the world was "very insular," and he tended to see international politics largely in personal terms. If a country did not have a strong leader, it was difficult for him to gain a clear impression of that country. After personal contact, however, his perception of a certain country became clearer. Nevertheless, he had "no context, no critical faculty" with which to assess trends and events within specific countries. As a former Johnson aid put it, the President simply did not have the "mental furniture" to grasp the complexities of international affairs.[48]

As Vice President, Lyndon Johnson had attended Senegal's independence ceremonies in 1961 and had been impressed by the erudition and eloquence of Senegalese President, Leopold Senghor. Nevertheless, his understanding of Africa was "imprecise and rough," "untutored", and "primitive," according to a key White House adviser."[49] As a result, Johnson tended to view Africa as he did Israel, Ireland, and India: they were important primarily because of their large constituencies within the United States. His perception of Africa, as with much of the rest of the Third World, was shaded by his impoverished childhood in the Texas hill country outside Austin and his experience as a New Deal politician. He believed that if his hometown of Johnson City could be "turned around" with electrification and other infrastructure programs, so could Southeast Asia, Africa, and Latin America.

Despite his lack of interest in African matters, some of Johnson's advisers concluded that the President's lack of interest in the continent could be a liability, especially in the minds of those who compared Johnson to Kennedy. In the early spring of 1965, Ulrich Haynes, who had replaced William Brubeck as the NSC staffer with responsibility for Africa, was interviewed by a correspondent, John Midgley, from the weekly British news magazine, *The Economist*. Midgley, who was doing a story on US policy toward Africa, expressed the opinion that President Kennedy had left a legacy of personal concern and identification for the welfare of the newly independent nations on the continent. He asked whether President Johnson shared this concern. Haynes assured Midgley of the President's deep interest in Africa and pointed to the recent state visit of President Maurice Yameogo of Upper Volta. Midgley remarked that it seemed as if the President had put on a "big show for some rather small fry." He asked whether the reception had been staged to impress American blacks. Haynes vigorously denied this and said that "most American Negroes do not identify with Africa to the same extent that other immigrant Americans identify with a 'mother country.'" Haynes assured Midgley that Lyndon Johnson was "not one who would think of tailoring his hospitality to the size or relative political importance of his guest."[50]

Haynes' assurances notwithstanding, Johnson was as willing as Kennedy to utilize African issues to cultivate the allegiance of black and liberal voters. At the same time, Johnson let it be known in the White House that he did not want to see the emergence of a new pressure group on African issues. Years before entering the White House, he had concluded that foreign policy was the prerogative of the President alone and was not a matter for protracted public discussion. As he saw it, "When they lead your boy down to that railroad station to send him into to boot camp and put a khaki uniform on him to send him some place [from] where he may never return, he doesn't debate foreign policy . . . . They send you to defend the flag and you go."[51]

Johnson's sensitivity to domestic pressure groups forming on foreign policy issues led to several meetings between senior administration officials and civil rights leaders who were calling for a more pronounced Africa policy. The administration was well aware that these groups were "fully capable of creating a 'flap' if they get the feeling that the White House is not willing to give them an audience."[52]

The White House faced a choice in dealing with civil rights activists who wanted the administration more involved with African issues. These groups could be ignored in hopes that they would disappear, which was a distinct possibility as the White House saw it, because such groups had little financing or staff. The other choice was to convey the administration's concern over "racial lobbies" to the leaders of the civil rights movement.[53] In the end, the administration decided to placate the activists through off-the-record meetings. Nevertheless, within the White House, the President made know his "strong views" on African Americans becoming a special interest group on foreign policy:

"The President's view is that since he is working to make the American Negro fully a part of American society, he doesn't think it is at all a good idea to encourage a separate point of view on foreign policy. We don't want an integrated domestic policy and a segregated foreign policy . . . . They should be interested in the totality of American policy."[54]

Although Africa policy received attention from the civil rights leadership, the issue of Portuguese colonialism was not at the top of their agenda either. The matter was touched on in one meeting between Dean Rusk and Roy Wilkins and other representatives from the Negro Leadership Conference. Rusk remarked that "the problems of Portuguese Africa were thorny because of the importance of the Azores to NATO." Yet Portugal was only one subject of many that was discussed in the course of a "quiet and friendly meeting."[55]

The Need for an Africa Policy

The end of the Kennedy administration and the beginning of the Johnson era in US-African relations was marked by a joint United States–Belgium paratroop operation in the Congo in November–December 1964. Its purpose was to rescue several hundred white hostages who were being held in the Katanga province by rebel forces. From the American point of view, the rescue operation was a "necessary and humanitarian action." It was undertaken with the explicit approval of Premier Moises Tshombe to prevent the break-up of the country.

From the African perspective, however, the military operation preempted African efforts, which were led by the Organization of African Unity and the Congo Conciliation Commission, to negotiate the hostages' release. The operation exposed the inability of some of the new African states to protect their own sovereignty and raised the prospect of the much distrusted Belgian Government reasserting itself in its former colony, with American complicity. This emotionally charged event, sandwiched between the Gulf of Tonkin incident in August 1964 and the intervention into the Dominican Republic in May 1965, suggested to a number of African leaders that the United States had embarked on a policy of aggressive unilateralism at the expense of all political considerations.[56]

Also, under Johnson, many of the opinionated and outspoken political appointees that Kennedy had charged with implementing his Africa policy were slowly being replaced by career foreign service officers, especially those in ambassadorial posts. Some who refused to conform to this new order, such as Assistant Secretary Williams, found themselves battling speculative leaks from within the administration about when they would be resigning.[57] The advocates of Africa policy, Williams, Fredericks, and, more recently, Goldberg, were being "smothered" by those senior officials who wanted a low-risk, low-cost Africa policy. The most influential of this group was George Ball, who believed that American ties with Western Europe should set the context for American policy toward Africa. As the President and Secretary of State had little interest in Africa, and Averell Harriman was, with growing frequency, being dispatched on diplomatic missions to generate support for American policy in Vietnam, Ball had become an increasingly crucial figure in shaping the American approach toward Africa.

By early 1965, it was apparent to Johnson's senior foreign policy advisers, including Robert Komer and Ulrich Haynes, both on the NSC staff, that "U.S. prestige and influence on the African continent had never been lower." They told the President that African leaders were "personally" concerned about the lack of interest that the American government appeared to have for Africa's welfare. Komer and Haynes reminded Johnson that no senior American official had ever visited the continent whereas both the Soviet Union and the People's Republic of China had sent high-level envoys on several tours of African capitals.[58]

As African officials were becoming disenchanted with Washington, morale was dropping in American embassies on the continent and in the

Bureau of African Affairs. This stemmed, in large part, from confusion over who was in charge, Harriman or Williams, and the uncertainty surrounding Williams in general. McGeorge Bundy addressed the problem directly in a memo he sent to Johnson in an effort to arrange a "two-minute call" for G. Mennen Williams before the assistant secretary left on a trip to Africa. As Bundy wrote to the President, "I know the problem he represents, but I think it is important that while he is Assistant Secretary, he be seen as *your* Assistant Secretary . . . ."[59]

Komer and Haynes persuaded Bundy that if the administration did not respond to the morale and confidence problems, the United States could jeopardize its strategic, economic, and political interests in the continent despite the more than three billion dollars worth of aid that the US had "poured into Africa." The problem was exacerbated by the "violent African reaction" to the Congo operation as well as "the activities of such Negro extremists as Malcolm X."[60] Johnson had one other inducement to refurbish his Africa policy, according to his NSC staff. Increasingly, pundits were engaging in "restless talk" that the President was not involved in foreign affairs.

McGeorge Bundy made the decision to place American relations with Africa on a new footing. Bundy and his advisers on the NSC suggested that the President announce that the Vice President or the Secretary of State soon make a two-week "friendship" tour of six African nations. His White House advisers encouraged Johnson to give an informal "pep talk" at the State Department to Foreign Service professionals who were concerned with Africa. He was to stress his confidence in their ability to advance US objectives in the region and his own "long-standing and continued personal interests in African affairs." They further urged Johnson to hold a reception for African ambassadors much as he had done with the ambassadors from Latin America the year before. In the end, however, neither the Vice President nor the Secretary of State made the "friendship" visit. Instead, Carl Rowan, director of the United States Information Agency, was dispatched on a two-week, five-nation public relations tour.[61]

A Policy in Search of Direction

In spite of his reluctance to send Vice President Humphrey or Secretary Rusk to Africa, Lyndon Johnson, who "trimmed his sail to every wind,"[62] was receptive to the urgings of his foreign policy advisers to redefine his Africa policy. Williams, White House advisor

Bill Moyers, and NSC aid Haynes, initiated the process by drafting a circular cable that was sent to all diplomatic posts on the continent, including the consulates in Luanda, Angola and Maputo, Mozambique. The cable stated that "the President has encouraged [the] Department [to] take [a] new and critical look at overall African policy as well as country-by-country review . . . . He wants [the] Department to shape future U.S. policy toward Africa with [the] same energy and imagination that generated [the] programs of 'The Great Society' at home." Johnson thought that an effective Africa policy could be developed by eliminating or reforming existing programs, though he allowed that new goals and areas of action might need to be introduced. The emphasis was to be placed on regional cooperation so that African states could more effectively share and utilize their abundant resources in their development efforts. In stark contrast with the Great Society program, Johnson's call for a new Africa policy was predicated on the condition that there would be no new budgetary expenditures.[63]

As far as the White House was concerned, the initial response to the circular from the field was less than satisfactory. For example, William Atwood, the American ambassador to Kenya, cabled that "US policy in Africa should be anchored to four words—firm, frank, friendly, fast."[64] To Ulrich Haynes, this typified the "preliminary thinking" from the Africa Bureau on the "New Program for Africa," as it had come to be called. In his view, the recommendations suffered from several problems: there was something to satisfy every bureaucratic agency, the recommendations lacked direction, and the recommendations were silent on "how" American objectives in Africa were to be achieved. With a skepticism that would be borne out, Haynes, whom Bundy considered "unusually clear-headed about African affairs," signed off on a note to his boss expressing the doubt that the "'New Program . . .' can be pulled down from way up there in the clouds."[65]

The NSC's frustrations at formulating a new Africa policy obscured the genuine consensus of views on a new approach that existed among officials in the Africa Bureau and the ambassadors in the field. There was agreement that the era of "easy independence" was over and African states were now confronted by the more difficult tasks of nation-building. A Chiefs of Mission meeting in Addis Ababa in May 1965, however, concluded that the present policy was basically sound. The American ambassadors recommended that the United States utilize economic aid as a political weapon with more aid going to friends than to critics but that a small amount of aid should go to all African countries. The ambassadors felt that the existence of a bilateral aid program was essential if the US was to exercise influence in individual African countries. (At this time, fifty percent of American aid in Africa went to four countries: Nigeria, Tunisia, Congo-Kinshasa, and Morocco.) The ambassadors also underscored the importance of a "strong US posture on African aspirations," such as self-determination in southern Africa that was seen as "the toughest potential problem" for US–African relations. The ambassadors also suggested that "political action programs" be expanded as an alternative to escalating violence in the region. Finally, the ambassadors warned against announcing a "New African Program" until new resources had been allocated to warrant the use of such a term.[66]

Ulrich Haynes, who participated in the Chiefs of Mission meeting in Addis Ababa and another one in Lagos, reported back to Bundy that the meetings were a "qualified" success. Although they provided a feel for the political and economic climate in Africa, "both conferences failed to generate significant, new or imaginative ideas around which a 'New Policy for Africa' could be built."

The ambassadors in Africa also recognized this and urged Williams to substitute the term "strengthened" for "new" as the appellation for their policy recommendations. As far as Haynes was concerned, no new Africa policy should be announced unless it had the substance of a Marshall Plan or an Alliance for Progress. To do so, would only create disappointment in Africa. It would also undermine Johnson's newly acquired "positive image" in Africa and the favorable climate of US–African relations, which had been improving since the Congo parachute drop, according to the ambassadors.[67]

As Bill Moyers informed the President, appealing to his unquenchable ego and desire for accomplishment, "The key to an American President's standing in Africa is his relationship at home to the civil rights movement. Your voting rights speech . . . coming after 98% of the Negro voters cast their ballots for you [in the 1964 presidential elections] makes you a hero to the Negro at home—and it has spilled over into Africa."[68]

The administration was unable to reach agreement over a new policy because it was not prepared to devote new resources and there was no agreement within the US government about what a new American policy should achieve. Those involved in formulating Africa policy generally believed that the US should nevertheless "do something." As Robert Komer quipped to the President, "Our experience to date has been that most African states which tasted the fruits of Communist support in the first flush of breaking away from the UK or France have tended to get a stomachache (Morocco, Guinea, Mali, and Kenya are cases in point)."[69]

The debate over Africa policy was no longer sustained by bold interpretations of the national interest. The growing involvement in Vietnam, the President's overriding interest in his domestic programs, and the new decision-making alignment in the government militated against anything but a traditional interpretation of American interests in Africa. The policy debate no longer revolved around Angola and the Azores, but whether new expenditures could be afforded and whether there should be a "new" Africa policy or one that had been "strengthened."

African issues remained on the American foreign policy agenda for reasons that had little to do with America's strategic interests. Not only did the Administration perceive a forward-looking Africa policy to be useful in gaining political support from African Americans, but it could also contribute to the image of a President who was in control of all aspects of foreign policy. There were also the thirty-seven votes in the United Nations to consider. To Johnson, Africa was important for very different reasons than had existed for the Kennedy administration. The specific issue of Portuguese colonialism, however, was an increasingly distant one in the minds of key policymakers.

The Fragile Opposition Parties

The lack of a cohesive political opposition in Portugal contributed to Washington's disinterest in Portuguese affairs. By the mid-1960s, public opposition in Portugal to the government's African policies had virtually ceased. Except for a manifesto issued by 101 Catholics claiming that the defense of Christian values was not to be confused with the activities of Portuguese colonialism, there was little active protest against the regime. Nevertheless, the crisis of the stability of the Portuguese regime, which American analysts had spotted as early as 1961, was in fact deepening. The period of compulsory military service had been increased to four years and officers were now being compelled to serve successive tours of duty with little more than a month of home leave between each tour. Overt opposition to the regime, not to mention all avenues of legitimate protest, had been smothered through censorship, political intimidation, the proscription of opposition political parties, and government control of the labor unions. It was for this reason that some in the opposition found "the last years of Salazar drab and difficult."[70]

The mantle of protest was largely left to the Communist Party, the most determined and enduring of the political opposition. Originating in 1921, the Portuguese Communist Party (PCP) by the mid-1960s drew support from industrial workers in the larger urban areas—especially around Lisbon—as well as from rural laborers in the south and from the intelligentsia. Yet, the PCP was doggedly and vociferously pro-Soviet, which further polarized the already fragmented opposition as many opponents of the Salazar regime were liberals, social democrats, or socialists. The strict adherence by the PCP to Soviet ideology also led to an "intellectual sclerosis," which constrained the ability of the Communists to adapt to changing conditions in Portugal.[71] Nevertheless, the PCP dominated the opposition to Salazar. As expressed by Mario Soares, the leader of the Portuguese Socialist Party, "The Communist Party has an extensive following among the working class in Portugal and without the Communist workers there can be no unanimity of the left . . . . The regime has relegated [the Communists] to a ghetto, and for the good of Portugal we must deliver them."[72]

Elsewhere in the virtually invisible opposition were the Republicans on the right, the Catholic democrats, and the communist splinter groups including disciples of Mao Tse-Tung, Leon Trotsky, and Che Guevara. The most notable characteristic of the student population, which was so deeply affected by compulsory conscription into the military, was "the moderation of their demands . . . as well as the slowness of their subsequent radicalization."[73] This amalgam of political factions was of greater concern and interest to independent observers than it was to officials in the American government. A journalist for the *New York Times*, Marvine Howe, who was stationed in Lisbon, was compelled to point this out to the Johnson administration. In a letter to Bill Moyers, Howe said that "there are qualified spokesman here [for the opposition], and if you'd like a name or two I'd be glad to submit them. After all, Premier Salazar is 76 and cannot last forever, and so the U.S. may have to deal with somebody else."[74]

In comparison to the factions in Portugal, the nationalist movements in Mozambique and Angola had established themselves as active opposition groups. FRELIMO had initiated its armed struggle in Mozambique in September 1964 with only 250 trained and equipped militants. By 1967, the FRELIMO fighting force had reached a strength of eight thousand combatants. During the same period the Portuguese armed forces in Mozambique had doubled to seventy thousand.[75] While FRELIMO successfully engaged the Portuguese in the northern provinces of Cabo Delgado and Niassa, their militants had also begun to establish embryonic educational, health, and economic structures in these areas, which they referred to as "liberated areas." These social programs, however rudimentary, established FRELIMO as a credible alternative to the Portuguese in the eyes of the illiterate peasantry within Mozambique. Internationally, FRELIMO used its social, political, and military successes as a rationale for support not only from the Eastern bloc nations, but from NATO members Holland, Norway, and Denmark, as well as Sweden. Although the Western countries classified the assistance as humanitarian and relegated it solely for nonmilitary purposes, it was a vital form of political and diplomatic legitimacy being extended to the Mozambican nationalists—at Portugal's expense.[76]

Whereas FRELIMO's credibility was on the rise internationally and within Mozambique, the same could not be said about its relations with the American government. With the exodus of appointees who had served President Kennedy in the developing US policy toward Africa, especially Robert Kennedy, and the escalation of the American involvement in Vietnam, it was no longer as easy to "move around" Washington and to get African visitors into the White House to see the President. Mondlane's access to influential American policymakers also diminished. This was typified by the response to a letter that Mondlane wrote to Lyndon Johnson on the eve of the first anniversary of FRELIMO's guerrilla war in which he asked the President to show some public sign of support for FRELIMO's struggle. In a memorandum to McGeorge Bundy, the State Department recommended that it is "not appropriate to reply to [the letter]. There is a possibility that any reply would be misrepresented or otherwise misused by Mondlane."[77] The message that was imparted to Mondlane was exactly what African leaders had feared: at the highest levels of government, the United States was not interested in Africa's welfare.[78]

As FRELIMO scored some important military and political successes, the same could not be said for the Angolan nationalists. By early 1964, there was a serious rift within GRAE. It centered on the personality, ethnic, and regional differences between Holden Roberto and his foreign minister, Jonas Savimbi. In contrast to Roberto, Savimbi was a bright, dynamic, and charismatic leader of the Ovimbundu that made up about one-third of the Angolan population. Factional suspicion and hostility escalated rapidly and within a short time the two leaders were openly conspiring against each other. Savimbi charged Roberto with tribalism, racism, and corruption—in short, all the accusations the MPLA had made in trying to stave off the OAU recognition of GRAE.[79] Savimbi's highly public and contentious resignation from GRAE in July 1964 was a devastating blow to Roberto's self-proclaimed leadership of Angolan nationalism. Within two years, Savimbi's political acumen led him through the perils of exile politics to the formation of the third significant Angolan nationalist movement, UNITA (National Union for the Total Independence of Angola).

Moises Tshombe, the Congolese Prime Minister and Roberto's host and nemesis, did not hesitate to exploit Roberto's difficulties with Savimbi. Though Tshombe was not prepared to shut down GRAE's camp at Kinkuzu in return for Portuguese aid, he interrupted Roberto's supply of arms and ammunition while encouraging the anti-Roberto activities of other Bakongo nationalists. Yet Roberto, who seemed to survive solely by twists of fate, gained another reprieve when Congo President Joseph Kasavubu fired Tshombe in the fall of 1964 and installed Lieutenant-General Joseph Mobutu as head of government. Mobutu, Roberto's political ally, personal friend, and relative through marriage, assumed the undisputed leadership of the Congolese government in a successful overthrow of Kasavubu several months later.[80] Mobutu's total backing for Roberto enabled the Bakongo leader to arrest and incarcerate all his opponents. Although it helped Roberto to rebuild his predominance within UPA/FNLA, Mobutu's blind support only further accentuated Roberto's parochial and demagogical qualities.

During the period when Savimbi left GRAE and established UNITA, the MPLA was able to regroup and reenter the fray of Angolan nationalist politics. The turning point was Agostinho Neto's consolidation of the leadership of the MPLA and his successful petitions to the OAU for assistance. The OAU continued to pressure the two movements to reconcile their differences. Although the OAU refused to "de-recognize" GRAE, it did begin to support the MPLA militarily and financially. The MPLA had some success in engaging the Portuguese militarily in the enclave of Cabinda and was also active politically inside Angola in urban areas such as Luanda, Nova Lisboa, Malange, Benguela, and Cubal.[81]

The MPLA's fortunes were further boosted by the Soviet Union's decision to resume the active support that they had curtailed following the MPLA's apparent demise in 1963. Whereas China carefully limited its support to Savimbi and Roberto, the MPLA established close relations with Cuba. This was the result of a 1965 meeting in Brazzaville between Agostinho Neto and Che Guevara, who was on a tour of Africa. The meeting cleared the way for MPLA militants to undergo training when nearly one thousand Cuban troops were sent to Congo-Brazzaville to assist the development of that country's military forces. Cuban assistance to the MPLA, which consisted of arms and training, would remain relatively constant for the next ten years, in contrast to fluctuating Soviet support.[82]

In Washington, as the American involvement in Vietnam escalated to one-half million troops and the federal budget was in the process of quadrupling in size, national security planners paid little attention to the continuing wars in Portuguese Africa and the emergent if fragmented opposition in Portugal. After all, Africa no longer seemed to be "the greatest open field of maneuver in the world-wide competition between the [Communist] bloc and the non-Communist world." Furthermore, the issue of Portuguese colonialism was peripheral at best to civil rights groups, and the administration had concluded that the costs of pressuring the Portuguese on their colonial policies was too high. To the degree that African issues had any visibility on the foreign policy agenda of the Johnson administration, it was because of the President's perception that they could be used for domestic political purposes.

"Evolving a Story on Africa"

By the middle of 1965, it was evident to the White House that the administration had an "information problem" in foreign policy. This problem initially arose from criticism over military intervention in the Dominican Republic, but it also came to include the administration's lack of activity in Africa. In response, the White House tried to generate favorable press on Johnson's existing Africa policy while Johnson's advisers sorted out the tone and content of a new program for Africa. After all, cultivating the press corps was a preoccupation with Lyndon Johnson, and he expected journalists "to play ball" with him. It was inconceivable to him that any journalist could be aloof to "the treatment" of focused presidential attention that he liked to lavish on key reporters.[83]

Therefore, on Bill Moyers' instructions, Rick Haynes and Robert Komer "evolved a story" of Johnson's interest in Africa. Haynes "found a friendly UPI correspondent," George Weeks, and gave him the story on background basis. Apparently without much difficulty, the thirty-four-year-old National Security Council adviser convinced the sympathetic Weeks that "the President's personal contacts with African leaders over the past six months was certainly an indication of his keen interest in and concern for African affairs." As evidence, Haynes pointed out that Johnson had exchanged letters with leaders from eleven African countries, he had hosted a "highly successful" yacht trip on the Potomac for African ambassadors, and he had sent astronauts Peter Conrad and Gordon Cooper to Kenya, Ethiopia, Malagascar, and Nigeria as Presidential good-will emissaries. Furthermore, Haynes informed Weeks, the President sent personally signed copies of his voting rights speech to all African leaders in addition to meeting with seven high level African officials over the previous six months. At the end of the meeting, Weeks assured Haynes that he would do a story that weekend on the President's active interest in Africa.[84]

Contrary to the efforts of the Johnson administration to show its interest in Africa, the United States was the target of growing criticism, especially as it concerned the Portuguese territories. At a meeting of the UN's Committee of 24, which had evolved from the Committee of 17 to oversee the decolonization process on behalf of the UN General Assembly, held in Dar es Salaam, the US "bore the brunt of much of the extremism . . . ." Evidence of the fundamental American "antipathy to the aspirations of the African inhabitants" took the form of American economic interests in the Portuguese territories and its NATO relationship. These ties and the American vote against a resolution calling for sanctions and an arms embargo on Portugal did little for Johnson's newly found "positive image" in Africa. On the contrary, it led American officials to consider withdrawing from the UN Committee.[85]

At the United Nations, through much of 1965, Arthur Goldberg tried to be as constructive as possible on the question of the Portuguese territories. His strategy was to push for a renewal of the dialogue between Portugal and the African delegates. At the same time, the American delegation was instructed to remain silent during the Security Council debate and abstain on any resolution. The Ambassador's primary concern was not to undermine the initiative that Anderson was pursuing in Lisbon with Salazar.[86]

From Goldberg's point of view, there were other reasons not to expend much effort pressuring Portugal. He was more concerned about the mounting pressure from African states that were calling for the use of military force against Ian Smith's illegal government in Rhodesia. The American ambassador was also preoccupied with keeping a majority of states in the General Assembly from voting to "restore" the seat of the People's Republic of China. Although it required a two-thirds majority to seat Beijing, Goldberg believed that "the repercussions of losing the majority . . . would be very powerful."[87] The American delegation had no incentive or, more important, instructions to undertake a new negotiating effort on self-determination in Angola and Mozambique. Therefore, Goldberg continued to urge a resumption of Afro-Portuguese talks on the basis adopted in 1963.

By all accounts, the White House failed in its effort to overcome its "information problem," and to demonstrate, both in the United States and Africa, that Johnson had a personal interest in African affairs. The administration was no more successful in generating a positive image in Portugal. Not infrequently, Goldberg was the subject of vicious attacks in the Portuguese press. On one occasion, Anderson received Nogueira's "official and personal apologies." Nevertheless, Washington's view of Portugal was reflected in the frustrated and dismissive tone of a US embassy official in Lisbon who concluded that "the Portuguese . . . are not a logical people by U.S. standards."[88]

The "Jugular Problems" of Southern Africa

As discussion of a strengthened Africa program continued into the fall of 1965, G. Mennen Williams realized that without increased expenditures and a strong and visible personal association by the President with the principle of self-determination, any revitalized Africa policy would have little chance for success. In an action memorandum to the Secretary, Williams argued that "budget increases" were justified because of the five year decline in assistance to Africa as well as the great disparity between what the United States was spending for assistance in Africa compared with other underdeveloped regions. Williams also pointed out to Rusk "two pertinent reasons" to increase expenditures: ". . . to secure African support of general U.S. policy objectives such as Chinese representation [at the UN], Vietnam, etc., and second, to enable the President to create his own African image." The embattled assistant secretary cautioned Rusk that the United States would not be able to "buy African votes," but it would "help to create the climate of concern [for] their problems that will permit us to get a hearing and argue our points."[89]

One of Williams' primary assets in convincing Rusk was that he had the concurrence of eight government agencies including the Agency for International Development (AID), the European Bureau, and Walter Rostow, the head of the policy planning staff. Still, this did not quiet opposition to his efforts. William Lang, Deputy Assistant Secretary of Defense for International Security Affairs, warned Williams that if Johnson were to support publicly self-determination in Africa, it "would be interpreted by South Africa and Portugal as [being] sharply critical of, and interfering with, their internal affairs." The Defense Department questioned whether such an endorsement would assist a peaceful, evolutionary solution to the problems in Southern Africa, or in fact, widen the breach.[90]

On the other hand, Robert Komer, McGeorge Bundy's deputy, who would shortly become General William C. Westmoreland's civilian deputy in Vietnam in charge of "pacification," criticized the proposals for not being strong enough. "What positions we take on Southern Rhodesia, the Portuguese colonies, Southwest Africa, and ultimately South Africa will be more influential . . . than any billion dollar 'Marshall Plan for Africa' (were such a grandiose project even feasible)". Komer warned the President that these issues would be the "chief test" of any country's policy toward Africa. He advised Johnson that "to the extent that we can stay slightly ahead on these issues instead of being reluctantly dragged toward the inevitable, we can keep our African affairs in reasonably good repair."[91]

Although Komer understood the key issues in Africa, he too was unable to translate opposition to colonial and white minority rule into a coherent American policy toward Africa. On 14 October 1965, the Secretary of State submitted a series of recommendations to Johnson for a "Strengthened African Program," which included increased expenditures of forty million dollars to allow for more active programs in information, education, cultural exchange, and economic aid. The program also called for visits to Africa by high level American officials and a major speech or speeches in which Johnson personally identified himself with US policy in Africa.

The essence of Rusk's reasoning to Johnson was that the peaceful transition from colonial rule to self-determination in Africa "would significantly extend the area of freedom in the world, thus making our own democratic freedoms more secure." Facilitating the transition to independence would also reduce the need for large military outlays to resist "Communist encroachments (perhaps 'Wars of Liberation') in Africa." Finally, the State Department told Johnson that he should publicly associate himself with the aspirations of Africa's leaders because "in Africa, perhaps more than in any other part of the world, relations between governments are viewed as personal relations between leaders." This rationale was calculated to appeal to a president for whom the practice of politics and government was, in essence, a network of loyal and effective individuals.[92]

In a briefing memo to the President on the Rusk-Williams proposals, an exasperated Bundy and Komer told Johnson, "We have held it up briefly, so as not to burden you with what is regrettably a mouse." To the NSC adviser and his deputy, the proposals suffered from the same problems they had eighteen months before: they were not adequately far reaching nor did they have sufficient focus. The two advisers were skeptical that "beefed up" aid and information programs, high-level visits, and a speech, spread over thirty-seven countries, would amount to "a bold new program." They maintained that there were important considerations that merited a strong American position on self-determination. This included the African votes at the UN, the need to maintain the support of civil rights groups in the US, and competition for influence with the Soviet Union and China, "who will jump to exploit too much US waffling on these issues." They advised the President "that the best and cheapest way to advance U.S. interests in Africa would be a clear U.S. stance on the southern third of Africa." As they emphasized in their memo to Johnson,

> In our judgment the success of US policy and the extent of US influence (in Africa) will depend primarily on the position we take on those political issues of overriding interest to the Africans themselves . . . . African majority rule is sooner or later inevitable and we ought to be on the winning side. The battle was really lost when two-thirds of Africa became independent; the completion of the process is historically inevitable. It will be painful, but there's no stopping it (except perhaps in South Africa for a time).[93]

Acting on their recommendations, Johnson instructed Rusk and Williams to strengthen the proposed speech, restating more forcefully US support for majority rule and independence. Echoing Bundy and Komer, Johnson wrote Rusk that "the prime determinant of US influence in Africa will be that stance the US takes on those political issues of primary concern to the Africans themselves. US concern for African problems must be demonstrated by actions, and in terms, which will have an immediate appeal to the people of Africa."[94]

Although Bundy and Komer correctly understood the vital issues influencing politics in Southern Africa and their impact on the regional balance of power, they were powerless to act. McGeorge Bundy was in the process of leaving the administration and Robert Komer was increasingly involved with Vietnam. As well, the influence of G. Mennen Williams was increasingly circumscribed. Before resigning in 1966, Secretary Williams testified in Congress on South Africa policy, stating a lifeless rendition of US opposition to South Africa's racial policies. Williams' flaccid testimony was echoed in a subsequent speech in Canada by Defense Secretary Robert McNamara, who said that "the United States has no mandate on high to police the world and the inclination to do so. There have been classic cases in which our deliberate nonaction was the wisest action of all." In short, Williams appeared to be trying to camouflage with low-cost rhetoric the immobility of the administration's position on the issues of most importance to the US in Southern Africa; McNamara only affirmed this paralysis.[95]

Nonetheless, on 28 November 1965, Johnson instructed Rusk to submit a revised proposal within two weeks. The urgency was marginally related to events in Africa, even though the month before Ian Smith precipitated an international crisis when his Rhodesian Front Party unilaterally declared independence for Rhodesia from Great Britain. More important was the desire of the White House to show a president fully engaged in foreign affairs and not just Vietnam, where the American military presence had increased from 25,000 to 165,000 in the year since his landslide electoral victory.

Unfortunately for Johnson, his nascent Africa policy offered little opportunity to deflect attention from Vietnam. On 23 December 1965, the Africa Bureau submitted the revised proposals to Rusk through George Ball, who had replaced Averill Harriman as overseeing Africa policy. Williams's proposals still were considered to be to general and not sufficiently focused on the "jugular problems" of Southern Africa. Disheartened and defeated, he submitted his letter of resignation to Johnson on 1 March 1966.[96]

With Williams's resignation, the deepening involvement in Vietnam and the demise of Africa's perceived strategic importance,

Rusk and Ball wanted an individual who could manage the Africa Bureau and keep the continent's problems "away from the Secretary." Wayne Fredericks, Williams's able deputy, was considered by many to be the logical choice as successor but others thought him to be too partisan, "too committed," to African issues. Rusk and Ball feared that Fredericks would try to do more in Africa than they wanted, especially as the Africa assignment was notorious for its bureaucratic autonomy. Fredericks would resign from the Administration and return to New York in September 1967. The White House concurred with the selection of Joseph Palmer as assistant secretary over a disappointed Fredericks. Palmer, a career foreign service officer and a former ambassador to Nigeria, was selected on his reputation as being a judicious and cautious decision-maker and for the high marks he received on the Congo Task Force.[97]

The appointment of Tapley Bennett to succeed George Anderson as ambassador to Portugal did little to disturb the bureaucratic tranquility over Portugal and Portuguese Africa. Bennett had been criticized for overreacting and overestimating the communist danger that led to the American intervention in the Dominican Republic. Although he remained in Johnson's favor, he was given a European post where there was little chance of "excitement." Bennett, like Anderson, came to be an admirer of Salazar and his tenacity in Africa. Bennett realized, though, that Salazar's tenacity had made Portugal a "pariah in the club" of NATO and the object of scorn at the UN.

One difference between Tapley Bennett and his predecessor was a sense of the need to be in touch with members of the political opposition. In a meeting with Nogueira, whom he viewed as a man of "firm and stern principles," the studiously correct Bennett asked whether the Portuguese government objected to the American Embassy having contacts with individuals from the opposition.

The Foreign Minister responded that the embassy could meet with whomever it wanted though it would be "unacceptable" to give political advice or material support. Bennett assured Nogueira that any contacts with opposition members would "always [be] orthodox." This green light led to surreptitious meetings between embassy personnel and individuals such as Mario Soares in parks early Sunday morning or at obscure cafés late at night. Nevertheless, because of PIDE's constant pressure and vigilance, it was difficult to maintain any meaningful contacts.[98] Whether it was Portugal, Angola, or Mozambique, the importance of maintaining effective ties to those opposed to the Portuguese dictatorship was of little significance to Washington.

Goldberg Weighs In

The Africa Bureau's frustration in its effort to devise a new policy toward the region did not prevent Arthur Goldberg from writing Johnson an incisive and highly confidential letter that argued that the time was "opportune for a 'Johnson plan' for the economic development of Africa." In the view of the esteemed ambassador to the UN, "the Chinese Communists [had] overplayed their hand in Africa," as had the Soviet Union, which made it a propitious time to support actively the moderate forces on the continent. Secondly, Goldberg reasoned, "It is highly desirable, in light of the international political difficulties we will continue to have over Vietnam, for you to take a new and constructive initiative in foreign policy which will attract those who are most disquieted about Vietnam and who believe we can only act vigorously in reaction to a 'Communist menace.'"[99]

Goldberg's plan was more specific than what Williams had produced. Drawing on conversations with George Woods, president of the World Bank, Goldberg told Johnson that Africa had four priority needs: the development of transportation networks, a telecommunications system, a continent-wide plan for power generation and distribution, and an imaginative program for mass education in Africa. The Ambassador envisioned that this program could be implemented and financed by an international consortium, including the World Bank and the African Development Bank, so as to avoid the "accusation that this is a white man's plan under white control." Comparing it to Johnson's Mekong River Program in Vietnam, he also suggested that the Soviet Union be invited to participate.[100]

The key aspect of Goldberg's plan and the fundamental difference with what the Africa Bureau was putting forward was the absence of illusions that this would resolve the difficult problems in Southern Africa. As Goldberg told Johnson, it would still be necessary for the United States to demonstrate its support of majority rule and self-determination independent of any aid program. In essence, Goldberg was arguing that the United States should try to develop a reserve of political "good will" in Africa by concentrating its "natural assets and great experience" in economic development.

On the same day that Johnson received Goldberg's letter, the newly appointed Joseph Palmer received a Presidential directive stating, "The President wants as soon as possible a design for an African alliance for progress, perhaps involving the expenditure of several hundred millions of dollars over some years. The President emphasized that he wants fresh study groups including the best people in and out of government." Palmer's instructions were to submit a progress report within six days.[101]

Not only were Goldberg's proposals far-reaching and specific, but few people in government had as much influence with Lyndon Johnson as did Arthur Goldberg. Much of this leverage had been accumulated when Johnson persuaded him to leave the Supreme Court for the United Nations. Not only did the President consider this a tremendous "victory," but, in Johnson's view, Goldberg was loyal, a "Johnson man," as well as the ultimate "can-do" professional. Goldberg would use this leverage as best he could because, as far as he was concerned, he was primarily responsible to the President and not to Rusk.[102]

Goldberg's timing was propitious as it coincided with the overall reshaping of the foreign aid program within the administration. In Johnson's view, the United States "had been dealing with Africa on a buckshot basis—a loan here, a dam project there, a technical assistance program somewhere else."[103] It was time to deal with Africa as a whole and strengthen regional cooperation as much as possible. Under the direction of David Bell, director of the AID, there had been a determined effort to rechannel aid through multilateral development institutions such as the World Bank. Bell and his associates believed that the problems of aid dependence could be reduced by utilizing international development institutions, which would minimize perceptions that the US was trying to replace the former colonial powers of Europe. Instead, American resources could be concentrated on infrastructure and technical assistance. For some foreign-aid theorists in the administration, multilateral institutions, especially the Asia Development Bank, held out the glimmering chance that the Soviet Union could be induced to join and, ultimately, to collaborate in the containment of China.[104]

Although Portugal and its colonial policies in Africa were attracting little attention in Washington, the same was not the case for Africa in general. Goldberg had been able to articulate the problem and prescription for American policy in a way that Williams had not.

The Johnson Plan for Africa

Goldberg's proposals for a revitalized Africa policy energized the planning that was already underway. The administration also sensed that "Africa's mood at the moment [was] one of drift and doubt" and that African leaders were "groping for new answers and reassuring guidelines."[105] Johnson sent Palmer an article from *The Economist* that concluded with the comment that "it is our turn now in the Third World; are we going to miss it?" Palmer dutifully reported back to the President that the thesis of the article, that the tide of events in Asia and Africa were moving in favor of the West, was a "sound assessment" and would figure prominently in his thinking and planning.[106] In short, the time seemed ripe for Johnson's long discussed "Strengthened Africa Policy" to be unveiled in a major presidential address. The White House selected Thursday, 26 May 1966, the third anniversary of the founding of the Organization of Africa Unity, for the address.

In conjunction with the speech, Rusk and Rostow suggested to Johnson that numerous benefits could be gained from a White House reception for African ambassadors and chiefs of mission. Besides giving USIA an opportunity to underscore the President's interest in Africa, the speech would provide an early opportunity for Johnson to publicly associate himself with the new assistant secretary for African affairs, Joseph Palmer. Furthermore, a reception would contribute to that "reserve of good will among African governments" on which the US would need to draw to achieve its objectives at the UN. Johnson's advisers also told the President that he had to counter "the growing incorrect belief that you spend ninety-five percent of your time on Vietnam, and have been somewhat ignoring Latin America, Africa and particularly Europe."[107]

At 3:00 A.M. on the morning of the day that Johnson was "to lay the foundation for a Johnson Doctrine for Africa," Bill Moyers wrote a memo to the President reminding him of the other political advantages that his speech would realize, besides being "big news throughout the world." In language calibrated for Johnson's ear, Moyers told the President that his speech would be important "for its impact on the civil rights people at home; it is a cheap way to keep them quiet at least on one issue . . . . There is also another reason. Bobby Kennedy goes to South Africa next week. He will try to get ahead of you on the question of political liberty for Negro Africans. Your speech preempts the stage. I think it would be wrong for us to simply offer economic assistance and material aid while Kennedy trots off making hay on the intangible issue of the rights of man."[108] As one former Johnson aide put it, this was the way to inform the President that "he could hit 19 birds with one stone, instead of only ten."[109]

As Johnson's speech was being prepared in the weeks prior to 26 May, the State Department decided to bring Edward Korry, the US ambassador to Ethiopia, back to Washington to lead a task force to implement the new aid initiatives that Goldberg had suggested. As the date approached, the State Department readied itself to reap from the initiative all the political benefits that it could. On the morning of the 26th, the State Department instructed American ambassadors in Bonn, Brussels, London, Ottawa, Paris, and Rome to discuss the implications of the new American program in Africa with the highest appropriate host country officials. The American diplomats were to ensure the Europeans that the President would acknowledge their efforts in African economic development and that the United States was not trying to displace them. In Africa, American officials in all capitals except Pretoria informed the various heads of government of the President's speech and new policy initiatives. In Washington, two and a half hours before the reception began, White House officials gave a briefing in which they bluntly described the speech as an effort to show "that the President intends to carry forth a global policy despite the burdens of Vietnam."[110]

The speech itself was an eloquent, nonconfrontational testimony of American sensitivity toward self-determination in Africa. Echoing Kwame Nkrumah's famous dictum that Africans "prefer independence with danger to servitude in tranquility," Johnson said, "Across the continent the majority of people prefer self-government with peril to subservience with serenity. This makes all the more repugnant the narrow and outmoded policy which in some parts of Africa permits the few to rule at the expense of the many." The President also affirmed that the United States "would not support policies abroad which are based on the rule of minorities . . . ."[111]

Despite the veiled reference to the racial policies of South Africa and Portugal, Rhodesia was the only African country that was specifically mentioned. The thrust of the speech was built on the aid proposals that had been under consideration for the previous year. In deference to Congress, which was threatening to cut foreign aid assistance drastically, Johnson did not announce any new expenditures, only a rechanneling of existing funds. Even Goldberg's influence had its limits. Johnson pledged to strengthen the American commitment to regional economic institutions such as the African Development Bank and the East African Economic Community. He also proposed to increase the number of Africans receiving advanced technical and academic training by making certain universities regional training centers. Johnson announced that Ambassador Korry would be working full-time on the implementation of these proposals.[112]

Although the White House was optimistic about the impact of its "ringing statement of principles" that followed "long months of planning and a rigorous examination" of existing policy, the reaction in the United States and abroad was decidedly indifferent. Editorials in American newspapers were confused over whether the President was simply making a declaration of principles or announcing a new policy. Many editorials asked what practical results could be expected. In Africa, a few leaders such as President Sangoulé Lamazina of Upper Volta, President Nicolas Grunitzky of Togo, and Kenneth Kaunda of Zambia, were quite enthusiastic about Johnson's "memorable" speech. In general, however, the attitude toward the aid program was one of "wait and see." As it concerned the political problems of Southern Africa, American diplomats reported "a degree of skepticism," given previous American policies. As the *Financial Times* of London remarked, "The most striking thing about the speech is the absence of concrete initiatives to back up the words."[113]

In spite of the lukewarm reaction and negligible impact, the White House instructed its speech writers to refer to Johnson's speech as "the boldest statement on Africa by any Head of State."[114] In fact, the administration's much belabored policy pronouncement was more posture than substance and more an explication of empathy and intentions than specific measures that addressed Africa's economic and political problems. Administration officials were constrained by the war in Vietnam not only financially but also to the degree to which it could embark on potentially controversial new steps.[115] The Africa initiative also suffered from the tendency of Lyndon Johnson and some of his advisers to confuse public relations with an effective, sustainable policy. This was typified by Walt Rostow's response to Senegal's ambassador to the US, Ousmane Diop, who had sent a note to the President thanking him for the speech and reception. Rostow informed the President that he had written the Senegalese diplomat "a bread-and-butter reply acknowledging his thoughtful gesture. There is nothing of substance in this exchange. It is merely an exercise in good public relations directed at a continent which tends to feel ignored."[116]

Johnson was convinced that a revitalized Africa policy would serve numerous objectives. Most important, the speech would demonstrate to the country and the international community that his administration was not paralyzed over Vietnam. The speech would also show the civil rights lobby that he had their interests at heart. A bold policy would also give Arthur Goldberg some badly needed leverage at the United Nations. Finally, it would satisfy Johnson's closest advisers who felt there was a genuine need to take a strong position on a vexing problem. The president failed, however, to realize any of these objectives and in the process revealed a lack of commitment to implementing an otherwise prudent policy.

The Twilight of Concern

In Lisbon's absorbing and cloistered tranquility, Salazar and Nogueira took little notice of Johnson's speech. As Franco Nogueira said, "it didn't impress us." From Lisbon, it appeared that the President of the United States was completely immersed in his domestic programs and the war in Vietnam. The Portuguese impression of Johnson was that he did not have strong ideas about independence in Africa nor did he appear to attribute the same importance to the American image in the Third World as had Kennedy. To them, Johnson's policy toward Portuguese colonialism seemed to be neutral, if not indifferent. Indeed, as Tapley Bennett remarked, he used to visit with Johnson whenever he returned to Washington but could not remember the President ever discussing the situation in Portugal's African colonies.[117]

Following the failure of the "Anderson Plan," the United States virtually abandoned any hope of pressuring the Portuguese to move toward some early accommodation with self-determination in their colonies. The costs of doing so were perceived to be too high, even though more sophisticated military aircraft were rendering the Azores as a less strategic base. When it came to Africa policy, the seemingly intractable problems in Rhodesia, South Africa, and Namibia; a reduced British presence in the region; and an escalating civil war in Nigeria helped to relegate the problem of Portuguese Africa to a very low priority on the American foreign policy agenda.[118]

Even personal appeals lacked bite. At a NATO meeting in Paris in December 1966, Rusk spoke with Nogueira in the "gentle, gracious" manner for which he was known—and also criticized. The Secretary of State told the Foreign Minister that the Portuguese presence in Africa could best be assured if Portugal accelerated its program of political and social reform leading toward self-determination. Using the Africans' proposals, Rusk told Nogueira that this could include all options: continued association with Portugal, some sort of commonwealth relationship, independence, or some other political arrangement. Yet as before, the tough and self-assured Nogueira remained unmoved by Rusk's requests. To him, this was but another repetition of a frequently heard complaint and could be ignored. It seemed to Salazar and Nogueira that Johnson had "discarded" Africa from America's concerns.[119]

Rusk was not the only one within the administration to treat the Portuguese with gentility. In March 1966, National Security Advisor Walt Rostow signed off on a memo that allowed for a telegram to be sent to Salazar, congratulating the Prime Minister on the occasion of his seventy-seventh birthday. The State Department had to obtain special permission because Salazar's birthday fell under the "multiple of five" rule that stipulated that certain leaders were to receive such greetings only every five years. But the congratulatory message of the year before had been "particularly well-received," Rostow was advised, and other European leaders, such as Franco and De Gaulle, would be sending salutations. As the State Department cautioned Rostow, the Portuguese "are extremely sensitive and would, if any opportunity for misinterpretation existed, exploit omission by the United States."

Rostow had good reason for not wanting to irritate Salazar. Four weeks before, the Prime Minister had warned Western powers that they should no longer expect "automatic cooperation" from Portugal. In an interview that was published on the front page of the *New York Times*, Salazar told journalist Tad Szulc that NATO had become totally "inadequate" for protecting Portugal's security needs and accused Washington of undermining its allies, especially Portugal. The Premier omitted the United States from a list of countries with which its government had "satisfactory" relations. Included on the list were Brazil, France, West Germany, and Spain. Playing the trump card once again, he also raised the possibility that Lisbon would terminate the "day-to-day" arrangement under which the United States was using the Azores.[120]

Salazar's threats followed by days Charles de Gaulle's announcement that France was withdrawing its troops from the integrated NATO command and expelling from France all foreign units and installations that were not under French control. Lyndon Johnson, determined to leave office with NATO stronger than when he had assumed the presidency, could not afford to allow Portugal to leave the alliance as well. In reality, Portugal was unlikely to follow such a course. Despite Salazar's bombast, the United States had largely normalized its military relationship with Portugal. Between 1963 and 1968, Portugal received a total of $33 million in military assistance and an additional $54.9 million in economic aid. In a 1968 appearance before the House Committee on Foreign Affairs, General Lyman Lemnitzer said that American military aid to Portugal "is designed to train key Portuguese military personnel and to provide maintenance support materials." The United States had restored its support and training of Portuguese military personnel in numerous areas and had increased the Military Assistance Advisory Group (MAAG) stationed in Lisbon to twenty-four individuals. The Portuguese Navy had also been given the use of three destroyer escorts for deployment in the colonies. In the words of Vice-Admiral L. C. Heinz, "Our modest military assistance has helped to foster close working relationships with the Portuguese military."[121]

With the closer political and military ties, came a larger economic involvement by American corporations. Their focus was not Portugal, but Angola and Mozambique. Spurred on by Portugal's relaxation of foreign investment laws, and Gulf Oil's successful oil strike in the northern Angolan province of Cabinda in 1966, there were more than thirty American companies operating in the two territories by the late 1960s. Most of the activity was in mineral prospecting, oil exploration, and oil production. By 1968, the total trade between Angola and the United States was one hundred million dollars, more than double what it had been in 1963, and twenty-eight million dollars with Mozambique.[122]

Next to the Gulf Oil operations in Cabinda and the iron mines at Cassinga in southern Angola, the most important project to the Portuguese was their effort to build a massive hydroelectric power plant at Cabora Bassa in Tete province in Mozambique. The dam was intended to generate two-thirds more power that the Soviet-built Aswan Dam. For Portugal, the Cabora Bassa project was an "essential strategic undertaking." International capital was necessary for the construction of the dam, and Lisbon saw this as an implicit vote of confidence in Portugal from the participating Western countries. The electricity generated by the dam would be sold to South Africa, which would make the project financially viable and further cement the economic and political alliance between Lisbon and Pretoria. Lisbon also talked of settling one million white immigrants in newly irrigated areas so as to provide another line of defense against FRELIMO incursions.[123]

In response, FRELIMO made its vigorous opposition to the proposed hydroelectric scheme a test of diplomatic strength vis-à-vis Portugal. Although the nationalist organization was able to dissuade some would-be participants, such as Italy, it did not have the military or political strength to prevent the dam from being built.[124] The United States decided not to participate in the project, though it was not for Admiral Anderson's lack of effort. Before leaving his post in Lisbon, the American ambassador cabled George Ball, "I cannot support this project too strongly." Anderson told Rusk that General Electric was considering a role in the project and he hoped that the "temporary political problems" with South Africa, not to mention Portugal, would not cause the American government to discourage the support of the Export-Import Bank. Such a role in the $250 million project would help the American balance of payments as well as generate "great benefits" for the Africans in the area. Unfortunately for Anderson, Rusk declined to approve the involvement of the Export-Import Bank.[125]

Although Portugal welcomed this unspoken rapprochement with Washington, the Salazar regime had insulated itself from the possibility that Washington might return to the aggressive policies of the early 1960s. In 1964, Portugal concluded vital bilateral military agreements with France and West Germany. France was permitted to build a missile tracking station on the Azores island of Flores and Germany was allowed to build a jet air base at Beja in southern Portugal. In exchange, the two countries provided Portugal with materials for its African wars, including jet aircraft, helicopters, frigates, and submarines.

The Demise of a Policy

In a futile effort to salvage the American position in Africa, Under Secretary Nicholas deb Katzenbach was dispatched on a hurried twelve-nation tour of the continent in May 1967. After returning, he blandly reported to a meeting of the NSC on 13 July, with President Johnson in attendance, that "the Portuguese cannot hang on forever to their African colonies."[126] Katzenbach's judgment came at a difficult time for the Johnson administration, which had been jarred from its preoccupation with Vietnam by the outbreak of the Six-Day War in the Middle East. Several weeks after the war's conclusion on 10 June, Johnson held a summit meeting with the chairman of the Soviet Council of Ministers, Aleksei Kosygin, at Glassboro, New Jersey. Amidst these events, Tapley Bennett, who had come from Lisbon to Washington for brief visit, requested an appointment with the President. Francis M. Bator, an NSC advisor who worked partly on West European matters, was against it. As he wrote Marvin Watson, Johnson's appointment secretary, "I see no need to bother the President with this. Nothing is happening in Portugal that need worry him. Things are a bit hotter in Portuguese Africa, but there is little we can do about it."[127]

Ironically, Bator's perceptions would reflect American policy toward Lisbon for the next several years even though fifteen months later that country passed through a momentous transition. On 6 September 1968, Salazar was rushed to the Red Cross Hospital in Lisbon with a brain hemorrhage that he had suffered in a fall several weeks earlier at his summer home near Estoril. Despite a flurry of wild rumors and expectations of chaos and upheaval, Lisbon remained calm, almost sluggish, in the airless September heat. On 25 September, President Americo Tomas appeared on national television. He told the nation that Salazar, who lay nearly comatose in the hospital, had "served the nation with genius and with total and unflagging dedication for more than forty years, but he must now be replaced." The new prime minister, Tomas said, would be Professor Marcello Jose das Neve Alves Caetano.[128]

The transition from Salazar to Caetano in fact led to an improvement in US-Portuguese relations. For one, Portugal had already agreed to replace France as the site of the NATO Iberian Atlantic Command (Iberlant was responsible for coordinating the protection of 410,000 square miles of ocean extending west from the Iberian peninsula to the Tropic of Cancer). Also, within two months after Caetano became prime minister, Portugal and the United States announced that they would begin to work on a new treaty to govern the American use of the military base on the Azores.[129] Such a development, however, had little significance for President Johnson who had announced on 31 March 1968 that he would not seek reelection. His last months were consumed by Vietnam, the Soviet occupation of Czechoslovakia, domestic legislation, and civil strife following the assassination of Martin Luther King, Jr. Given the smoothness of the transition, and having never met Salazar or Nogueira,

Johnson and Caetano had a perfunctory exchange of notes expressing the hope that close ties between the two countries would continue.[130]

The fervor with which the administration had once cultivated ties with the nationalists in Angola and Mozambique was, like the Africa policy in general, a victim of more salient imperatives. In fact, by 1968, the established policy toward Portugal and Portuguese Africa was one of studied neutrality, as Nogueira had surmised. On 16 January 1967, Rusk approved the "National Policy Paper on Portugal," which was the first national policy study to be completed for a European country. The Paper reaffirmed the US policy objectives of: (a) keeping Portugal in NATO and the UN; (b) urging Portugal to adopt a policy of self-determination in its African territories, based on the "Anderson Plan;" (c) maintaining normal commercial and trade relations with Portugal and Portuguese Africa; (d) providing additional military assistance to Portugal in exchange for access to existing military facilities; and (e) restricting the use of American military equipment, granted or sold to Portugal, to NATO purposes.[131]

Financial support for Roberto and Mondlane continued as well, though there was no increase in the size of disbursements. What was once seen as a bold policy initiative, however, was now a program viewed by the White House as a series of political bargaining chips, or "flag money," to protect American interests in a slowly deteriorating situation.[132]

Yet American interests were getting little protection in Africa. This became evident in a meeting between Eduardo Mondlane and Wayne Fredericks, then an official at the Ford Foundation in New York, at a conference sponsored by the African American Institute in September 1968 in Nairobi. Mondlane was, on the surface, in a strong position. In July, at FRELIMO's Second Congress that was held in Niassa province in a "liberated area" inside Mozambique, Mondlane was reelected as FRELIMO's president. Nevertheless, this was a period of internal crisis for the nationalist movement. One faction within FRELIMO wanted to declare "independence" for the province of Cabo Delgado, much as had Biafra in Nigeria. Difficulties also surfaced at the Mozambique Institute in Dar es Salaam, forcing it to be closed. Finally, before Mondlane left his home in Dar es Salaam for Nairobi, for what he had said would be a meeting with Kenyan President Jomo Kenyatta, an article appeared in *The Nationalist*, the main English language newspaper in Dar es Salaam, that attacked him for being an agent of the CIA.[133]

At a private meeting in a Nairobi hotel room during the course of the African American Institute conference, Mondlane "did not conduct himself" in front of the assembled influential Americans (which included Elliot Osborne, who was editor of *Newsweek*) in a way consistent with how Fredericks perceived the nationalist leader. Mondlane appeared "tense and preoccupied," by the difficulties in FRELIMO and Dar es Salaam.[134] Mondlane was also frustrated by the inability and, now, the unwillingness, of the American government to be more aggressive and effective in its pressures on Portugal.[135]

The Nairobi meeting would be the last time that Fredericks saw Mondlane. It marked the end of official American contact with the nationalists who were fighting for independence in Mozambique, as well as a close friendship. Several months later, late on the morning of 3 February 1969, Mondlane was assassinated by a package bomb that exploded as he was going through his mail at a small beach house in Masasani, on the outskirts of Dar es Salaam. The assassination was the combined work of PIDE and dissidents within FRELIMO.[136]

In Angola, where the situation was implacably diffused by ethnic, ideological, cultural, class, and racial differences, Washington saw its interests as increasingly coincident with those of Portugal. During Tshombe's rule in the Congo (1964–1965), the Portuguese had effectively infiltrated factions, enflamed dissension and nourished secessionists and collaborators within the Angolan exile community. Even though the United States retained its tie to FNLA leader, Holden Roberto, it was of little value as Roberto would not even venture into Angola from the Congo. Roberto remained in the relative security of the the Congo where he "maintained a distrustful eye over all FNLA affairs from behind the defensive barricade of ever-present dark glasses." The movement's structure and military effectiveness, which was never strong, only withered further during this period.[137]

The MPLA, on the other hand, drew a breath of life by opening a military front in eastern Angola in 1966 under the guidance of Daniel Chipenda. Though the front was militarily important, it created problems for the organization. For one, it spread the MPLA's leadership out among offices in Brazzaville, Dar es Salaam, and Lusaka. Second, it led to faulty communications, competing ambitions, and inadequate reserves. Social tensions within the movement also persisted due to the large number of Luandan *mestizos*, who dominated the upper ranks of the movement.

Only Jonas Savimbi was able to sustain any military initiatives, though this also created difficulties for him. On Christmas day, 1966, Savimbi and his UNITA militants cut the Benguela railroad, a lifeline for Zambian and Zairian mineral exports, at the border town of Teixeira de Sousa, in an effort to force the Portuguese to take notice of his entry into the anticolonial war. When the attacks on the railroad continued, however, Kenneth Kaunda, Zambia's president, responded by having Savimbi arrested and imprisoned, and ultimately expelled from Zambia. This loss of an external base forced Savimbi back into the Angolan bush where he would continue to conduct his war against the Portuguese and not infrequently against the MPLA.

While Savimbi was trying to accumulate whatever armaments he could, he also persisted in his effort to form an alliance with his old mentor, Holden Roberto. Much of his desire for a union was based on a fear of becoming the victim of an FNLA-MPLA alliance. Nevertheless, despite various schemes pursued by the OAU, Kaunda, Mobutu, and the Egyptian government, no political accord reached between any of the members of the movement ever lasted beyond the drying of the ink.[138]

In January 1968, four years after Williams's first request, Vice President Hubert Humphrey made a nine-nation tour of Africa, which attracted little attention from the American press. Given the escalation of the Vietnam war following the debacle of the Tet offensive and submission to Congress of the Administration's aid budget, which was the smallest in twenty years, Humphrey had little with which to illustrate America's commitment to Africa's well-being. Instead, in a speech in Lusaka, Zambia, he criticized the "retrogressive policies" of Portugal, Rhodesia, and South Africa that "had turned their faces away from the inevitable triumph of self-determination."[139] Inexorably, America seemed to be following suit.

Chapter 3

Nixon, Caetano, and Spínola: Partners in Uncertainty

The Structure of Peace

The most immediate challenge that Richard Milhous Nixon faced when he assumed the presidency on 20 January 1969 was the need to repair the national consensus on America's role in the world that had been shattered by Vietnam. Nixon and his chief foreign policy adviser, Henry Kissinger, saw their principal task as extracting the United States from Vietnam, the country's first experience with an unsuccessful war, while keeping America's prestige as a leading global power intact. Underlying this, in their view, was a need to reassess America's purpose in a world where its nuclear superiority was eroding, its economic strength was being challenged, and its understanding of forces shaping the developing world was insufficient. At the same time, Nixon and Kissinger saw a major opportunity for the United States in the split between People's Republic of China and the Soviet Union, which diminished Moscow's global influence and that of the international communist movement.[1]

Richard Nixon, who in Kissinger's view possessed a greater knowledge of international affairs than any other American president, subscribed to the worldview developed by the architects of containment. The world was divided between friends and enemies and between arenas of cooperation and competition. As Nixon wrote in his memoirs, "I could see that the central factor in 1968 on the eve of my presidency was the same as it had been in 1947 when I went to Europe with the Herter Committee: America, now, as then, was the main defender of the free world against the encroachment and aggression of the Communist World."[2]

Nixon counted on a balance of power to produce stability among nations and depended on a strong America—with strong allies—as essential to the global equilibrium. The president translated this view into policy on 25 July 1969, on the South Pacific island of Guam, where he enunciated what came to be known as the Nixon Doctrine. While reaffirming America's commitment to existing treaty obligations and a willingness to provide a "shield" if a nuclear power (i.e., the Soviet Union) threatened a key American ally, the Nixon Doctrine was designed principally to address crises in the Third World, such as had occurred in Korea in the 1950s and in Vietnam. In such instances, the United States would "look to the nation directly threatened to assume the primary responsibility of providing the manpower for defense."[3]

The Nixon administration seemed to be signaling its allies, such as Portugal, that the US would become more selective about engaging in Third World conflicts. As Kissinger subsequently noted, "The Nixon Doctrine was . . . primarily relevant to crises in the peripheral areas not covered by formal alliances and threatened by Soviet surrogates, of which, as it turned out, there were very few."[4] The Nixon administration, therefore, sought to design a diplomatic strategy that would prevent the US from being drawn into Third World trouble spots but that would also forestall Soviet advances in the developing world, especially where US allies might not be able to strengthen their defenses.

This strategy was predicated on "linking" an expansion of the areas of cooperation—such as an increase in diplomatic ties, commercial activity, and cultural and scientific exchanges—with Moscow to a more restrained Soviet policy in the Third World. A primary objective of this policy of "détente" was to prevent the Soviet Union from seeking unilateral gains in "peripheral" areas.

As part of his effort to implement the policy of détente, Nixon instructed Kissinger to obtain Soviet agreement on "the need for a single standard" of international conduct. As he left Washington on 20 April 1972 to finalize the agenda of a summit meeting that was to be held the following month, Nixon told Kissinger that the United States "could not accept the proposition that the Soviet Union had the right to support liberation movements all over the world . . . ." Nixon's objective of gaining Moscow's agreement on a code of international behavior in Asia, the Middle East, and Africa was, on the surface, realized in the signing of a document called the "Basic Principles of US-Soviet Relations." As Kissinger said in a press conference in Moscow following the summit meeting, these principles "state that both sides will attempt to their utmost to avoid military confrontations [while] recognizing that the attempt of traditional diplomacy to accumulate marginal advantages is bound to lead to disastrous consequences in the nuclear age."[5]

Article 2 in the agreement contained Nixon and Kissinger's repeated exhortation to Moscow to forego "efforts to obtain unilateral advantage" at the expense of the West and "to exercise restraint" in Soviet foreign policy. Yet the accord was a "psuedoagreement" that allowed "each side [to] read its own hopes and desires" into the document that served as a framework for Soviet-American relations. As for Nixon's desire to have Moscow desist in its support for liberation movements in various parts of the world, Kissinger and his colleagues tended to think of this as "the same old rhetoric," according to Walter Stoessel, the US ambassador to the Soviet Union at the time. As a result, the issue of Soviet support for Third World liberation movements was "sloughed over" in the negotiations that produced the Basic Principles Agreement and was not included in the final document.[6]

Nonetheless, Kissinger would subsequently describe the Basic Principles Agreement as "a yardstick" against which to assess Soviet-American relations. The Agreement also enabled the administration to prioritize issues, especially in terms of their impact on Soviet-American relations. Accordingly, the problems in Portugal and Portuguese Africa attracted virtually no attention from the Nixon White House. Washington expected the former colonial powers—Britain, France, and Belgium—to take the lead in responding to crises on the continent. Moreover, African issues more generally were beyond Kissinger's policy or intellectual interests. He typically asked, for example, "What have African states done for us lately?" in reference to their support for larger American objectives.

An equally significant dimension of Nixon's "structure of peace," which he pledged in his 1969 inaugural address that his administration would create, was the opening of relations with the People's Republic of China. Once the Shanghai Communiqué was signed with China in February 1972, the US found itself in a position closer to each of the communist giants than they were to each other. Moreover, the Soviets were now faced with threats on two fronts: NATO in the West and China in the East. Increased tensions with the US would only accelerate

US–China rapprochement that, in effect, worked as an added brake on Soviet ambitions in the Third World. Thus, at the zenith of its conduct of geostrategic diplomacy, the Nixon administration pursued this triangular balance of power foreign policy in an effort "to solve practical problems with the Soviet Union while maintaining a dialogue of global concepts with the Chinese."[7]

Following the dramatic opening of relations with China, Nixon and Kissinger's foreign policy successes appeared to be unrivaled by any other American administration in the twentieth century. Less appreciated in Washington was the fact that the opening of diplomatic ties with Beijing helped to spark a new scramble for influence between the Soviet Union and China in Sub-Saharan Africa, principally in Central Africa. Ironically and unfortunately, the "peripheral" area of Angola would come to be the focal point of this superpower competition that eventually drew in the United States, the Soviet Union, and China and would undermine the carefully crafted policy of détente.

The New Portugal

Marcello Caetano inherited a government that was a captive of the Salazar legacy. Neither the former law school dean nor his ministers were able to comprehend, much less adapt to, the new currents that were transforming Portuguese society. Most significant was Lisbon's weakening grip on its empire in Africa.

During the 1960s, Portugal strengthened its commercial ties to Western Europe at the expense of its economic links to its colonies in Africa. Epidemic emigration to Western Europe from Portugal accompanied the shift in trade flows. Between 1960 and 1971, nearly one million Portuguese left the country. Most of these emigrés were between eighteen and thirty-five and subject to conscription. The commitment to defend "the nation" was waning, especially among those youths who had to leave the comforts of their villages and universities for the perilous uncertainties of war in the African bush.

The reorientation of the Portuguese economy away from Africa was accompanied by a large infusion of foreign direct investment from Europe. In 1959, foreign investment accounted for less than one percent of the nation's gross capital formation; by 1970 its share had risen to more than twenty-seven percent. These trends stabilized Portugal's balance of payments, but they fueled the already spiraling rate of inflation. This further strained depressed urban salaries, working conditions, and living standards and contributed to the depletion of the labor market, especially in the rural, agricultural provinces.[8]

The shift toward Europe brought popular Western culture to Portugal's towns and cities. Pop groups, beauty contests, and television shows became as commonplace as rebel priests who challenged celibacy laws and dogmas about birth control. The popularity of the mournful *fado* was overshadowed by folksingers protesting the iniquities of colonial warfare and poverty. The exchange of ideas, literature, and information with the outside world was more vibrant than it had ever been, fuelled in part by the more than two million tourists who visited Portugal in 1968.

Spurred on by the political and cultural upheavals in the rest of Europe, and by a generation of youths that had become familiar with PIDE's techniques of surveillance, a political underground spawned in Portugal among students, journalists, and other professionals. Previously unheard of strikes became more frequent among workers, as did student protests. Revolutionary "commandos" began periodically attacking symbols of colonial rule and NATO.[9]

The challenge to Marcello Caetano was to harness and channel this nascent dynamism. Unfortunately, he inherited a government that was created to resist liberalism and free market capitalism and a bureaucracy that had come to a virtual standstill during the last years of the Salazar regime. Indeed, the Portuguese government was "sluggish to the point of stupor."[10]

When he first came into office, the new prime minister tried to respond forcefully to the country's changes and growing problems. In an effort to distance himself from Salazar's legacy, the only legal political party, the National Union, was renamed Popular National Action, and the *Estado Novo* [New State], became the *Estado Social* [Social State]. PIDE was renamed the Directorate General of Security (DGS), the Propaganda Secretariat became the Information and Tourist Office and the Censorship Board was renamed the Previous Examination Board. He also permitted the return from exile of two popular critics of the Salazar regime, Mário Soares and the Bishop of Oporto, Dom António Ferreira Gomes.

A more significant "renovation" came with the decision to allow labor unions the right to select their own leadership without government approval. Within months, the trade unions, or *sindicatos*, were transformed from listless agencies into vibrant unions controlled by the rank and file. Caetano's response was to reverse the policy and ban union rallies on the pretext that they were "fomenting class struggle." This led to the formation of unofficial trade unions throughout the nation's major industries that united under a broad umbrella organization called the *Intersindical*. As the government tried to outlaw the *Intersindical*, it moved underground where it quickly came to be dominated by the similarly clandestine Portuguese Communist Party. By 1973, forty major strikes succeeded in distracting Caetano from Portugal's war effort in Africa and undermining many of his social reforms.[11]

True to his liberal pretensions, Caetano allowed the political opposition to contest the November 1969 National Assembly elections. Even though opposition candidates were denied free access to newspapers, television, and large assembly halls, they accepted Caetano's offer. As Mário Soares put it, "In a country that was politically asleep, the point was not so much to win as to wake up." The opposition, largely because of its internal split, had little success on either score. In the final results, the Democratic Electoral Committee (CED), an alliance of progressive Catholics and liberals, and the Electoral Committee of Democratic Unity (CEUD), a more moderate coalition of liberals and socialists, gained only twelve percent of the vote while candidates endorsed by the government received the rest. As less than twenty percent of the voting age population were registered voters and nearly half this group stayed home from the polls, the elections had virtually no significance as a referendum on the policies of the government or opposition parties.[12]

The election was important in two respects, however. For the first time in ten years, more than three thousand members of the opposition held a legal rally at Aveiro in Oporto, where they were able to express their demands publicly for more liberalization at home and in the colonies.The elections also created an opportunity for new democratic political figures to surface, however briefly. This included individuals such as Sá Caneiro, a brilliant lawyer from Oporto, and Francisco Pinto Balsemão, a wealthy journalist and publisher from Lisbon. Another individual who unsuccessfully contested the elections was Melo Antunes, an articulate and activist junior army officer from the Azores. All would play significant roles in Portugal's transition from dictatorship to democracy.[13]

For Caetano, the November 1969 elections were essentially a referendum on the issue of Portugal's presence in Africa. To underscore the seriousness of the poll, President Americo Tomas told the new prime minister that if the referendum was not a success, the reins of government would be transferred to the armed forces.[14]

In fact, no issue was as difficult for Caetano as was Portugal's continuing hold on Angola, Mozambique, and Guinea-Bissau. As Caetano would later write from exile, "All my actions of governance were conditioned by the question of the *ultramar* (or colonies)."[15] On becoming premier, Caetano gave the military assurances that he would not press his earlier federalist ideas. His tour of Africa in April 1969, a trip that Salazar never took, was designed expressly to demonstrate his commitment to sustain and protect Portugal's presence in Africa. As Caetano proclaimed in a speech to the National Assembly in September 1970, the defense of Portuguese Africa "is a sacred duty . . . that cannot be either ignored or forgotten by the Portuguese people."[16]

Although opposition figures made an unprecedented appearance on the Portuguese political scene in the 1969 elections, the government's tight control of the media blunted their effort to illuminate the economic and social pressures straining the country. By 1970, Lisbon was spending about $400 million a year, or forty-five percent of the national budget, on defense and security. This, in effect, curtailed all public spending on housing, education, and health in the country in which the standard of living was already Europe's lowest. The three wars in Africa also imposed serious manpower costs. With a military force of about 140,000 in a population of 9.5 million, only Israel and South Vietnam had a larger percentage of its populace under arms at the time. There was also an increasing popular disaffection for the war effort that was reflected in the fact that only thirty percent of the young men who were called for the draft appeared. Moreover, conscription, which had been extended from one year to four under Salazar, was supplemented by new legislation that allowed for the recall of officers drawn from the past four draft calls and for an unlimited period if necessary. The conditions that the soldiers encountered in Africa were very harsh. As one American diplomat who visited Angola in 1973 said, military service in the colonies was "a dreadful, dreadful life."[17]

Portugal's image as a haven for tourists seeking economy, tranquility, and simplicity belied serious strains and divisions in virtually every aspect of society. On the one hand, Caetano's reforms had little effect on the problems for which they were designed. On the other hand, the reforms created strong opposition within the military and among those supporters of Salazarist dogma who suspected that Caetano was preparing to abandon the colonies. Although the

US ambassador to Portugal, Ridgeway Knight, had reported to the State Department that there were rumors of "displeasure" in the armed forces to some of Caetano's initiatives,[18] Washington had no comprehension of the pressures that were building in Portuguese society.

Friends in the White House

As far as Richard Nixon was concerned, the Kennedy administration's hostility toward Portugal and the Johnson administration's "benign neutrality" were a thing of the past. The new American president made this explicit to Prime Minister Caetano, who represented Portugal at President Eisenhower's funeral following his death on 28 March 1969. Nixon met with the Portuguese leader while he was in Washington and promised him unqualified American support.

Following the Nixon-Caetano meeting, the White House issued a directive terminating all American contacts with the nationalists who were fighting for independence in Portuguese Africa. Relations with FRELIMO were severed and Holden Roberto was "deactivated" as an intelligence asset, although he kept his monthly ten thousand dollar retainer at the insistence of the CIA, which wanted to maintain a minimal presence in Angola.[19]

Nixon further signaled his openness to Lisbon by receiving Franco Nogueira in the Oval Office on 6 April at a meeting that was also attended by the National Security Affairs adviser, Henry Kissinger. Nixon told Nogueira that Portugal did not deserve to be pressured by the United States and that such a policy was not consistent with American interests. That evening at a gala White House dinner celebrating NATO's twentieth anniversary, Nixon came up to Nogueira and repeated his belief that the previous American attitude toward Portugal had been "unjust." Bracing Nogueira's shoulders, Nixon said, "Just remember, I'll never do to you what Kennedy did."[20]

Nixon was no neophyte on the issue of Portugal and its African colonies. During a visit to Lisbon in June 1963, ostensibly on behalf of General Tire, he pleased Franco Nogueira—and angered the Kennedy White House—by saying that independence was "not necessarily the best thing for Africa or the Africans." From his perspective, Portugal, as a member of NATO, was entitled to American loyalty and respect. Nixon was also cognizant of the importance of the Azores to the American security network. He was sympathetic to the argument that Portugal was a bulwark against the spread of communist influence in

Africa. As importantly, the Portuguese leaders, especially under Salazar, had shown themselves to be decisive and unambiguous in their actions, which was a trait that both Nixon and Kissinger admired and valued in an ally. In the geostrategic calculations of the Nixon White House, the Portuguese were seen not only as a trusted NATO ally but as a source of order and stability in Southern Africa.[21]

Nixon's first exposure to African issues came during his tour of eight African nations in 1957, during which he led the official American delegation to Ghana's independence celebrations. In his report to President Eisenhower, the Vice President had described Africa as "a priority target for the international communist movement . . . . The course of its development . . . could well prove to be the decisive factor between the forces of freedom and international communism."

In the wake of his visit to Ghana, Nixon became a strong proponent of upgrading the quantity and quality of American diplomatic representation in Africa. This was in part due to the Communist threat, which justified "the wisdom and necessity" of actively assisting African countries in every way to maintain their independence. It was also provoked by several USIA officials who had run afoul of the Vice President, which prompted Nixon to refer publicly to the American diplomats as "corn-balls." This remark set off a minor uproar in Washington when accompanying American journalists included it in their dispatches back to the United States.[22]

Richard Nixon, accompanied by aide Patrick Buchanan, revisited Africa in 1967 as part of four trips that he used to prepare for his successful presidential bid. On this occasion he found a different Africa. No longer did he call for top-grade diplomatic personnel because, as many in the Johnson administration concluded, Africa was not the cutting edge of the East-West struggle as it once had been. As he wrote in his memoirs, "I was discouraged by the fact that, with a few exceptions, the new black African nations simply did not have the trained leadership to achieve their goals in the foreseeable future."[23] Except for issues such as Biafra, which evoked Nixon's sympathies and attention, Africa's problems in 1969 did not appear to be complicated by the advances of the Soviet Union and China. The quiescence of America's strategic rivals and the region's lack of socioeconomic development were key reasons that Africa did not figure prominently in the new administration's foreign policy calculations as Nixon assumed the presidency.

Another reason was the "squalor of prejudice" and "pall of racism" that hung over the West Wing basement and Oval Office. On occasion, when Roger Morris, the new aide for Africa on the NSC staff, would enter the Situation Room, Kissinger's staff assistant, Alexander Haig, would begin to beat his hands on the table as if pounding a drum. In another instance, when Nixon was putting the final touches on his first presidential message to Congress on foreign policy, the President turned to Kissinger and asked, "Is there something in it for the jigs?" During a National Security Council meeting when the administration was discussing its policy toward Southern Africa, Vice President Spiro Agnew read a statement about how "South African independence" in 1965 *[sic]* was similar to that of the United States in 1776, when blacks did not have the vote. Following the embarrassed silence at the end of the Vice President's intervention, Nixon leaned forward and said, "You mean Rhodesia, don't you, Ted?" This strain of bigotry and ignorance about Africa, along with Africa's perceived geostrategic irrelevance, provided the setting against which US policy toward Portugal, Angola, and Mozambique was formulated during the Nixon administration.[24]

Designing "Tar Baby"

It took little time for the President's sentiments toward Portugal to become enshrined in policy. On virtually the same day that American diplomats were instructed to cease contacts with the Angolan and Mozambican nationalists, Henry Kissinger issued National Security Study Memorandum 39 (NSSM 39). This was one of eighty-five policy reviews that the administration would undertake in its first year. Assigned to the National Security Council Interdepartmental Group for Africa, NSSM 39 was intended to be a comprehensive review of American interests and policy options in Southern Africa—which included Rhodesia, South Africa, the Portuguese territories, and adjacent states south of Zaire (as President Mobutu renamed the country in 1970) and Tanzania. The policy review was to be completed in two weeks. As one participant would later write about the process, "The conduct of the review was alternately childish, venomous, dull, colossally wasteful of official time, and very much the daily stuff of government in foreign affairs." Moreover, as Kissinger would subsequently acknowledge, the review "consigned" Africa to the bottom of the American foreign policy agenda.[25]

From the outset, two "arrogant and energetic" staffers, Roger Morris and Richard Kennedy, respectively representing the NSC and the Defense Department, took the lead on NSSM 39. The initial impetus was supplied by Roger Morris who, in the reforming zeal of the new White House, was eager to showcase his talents and loyalties to Kissinger. Already aware of Nixon's determination "to stop lecturing the Portuguese" and to suspend contacts with the liberation movements, Morris also believed that no American president, least of all the conservative and relatively uninterested Richard Nixon, would be willing to undermine the white-ruled states of Southern Africa. Second, it was "a clear historical lesson" to Morris, who recently had completed a Ph.D. in government at Harvard, that outside coercion would only harden the resolve of the besieged white minority regimes. Therefore, in his opinion, any new American policy would have to be based on the "twin premises [of] accepting the expedient American stakes in the tyrannies [while] using that presence wherever possible to encourage racial progress in the region." Richard Kennedy shared Morris's belief that there should be more communication with, and a partial relaxation of, American measures against the white minority regimes as well as a more restrained position at the United Nations.[26]

To retain influence in the policy process and to garner some "bargaining advantage" of its own the State Department's representative to the policy process initially tried to recycle a 1968 National Policy Paper on Southern Africa. Yet the document was a bland and shallow codification of existing policy that the White House viewed as "aimless and overtaken." The NSC staff in the Johnson administration had been unwilling to clear it and its fate was no different in the Nixon administration.[27]

Kissinger had instructed Morris to make sure that all existing policies and assumptions were examined and challenged. In response, Morris ordered his bureaucratic counterparts to inventory every American interest, program and political relationship of the US in the region. According to Morris, the various bureaucratic agencies spent the summer of 1969 jostling, battling, and maneuvering in an effort to define two or three legitimate policy choices between the two extremes of aligning with the white states or condoning their destruction through guerilla warfare.

When the new assistant secretary for African Affairs David Newsom assumed his position in the State Department in July 1969, he found the policy review well under way. Newsom, who had most recently been ambassador to Libya, was familiar with the broad range of African issues. Quickly, he came to see his job as preserving the general thrust of American policy toward Africa as defined by the Kennedy and Johnson administrations against Kissinger's bureaucratic gladiators who wanted to make substantial changes. Newsom was caught between the White House and the Defense Department, who were willing to accept Portugal's continued presence in Africa with little debate, and the less influential African constituency in the American government, who wanted to work more closely with the African governments to facilitate the transition to independence in Angola and Mozambique. Newsom viewed his task as maintaining American credibility with African leaders such as Julius Nyerere and Kenneth Kaunda, who were Africa's most respected and moderate advocates of self-determination, while trying to modify the extremes to which the Nixon White House was prepared to go.[28]

By mid-August, Morris's interagency team completed a draft response to NSSM 39. It consisted of essentially five options. The first of these was the so-called "Acheson option," which was based on a paper that the former secretary of state had given Nixon that spring advocating a normalization of relations with the white minority-dominated regimes. Acheson believed that condemnation of the racist regimes was as example of excessive moralism in diplomacy. The second option advocated a broader association with white states, in an effort to encourage moderation, and with the black states, in an effort to enlist their cooperation in reducing regional tensions and cross-border violence. Option three called for increased identification with and support for the black states in the region, as a precondition to pursuing American economic, strategic, and scientific interests with the white states. A fourth option advocated decreased contacts with the white regimes, and a fifth suggested the possibility of severing all ties to the region to avoid involvement in an expanded conflict.[29]

There was little secret about the White House's preference for Option Two, as Kissinger was skeptical that external pressures would change conditions in the white minority states. Caustically labeling the proposed option "tar baby," the Africa Bureau argued that Option Two reversed a decade of American support for self-determination in Africa and that the United States would be unable to abandon the policy if it did not work. In a last-ditch effort to soften its impact, Newsom unexpectedly introduced a "new" option at the Review Group meeting in November 1969. Outlining an approach similar to Option Two,

Newsom suggested that the United States consult with black African leaders to seek their approval *before* adopting the posture. Punctilious in front of the Review Group, Kissinger raged at the "intellectual squalor" of the State Department once in the privacy of his office. It was enough to make him a firm advocate of Option Two.

The full National Security Council met on 17 December 1969 to consider American policy toward Southern Africa. Attending the meeting, among others, were Nixon, Vice President Spiro Agnew, Attorney General John Mitchell, Secretary of State William Rogers, Under Secretary of State Elliot Richardson, Director of the CIA Richard Helms, and Kissinger. Nixon opened the meeting by remarking that the subject was a complex foreign policy problem of extraordinary moral and political dimensions. Rogers then mentioned that the issues involved could not be that difficult because so many around the table were "lawyers who must have had clients in South Africa . . . . I know I did."

Rogers' otherwise obscure point in fact reflected the "cliency," or vested interests, that also colored the bureaucratic debate over NSSM 39. This was particularly evident in the presentation made by CIA director Richard Helms. His analysis was "transparently pro-white . . . disdainful of the black opposition," and fully reflective of the views of the security services in South Africa, Rhodesia, and Portugal on whose reports the CIA based much of their analyses. The US intelligence agencies were unable to produce information from the black perspective or about groups that the US was not supporting. Charles Yost, Ambassador to the UN, who was also at the meeting, was no less accommodating to the general tone of the discussion when he told Nixon that "we can live with the Portuguese problem" at the United Nations.[30]

The only divergent perspective was supplied by NSC adviser, Winston Lord, who had written a special briefing paper on "Domestic and Moral Factors" in Southern Africa. Lord had been encouraged by Kissinger to write analyses on various issues independent of the review process to highlight considerations that may have been "glossed over and blanched out" of the policy study. Perceptively, Lord warned that the Southern Africa issue could have significant domestic consequences within the US if the crisis in the region, especially in South Africa, were to escalate significantly. Therefore, Lord argued for disengagement, contending that the US did not have interests in the area "sufficiently important to run even the potential risks of southern Africa becoming a serious and divisive domestic issue."[31]

"The Whites Are Here to Stay"

Lord's recommendation for US policy toward Southern Africa was appreciated by his boss, Henry Kissinger, but ignored. As Donald McHenry, then a State Department official familiar with the policy process would later testify, NSSM 39 was produced by "individuals possessing African expertise [who] had less influence than those interested in selling planes, buying chrome or in renewing contracts."[32] Morris and Kennedy, in tandem with representatives from NASA, Commerce, and the CIA, lobbied effectively for a relaxation of restrictions against and a greater communication with the white minority regimes. NASA had a valued tracking station in South Africa; the CIA had close relations with the intelligence services in Portugal, Rhodesia, and South Africa; and Commerce was not willing to jeopardize American investments in South Africa that amounted to approximately one billion dollars. The Africanists at the State Department were no match against this alliance of interests.

Moreover, Kissinger had developed contempt for the Africa Bureau during his first week in the White House when the administration tried, unsuccessfully, to articulate a policy toward Nigeria and the civil war in Biafra. As a result, "no field officer had anything to do with NSSM 39."[33] In the view of the White House, the US embassies in Africa produced analyses and intelligence that were predictable at best.

Subsequent reports from the field, however, did contradict the conclusions that were being reached by the NSC. On 12 October 1970, Consul General Richard Post attended a briefing by the Portuguese High Command in Angola that was a "sober report" and almost diametrically opposed" to the picture that Portugal had presented publicly. The report indicated that the insurgency had increased substantially over the last year.[34] The Bureau of Intelligence and Research (INR) was drawing similar conclusions. Analysts in INR perceived that "the rebels [in Angola] show no sign of weakening, despite their inability to mount concerted actions or to unite in a common front."[35] As for the insurgency in Mozambique, INR concluded an October 1969 study with the assessment that "FRELIMO has successfully carried the insurgency to a third front. The Portuguese may be able to contain FRELIMO in Tete, but may be faced with more widespread land mine and ambush activity. As a result of this pressure, the Portuguese military will probably be more ready in the future to accept Rhodesian and possibly South African assistance."[36]

Nevertheless, Option Two, or "tar baby," embedded the status quo into American policy toward Southern Africa. Most significantly, it overlooked the strains that waging war on three fronts was having on Portugal. The option concluded that:

> The Whites are here to stay and the only way that constructive change can come about is through them. There is no hope for the blacks to gain the political rights they seek through violence, which will only lead to chaos and increased opportunities for the communists. We can, by selective relaxation of our stance toward the white regimes, encourage some modification of their current racial and colonial policies . . . .[37]

In January 1970, this view, which laid the conceptual groundwork for American policy toward Portugal and its African territories, Rhodesia, and South Africa, was strengthened by other events. For one, it seemed to Morris that African leaders, such as Haile Selassie in Ethiopia, General Yakubu Gowon in Nigeria, and Jomo Kenyatta in Kenya, were too preoccupied with domestic matters to fan the flames of insurrection in Southern Africa. Second, with the turmoil in the Angolan and Mozambican nationalist movements and the death of Eduardo Mondlane there was the appearance that these guerrilla organizations were floundering and could never threaten the stability of the colonial and white-minority regimes, INR's analysis notwithstanding. Moreover, leading American analysts were reaching similar conclusions. In their authoritative review of Portuguese Africa, David Abshire and Michael Samuels concluded that for the "foreseeable future," Portuguese dominance in the colonies would continue. Another influential voice was that of Herman Kahn, a well-known futurist. Following a trip to Angola in August–September 1969, Kahn and a group of analysts from the Hudson Institute argued that a "premature" withdrawal from Africa would be "irresponsible."[38] Dean Acheson also went public with the Southern Africa policy advice that he gave to Nixon. Testifying before Congress, Acheson warned that the US would bring chaos to Portuguese Africa and a revolution to the Iberian Peninsula if it interfered with Portugal's Africa policy.[39]

As events would show, NSSM 39 represented a partial and incorrect reading of the situation in Portuguese Africa, not to mention Rhodesia and South Africa, as Morris would later admit. In fact, since the beginning of its anti-colonial war in 1964, FRELIMO had grown from a guerilla group of 250 to an armed force of about ten thousand. In Guinea-Bissau, which was generally outside the scope of American foreign policy considerations even in Africa, a force of four thousand PAIGC (*Partido Africano da Independência da Guiné e Cabo Verde*, or the African Party of Independence of Guinea and Cape Verde) militants were holding down the Portuguese army of forty thousand. It is ironic that individuals such as Roger Morris, who would later criticize foreign service officers for their "appalling ignorance of Southern African history and politics," would himself be guilty of these lapses.[40]

Unaware or unconcerned by these trends, Nixon expressed his satisfaction at the results of the policy review, which became National Security Decision Memorandum 39 when completed, by scribbling "excellent staff work" on the memorandum entitled "Southern Africa Policy Decisions," which Kissinger submitted to him on 15 January 1970. As was his style, Nixon made the final decision in the privacy of his office or in consultation with Kissinger.

In this January memo, Kissinger pointed out that even though there "may have been several instances" in which the Portuguese violated their pledges not to use NATO equipment in Africa, "the Portuguese have, in general, kept their assurances." Kissinger also repeated to Nixon Lisbon's argument that "they are a NATO ally defending the West on its African flank." He then made the erroneous point that Africans viewed Lisbon in a "somewhat more benign way" than they do South Africa, implying that a closer relationship with Lisbon would be less damaging to US relations with African governments than closer ties with Pretoria. In fact, such a distinction was meaningless as both governments were pariahs in the eyes of most African governments.

Despite a concern that NSSM 39 would leak to the public, Kissinger suggested that "a slight loosening of arms supply policy would be a useful gesture to tell Caetano [as the Azores negotiations come forward] that we mean what we say about a less doctrinaire approach." Thus, "on policy grounds," Kissinger recommended to Nixon "that you (1) maintain the arms embargo on South Africa for the time being, and (2) relax the embargo on Portugal by excepting non-lethal equipment which has dual civilian and military uses." With little delay, Nixon initialed the space next to "Approve,"[41] but subsequently included South Africa in the relaxed arms embargo.

The normalization of relations with Portugal was completed on 17 August 1970 with the issuance of National Security Study Decision Memorandum 81, entitled "Implementation of Arms Embargo on South Africa and Portuguese Africa Territories." The White House had decided that, in regard to Portugal and South Africa, "Non-lethal dual-use items which are *preponderantly employed for civilian use* will be licensed to either civilian or military buyers . . . . Non-lethal dual-use items which are *preponderantly used by military forces*," can be licensed to civilian and military buyers with concurrence by the Departments of Commerce and State.[42]

Within twelve months of assuming office, the Nixon administration had embraced Lisbon and given tacit support to its policies in its African territories. Washington's endorsement was predicated on the president's sympathies for the Portuguese government and his belief that their presence in Africa was important for stemming an expansion of Soviet influence, not to mention his disdain for African nationalism. The process that designed the new policy was supposed to have been comprehensive and inclusive but, in fact, was exclusive and skewed. As a result, the accommodating policy of the Nixon administration ignored subtle but apparent and disturbing trends in Angola, Mozambique, and Guinea-Bissau. The consequences would be profound not only for Africa, especially Angola, but for US relations with Africa and, as importantly, the Soviet Union.

A Ticket to the Azores

Franco Nogueira announced his resignation as foreign minister at a press conference in Lisbon on 10 June 1969. In summarizing his tenure, he declared that Portugal had "all the connections and international acceptability that is necessary to the country."[43] The statement poignantly reflected Nogueira's skill at protecting Salazar's interpretation of the nation's interests. Nogueira had adroitly maneuvered around international sanctions and rebuffs while parlaying the inherent weaknesses of a small state into specific advantages. Yet his accomplishments and the view of Portugal and its colonies to which he was wedded would soon be violently overtaken by the events he had so brazenly tried to control. Nogueira's legacy was his ability to outlast and frustrate his diplomatic interlocutors and to forestall, at great cost to Portugal and Africa, self-determination in Angola, Mozambique, and Guinea-Bissau.

At the time, however, Nogueira was right. Portugal did have a new acceptability to the United States, but that was due more to changes in Washington than in Lisbon. The number of Portuguese military trained by Americans nearly doubled, from seventy-four in the last year of the Johnson administration to 130 in the first year of the Nixon administration. Within months of the approval of NSDM 81, the administration allowed Portugal to purchase several Boeing 707s and 747s, which were used to transport troops to Africa. Portugal also bought Bell helicopters for agricultural spraying and dusting in Africa in spite of liberation movement protests against Portuguese defoliation raids and unusually large herbicide imports. As the US ambassador to the UN, Charles Yost, testified in Congress, "We have had no evidence presented which has been convincing to us that there have been violations" of the American arms agreement with Portugal. American investments in Portugal and Portuguese Africa had grown form $183 million in 1968 to $368 million in 1970. Gulf Oil, with its interests in the Angolan enclave of Cabinda, was the largest single investor in the colonies.[44]

The rapprochement between Portugal and the United States was solidified by the signing of a new agreement on the Azores on 9 December 1971 in Brussels. The arrangement, which extended the rights of the US to the air base in Lajes until 3 February 1974, was concluded by Secretary of State William Rogers and Nogueira's successor as foreign minister, Rui Patrício, who was also Marcello Caetano's godson. A week later, Caetano joined Nixon and French President Georges Pompidou in talks at Lajes on the relative values of the French and American currencies. The decision to hold the Nixon-Pompidou talks on the Azores was a compromise choice that had little to do with Portugal. Nixon could not go to Europe without visiting other allies and Paris was hesitant to receive Nixon on a European tour.[45] The speed with which American negotiators concluded the otherwise lengthy and difficult negotiations tended to underscore the Nixon administration's inclination to view Portugal primarily as "a ticket to the Azores."[46]

The $436 million agreement seemed to represent a new era in Portuguese-American relations. It consisted primarily of a $400 million Export-Import Bank line of credit to cover the costs of development projects that the Caetano government planned to undertake in Portugal.

The rest of the agreement provided for surplus agricultural commodities, a modest amount of excess nonmilitary Defense Department supplies (such as earthmovers), and one million dollars for the Portuguese education reform program in Lisbon.

Abroad and at home, advocates of self-determination in Portugal's colonies criticized the Nixon administration for its "deadening hand of indifference" and what appeared to be direct financial support of Portugal's war effort in Africa.[47] The United Nations Security Council, which was holding meetings in Addis Ababa, warned Washington that it was "in deep trouble with Black Africa." In Washington, Congressman Charles C. Diggs, Jr., chairman of the Congressional Black Caucus, sent a letter to President Nixon signed by eighteen other legislators that criticized the accord and its implications for American policy in Southern Africa. Four days later, Diggs publicly resigned from his position as a member of the United States delegation to the UN in protest over the Azores agreement that he denounced as an "open alliance with Portugal." A week later, William Rogers dismissed Diggs' action by saying that "our support for Portugal, and with particular reference to the Azores base . . . is unrelated to Africa."[48] In Rogers' view, the American standing with most African countries was in fact improving. He cited the trip he had taken to Africa a year earlier and the visit that the First Lady, Pat Nixon, was about to make to the Ivory Coast, Ghana, and Liberia, as evidence of the "positive relations" with Africa.

Lisbon truly wished that Nixon's critics were right. Even though Caetano publicly expressed his happiness that Portuguese–American relations were back on solid footing, there was still much displeasure within his government over the new agreement. Under Salazar, it had been Portugal's policy not to charge the United States rent for use of the base. Not only did Portugal believe it was performing its role as an ally but it valued the leverage and freedom that such an arrangement created. Yet times had changed, as evidenced by Caetano's assurances during his regular Sunday broadcasts to the nation that Portugal had not been bought by the United States. The real problem from Lisbon's point of view, however, was the unwillingness of the American government to give Portugal the unqualified political support that it so badly wanted for its war effort in Africa.[49]

In practical terms, the Azores agreement turned out to be worthless to Portugal. The materials that the Defense Department made available were not relevant to Portugal's military needs. Also, developmental financing was available at better terms elsewhere in Western Europe. One American diplomat involved in the negotiations sardonically, but accurately, compared the agreement to an individual who donated a ten-year-old suit of clothes to charity and took a tax deduction for the original value of the clothing.[50]

Rogers in Africa

In an effort to put the best face on the still secret NSDM 39 and to put his personal mark on American policy toward Africa, Secretary of State Rogers left Washington in February 1970 for a ten-nation tour of the African continent. His goal was to demonstrate a "new interest in Africa" on the part of the Nixon administration. The effect, however, was to signal to Africa the administration's unwillingness to involve itself in the region's most complex issues. In meetings with leaders such as Kenyatta in Kenya, Kaunda of Zambia, and Mobutu in Zaire, Rogers repeatedly reminded them that there "was a limit to what the US could do" in ending the conflicts in the white-ruled states. He told African leaders that violence was not the answer and that the United States would take no active role in the liberation struggles of Southern Africa. As for American aid, Rogers informed the African leaders that the days of large American aid programs were finished. Rogers said that African nations had to become more self-reliant and willing to cooperate regionally.

In Lusaka, Zambia, Kenneth Kaunda asked Rogers to use his influence to get Portugal to respond to the Lusaka Manifesto, a moderate document issued by thirteen East and Central African states that called for a peaceful settlement to the tensions in Southern Africa.[51] Rogers remained noncommittal even though President Nixon's 1970 report to Congress on American foreign policy had "warmly" welcomed the Lusaka Manifesto as a "statesmanlike document." The Portuguese, however, blasted the manifesto and rejected "the insulting accusations" that they contended it contained. Rogers was unwilling to agitate Lisbon. Indeed, Rogers concluded on his return from Africa that "the declared Portuguese policy of racial toleration is an important factor" in the quest for self-determination. "We think this holds genuine hope for the future." Given the American position, Caetano and Patrício found that their discussions with Rogers in Lisbon in June 1970 made "a major contribution to removing (American) misunderstanding" about Portugal's role in Africa.[52]

Rogers' desire to demonstrate a new interest in Africa was undercut by his inability to align the United States with the right to self-determination and, of course, the pervasive influence of the Nixon policy toward Southern Africa that was predicated on working through Lisbon and the white minority regimes for political change. In fact, Washington was prepared to support Portugal at the expense of its ties to black Africa. For instance, the Nixon administration avoided criticizing Portugal when on 22 November 1970, five hundred Portuguese commandos staged an attack from the sea on Conakry, the capital of Guinea, adjacent to Guinea-Bissau. The Portuguese objective was to overthrow the Guinean government, attack the headquarters of the PAIGC, and free Portuguese soldiers who had been taken prisoner of war. Although the United States condemned the raid and said it must not be repeated, the Nixon administration abstained on a subsequent Security Council resolution that condemned Portugal "because it tended to commit the Council to actions in future situations." As if to underscore its contempt for its Third World critics, the US also withdrew from the Committee of 24 at the United Nations.[53]

In June 1971, the Administration again underscored its favorable disposition toward the regime in Lisbon when Vice President Spiro Agnew visited Portugal at the end of a ten-nation "goodwill tour." Caetano had hoped to use his meetings with Agnew to move along the then stalled Azores negotiations and to shore up American acquiescence in, if not support for, Portugal's continued control over Angola, Mozambique, and Guinea-Bissau. Agnew, however, was under instructions only to tell the Portuguese what he had told the other leaders with whom he had met: that President Nixon still retained his interest in these states despite the reduction of American overseas commitments in the wake of the Vietnam war and a rise of isolationist sentiment in the US. Agnew also told Portuguese officials that the Nixon administration would stand by Portugal even though the United States was determined to withdraw from Vietnam and was developing a new relationship with the Soviet Union and other nations.

The Stalemated Guerrilla Wars

Washington's embrace of the Caetano regime obscured the deteriorating situation in Portuguese Africa. According to the American Consulate in Maputo, the anticolonial struggle had spread into Niassa and Tete provinces, and FRELIMO was active in more than half the country. This report came at the conclusion of a major military operation, Operation Gordian Knot, directed by the new Portuguese Commander in Chief in Mozambique, General Kaúlza de Arriaga. The Consulate concluded that the Portuguese military campaign, waged by thirty-five thousand Portuguese troops had destroyed FRELIMO's bases and supplies, "but there are no signs that they [FRELIMO] are ready to quit." To the contrary, the Consulate noted that the Portuguese military was tiring from the war because "this stalemate is costing too much."[54] Moreover, it was apparent that the Portuguese armed forces could not contain or seriously inhibit FRELIMO's movement throughout the northern half of the country. As a result of this essential military failure, a senior Portuguese military leader would later admit that Operation Gordian Knot in fact transferred the "operational initiative" to the enemy camp.[55]

The situation in Angola had evolved into a "conflict of mines and helicopters that no one seemed able to win or lose." The Consul General in Luanda, Richard Post, reported that during the late 1960s that the liberation movements had increased their military capabilities. The Bureau of Intelligence and Research noted in 1970 that the guerilla activities in the past several years had more than offset government gains in reducing the insurgency. In Angola, as in Mozambique, there was little evidence of any weakening of the guerilla movements. "The two major and rival movements—GRAE and the MPLA—have sizable and well-armed guerilla forces, as well as financial resources." In contrast, the Portuguese military was beginning to experience a shortage of officers as it tried to expand its operations in Africa. Fewer students were entering the military academies and the government was forced to increase the number of university-aged males that were drafted into the military. The military no longer was the respected and eagerly pursued career that it had been in Portugal.[56]

The Bureau of Intelligence and Research concluded, on the strength of reports from the field, that the MPLA "has developed into the best disciplined and most effective of the three movements."[57] The Portuguese also acknowledged that the MPLA had the most effective leadership among the nationalists. Most of this assessment came as a result of the new front that the MPLA had opened in eastern Angola under the command of Daniel Chipenda. It forced the Portuguese military into armed, island-like outposts that were tenuously linked by mined and rutted dirt roads. The isolation and harshness of the conditions in the African bush fed a sense of resentment among the young, conscripted soldiers who were becoming an internal source of opposition to the Africa policies of the Portuguese government.[58]

The MPLA's success was due in part to the three thousand-strong guerrilla force it was able to maintain with support from the Soviet Union, Algeria, Tanzania, Cuba, and Yugoslavia. The FNLA, on the other hand, was primarily reliant on President Mobutu's support and the more than three hundred thousand Bakongo refugees in the southwestern area of Zaire. It was able to field a fighting force of about two thousand on the northern Angolan border.[59]

The most enigmatic of the three Angolan nationalist movements was UNITA, led by Jonas Savimbi. UNITA operated contrary to the laws of guerilla warfare as it had no meaningful outside support, no external sanctuary and a political line that vacillated between support for "anti-revisionist marxism" and a black socialist republic. Ironically, this lack of external support may have worked to Savimbi's long-term advantage as he was forced to establish operational headquarters inside Angola. In addition, his considerable leadership skills helped him to consolidate a strong political base among the Ovimbundu in central Angola. In the near-term, however, it left UNITA an unknown entity to the diplomatic community both in Luanda and internationally.[60]

The PAIGC in Guinea Bissau posed the most serious challenge to Portugal's military dominance in the colonies. Ambassador Tapley Bennett recognized the seriousness of the situation when he visited the territory in 1969 before leaving his post in Lisbon. The Governor General and Commander in Chief of the Portuguese Armed Forces in Guinea-Bissau, General António de Spínola, told Bennett that the war in the province could not be won militarily and that it required a political solution. The PAIGC had been formed in 1956 and three years later began to prepare for military conflict with the Portuguese. By 1969, the movement, led by Amílcar Cabral, one of Africa's leading intellectuals and theoreticians on anticolonial warfare, controlled half the territory. The PAIGC's success was measured in part by the fact that in 1961, the Portuguese had a military force of one thousand in the colony; by 1969, it had grown to forty thousand. Although the size of the Portuguese military was larger in Mozambique and Angola, the casualty rate was highest in Guinea Bissau.[61]

American policymakers had little contact with the PAIGC. As members of the Africa Bureau in the Kennedy and Johnson administrations told PAIGC supporters who were lobbying for more attention from the State Department, it was difficult enough to convince senior officials of the importance of Angola and Mozambique—Guinea-Bissau was out of the question.[62] Moreover, the Nixon administration was tilting visibly toward the white minority regimes. In a visit with General Kaúlza de Arriaga in Mozambique in December 1972, Clark MacGregor, who had been chairman of Nixon's reelection campaign, stated that "the ties that connect Portugal and the United States are strong, and they will become stronger in the future." MacGregor, who met with Nixon immediately upon his return, told the President that he was "happy to confirm all the fine things he had understood constituted Portuguese policy in Africa." MacGregor's comments contrasted sharply with INR's prognosis of two years earlier that "despite their superiority in numbers, equipment and logistics, few Portuguese expect a successful military conquest."[63]

By the end of the first Nixon administration, American ties with Portugal were stronger than at any time since the Eisenhower administration. As for the prospects for political change in southern Africa, the Administration accorded little chance. As Nixon said in his annual statement to Congress, "No one who understands the complex problems of Southern Africa believes that solutions will come soon or easily. Nor should there be any illusion that the United States can transform the situation, or indeed, that the United States should take upon itself that responsibility."[64]

A New Desperation in Lisbon

Washington's unquestioning support of the Caetano government and its preoccupation with other issues obscured the fact that the Portuguese prime minister was being torn by forces he could not control and opportunities he could not seize. The resolve of the military was erratic and diluted, and the Government was polarized between "Ultras," who believed in "Africa first," and those who advocated a negotiated solution to the wars in Africa.

Lisbon faced a major crisis in early 1972 when the United Nations announced that it was sending a fact-finding team from the UN Decolonization Committee to Senegal and the "liberated areas" of Guinea-Bissau in March. In its July report to the General Assembly, the mission concluded that "Portugal no longer exercises effective administrative control of Guinea [Bissau]," and found widespread support for the PAIGC. Underscoring the point of Portugal's lack of control, the PAIGC organized elections for a Popular National assembly in areas under its control. The UN General Assembly subsequently recognized the PAIGC as the sole representative of the people of Guinea-Bissau and Cape Verde, ninety-eight votes to six, with the US casting a negative vote.[65]

In the wake of the UN visit to Guinea Bissau, and in response to the pressure it generated, Caetano authorized General Spínola to respond to President Léopold Senghor's persistent efforts to arrange a negotiated solution to the war in Guinea-Bissau. In 1970, Senghor had made public a three-step plan for peace based on a cease-fire, negotiations for self-determination, and independence within the framework of a Luso-African community.[66] In mid-1972, therefore, at a small town called Cabo Skirring on the Senegal-Guinea border, Senghor put his plan before the monocled Portuguese general and further proposed that Spínola meet with Cabral to negotiate a cease-fire and terms under which the PAIGC could collaborate with the Portuguese in governing the territory.[67]

Spínola returned to Lisbon immediately following his meeting with Senghor to present what he thought was a genuine and viable proposal. Caetano, however, disagreed and told the popular General that a cease-fire followed by the negotiation of an accord for independence would only set a precedent for the other territories. Caetano asked Spínola whether it was not preferable to leave Guinea by "a military defeat with honor" rather than to negotiate an accord with "terrorists" that would lead to other unwanted negotiations. A stunned and offended Spínola asked the Prime Minister whether he was willing to accept a military defeat in Guinea.[68]

Spínola's support of Senghor's proposals provoked alarm in the Portuguese ruling hierarchy. Caetano convened a meeting of the highest officials in the Portuguese government to discuss the Spínola-Senghor contacts. In a further rebuff to Spínola, there was unanimous support for the argument put forward by the Chief of the General Staff of the Armed Forces, General Venancio Deslandes, who contended that the situation in Guinea was not so bad as to warrant further consideration of Senghor's proposals.[69]

Spínola did not hide his frustration with his superiors. He returned to his command in Bissau and began writing the book that would jolt the government from its romantic notions about its colonies. Stories of Spínola's rebuff began to spread, and the fear grew in military circles that the civilian government would accept military defeat in Africa over a political settlement and would use the army as a scapegoat, as it had following the loss of Goa in 1961.[70]

American officials, who in the early 1960s had longed for a serious proposal for decolonization that the Portuguese would even consider, were unaware of this initiative and the turmoil it provoked within the ruling hierarchy. Indeed, Assistant Secretary of State for African Affairs David Newsom had no clear mandate from the White House when he met with Prime Minister Caetano, Foreign Minister Patrício, and Minister of the Overseas Territories Silva Cunha for two days in Lisbon on 19 and 20 March 1973. The assistant secretary did not think that his talks "or any precise steps we might take," could pressure Portugal into changing its policies in its colonies. His very limited objective during that visit was to convince the Portuguese of the American view that without some move toward self-determination in the colonies, "Portugal and its friends run the increasing risk to their interests in a polarized Africa."[71]

The Portuguese, in return, complained to Newsom with a new sense of desperation that the Nixon administration had not sold them the arms they needed to pursue their objectives in Africa. They characterized the arms embargo as being "one-sided" as the US sold arms to some African nations. Moreover they felt that Washington did not take into account the vigorous Portuguese defense against the expansion of communism in Africa. The Portuguese officials were also adamant in their stand against any discussion of negotiations with the liberation movements. As Caetano had said previously to Spínola and reiterated to Newsom, it would be "disrespectful" to the Portuguese nation to negotiate with "terrorists." Moreover, the officials in Lisbon did not see the liberation movement leaders as valid representatives and, in any case, thought they posed no long-term military threat.[72]

Despite Lisbon's brave stance toward Washington, the Portuguese government was increasingly on the defensive not only militarily in the colonies but also in the international political arena. In June 1971, Amílcar Cabral, Agostinho Neto, and Marcelino dos Santos of FRELIMO inflicted a stunning public relations defeat on Lisbon when they were photographed in the presence of Pope Paul IV during a conference in Rome. At NATO ministerial meetings, Holland, Norway, and Denmark attacked Portugal with increasing frequency for its use of NATO weapons in Africa. West Germany, previously a strong Portuguese ally, announced that it would no longer sell NATO weapons to Portugal. Equally devastating was the 105 to 5 vote in the UN

General Assembly in October 1972 to recognize the PAIGC as the sole legitimate representative of the Guinean people.[73]

Lisbon's difficulties came to a head in July 1973 when Prime Minister Caetano led a delegation to London to celebrate the six hundredth anniversary of the Anglo-Portuguese Treaty, the oldest continuous pact between any two nations. The Caetano regime was counting on a strong display of support from its most important ally. To Caetano's bitter frustration, however, allegations of a horrendous massacre committed by Portuguese troops in northern Mozambique began to circulate in the British press as he and his delegation were preparing to leave for London. The press alleged that the Portuguese military had killed more than six hundred unarmed Africans in a town called Wiryiamu.

Instead of the heroes' welcome for which the Portuguese had been looking, Caetano's delegation repeatedly encountered throngs of angry protestors. What was to have been a moment of triumph for Portugal became an embarrassing and painful experience. The failure of the trip was underscored by a narrowly defeated resolution in the House of Commons condemning Caetano's visit.[74]

While Caetano was being humiliated overseas, he was being undermined at home. In an effort to expand the depleted officer's corps of the armed forces, Defense Minister Sá Viana Rebelo, announced a new law, decree law 353/73, which would increase the pay and status of those conscripted officers who reenlisted or joined the permanent corps. It created an explosive situation, however, between those professional officers who had climbed the ranks from the military academies and those short-term conscripted officers who were suddenly being extended equal status. A month later, following a torrent of protest from the permanent corps, or Quadro Permanente, the government tried to rectify the situation by ensuring that officers above the rank of captain had their seniority protected. The damage to the pride of Portugal's tradition-bound officer corps was not assuaged by the move.[75]

On 18 August 1973, a group of captains, all of them "Spínola's boys," met at the Military Club in Bissau to discuss the ramifications of the new laws. Within a week they produced a letter signed by 136 captains in the Portuguese military and sent it to senior government officials including Prime Minister Caetano and President Tomas. The letter expressed "profound grief" and a sense of lost prestige and pride on the part of the officers who now shared similar privileges with those who had sacrificed much less and spent much less time in the army.

Within a month, officers in Portugal, Angola, and Mozambique sent identical letters with nearly four hundred signatures to Caetano and Tomas.[76] On 12 October, in an effort to quell the growing crisis, the new Defense Minister, Silva Cunha, who was formerly the Overseas Minister, suspended the laws and established a commission to study and resolve the problem.

The damage had been done, however. On Sunday, 9 September 1973, a group of 136 officers, calling themselves the Movimento das Forças Armadas (the Armed Forces Movement, or MFA), met in Evora, Portugal to discuss their grievances. Although they shared a tremendous dissatisfaction with the government, it would not be until the MFA's meeting on 10 December in the ancient walled town of Óbidos, that a coup d'etat was suggested as the answer to the officers' problems. The proposal, however, was defeated in favor of a plan that called for continued protest in the confines of the law.[77]

Although initially reluctant to directly challenge the central government, the MFA had solid grounds for its grievances. In 1972, the seventy-eight-year-old President, Americo Tomas, was "reelected" for another seven-year term. The uncharismatic and extremely conservative Tomas was a strident Salazarist and protector of the old order. That things were not going to change in Africa were apparent from the constitutional review of 1973. Caetano introduced legislation that allowed for a somewhat larger degree of political decentralization in the colonies. Mindful, however, of the ultra-rightists in the regime whom he had to placate, the reforms also reaffirmed the "pluricontinental and pluriracial character of the Portuguese state."[78]

The frustration of Portugal's increasingly politicized electorate spilled over in April 1973 at the Aveiro Congress for opposition parties. Their disenchantment with the government was stimulated by the delegates' general awareness that Portugal was lumped together with Rhodesia and South Africa as international outcasts. The Congress established a united broad-left political front to contest the National Assembly elections on 28 October. After using the electoral campaign to mobilize opinion against the government, the opposition pulled out of the elections so as to avoid legitimizing the polls as had happened in 1969. Portugal was no longer sleeping.

Focusing the Attention of Washington

Even though the political opposition in Portugal was increasingly assertive, the Portuguese government's most immediate crisis was on the battlefield in Guinea. Following the rebuff of Spínola and the Portuguese-sponsored assassination of PAIGC leader, Amílcar Cabral, on 20 January 1973, the Caetano regime felt that it had strengthened its hand militarily in the territory. On 23 March 1973, however, the PAIGC stunned Lisbon when it brought down two German-made Fiat G91 aircraft with Soviet-made SAM-7 ground-to-air missiles. The introduction of the SAM-7s, which the PAIGC had received at the end of 1972, instantaneously transformed the military situation in Guinea because it denied the Portuguese their previously unchallenged air superiority.

Within a year, the PAIGC would claim to have shot down thirty-six aircraft. Portuguese pilots became reluctant to fly on missions. The morale of the military, already riddled with defeatism, resentment, and conspiracy, sunk even lower after the introduction of the missiles.[79]

By the fall of 1973, the frustration of the Lisbon government was palpable. The PAIGC consolidated its military breakthrough and scored a diplomatic victory at the UN by gaining the official recognition of more than eighty-eight nations. Even though the United States opposed the PAIGC's declaration of independence, it was not enough for Lisbon. Angered by the lack of support and frustrated at not being able to arrange a meeting with the new secretary of state, Henry Kissinger, Foreign Minister Ruí Patrício announced at a press conference at the UN on 6 October that the Portuguese government hoped the United States would renounce utilization of the Azores when the treaty expired in February 1974. In Lisbon's view, it would rather have fewer ties with the US than weak commitments.[80]

Patrício's outburst, which had Caetano's full support, went virtually unnoticed in Washington. However, several days later, with the outbreak of war between Israel and Egypt, Lisbon and Washington found themselves enveloped in an intense diplomatic exchange.

When the US began to resupply Israel one week into the war, all NATO members and Spain—which collectively received about eighty percent of their oil from the Middle East—refused to allow American aircraft to refuel on their territory. On Friday, 12 October, Kissinger approached the Portuguese for permission to use the base at Lajes.

Prime Minister Caetano's response was negative; he felt rejected by Washington and did not want to imperil the country's energy supply. Nevertheless, in the cavernous office of the secretary general of the foreign ministry, Portugal's top officials worked feverishly to utilize the request to their advantage. They drafted a reply that reminded the State Department of the costs Portugal would incur for allowing the United States to use Lajes. Not only would it undermine Portugal's ties with the Arab states and perhaps lead to terrorist attacks on Portuguese targets, but it would probably result in a denial of oil from Middle Eastern states. Furthermore there was anti-Portuguese legislation pending in Congress, the Tunney-Young amendment, which Lisbon regarded as extremely hostile. Also, in Lisbon's view, the recently negotiated Azores accord had been a "deception." Obviously, to permit the United States to utilize the Azores would jeopardize Portugal's most vital security concerns. Nevertheless, Lisbon inquired, would Washington be prepared to assist Portugal if these negative developments occurred? More specifically, would Washington be willing to supply Portugal with the armaments it needed to regain the offensive in Guinea in return for access to Lajes?[81]

When briefed on the Portuguese response, Kissinger was furious at their efforts to extract commitments from Washington. He cabled Richard Post, the acting chief of mission in the American embassy in Lisbon, early in the morning on 13 October and told him to communicate the following points to Portugal's Foreign Minister: Portugal would greatly strengthen its position in Congress and undermine its enemies sponsoring the hostile legislation by supporting the US in this difficult hour; peace in the Middle East was in Portugal's vital interests; the secretary's inability to meet Patrício was the result of a lack of time and should not be regarded as a slight against Portugal; and "should it develop that Portuguese concerns [about the military crisis in Guinea-Bissau] have a basis in fact, we should be prepared to consider together with the Portuguese government what might be done to restore the situation." Kissinger then instructed Post to remind the Foreign Minister of the urgency of this request and that the US wanted to begin resupplying Israel immediately.[82]

Several hours later, Rui Patrício responded in a way that evoked Franco Nogueira's draining obstinacy of a decade before. He cabled Portugal's ambassador in the US, Joao Hall Themido, and instructed him to remind the Secretary of State of several points "of major importance." This included Portugal's traditional position of neutrality in Arab-Israeli conflicts, Portugal's historic ties with the Arab world and its geographical proximity to the Middle East, and the extraordinary risks that Portugal would incur if it granted Washington permission to use Lajes. Patrício also instructed Themido to remind Kissinger of several events over the previous two years, particularly the maintenance of the arms embargo, Washington's "unscrupulous" renegotiation of the Azores accord, and the anti-Portuguese legislation in Congress.[83]

Finally, Themido was to tell the Americans that the use of the Azores would be dependent on a "satisfactory response" to several conditions: (1) a specific commitment from Washington as to how it would respond if hostile actions were taken against Portugal, (2) the degree to which the administration would guarantee that the anti-Portuguese legislation would not be approved; and (3) a position "more frank and positive" in the UN Security Council on the question of Guinea-Bissau's admission to the UN. Portugal's key demand, however, which it needed "with the utmost urgency," was the capability to neutralize the PAIGC's military superiority. Therefore, Portugal wanted American-made RedEye antiaircraft missiles to be delivered immediately to the Azores for transfer to Guinea-Bissau.[84]

Kissinger was unmoved by Portugal's pressure tactics. He responded to Caetano with a presidential letter that amounted to a virtual ultimatum. The letter, which was received by the Prime Minister at noon on Saturday, refused the request for military supplies and "threatened to leave Portugal to its fate in a hostile world." Several hours later, Lisbon capitulated and granted the United States unconditional use of the Azores.[85]

Despite Kissinger's formal toughness, Caetano's decision was eased by a meeting between Ambassador Themido and several Kissinger aides, including Assistant Secretary for European Affairs Wells Stabler and Helmut Sonnefeldt, that took place at the State Department during the frantic exchanges. Privately, the Americans promised Themido that if permission were granted to use the Azores to resupply Israel, the United States would allow Portugal to purchase from the US, once the Middle East crisis was resolved, the planes and missiles it needed.[86]

Following the resolution of the October War between Israel and Egypt, senior American officials began to search for ways to compensate Portugal. Portugal had attracted Kissinger's attention and gratitude as a loyal ally. As he wrote in his memoir, "I owed the Portuguese government a show of support for its assistance during the airlift."[87]

This show of support initially resulted in a photo session between Themido and Nixon and Kissinger that was scheduled for fifteen minutes but lasted nearly an hour.[88] The Portuguese were undoubtedly more pleased when, on 13 December 1973, Secretary of State Kissinger visited

Lisbon, en route from the Middle East to Geneva, to express his personal appreciation. In a private meeting after a sumptuous dinner, Foreign Minister Patrício once again explained to Kissinger how their air superiority in Guinea had been neutralized because of the SAM-7s that the PAIGC had acquired from the Soviet Union. Patrício told Kissinger of the devastating psychological effect that the missiles had had on the Portuguese pilots who were unable to defend themselves, and asked if it were "fair" for communist countries to supply their allies while Portugal's allies did nothing. In gratitude, and mindful that the Azores accord would expire once again in two months, Kissinger repeated earlier American promises to help Portugal get the armaments it needed.

Several weeks later, a West German firm approached the Portuguese with an offer to sell the Portuguese the antiaircraft missiles that they so desperately wanted. Delivery was set for several months later, in late April 1974. On his return to Washington, Kissinger instructed the State Department to develop options for loosening further the arms embargo on Portugal further than had been done at the beginning of the Nixon administration. In Congress, Senator Hubert Humphrey, chairman of the Africa subcommittee, rewrote the Tunney-Young Amendment weakening it significantly by requiring the administration simply to report to Congress on its dealings with Portugal.[89]

Kissinger's pledge to help Portugal obtain the weapons it needed defied the arms embargo that had been in place since 1961 and extended the more favorable conditions already adopted by Nixon in 1970. There was no discussion and no debate within the Nixon administration on this action. Indeed, Nixon was less involved with foreign policy because of his problems with Watergate, and Kissinger's authority was at its zenith as he was still officially national security adviser in addition to being secretary of state. As one White House official put it at the time, "Given the pros we have in the top jobs now, we can do with a nod what used to take three hours of discussion."[90] In this instance, American policy toward Portugal changed dramatically with little more than a nod.

The Coup in Portugal

Unfortunately for the United States, the American embassy in Lisbon was as unaware of the severity and complexity of Portugal's problems as was Kissinger. The days of C. Burke Elbrick and active involvement with the highest Portuguese officials belonged to an era in the seemingly distant past. The embassy had been without an ambassador for all of 1973 as Ambassador Ridgeway Knight completed his tour in Lisbon at the end of 1972. What may have been a bureaucratic oversight in Washington was interpreted in Lisbon as further evidence of Washington's low regard and lack of support for Portugal. Moreover, Knight had never been very comfortable in Lisbon and did not have close ties to the Portuguese leadership.[91]

To complicate the situation, Knight's successor was chosen by accident. Stuart Nash Scott, a sixty-eight-year-old New York lawyer who had been an associate of Thomas Dewey, was asked in the spring of 1973 by Secretary Rogers to become the State Department's legal adviser. Yet as Kissinger consolidated his hold over the Department in the summer of 1973, he decided to appoint his own legal adviser. Kissinger was nevertheless prevailed upon to give Scott, who had concluded his affairs in New York and was poised to move to Washington, another appointment of equal stature. As embassies in Stockholm and Lisbon were open, Kissinger decided to offer Stuart Nash Scott the position as ambassador in Portugal.

Scott's arrival in Lisbon on 10 January 1974 was difficult, to say the least. His first meetings with Rui Patrício were rather unpleasant for the new ambassador as they "consisted almost entirely of severe dressings down." The Foreign Minister was particularly irate that Secretary Kissinger "had made a number of promises" when he passed through Lisbon the previous month and not only had he not kept them but he had not communicated with Patrício in any way, directly or indirectly.[92]

On 22 February, almost one month after Scott presented his credentials to the Portuguese government, General António de Spínola sent shock waves through the country with the publication of his book, *Portugal and the Future*. When Prime Minister Caetano read the book two days before it went on sale, he finally accepted that Portugal's empire in Africa was in its dying moments. As he later wrote, "I did not stop until the last page, which I read in the small hours of the morning. And upon finishing the book, I had understood that the military coup, whose march I had foreseen several months before, was now inevitable."[93]

Spínola was legendary in Portugal for his bravery, camaraderie, and achievements as a military officer and colonial administrator. Spínola's father had been one of Salazar's most trusted advisers and Spínola himself had fought with General Franco's army during the Spanish civil war and with Hitler's on the Russian Front during the

Second World War. As a result, Spínola had impeccable credentials as a loyalist to the Portuguese government. At the same time, his skill as a courageous cavalry commander and his reputation as a benevolent colonial administrator won him high respect from soldiers in the field and the public in Portugal. His aura was accentuated by his monocle, riding whip, and brown gloves, and, on occasion, the government censor would intervene to cut down the General's appearances in the Portuguese press. In short, Spínola was "the ideal man to state the unstatable."[94]

The message in Spínola's book, an instant bestseller in Portugal, was hardly revolutionary; nevertheless it had an electrifying effect on the entire nation. The General wrote that the government should admit what everyone knew: the wars in Portuguese Africa could not be won through military means within an acceptable period of time. He called for a political solution and for Lisbon to hold a referendum in the colonies to determine their future relationship with Portugal. Spínola was convinced that when given the choice, the colonies would choose to remain connected to Portugal in a federation of autonomous states.[95]

The crisis that enveloped the Portuguese government following the publication of Spínola's book was total. The general's challenge to the stunned and indecisive Caetano was exacerbated by rumors on the right that General Kaúlza de Arriaga was planning to wage a coup against the regime. On 5 March, in an effort to regain control over the situation, Caetano delivered to Parliament an impassioned defense of Portugal's Africa policy. In an unprecedented move, he asked for and received an oath of loyalty from one hundred twenty generals and admirals. Ominously for Caetano, the Chief of Staff of the Armed Forces, General Costa Gomes, and his deputy, Spínola, refused to make the pledge. They were promptly dismissed from their positions and, along with a number of other officers thought to be disloyal to the government, were dispersed to remote areas of Portugal.[96]

On the same day that Caetano delivered his speech defending his policies in the overseas territories, a clandestine meeting of the Armed Forces Movement in Cascais, just outside Lisbon, approved what would become the basic document of the revolution. Populist in tone, it called for democracy and development in Portugal and decolonization in Africa. Beyond this, the results of the MFA meeting were not conclusive, but the majority of the officers present were firmly convinced that the old regime had to be overthrown.[97]

Following the publication of Spínola's book and Caetano's appearance before Parliament, Portugal's most senior government leaders constantly reassured themselves that they were pursuing the correct course in Africa and that they had the support of the military. Yet in a bizarre statement, Caetano announced on 15 March in a speech at São Bento, that the country could be "secure" without the support of the armed forces.[98] Whatever confidence Caetano had been able to muster was totally shattered the next day when the 5th Infantry Regiment based at Caldas da Rainha, about two hours north of Lisbon, mutinied and began to march on Lisbon. The spontaneous action was easily quelled by troops loyal to the regime. Although there was no apparent connection between the removal from command of Costa Gomes and Spínola, the uprising reinforced the mood of desperation in Lisbon. As one journalist noted at the time, "The Prime Minister's political resources are almost exhausted."[99] Caetano's resources expired completely in the early morning hours of 25 April 1974 when the Armed Forces Movement waged a successful coup and overthrew the Portuguese regime.

Misreading the Conspiracy

In 1961, the United States government had been on the inside of the unsuccessful conspiracy fomented against the Salazar government. On 25 April 1974, Washington was completely surprised by the coup, as was practically every other government in Western Europe. Ellwood Rabenold Jr., director of the office of Iberian Affairs at the State Department, acknowledged six weeks before the coup, in testimony before Congress, that the publication of Spínola 's book and the uprising at Caldas da Rainha did "indicate probably a degree of ferment" in Portugal. Rabenold went on, however, to reassure the House Subcommittee on African Affairs that "change in Portugal occurs very, very slowly and I don't think one can assume that anything, even [Spínola's] book, can bring about a drastic change rapidly."[100]

Rabenold's comments reflected Washington's "wait-and-see" attitude. As long as access to the Azores was assured and US interests were not being threatened in any other way, senior officials were not disposed to pay too much attention to tremors of revolution in Portugal. After all, rumors frequently ran rampant in Lisbon and the seemingly low level of unrest could continue for years. As Ambassador Stuart Nash Scott subsequently remarked with great understatement, "We really weren't as awake as we should have been to the discontent in the army."[101]

State Department officials in Washington were not the only ones in the dark. CIA officials would later testify that they were so dependent on the Portuguese security services for information that they had no opportunity to obtain independently and verify intelligence from other sources. The National Intelligence Officer (NIO) for Western Europe did attempt to undertake a comprehensive analysis of Portugal in the weeks prior to the coup. Even so, the report, entitled "Cracks in the Façade," did little to illuminate or explain the real causes of discontent in Portugal, not to mention the potential ramification of the discontent. As the Pike Committee concluded, "The intelligence community . . . was too preoccupied to closely examine the Portuguese situation." Those who had responsibility for writing current intelligence reports had deadlines to meet, meetings to attend, and little time or incentive to speculate on events in the previously sleepy Caetano dictatorship.[102] This mindset also precluded the intelligence community from reviewing their analyses of a decade before which, indeed, seriously considered the possibilities of a military coup.

William G. Hyland, who was then director of the Bureau of Intelligence and Research, said that Portugal's history of internal stability over fifty years "would almost certainly have tempered any intelligence warning, even if there had been more precise analysis." Keith Clark, a senior CIA analyst, said the "chief defect" in not predicting the coup was that no one provided "a full picture of the plans, program, ideological orientation and differing philosophies of the members" of the MFA. Hyland added that "the analysis was more at fault than the information. There was enough information to suggest trouble, but it wasn't subjected to a detailed analysis and a projection of where trends might be going."[103] After all, "as a friendly country," Portugal was not a target of major intelligence attention.

The six Defense attachés in the embassy, who were responsible for ties with the Portuguese military, were no more informed than anyone else. They had reported to the Defense Intelligence Agency on 26 October 1973 rumors of a coup plot and discontent among Portuguese military officers. The rumors were judged not to be serious. However, there was no evidence that the attachés understood the junior officers in the Portuguese military or had relationships of any significance with them. As Lt. Gen. Samuel Wilson, who was chief of staff to CIA Director William Colby, testified, "There are rules of propriety when you are dealing with an allied country." This meant that if an American attaché wanted to meet with a Portuguese military officer of the middle or lower level rank, it would have to be arranged through the Portuguese liaison office, and only those whom the Portuguese selected could meet with the American attachés.[104]

Nevertheless, in February 1974, the attachés forwarded information from December 1973 on the Portuguese government's response to a petition of complaints signed by over 1500 junior military officers. Once more, however, there was no effort to identify the leaders of the petition campaign or contact any of the signers. On two occasions before the coup, the Defense Intelligence headquarters at the Pentagon instructed the six officers in Lisbon to travel more around the country and to frequent the party circuit less. Yet many of these officers were at the ends of their careers and were not motivated for such activity. This reinforced the notion that for many American officials, Lisbon was little more than a highly sought after "retirement post" where careers could be concluded in the country's leisurely and pleasant ambience. In general, there was little incentive to know the political opposition in Portugal. Both Tapley Bennett and Ridgeway Knight did allow lower level embassy officials to have contact with opposition political figures, even though Knight was "nervous about it." The opposition figures with which they met, however, were the "acceptable" ones, such as social democrats, and not the "dissidents," such as communists or radical soldiers.[105]

Unfortunately for Stuart Nash Scott, he came to symbolize the American policy and intelligence failure surrounding the coup, at least to some. On 21 April 1974, Scott left Lisbon to preside at the annual meeting of the Harvard Law School Association, scheduled to be held on 25–26 April. Scott decided to use this opportunity to pay an official visit to the base at Lajes. On the morning of 25 April, Scott was awakened in his room at Lajes by a phone call from Richard Post, the deputy chief of mission in Lisbon, who told him of the successful coup. Scott was also informed that the Lisbon airport was closed indefinitely as was the border with Spain. Scott decided that there was "no point in sitting around the Azores" and proceeded to the United States to fulfill his obligations at Harvard. He arrived back in Lisbon a 9:00 A.M. on 29 April.

For Scott's brief diplomatic career, as well as for Richard Post, the decision to proceed to Cambridge, Massachusetts was disastrous. At 11:00 A.M. Lisbon time on 25 April, Post informed the State

Department that the city was "tense but calm" following the coup and gave the phone number in Cambridge where Scott could be reached. Kissinger and his advisers on the seventh floor of the State Department immediately began to question the embassy's professionalism. With the questioning, Scott's credibility and that of the embassy evaporated in Washington. When the State Department's press spokesman was asked at the noon briefing on 25 April whether the embassy had been in contact with the new government, he replied, "We're in the ancient position of trailing the wire service reports . . . you [journalists] are so much better than we at finding out what is going on at these posts."[106]

In an effort to limit public perceptions of an administration caught unaware by events in Portugal, State Department officials told the *New York Times* that the coup leaders were "well-known in Washington" and were "very pro-Western." It was acknowledged that the overthrow of the Portuguese Government would probably have "an important impact on Africa," but it would not lead to any changes in Portugal's membership in NATO.[107]

The Revolution of Red Carnations

When Marcelo Caetano surrendered to General António de Spínola in the early morning of 25 April, Caetano told Spínola, "You must maintain control. I am frightened by the idea of power loose in the street." Fortunately for Caetano, he, along with several cabinet ministers, was sent into exile that night to Madeira and later to Brazil, and so he did not witness the national outpouring of emotion, euphoria, and upheaval that followed the end of forty-six years of smothering dictatorship.

At 7:50 P.M., the rebel broadcasting station, *Radio Clube Portuguese*, announced confirmation of the fall of the Caetano government and that Caetano had given unconditional surrender to General Spínola. At 1:20 in the morning of 26 April, General Spínola made his first public appearance on television with the Junta of National Salvation (JSN) and read the MFA program to the nation. On his return by train from exile on 28 April, Mário Soares appeared at the window of Lisbon's Apollonia Station waving victoriously to swarming crowds. The leader of the Portuguese Communist Party, Alvaro Cunhal, arrived by plane from Paris on 30 April. At the airport, he clambered atop an army tank and announced that his party "is ready to assume responsibility within the government . . . to create a democratic society [and] reinforce democracy in Portugal."

What would become sharp and bitter political differences between the two leaders were all but swallowed in an emotional embrace, with Soares proclaiming Cunhal a national hero.

The national jubilation that followed the coup led immediately to a loosening of the regime's social mores. Previously banned films appeared in Lisbon cinemas, songs that had been forbidden were heard on the radio, and people began protesting for the right to divorce, which previously had been opposed by the Church and the Portuguese government. Political debate permeated every aspect of life once the secret police was forced to surrender to the MFA. Portuguese soldiers more often than not had red carnations sprouting from the muzzles of their carbines.

General Spínola presented a reassuring image to the nation. Indeed, the embassy in Lisbon reported on 26 April that "the present regime seems likely to be more favorable to US interests than its predecessor." A day later the embassy strengthened its positive view of the new government by describing the Junta as "a group of basically conservative men who . . . [will] not stand for any nonsense . . . . Their emphasis is likely to be on caution and careful testing of the way" toward democracy. Implicit in this endorsement was the recommendation that Washington "respond affirmatively" to a likely request from the Portuguese government for recognition.[108]

The embassy's reporting, sympathetic to the new government, obscured a bitter political struggle for political power that accompanied the coup. The struggle initially focused on the decolonization process and foreshadowed the divisive political conflicts that would characterize the revolution in Portugal. On 26 April, the Lisbon journal *Republica* published one version of the MFA program with a clause that recognized the right of the people of the Ultramar to self-determination. On the same day, the government-run newspaper, *Diário do Governo*, published the same MFA document without the clause on the right to self-determination.[109]

The new president of the JSN, General António de Spínola, represented a faction of conservatives and centrists who advocated the return of the military to the barracks, the dismantling of the MFA, and the installation of a civilian-dominated regime committed to democratic government. The "Spínolistas" also shared the belief that Portugal's future relationship with its colonies should be a federation resembling the British or French post-colonial relationship.[110]

The popular and vainglorious general repeated this on 26 April when he read a message to the nation introducing the members of the JSN and said that their duty was to preserve the survival of the nation and the "pluricontinental fatherland." He maintained this position when he was sworn in as President of the Republic in the First Provisional Government on 15 May in the ornate Hall of Mirrors at Queluz on the outskirts of Lisbon. In his inaugural address, Spínola said that there could only be self-determination in the territories when there were functioning democratic institutions. Because these did not exist, he continued, immediate independence would be a denial of the spirit of the MFA. Spínola's strategy envisioned the cessation of hostilities, to which the liberation movements had agreed at the toppling of the Caetano dictatorship, as a period during which the Provisional Government would arrange for a referendum.[111]

Spínola and his supporters, primarily the centrist Popular Democratic Party which was formed immediately after the coup, were opposed by a coalition of junior officers from the MFA, the Portuguese Socialist Party (PSP), and the Portuguese Communist Party (PCP). They argued that outright recognition of the right to independence in the colonies was the only position the Portuguese Government could adopt. As Mário Soares, the new foreign minister and leader of the PSP said, "The new Portuguese government is for decolonization, and not for neocolonialism."[112]

The liberation movements in the colonies strengthened Soares' hand as they refused to consider a permanent cease-fire until Lisbon recognized the right of independence and self-determination in Africa. The Communists and the MFA also supported this position and thought they could utilize it to gain control of the Provisional Government.

The pressure on Spínola began to mount in the end of May when a Portuguese delegation, led by Mário Soares, failed to reach an agreement on the decolonization process with the PAIGC in London. Soares was constrained by the vagueness of his Government's position on the colonies and, as a result, could not simultaneously address the question of cease-fire and self-determination as the PAIGC insisted.[113] The Socialists made veiled threats to withdraw from the Provisional Government if negotiations with the liberation movements failed because of the confusion in Lisbon. Several weeks later, Soares met with the top FRELIMO leadership in Zambia to initiate negotiations about the future of Mozambique. These talks were no more successful than the ones with the PAIGC. Soares and FRELIMO jointly issued a communiqué that stated that a cease-fire depended on a "previous global accord," an unsubtle reference to a commitment to self-determination. To increase the pressure on Spínola, the communiqué included a clause that stipulated that there had to be progress between the Portuguese and the PAIGC before further conversation could take place between Portugal and FRELIMO.[114]

Spínola fought back by trying to assume more political power for himself and his prime minister, Adelino Palma Carlos, a highly respected Lisbon lawyer. Indeed, doing Spínola's bidding, Palma Carlos proposed immediately holding a presidential election to legitimize and secure Spínola's position. He also proposed to delay Constituent Assembly elections, which would elect representatives to draft a new constitution, from March 1975 to March 1976. When the Council of Ministers rejected these two measures, Palma Carlos resigned as prime minister along with four moderate ministers. This brought down the First Provisional Government after only fifty-six days, which forced Spínola to form a new government.

Spínola's political options narrowed following his clumsy reach for more power. His choice for the next prime minister was Lt. Col. Firmino Miguel, a moderate who had been the Minister for Defense in the First Provisional Government. Yet the increasingly powerful Armed Forces Movement wanted a prime minister who reflected their views. They chose Vasco dos Santos Goncalves and, at the last minute, prevailed on Spínola to appoint him. Goncalves, a committed Marxist and supporter of the Portuguese Communist Party, had been a leader in the MFA and one of the main proponents of the MFA program. The demotion of Palma Carlos, the accession to power of the Marxist Vasco Goncalvez and several other officers in the Second Provisional Government, assured a dominance of the left over the center in a Portuguese government that was inexperienced, uncertain, and very divided. The left's burgeoning preeminence was strengthened further by the creation of a special paramilitary force called COPCON (Continental Operations). COPCON was placed under the control of the quixotic and leftist Otelo Saraiva de Carvalho, the military governor of Lisbon, who had directed military operations during the coup. Increasingly isolated in his own government, Spínola announced on 27 July 1974 that independence in the colonies would be granted immediately.

"If you kick Portugal hard enough . . . "

While the Portuguese Government was trying to stabilize itself amidst the escalating power struggles, Washington was mired in the nightmare of Watergate. The American government was paralyzed and virtually all foreign policy initiatives were put on hold except for those that would bolster the presidency. In addition to the crisis in the Nixon administration, Kissinger was concerned about ominous trends in Europe. Not only had the 1973 "Year of Europe" failed to strengthen European-American relations, but Western European communist parties were becoming increasingly influential in several key countries. The practitioners of what came to be known as Eurocommunism were different from their communist predecessors in two vital respects: (1) they advocated participation in ruling coalitions and embraced the idea of the parliamentary road to socialism, and (2) they also sought to defuse East-West tensions in part by asserting independence from the Soviet Union.[115] In the view of the Washington foreign policy establishment, however, Eurocommunists were still communists.

To the American Secretary of State, Eurocommunism was little more than a smokescreen for the advance of Soviet influence in Western Europe and a grave threat to the Western Alliance. Moreover, the Eurocommunist movement seemed to be strengthening. In March 1973, the French Communist Party allied with François Mitterand's Socialist Party to unseat the Gaullist majority. Mitterand then narrowly lost the May 1974 presidential election as the candidate of the united left. In Italy, electoral gains in the spring of 1974 buoyed the communists, and, to Kissinger, the situation "was analogous to that of the Weimar Republic of the early 1930s which led to the collapse of democracy in Germany."[116] The Spanish Communist Party also seemed to be gaining strength as Franco's health declined.

When the Caetano dictatorship was overthrown, Washington cautiously welcomed the new Junta. Two weeks later, however, when the First Provisional Government was sworn into office, Kissinger's worst fears about communist influence in Western governments seemed to be coming true, and in Portugal of all places. Kissinger was most exorcised by the fact that Portugal's first democratic government in fifty years included Alvaro Cunhal, the head of the Portuguese Communist Party, as minister without portfolio, and Avelino Pacheco Goncalves, a ranking PCP official, as minister of labor. Kissinger believed that a communist-dominated government in Portugal would lead to "a southern Europe domino theory," which would begin in Portugal and lead to communist-controlled cabinets in Italy and France and a legalized communist party in Spain. The Soviet Union would, for the first-time in the post-World War II era, have allies in NATO. In Kissinger's view, this would result in the demise of the Atlantic

Alliance and the network of security arrangements between the US and its allies in Europe. Therefore, Kissinger concluded that if he were to "kick the Portuguese hard enough," it would get the communists out of the government. Only this type of action would send the correct signal to other Western European nations where communists were poised to use the electoral process to gain a share of political power.[117]

Spínola had advised Western embassies in Lisbon that he wanted to form a coalition government of national unity in which all principal political parties would be represented. Given the unstinting opposition of the Portuguese Communist Party to the Salazar-Caetano dictatorship and their long-standing collaboration with other political parties, especially the Socialists, there was a groundswell of sympathy in Portugal to include the Communists in the new government, to which Spínola yielded. Spínola also believed, naïvely, that including the PCP in the government would demonstrate how little support they had. As Spínola would later admit, not only had he never had experience with the Communists, but he wrongly concluded that the PCP would play by the "rules of the game."[118] Moreover, Spínola and his advisers gave no thought to how the US and other allies of Portugal would react to the inclusion of communists in the new government.

On 12 June 1974, General Spínola met in the Azores with a beleaguered Richard Nixon, who was returning from a grueling trip to the Middle East. Nixon became the first foreign head of state to visit Portuguese soil since the toppling of the Caetano regime. In a private two-hour meeting, which was attended only by an interpreter and the two heads of government, Nixon, in essence, expressed his support for the new Portuguese government. He told Spínola that an "independent, free, prosperous Portugal is vital to the interests of the United States." Nixon was also eager to renew the Azores agreement that had expired the previous February. Although Spínola agreed to begin the negotiations the following month, he could not assure the United States permission to use the base to refuel planes on their way to Israel. The Portuguese president told Nixon of his desire for continued close ties with the United States and NATO. The General also requested financial support from the United States, which would help stabilize Portugal's economy. Nixon told Spínola that he was unable to commit any funds to Portugal but reaffirmed his belief that Portugal had to remain independent and a full member of NATO. Nixon also expressed support for Spínola's plan to hold a referendum in the colonies as a way to move forward on an orderly and controlled process of decolonization.[119]

While Nixon was telling Spínola he wanted Portugal to remain a member of NATO, Kissinger was in fact beginning to isolate Portugal within the NATO alliance. Portugal was cut off from highly classified military and nuclear information to which it had previously had access. Kissinger strongly opposed the idea of members of the Portuguese government discussing sensitive NATO information with their communist counterparts who would then pass it along to their allies and financial benefactors in Eastern Europe and the Soviet Union. As a result, the Portuguese did not take their seat on the NATO Nuclear Planning Group in June 1974, to which they had been previously entitled.

Kissinger's distrust of the Portuguese Government was accentuated by his intense dislike for Portugal's Foreign Minister and leader of the Portuguese Socialist Party, the voluble Mário Soares. The two met for the first time at a NATO Ministerial Meeting in Ottawa in June 1974. To Kissinger, Soares was untried and untested. Soares's grandiose and hyperbolic style of expression seemed to confirm his reputation as a "drawing room liberal." Kissinger did not believe that Mário Soares had the ability "to play hardball" with the highly organized and hard-bitten communists in Portugal.[120]

Kissinger's pessimism over Portugal, which was "somewhere between very strong and adamant," was reinforced by reporting from the CIA station in Lisbon that suggested that the Communists were poised to make unprecedented gains in the Portuguese government. This helped to confirm the already low estimation that Kissinger had of competence of the embassy's political section. The Secretary became particularly incensed when Ambassador Scott met with Alvaro Cunhal, after the communist leader was sworn in as minister without portfolio. Scott was fascinated by Cunhal and in his cable to Washington reporting on the meeting characterized the Communist as "affable, intelligent, and most impressive." As well, Scott's deputy, Richard Post, believed that "the MFA was a group that the US could work with."[121]

Such sentiments were viewed in Washington as "unfortunate and inappropriate," because Kissinger would not tolerate US officials working with communists, in Portugal or anywhere else. The embassy's credibility vanished altogether when Vasco Gonçalves was appointed prime minister. Not only did this take the embassy by surprise, but the

American diplomats in Lisbon had no knowledge of Gonçalves and could not assess the significance of his appointment.[122]

On 18 July 1974, Kissinger summoned Ambassador Scott to Washington. Before leaving, Scott paid a visit to Spínola, Gonçalves, and Soares to see what messages they wanted to communicate to the Secretary. When the elderly ambassador finally met with Kissinger on 24 July, he started by giving the Secretary a "pretty upbeat" analysis of events in Portugal. Scott had been convinced by Spínola that the danger of a communist takeover was "nonsense." Scott told Kissinger that Gonçalves, whom the ambassador considered "a dedicated social reformer . . . [and in] no part . . . a communist," had repeated the MFA's call for strict fidelity to all international obligations, including NATO. Scott predicted a favorable outcome of events in Portugal and said that the United States should watch the actual performance of the new administration before concluding that there was a strong leftward drift.[123]

Kissinger was unconvinced by Scott's analysis. He responded with a lengthy statement about the problem of communist influence throughout Southern Europe. He reminded Scott that the problem was a very serious one in Spain, France, Italy, and Greece (where the military dictatorship had just collapsed), and that it was Portugal that had taken the unprecedented step of inviting communists into the government. Even in Italy, where the communists were the strongest party, this had not occurred.

Kissinger then instructed Scott to return to Portugal. He was to tell Spínola that the United States Government was greatly concerned over communist influence in Portugal and that it strongly objected to the presence of Portuguese Communist Party members in the Council of Ministers. Kissinger also told Scott to inform the Portuguese that future relations between the two countries would be determined by the way in which Lisbon dealt with this problem. Somewhat incredulous, Scott asked Kissinger if this meant that he was being directed to tell Spínola that he had to fire Alvaro Cunhal. Kissinger replied that it was "unacceptable" to the United States that there are communists in the government of Portugal. At this point, the meeting ended and Scott returned to Lisbon. Scott had no further direct contact with Kissinger.[124]

Chapter 4

Kissinger, Carlucci, and Portugal's Revolution

The Embassy's Credibility Problem

Upon returning to Lisbon, Stuart Nash Scott met with Spínola to deliver Kissinger's message that the presence of communists in the government of Portugal was "unacceptable" to the United States. Spínola tried to deflect Scott's concerns by telling the ambassador that the press had greatly exaggerated the strength of the Communists. In fact, Spínola predicted, the Communists would be so weakened by the time of the elections in March 1975 that they would not be included in the ensuing government. Scott relayed this message to Washington and again returned to the United States for six weeks of home-leave, until the beginning of September.

Scott's confidence in Spínola's predictions did little to allay Kissinger's fear that the crisis in Portugal would precipitate a "southern-Europe domino" action and lead to the collapse of NATO. From the Secretary's perspective, the defense of the Western alliance was not on the agenda of the Portuguese Communist Party or any other European communist party. The issue, as Kissinger saw it, was not the degree of independence of Euro-communists from Moscow, but the parties' internal organization and the communist ideology.[1]

The Secretary's concerns of dominance by the PCP were strengthened by numerous press reports that portrayed a virtual state of anarchy in Portugal with the Communists poised to take over. In fact the Portuguese Communist Party and its close ally, the Portuguese Democratic Movement (MDP), dominated hundreds of municipal councils throughout Portugal by mid-1974. PCP loyalists also gained key positions in the newly legalized labor federation, the *Intersindical*, as well as in the state-run radio and television network. Influenced by the Portuguese Communists, the ever more powerful MFA Assembly, a body of 240 noncommissioned officers and enlisted men of the three military services, was increasingly more vocal and radical in its demands.

Nevertheless, Scott urged Washington to pay closer attention to the actual performance of the new regime and not its rhetoric. The Ambassador was particularly encouraged by Spínola's efforts to align himself with the centrist and conservative political parties that had formed in the wake of the revolution. This included the Progressive Party (PPP), the Liberal Party, the Social Democratic Center (CDS), and the Popular Democratic Party (PPD). Scott also supported Spínola's desire to promote a rapid modernization of Portugal's economy and to raise the country's standard of living to a level closer to the European norm. Although the Communists shared this objective they vigorously opposed the allies on whom Spínola was depending, especially the individuals associated with the network of banks, industries, and financial institutions that had backed Salazar and Caetano.[2]

In Kissinger's view, both Scott and Spínola grossly underestimated the power and influence of the Communists and leftist military officers. Kissinger believed that Scott did not understand the threat that events in Portugal presented to Western security. Skepticism over the embassy's ability to represent the United States effectively continued to grow on the seventh floor of the State Department.

The embassy's credibility problem became worse as General Spínola again attempted to increase his control of government. Toward the middle of the September posters began to appear anonymously throughout Lisbon announcing a large rally in support of Spínola and the "silent majority." Coup rumors, which were daily occurrences in the aftermath of the revolution, began to run rampant. The strongest rumor alleged that the demonstration was being organized by Spínola loyalists and it would lead to a rightist coup that would remove the leftists, including Prime Minister Vasco Gonçalves, from power. There was intense speculation over whether Spínola was behind the rally, which was to be held on Saturday, 28 September, unaware of it, or simply, giving it his tacit support. The tension in Lisbon spilled over on the evening of 26 September when President Spínola and Prime Minister Vasco Gonçalves became embroiled in an arm-waving argument in the presidential box at Campo Pequeno, Lisbon's bull fighting stadium, over the wisdom of Spínola's rally. Outside Campo Pequeno, mounted units of the Republican Guard were jousting with left-wing demonstrators who had gathered to show their opposition to the rally.[3]

On the following afternoon, 27 September left-wing activists began manning barricades to prevent the expected 500,000 Spínola supporters from entering Lisbon. The prospect of armed civilians of the left and right facing each other in the streets of Lisbon grew with each hour. Throughout the night the entire Portuguese high command met at Belem Palace in an effort to defuse the crisis. Ultimately, Spínola was outmaneuvered and at mid-day on 28 September, he was forced to call off the rally of the "silent majority." On the evening of the twenty-ninth, the legendary Spínola, who had approached his presidency as a "military mission," announced his resignation as president of Portugal.[4] Once again, the embassy had failed to anticipate this event and Washington was forced to rely on press accounts as much, if not more, than reports from the embassy.

With Spínola's resignation, the fragile centrist coalition of military officers and civilians collapsed. General Costa Gomes was appointed by the MFA to succeed Spínola as president and, along with Vasco Gonçalves as prime minister, formed the left-leaning Third Provisional Government. The new government was characterized by a tense collaboration among the Popular Democrats (PPD), Socialists (PS), the Communists (PCP), and the revolutionary-minded military officers of the MFA. The influence of the left had become more pronounced than at any time since the beginning of the revolution, and Kissinger's worst fears seemed to be materializing.

Kissinger's Kerensky

Washington reacted promptly to Spínola's demise and the installation of the Third Provisional Government. Stuart Nash Scott was instructed to meet immediately with President Costa Gomes and to advise him "in the strongest terms" of Washington's increased concern over the leftward drift of the Portuguese government. During his meeting with Scott, Costa Gomes denied that there had been a "drift" of any kind. He said that the problems were over personalities and not over policies or political principles. The MFA was still committed to honoring its treaty obligations, including NATO, and to holding democratic elections. Costa Gomes emphatically told Scott that the influence of the Communist Party was being vastly exaggerated by the

American and foreign press. He did acknowledge that the Communists were strong in the industrial unions and in the Alentejo District, which consisted of large plantations employing lowly paid workers. In the north, which was populated by small family-owned farms, however, the people were implacably hostile to communism. The new president of Portugal, like his predecessor, predicted that the Communists would not get more than fifteen percent of the vote in the March 1975 election.[5]

In his report of this meeting to the State Department, Scott mentioned that he had asked to meet with Prime Minister Vasco Gonçalves to congratulate him on his reappointment. Washington sent Scott a "peevish" response that expressed incomprehension over his desire to meet with Gonçalves. In Kissinger's view, the only reason Gonçalves did not join the PCP was to avoid paying the dues. The ambassador was ordered not to make any more appointments with high Portuguese officials without advance clearance from Washington. As Scott later reflected, "This was undoubtedly the handwriting on the wall," indicating that his days in Lisbon were numbered.

Scott's demise had been foreshadowed by the appearance at the embassy, on twenty-four hours notice, by Vernon Walters, the Deputy Director of the CIA, on 9 August 1974. Dispatched to make a "personal appraisal" of events in Portugal during Scott's absence from Portugal, the veteran military and intelligence officer and diplomat met with numerous officials including Spínola, Gonçalves, and Soares. The tone of the report that Walters filed on his return to Washington was "pessimistic." He was especially concerned over the apparent radicalization of the MFA and its influence over Portuguese politics. A similar message was being communicated to Kissinger by retired Admiral George W. Anderson, who was chairman of the President's Foreign Intelligence Advisory Board (PFIAB). The former ambassador to Portugal was spending part of the summer of 1974 at his house on the Algarve. While in Portugal, he met with many of his old associates, mainly industrialists and wealthy Portuguese, who had grave reservations about Portugal's future. George Woods, a former president of the World Bank with business interests in Portugal, also conveyed to Kissinger opinions similar to Anderson's. Scott and his embassy were increasingly isolated within the Washington policy community engaged in formulating policy to Portugal.[6]

Following Spínola's resignation, a second investigative team was sent to Portugal, this time from the State Department. The delegation was headed by Alan Lukens, the new director of the Office of Iberian Affairs, and included Robert Ryan, a State Department monetary expert, and Michael Samuels, a government authority on Portugal's African colonies. The mission had several objectives. For one, it was a way of "gently equivocating" on an invitation to the president of Portugal to visit the United States. Spínola had been invited to Washington during September for a working visit. Yet, when he was replaced by Costa Gomes, whom few in Washington knew, the State Department did its best to discourage the trip. Second, some policymakers in the State Department were beginning to feel that Kissinger's "very negative gut reaction" to events in Portugal was unjustified. Nevertheless, it was difficult for them to present effective evidence for their policy recommendations because of the embassy's lack of credibility in Washington.[7]

The Lukens team agreed with the general consensus that the embassy needed a "new look." They were critical of the competence of the embassy staff as well as the access that embassy officials had to the numerous political groups and figures in Portugal. The image that Scott presented, with his hip ailment and cane, did little to reassure Washington that the ambassador could manage the rapidly shifting events in Portugal. Moreover, Washington lost faith in the deputy chief of mission, Richard Post, at the outset of the revolution when he advised Scott to proceed to the United States instead of returning to Portugal. As well, Post was supportive of decolonization in Africa, which Kissinger considered to be a communist theme and destabilizing to the status quo. Post's influence was further impaired by the fact he was considered to be an "Africanist," which to Kissinger was tantamount to being a dreamer and idealist. The Lukens team, in effect, corroborated Kissinger's impression that his top two diplomats in Lisbon were more like "flower children" than they were effective, communist-fighting diplomats.[8]

At the same time, the Lukens mission vindicated in part Scott and his embassy. In contrast to Admiral Anderson and George Woods, they shared Scott's perception that a Communist victory in Portugal was not a foregone conclusion. They reasoned that with effective political and material assistance from the United States and Western Europe, Portugal could emerge in a democratic, noncommunist direction. According to the Lukens delegation, there were politicians and military officers who could provide a stable base for the evolution of democracy and who would effectively oppose the Communist's revolutionary platform. This view was implicitly endorsed by the First National City Bank, which on 16 September announced a five-year, $150 million standby credit for Portugal.

Lukens' report also helped to persuade a reluctant State Department to agree to a Washington visit by Costa Gomes during his trip to the United Nations for the opening of the General Assembly. On 18 October, Costa Gomes met with President Gerald Ford for forty minutes at the White House with Kissinger in attendance. The General assured Ford that a pluralistic system would be maintained in Portugal and that elections for the Constituent Assembly would be held as scheduled the following spring. The new President of Portugal also told Ford that Spínola's resignation did not signify in any way Portugal's withdrawal from the West. In fact, Gomes added, Portugal's fragile economic and political situation could be helped significantly by American aid. In response, Gerald Ford affirmed his support for democracy in Portugal but made no commitment on aid.

The following day, 19 October, Kissinger hosted a lunch at the State Department for Costa Gomes and Foreign Minister Mário Soares. Grimly, Kissinger spoke: "I could talk about the weather and so on, but I must be frank . . . . You are allowing excessive Communist Party influence in the government. The labor minister, who is a Communist, remains in the new cabinet . . . . And, for example, you have just named a Communist named Cabral to be head of ANI [the government's national news agency]. I must be frank with you: you may be sorry about this."[9]

Turning to Mário Soares, the Portuguese Foreign Minister, for whom he had so much contempt, he said, "You are a Kerensky . . . . I believe your sincerity, but you are naïve."

Soares responded, "I certainly don't want to be a Kerensky."

"Neither did Kerensky," Kissinger replied.[10]

Like Ford, Kissinger remained ambivalent about economic assistance, although he agreed to send a delegation from the Agency for International Development (AID) to assess Portugal's most urgent needs. He stated emphatically that sending the experts did not signal commitment to an aid program. Moreover, he added, he would not support any aid to Portugal until he was satisfied with the political direction in which the country was heading.

Before sending material support to Lisbon, Kissinger fired Stuart Nash Scott as ambassador to Portugal. On 16 November 1974, four weeks after Kissinger's meeting with Costa Gomes and Soares,

Frank C. Carlucci III, the 45-year-old Undersecretary of Health, Education and Welfare and former foreign service officer, was appointed to be the new ambassador to Portugal. Carlucci was a skilled and forceful diplomat who had served in Zaire and on Zanzibar during the early 1960s when both experienced political upheaval and turmoil. For his service in Zaire, Carlucci earned the Department of State's Superior Service Award for his "resourcefulness and effectiveness" as a political reporting officer and for "his outstanding courage in the face of real danger." When asked how he managed to stay informed in a difficult place like Zaire, Carlucci told a reporter that "keeping informed is merely a process of getting to know the Congolese personally . . . . You've got to get out and shake their hands and talk to them."[11]

After his service in Africa, he was posted to Brazil where he developed a fluency in Portuguese. Throughout his career, Carlucci cultivated a broad range of influential political ties in Washington that made him "a rarity" among foreign service officers in the State Department. These contacts, plus his "youth and athletic energy, [that] have been assets in posts where courage and physical agility, have sometimes counted as much as statesmanship," and would be vital to his success as the American ambassador to Portugal.

Also picked by Kissinger on the recommendation of Vernon Walters were two individuals with whom Carlucci had served in Brazil. Herbert S. Okun was selected to be the embassy's political counselor and deputy chief of mission. Okun, whose daughter was Walters' godchild, was a specialist on Soviet and Communist affairs and also fluent in Portuguese. Robert Schuler was chosen to be the embassy's defense attaché. Kissinger and Walters also selected David Whipple, who had previously served with distinction in Phnom Penh and was regarded as a top Agency operative, as CIA Station Chief. As this team had the personal approval of Kissinger and Walters and the confidence of Kissinger's closest advisers, including William Hyland and Helmut Sonnenfeldt, the leadership in the embassy was assured, at least initially, a measure of influence that Ambassador Scott had never known. As Tad Szulc wrote, the Carlucci team "was a remarkable combination of talent, the best the State Department could have possibly marshaled for the Lisbon embassy."[12] Ironically, however, their influence almost became as negligible as Scott's.

The change in personnel at the embassy was announced as a groundswell of support in Congress mounted for extending aid to the fledgling regime in Lisbon. A leader of this groundswell was Senator Edward M. Kennedy, who had visited Portugal in the fall of 1974. When he returned to Congress, Kennedy, who was regarded as a leading Democratic contender for the presidency, introduced an amendment to the Foreign Aid Bill that included fifty million dollars in loans to Portugal and another five million in technical assistance to be divided between Portugal and her former African territories.[13]

As a result of Lukens' guardedly optimistic report, the appointment of the Carlucci team, and pressure from Congress, Kissinger's pessimism over Portugal began to thaw. On 13 December, the State Department announced that it was launching an economic aid program for the new government of Portugal as a "positive demonstration of United States support and confidence in Portugal's future." The State Department and the Portuguese Government also issued a joint statement that said that the program was intended as "an earnest indication of United States Government support in its effort to construct a free and democratic society."[14] The aid package consisted of a guarantee of twenty million dollars in private American loans for construction of new housing. The State Department also pledged to support Portugal in international bodies, such as the World Bank, and announced its support for Senator Kennedy's amendment to the Foreign Aid Bill.

Kissinger's turn-around was not intended to be a vindication of Stuart Nash Scott, even though Scott could legitimately claim it as such. The Secretary of State remained skeptical about the ability of Portugal's moderates to withstand Communist pressures. In December 1974, Kissinger met in Washington with the leaders of the Portuguese Popular Democrats, Sá Caneiro and Francisco Pinto Balsemão. The meeting was arranged by the Office of Iberian Affairs in the State Department in an effort to introduce Kissinger to moderate political leaders capable of directing Portugal back to the democratic center. In the short desultory meeting, however, Sá Caneiro and Francisco Pinto Balsemão criticized the Socialists for being weak against the Communists and Portugal's Western allies for not providing sufficient support. This did not help those in Washington who were struggling against Kissinger's fatalistic views about Portugal's future.[15] Nevertheless, Kissinger was compelled to support the aid to Portugal, which was intended to help Carlucci and Okun get off to a good start in Lisbon as much as it was a "down payment on the good behavior of the MFA." Kissinger would later write that he initially believed that the aid should only be extended after the radicals had been "squeezed out" of government so the moderates would get the credit. Nevertheless he supported the assistance as long as it was seen as a "Kissinger decision," to underscore his personal engagement in the issue. For Carlucci, who was experienced in the technical aspects of housing, it was an opportunity to demonstrate a genuine interest in the people of Portugal and to counteract any impression that he was an "evil genius" being sent by Washington to meddle in Portugal's domestic affairs.[16]

Carlucci Takes Over

Carlucci arrived in Lisbon on 18 January 1975 believing that Portugal could be brought back from the edge of anarchy. His assessment was based on more than his experience and considerable self-confidence. Portugal's location in Europe made it difficult for the Soviet Union to intervene as it had in Hungary and Czechoslovakia. Moreover, Portugal had few commercial or political ties with the Eastern bloc. Despite the Communist Party's estimated membership of sixty thousand, its leaders had spent many years in jail and exile. In Carlucci's view, they were isolated from popular Portuguese sentiment as well as the "modernized" Western European communist parties. The essentially conservative and religious nature of the Portuguese people, especially the small landholders in the north, was another significant obstacle to the potential gains of the PCP. Carlucci did not think the people of Portugal were prepared to exchange their loyalties to the Catholic Church and the village priest for an opportunity to join the Communist Party. In fact, Carlucci perceived signs of an emergent, viable noncommunist leadership even though it was not consolidated. Portugal's membership in NATO was also extremely important to the new American ambassador. Not only did this reinforce Portugal's diminished role as a member of NATO but it provided an opportunity to reestablish a sense of professionalism and pride in the fragmented military.[17]

Nevertheless, in a meeting at 4:30 P.M. on 7 January 1975, Carlucci met with the secretary of state to learn his "candid views" on how to deal with the government in Lisbon before departing for Portugal.[18] Kissinger was unambiguous. He wanted Carlucci to get the Communists out of the Portuguese government and keep them out.

Events initially played to Carlucci's advantage as he and his team assumed their posts at the cramped embassy on the Duque do Loule in the center of Lisbon. What had begun as an adolescent romance between between the Socialists and the Communists in April 1974 had developed into a bitter divorce by January 1975. The "crystallizing factor" was the PCP effort to make the *Intersindical*, an umbrella organization for the three hundred and twenty six legalized unions, the only legal labor union. The Communists controlled more than half the unions in the *Intersindical* and they claimed that more than one union would split the working class, making the defense of its rights more difficult. The Socialist Party and the PPD viewed this as part of the PCP's strategy to establish a communist-dominated state. They opposed it vigorously and argued for the right to establish "parallel" unions. Soares and his allies demanded a pluralist union framework that would prevent Portuguese trade unionism from being turned into a conveyor-belt for Communist Party directives.

Even though the MFA eventually backed the Communists on the trade union issue, the breadth of popular opposition to this initiative caused many officers in the MFA to reconsider their support of the PCP for the first time since the beginning of the revolution. It also provided the Socialists with their first real experience organizing the working class, with plotting strategy and "acting like a disciplined political cadre instead of a Lisbon conversation group."[19]

The PCP persisted in its efforts to capitalize on the weaknesses and disorganization of the noncommunist political groups while consolidating its relationship with the MFA. The Portuguese Communist Party was offering the MFA a strong political organization and loyal support among parts of the urban and rural working classes. In return, the PCP received a valuable measure of legitimacy through its cordial ties with a number of sympathetic MFA leaders, including Prime Minister Vasco Gonçalves, the chief of the army, Carlos Fabião, and Otelo de Carvalho, the head of *Comando Operacional do Continente* (the National Operational Command or COPCON). The crisis that this bourgeoning alliance represented to Kissinger was underlined by reports that the Soviet Union had asked Lisbon's permission to use the militarily strategic Portuguese port facilities for the Soviets' Atlantic fishing fleet.[20]

The Embassy and the State Department initially judged the significance of these events through a shared lens. In his first meeting with President Costa Gomes, Carlucci reaffirmed the US interest in going ahead with Exercise Locked Gate, a NATO maneuver at the mouth of the Tagus River and in view of Lisbon, that had been planned for 31 January to 7 February. For Washington, the exercise was a "litmus test" to determine Portugal's resolve to remain part of the Western alliance. Carlucci agreed with Kissinger that if Lisbon proved to be an unreliable member of NATO, Portugal ought to be informed by all NATO members that it no longer belonged to the alliance. Whereas Carlucci tried to communicate this to the Portuguese "as a fact and not a threat," Washington's strategy was to make Portugal feel like "outcasts within NATO, without casting them out."[21] In an effort to strengthen the message, a NATO warship was anchored at the mouth of the Tagus for most of 1975.

One of the embassy's first moves to counter the communist influence in the Portuguese government was to establish its own credibility with the seventh floor of the State Department. The embassy therefore worked quickly to establish contacts and relationships with a broad group of Portuguese, as Carlucci and Okun were operating under the premise that there was no central authority in Portugal even though there was a government in name. Embassy officials paid particular attention to the MFA, which they regarded as a microcosm of Portuguese society, and provided vital information about events, attitudes of key personalities, and insights into larger trends within the country. Contacts with the MFA enabled the embassy to alert Washington to developments before they appeared in the *New York Times*, even if it was by a matter of hours. Within a short time, the embassy had generated the impression in Washington of being "wired in," articulate, and very knowledgeable about the turmoil in Portugal. It was not that Carlucci's message was so different from Scott's, it was that the style of reporting was perceived to be highly professional. During the first six weeks of 1975, the embassy's cables were detailed, cautious, and tinged with optimism. Nevertheless, they had no influence on Kissinger's decision to isolate Portugal within Europe and NATO.[22]

In the wake of the *Intersindical* crisis, the new ambassador perceived signs that the PCP was being abandoned by its former allies. For one, Carlucci cabled Washington, the MFA was publicly distancing itself from its association with the PCP. At the same time, the Socialists, who at the end of 1974 had been in "near total disarray," had negotiated considerable changes in the draft labor law with the support of some in the MFA who otherwise would have sided with the PCP. Carlucci noted that these changes allowed the Socialists to work freely within the union despite communist control of its administration. In addition, the MFA offset public perceptions of a PS-PPD defeat on the union issue by announcing their intentions to hold elections by 25 April, the revolution's first anniversary. As Scott had reported several months before, Carlucci informed Washington on 22 January of Portuguese perceptions that the communists "will clearly lose [the] elections."[23]

The State Department remained unresponsive to the embassy's interpretation of the emergent political divisions. A week later Washington cabled that it had "reliable" reports that leftists and the PCP were planning actions to consolidate their power. Carlucci replied that such "phraseology" overstated the embassy's evidence. He also disagreed with Washington's perception that the MFA was hinting that it would cancel the elections. In a slightly less grim interpretation of the MFA's pronouncements, the ambassador allowed that the military leaders were "setting [the] stage for manipulating or modifying [the] outcome if [the] desired result does not occur."[24] He did not specify, however, what this "desired result" might be. Indeed, on 5 February, Costa Gomes announced that Constituent Assembly elections would be held by 25 April at the latest. As Carlucci pointed out to Washington, the government of Portugal evidently saw such announcements as having a "calming and reassuring effect" even though no precise date was fixed.[25]

In early March, after about seven weeks in Lisbon, Carlucci filed a "pre-election assessment" with Washington that was both thorough and decidedly upbeat. Based on the embassy's conversations with an array of moderate civilian and military leaders, Carlucci had "reasonable confidence" that the Communist grip on Portugal was weakening. In the ambassador's view, the noncommunist political parties had developed into "an independent political force" that was able to hold its own in negotiations with the military over the degree to which the MFA role would become "institutionalized" in Portuguese politics.[26] The Socialist Party and the PPD had shown political strength and acumen by negotiating a Press Law with the Communists that outlawed an ad hoc censorship commission.[27] Another important sign was the MFA's economic program that, despite its considerable socialist rhetoric, contained an immediate role for the private sector. Carlucci also suggested to Washington that the Junta's assumption of additional authority was a positive development. Although some saw this as an unfortunate increase in the military's power, he argued that it preempted Communist demands for more extensive powers to be granted to the younger and more radical MFA Coordinating Committee. As importantly, the government had made an effort to introduce "a small element of balance" into the state radio and television and remained publicly supportive of NATO. Carlucci also noted that there was "a steady momentum" toward elections despite efforts by the PCP and its allies to delay or postpone them. He praised President Costa Gomes as "a conciliator who is absolutely sure of his ground before he moves" and declared that even the Socialist Party was "in good shape now."[28]

The embassy ascribed importance to these "stirrings" because they provided a sense of direction, hope, and equilibrium "to the formerly disjointed and inchoate moderate forces." Moreover, they were perceived as a response to "a communist offensive of massive proportions" that had already made "deep if not decisive inroads" into the trade union movement and the media. Adding a note of immediate caution, however, Carlucci said that the nascent equilibrium could be upset by two immediate dangers: an attempted coup from the right and an escalating campaign of violence from the fragmented groups on the left. In fact, in the ambassador's view, "disruptive tactics by the extreme left are . . . the biggest short-run danger in Portugal."[29]

The fragile equilibrium emerged in an intensely fluid and chaotic environment. The country was buffeted by increasingly militant strikes, flowery and excessive political rhetoric, and an immense social uncertainty about what the future of the "revolution" would bring. Political violence and sabotage were daily occurrences and anti-American rhetoric was an integral part of the revolutionary culture. The frequency with which rumors spread about imminent coup attempts and physical attacks on candidates was "phenomenal."[30] As the center of political power was so diffuse, one could never be absolutely sure about what was real and not real. As one American journalist wrote, Portugal had become a place where Socialists were called Fascists, Marxists were called moderates, Marxist-Leninist became a code word for Maoist, Maoist became a code word for anything noisy and disruptive, where conservatives labeled the entire left Communists, and where Communists labeled the rest of the left conservative.[31] Against this backdrop, Carlucci came to regard his mission more broadly than had initially been defined. As he cabled Washington, "The pressures and forces that have been unleashed must be tempered and guided; they cannot be stuffed back into the tube."[32]

"The Communist Drive for Power"

Despite the embassy's guardedly optimistic reporting between January and early March 1975, Kissinger did not perceive any change in Portugal's drift toward a neutral, communist-dominated regime. In fact, he was unable to identify any factions or individuals in the Portuguese political scene who could keep Lisbon a viable member of NATO.

As far as Mário Soares was concerned, the Secretary of State's negative first impression of the socialist leader had only intensified in the months after their first encounter at the NATO ministerial meeting in Ottawa. To Kissinger, Soares was verbose, hyperbolic, and humorless.[33] More importantly, Kissinger did not believe that Soares had the ability or the will to stand up to the Communists; he had been forthright when he called Soares a "Kerensky."

Kissinger also distrusted those in the MFA whom the embassy was coming to regard as supporters of a democratic and pro-Western Portugal, especially Melo Antunes and Vitor Alves. To the Secretary of State, they were "crypto-communists" and highly suspect. Although they may have talked about democracy to Carlucci and Okun, they, along with Soares, were also advocating "a vigorous non-alignment away from big-power blocs."[34] Their objective was to emphasize Portugal's ties with the Third World, especially Africa. This was combined with an "Arab offensive" that was designed to overcome the difficulties created for Portugal when the United States used the Azores for refueling during the Arab-Israeli war in 1973. Responding to the Portuguese effort to diversify their relations, several Arab countries offered to invest $400 million in Portugal if Lisbon did not renew the Azores agreement with the US.[35] Kissinger was also concerned that in Lisbon's haste to decolonize, the Soviet Union would gain naval and air access to the Cape Verde islands. From Washington's perspective, such access would provide the USSR with an invaluable opening toward the south Atlantic.[36]

In the context of the Portuguese revolution, individuals such as Antunes and Alves, "who were once believed to be far leftist," were now considered moderates supportive of democracy in Portugal. Melo Antunes, in particular, had been one of the leading intellectual forces of the revolution, a member of the Coordinating Committee of the MFA, and the second choice to Vasco Gonçalvez to replace Palma Carlos as prime minister. In the second provisional government,

Antunes, as minister without portfolio, was one of the principal negotiators with the liberation movements over the process of decolonization. On 20 February 1975, the MFA unveiled its "Economic and Social Program," which had been authored by Antunes. It called for land reform, state intervention in key industries, foreign investment, and nationalization to fifty-one percent of all oil and gas wells and mines. Although the State Department may have seen it as an anticapitalist document, the Program represented a defeat for the PCP, which had advocated a complete takeover of the banks and insurance companies that were controlled by large family-owned conglomerates. Thus individuals such as Antunes and Alves, who called for nonalignment and a form of economic socialism, also helped to isolate the Communists from the noncommunists in the military and the civilian population. For the American embassy, they were allies in the fight to restore democracy; to Washington they were key elements in Portugal's "revolutionary vanguard" which threatened to undermine NATO's unity. This difference in perception was accentuated when Carlucci and Okun began to tell the State Department that with time and proper support, the Socialists and the noncommunist leaders will defeat the Communist Party and stabilize Portugal, a message very similar to the humbled former ambassador, Stuart Nash Scott. Kissinger could not dismiss Carlucci as he had Scott and, as a result, the message ignited a conflict with the embassy in Lisbon over the control and direction of American policy toward the Portuguese revolution.

Carlucci's effort to guide American policy through the Portuguese revolution was dealt a decisive setback at about noon on 11 March 1975. Scheduled to have lunch that day with Admiral Rosa Coutinho, head of the Angolan Transitional Government, Carlucci was forced to cancel when the embassy received a report that shooting had broken out between military units at the base of the MFA's most loyal and leftist unit, the Lisbon Light Artillery (RAL-1), near the Lisbon airport.[37] By 3:30 P.M., the embassy informed Washington that "as of now it appears that whatever was attempted via attack at the airport fizzled." Ten minutes later, there was a radio broadcast of a communiqué from President Costa Gomes that condemned the "adventure" against the revolution. Gomes said that the situation was calm, appealed for "civic maturity," and alerted the population to be on guard against activities that might lead to "fratricidal struggle."[38] This "adventure" turned out to be a failed coup attempt that had been staged by General António de

Spínola, who had become embittered and frustrated while watching events from the sidelines.

Twelve hours before the abortive coup, the embassy had sent a cable to Washington that said that Spínola was "still probably the most popular military figure" in Portugal, although it "bemoaned Spínola's conspicuous lack of political skill."[39] By the end of the afternoon, his failed effort and dramatic exit from Lisbon via helicopter, along with eighteen other officers, his wife, and cat, to a military base in Spain near Badajoz, removed from the Portuguese political scene what Carlucci referred to as the "principal, responsible rallying point [for] moderate forces." The embassy reported that Spínola's efforts had been "unbelievably ill-conceived, poorly led and disorganized . . . whatever the composition, origins, and motivations of [the] abortive coup attempt, [the] result can only be to strengthen [the] hand of [the] leftists. The pity is that it came just as the moderates were beginning to show some political strength. [The] main question . . . appears to be how much further leftward [the Government of Portugal] will swing . . ."[40] In a note of frustration, Carlucci added, "It is difficult to understand how Spínola allowed himself to get involved" in this operation.[41]

Two days later, Carlucci sent to Washington a more in-depth assessment of the implications of the abortive coup attempt. He recognized that it would "dismember" the extreme right, especially those parties with even the vaguest association with Spínola, and seriously weaken the moderate center while strengthening the radicals in the MFA. "My judgment is that the MFA radicals will score massive, but hopefully not decisive, gains." The ambassador also noted that the civilian political parties, with the possible exception of the Communists, had been wounded, "perhaps fatally." These events significantly raised the likelihood that Portugal would move toward an entrenched military rule based on populist policies with heavy procommunist overtones. International support is likely to be sought in the Third World and NATO ties, "at minimum," de-emphasized.[42]

Despite the bleakness of his analysis, Carlucci did not abandon his guarded optimism. There was a chance, he thought, that Costa Gomes' position would be strengthened as the Portuguese president would no longer have to compete with Spínola for the leadership of the centrist forces in the military. Although the American ambassador acknowledged that Costa Gomes was "no charger," he did point out that he was "a sure-footed, respected leader who will counsel moderation." The same could not have been said for Spínola.[43]

In straightforward terms, Carlucci recommended that US policy focus "on doing all we can do to limit the inevitable leftward shift." He said it would be a difficult and gradual process because the embassy had lost "a certain amount of credibility" by repeatedly warning about the dangers of a communist-led coup when it fact it emanated from the right.[44] Further, it was widely believed in Portugal that the US had been involved with Spínola's failed effort. Carlucci realized, however, that there was "respect and residual good will" for the United States in many circles, that Portugal's population was still conservative even though its voice had been muted, and that the bulk of the military officers had not yet been radicalized. He asked the State Department to reaffirm publicly the continuation of the aid program that, for the embassy, had been "the most useful tool to date." As Carlucci said in signing off, "We will need all the levers we can put our hands on in the weeks and months ahead."[45] What the ambassador wanted, above all, was public and positive reinforcement from Washington.

It did not take long for Carlucci's bleak scenario, in contrast with his guarded optimism, to become reality. Within days after the abortive coup, it was announced that "fringe parties" of the left and right would be banned, that the cabinet of the Provisional Government would be reshuffled, and that a new Supreme Revolutionary Council would take control of the country and be responsible only to the General Assembly of the Armed Forces Movement. Although the Portuguese government had indeed become a full-fledged military regime, the question for the American diplomats in Lisbon was the degree to which it was dominated by Communist military officers and sympathizers.[46]

Significantly, Commander Jorge Jesuino, Minister for Social Communication, said in a press conference the day after the coup attempt that the Constituent Assembly elections scheduled for 12 April would still be held, even though they might be delayed a week or two. On March 14, Prime Minister Vasco Gonçalvez announced on television the nationalization of the banks and insurance companies. Two days later, Lisbon announced that the government was considering a request by Moscow for refueling facilities for merchant ships at the island of Madeira, 780 miles southwest of the Straits of Gibraltar. Also COPCON arrested more than one hundred supporters of the previous regime including members of the Champalimud and Espirito Santo Silva banking families. As Carlucci noted, "The moderates appear to be cowed and unwilling at least for the moment, to stick their necks out for moderation."[47]

The diplomats in the American embassy were stunned. Rumors were widespread in Lisbon that Carlucci had given Spínola the green light to stage the coup and that Carlucci was working for the CIA and had been ambassador to Chile before coming to Portugal. Carlucci's own security was jeopardized when Otelo de Carvalho, the head of the MFA's security force, COPCON, who fancied himself as the "Fidel Castro of Western Europe," stated publicly that the safety of the American ambassador could not be guaranteed. As on numerous other occasions, the embassy became the focal point for demonstrators protesting what was seen as American manipulation of Portugal's internal affairs.

In an effort to reassert American leverage in the rapidly shifting events, Carlucci presented a demarché to Costa Gomes on 25 March that stated that Portugal's turn to the left was hostile to the interests of NATO and the US. While playing tough with the Portuguese, the ambassador cabled Kissinger in Jerusalem and warned against becoming involved in trying to influence the configuration of the new cabinet. To Carlucci, this was "a hopeless case and [the] wrong one on which we . . . should expend the slight influence we have . . . . If our concern is [the] more fundamental issue of future relationships between Portugal, NATO and [the] West, I have more hopes of exercising influence." He emphasized the importance of understanding the "psychology" of the Portuguese government, "at this moment," especially in light of the fact that the embassy gave no warning of a rightist coup "when everyone, including [the] Western press, knew one . . . was brewing."[48] The Soviets, for one, "were blatantly playing on this emotion," and their ambassador, Arnold Kalinin, offered formal congratulations for the defeat of Spínola and his accomplices. Carlucci recommended that the US indicate to Costa Gomes, who "has been substantially to the left of his cabinet colleagues," that "we understand the delicacy of the situation" and will maintain American support for his efforts. "The only [other] option I can see to starting on the shaky road of rebuilding [the] moderates," Carlucci opined, "is a policy of ostracizing Portugal."[49]

The day after Carlucci's demarché to Costa Gomes, the fourth provisional government was installed. According to Western embassies in Lisbon, eleven of the twenty-one members of the new cabinet were, or were perceived to be, Communist Party members or pro-Communist, including Melo Antunes as foreign minister. In a Washington press conference four days later, the Secretary of State ignored Carlucci's advice for positive statements and said that the recent developments "will of course raise questions for the United States in relationship to its NATO policy toward Portugal."[50] Kissinger continued by saying, "What seems to be happening now in Portugal is that the Armed Forces Movement, which is substantially dominated by officers of leftist tendencies, has now appointed a new cabinet in which Communists and parties closely associated with the Communists have many of the chief portfolios . . . . We are disquieted by an evolution in which there is a danger that the democratic process may become a sham, and in which parties are getting into a dominant position whose interests we would not have thought were necessarily friendly to the US."[51]

Convinced that Portugal was "lost," Kissinger sent the embassy in Lisbon a series of "very pessimistic" cables asking for scenarios other than a moderate victory. Senior administration officials leaked to the press that the US was considering the imposition of a "quarantine" on Portugal within NATO. At a staff meeting in Washington, Kissinger complained that Carlucci had failed to live up to his reputation as a hard-hitting diplomat who would expel the Communists from government and reverse Portugal's growing affinity with the Eastern bloc. In a fit of pique, Kissinger shouted at his staff, "Whoever sold me Carlucci as a tough guy?"[52]

It was during this period that Kissinger, in consultation with CIA Deputy Director Vernon Walters, focused considerable attention on staging another, but successful, coup from the right. This option began to receive active attention following Spínola's resignation as president on 28 September 1974, which sent Portugal into a period in which "nobody (in Washington) knew what was going to happen." Alternately referred to as "the Chilean solution," or the imposition of a "Portuguese Pinochet," the strategy's primary obstacle was that there was no figure on the right who could "handle the task," especially after Spínola's demise.[53] At the same time, individuals in Congress, such as Jesse Helms, the CIA, and the Defense Intelligence Agency, were actively encouraging the anti-Communist secessionist movement in the Azores. It was thought that the Azores could become an independent nation or, perhaps, join the United States as the fifty-first state. It was also reported that the CIA had established "extensive contacts" with the Azorean Liberation Front that advocated independence and was prepared to push for secession "if Lisbon goes communist." Although Washington claimed strict noninvolvement, middle-level State

Department officials received representatives of the secessionist movement.[54]

Senator James Buckley added a public voice of alarm when he told a Washington press conference on 21 March 1975 that military actions against Portugal would be one option for NATO should the Communists take full power in Lisbon. "There is nothing else going on in the world—not in Southeast Asia, not even in the Middle East—half so important and so ominous as the Communist drive for power in Portugal." Defense Secretary James Schlesinger echoed the sentiment on the same day when asked about NATO's relations with Portugal he said, "It will have to take some symbolic form-making them outcasts without casting them out."[55]

"The Only Game in Town"

Carlucci's difficulties with Kissinger over the appropriate policy toward the revolutionary government in Lisbon grew in tandem with the political crisis in Portugal. Washington had become impatient with Carlucci's cautious analyses and asked the embassy for a different and more in-depth report about what it expected for Portugal's future. Irritated by Kissinger's threatening public comments and his grim view of Portuguese affairs, Carlucci sent a cable to the Secretary of State saying that there were only two scenarios on which to base American policy: to immediately cut all ties with Portugal or to work with the moderate forces in the belief that they will defeat the Communists. The following day, Carlucci received a request from the State Department to develop the isolation scenario.[56]

Frustrated by the turn of events, Carlucci made his first public speech in Lisbon—without requesting permission from Washington—in which he stressed that the US still had confidence in Portugal and would continue its economic assistance. In a veiled swipe at Kissinger, the Ambassador said that it was "very easy to find the gloomy side of the picture" but that there were also favorable aspects of the situation such as Lisbon's continued attachment to NATO. Carlucci also told the packed house at the American Club that he did not work for the CIA and that the embassy had not been involved with Spínola's abortive coup attempt.

The ambassador's nascent public relations campaign sputtered, however, when *A Capital*, a leading afternoon paper in Lisbon, appeared several hours after his speech with a front-page story accusing the CIA of fomenting the recent right-wing coup attempt and organizing a so-called Portuguese Liberation Army. The Lisbon daily, *Diário de Notícias*, alleged that Carlucci was a prominent figure in the "agitation, sabotage, and overthrow of governments" and noted that he had been expelled from Zanzibar in 1965 for "subversive activities." Unfortunately for the ambassador, the left-wing controlled press in Portugal gave him credit only for his fluent, if Brazilian-accented, Portuguese, and not his efforts to counter rumors that he worked for the CIA.[57]

In spite of these controversies, no event had more significance for Portugal's political future and the American embassy's efforts to help restore democracy than the Constituent Assembly elections that had originally been scheduled for 25 March, then 12 April, and finally 25 April, the first anniversary of the revolution. In Washington, there was skepticism about whether the elections would be held at all. After the Revolutionary Council obliged the political parties to sign a "pact" with the MFA in which military dominance in political affairs was assured for at least three years, there was additional skepticism about whether they would have any meaning if they did occur. However, as Carlucci subsequently remarked, "I think it was the elections that turned things around."[58]

In the weeks following the debacle of 11 March, the embassy concluded that the noncommunist political and military groups and factions had not been dealt a decisive or fatal blow. In fact, as the embassy noted, "Developments of recent months had stiffened spines universally." Significantly, for the first time since the revolution, Portuguese religious leaders came forward publicly in opposition to the violence and chaos which enveloped the country. "Far from wilting in [the] face of mounting leftist attacks," Carlucci reported, "[the] Portuguese church hierarchy has closed ranks and decided on appropriate tactics to follow in regards to [the] challenges it faces." The clerics had adopted the position that voting on 25 April was as much a Christian duty as it was a civic one.

The Church was relying on locally delivered messages from parish priests, particularly in the north, to encourage parishioners to vote for those political parties whose philosophies reflected Christian values, primarily the Popular Democrats and the Christian Democrats. Particularly forceful in his public criticism of the left was the Bishop of Oporto, Dom António Ferreira, who had been a dogged opponent of the Salazar-Caetano regime.

In the embassy's view, the Bishops had been "unyielding," especially in their determination to retain control of the Catholic radio station, *Radio Renasçenca.* As Carlucci concluded in a telegram to Washington, "Probably the single greatest threat to a psychological electoral victory by democratic forces is massive abstention by [the] members of [the] conservative, particularly rural, 'silent majority.' The Church's get-out-the-vote message represents an important effort to assure that abstentions do not distort [the] true degree of [the] Left's popular support." The importance of the Church's actions was implicitly endorsed by the PCP that said that it welcomed "without reserve" those Catholics who would accept the PCP's "political line and discipline." In an opportunistic but futile departure from its Stalinist orthodoxy, the PCP also claimed support for freedom of religion and defended strong relations between Church and State.[59]

As election day approached, the American embassy in Lisbon cautioned Washington against making confident predictions about the future or even about those general trends that might develop. "Fifty years of dictatorship and economic stagnation have not prepared Portugal for instant democracy or comprehension of what 'instant democracy' is all about. [The] current military leaders have been either unwilling or unable to focus on human rights questions in face of [the] more urgently perceived priority of tending to political and economic problems . . . . Their attention has been fixed on [the] electoral campaign and [the] battle to survive as viable forces."[60] Indeed, the most immediate concern of moderates was the fifteen registered parties on the ballot, the "electoral smorgasbord," and that the populace would overlook the "main dishes," the major parties, as a result.[61]

This battle constantly pitted faction against faction, not only in the political arena but especially in the military. On 25 March, Lt. Ramiro Correira, a member of the Revolutionary Council and a leader of the MFA's Cultural Dynamization Campaign, issued a statement saying that persons who are undecided about for which party they will vote, might consider casting a blank ballot. Correira's remarks were endorsed by the National Electoral Commission (NEC), which stated that "A blank vote should not be confused with absenteeism."[62] What they did not say was that a blank ballot would be invalid.

Even more ominously, Carlucci reported that "most MFA leaders who had spoken on the subject of elections had made clear that they would not be bound by the results nor swayed from their present course regardless of the outcome." At the same time, the ambassador emphasized, a good showing by moderate parties will inevitably reinforce the moderate elements in the MFA. Mário Soares put it more starkly in an interview with the Italian newspaper, *La Stampa,* when he said that the upcoming elections would force the MFA to choose between adopting a more "elastic position or transforming Portugal into a new Albania."[63]

As 25 April approached, the moderate political parties repeatedly expressed their concern to the embassy that the MFA might undertake some action that would postpone or cancel the elections. Embassy officials, however, believed in the "sincerity" of those MFA leaders who said they wanted voting procedures to be as perfect as possible. Heavy penalties for voting fraud had been instituted as had checks and balances in the counting process in an effort to ensure honesty. Films explaining the mechanics of voting were being shown daily and, in the embassy's view, the MFA was "doing a good job" in preparing for the election.

A potentially destabilizing event was the 22 April release of the report on the 11 March coup attempt. Although the report "obliquely" linked the United States to the operation, the embassy regarded it as "milder than expected." Most significantly, it alleviated fears that the PS or PPD might be forced out of the election or that the election would be cancelled altogether.

Three days before the election took place, the embassy sent a cable to Washington once again predicting a Communist defeat at the polls. Its assessments were tempered by several factors. This would be the first free election in Portugal in almost half a century and the first for most of those voting. Polling data was difficult to ascertain because there were few reliable polling organizations. Many of those polled were suspicious of the interviewers and refused to answer pollsters. Another difficulty was evaluating the impact of abstentions or blank ballots especially in light of the MFA Party "pact." There was also the prospect of violence at the voting booths.[64]

By 25 April, the elections had essentially become a triangular popularity contest between the parties of the center, the parties of the left, and the MFA. The undisputed winner, in an election in which more than ninety percent of eligible population voted, was Mário Soares' Socialist Party. As Carlucci cabled to the State Department, "[the] Socialist vote exceeded [the] party's fondest hopes" and it has "now emerged as Portugal's dominant, civilian political force." Although the Socialists tended to be the "rightist" alternative to the Communists in the south, and the "leftist" alternative to the PPD and CDS in the north, it was in the central regions of the country and the major urban centers where they attracted most votes (thirty-seven percent). The unquestioned loser was the Portuguese Communist Party that received only 12.5 percent whereas its ally, the MDP/CDE, received an even smaller 4.1 percent of the vote.[65]

For Carlucci and the American embassy, as for Portugal, the election results were the most important event since the overthrow of Caetano's government. Nevertheless, the embassy was guarded in its reporting to Washington about the overall impact of the elections on national political trends. In Carlucci's view, the polls represented "two cheers for democracy;" the "missing third cheer" represented the "unknown" MFA reaction to the outcome.

To a skeptical State Department, Carlucci's sober analysis and Okun's precise predictions of the elections results added influence to the embassy's policy recommendations[66]. Yet it was not enough. Since arriving in Lisbon, the two American diplomats had made a concerted effort to coordinate their initiatives in Portugal with other embassies of Western European governments. Sometimes it was purely symbolic, such as when Olaf Palme, Sweden's prime minister, François Mitterand, and Willy Brandt visited Lisbon to reaffirm their support for Soares and the Socialists. On one occasion, in February 1975, on the day before he was to depart for a visit to Portugal, James Callahagn, the British Foreign Secretary, met with the Portuguese ambassador to Great Britian, Albano Nogueira, and asked what he was supposed to say to those with whom he would meet. Nogueira responded, "Mr. Secretary, when you arrive in Portugal just say one word, 'democracy, democracy, democracy.' Everything else will fall into place."[67]

A key source of support for the Socialists was its close relationship with the West German government, the Social Democratic Party, and the Frederich Ebert Foundation (FES). This stemmed from 1972 when Mário Soares' Acção Socialista, which he had founded in Geneva in 1964, became part of the Socialist International. The following year, with the support of the FES and the German Social Democrats, it was renamed the Portuguese Socialist Party. Following the demise of the Portuguese dictatorship, the PSP found itself with "not enough militants in [Portugal's] towns and villages, no tested and firmly established organization, no effective information media, and almost no money."[68] Therefore, in the months after the revolution when West German trade union officials traveled to Portugal, "it was not uncommon that they carried a suitcase full of money as a gesture of solidarity." As former West German Prime Minister Willy Brandt wrote in his memoirs, "We strove to lend concrete political and moral support [to] combat the defeatism that was gaining a hold in influential circles in the West."[69]

Due in large part to Soares' contacts in Western European capitals, the Socialist Party went from an organization which had little money and structure on 25 April 1974 to one that outspent all of its rivals a year later. The PSP received about two to three million dollars the year following the revolution from West Germany, Sweden, Holland, and Great Britain. The PCP also received a similar amount from the Soviet Union.[70] Most political parties in Portugal used external support to buy printing presses, to pay party activists, and to maintain party headquarters.

In spite of the moderate's electoral victory, Washington was still not persuaded that the Socialists were the country's dominant civilian political force. Kissinger had encountered numerous foreign service officers who had become "enamored" with tangential details in the countries where they were stationed. More specifically, as the Secretary was informed in preparation for a briefing on Portugal that he was to give President Ford, "The election measured Portuguese public opinion, but the radical leftists are still firmly in control of the government. At best, the moderates have survived with the hope that they will be able to fight another day." Although this view of political trends differed strongly from Carlucci's, Assistant Secretary of State Arthur A. Hartman, who prepared Kissinger for his briefing of the president, did communicate the embassy's strategy for American policy to the Secretary. Hartman pointed out to Kissinger that "it is easier for us to have a negative rather than a positive impact upon the political climate in Portugal. Punitive actions such as isolating Portugal in NATO or cutting off our nascent aid program . . . would be used by the radicals to justify policies even more hostile to the US than those now in effect."[71]

Frustrated by the series of "silly," pessimistic cables that the embassy was receiving from the State Department, and bolstered by the success of the elections, Carlucci returned to Washington for a high-level policy review and a showdown with Kissinger. Over the course of several meetings at the State Department during the second week of May, which coincided with the *Mayaguez* crisis, the determined American ambassador bluntly told the Secretary of State that his public comments were driving Portugal into the hands of the Communists. Moreover, Carlucci added, the moderates may not be all that he would desire, but if the administration "writes the place off, that's the end of it." In short, Carlucci told Kissinger, Soares, the Socialists, and the other moderates in the military were "the only game in town." With time and the right type of support, they would emerge victorious.[72]

Carlucci had prepared carefully for his battle with Kissinger. For one, he and Okun had made numerous trips to Washington in an effort to keep senior officials informed about developments in the country. Second, Carlucci and Okun had the confidence of an influential coalition of political allies, particularly Vernon Walters and Kissinger's other closest advisers. Not only did Carlucci know Ford personally, but he and Donald Rumsfeld, Ford's chief of staff, had been close friends since both were on the wrestling team as undergraduates at Princeton University.

Valuable assistance also came from General Alexander Haig, commander of NATO forces, who accepted the Ambassador's invitation to visit Portugal in February 1975 and subsequently became a supporter of Carlucci's efforts. The embassy arranged through Haig for an obscure but impressive military officer, Ramalho Eanes, to leave Portugal for a short NATO training program. Eanes would later gain national prominence by foiling an attempted leftist military coup. In 1976, he became Portugal's first freely elected president. As Carlucci would later comment, Haig "was very helpful in dealing with Henry."[73]

Another ally was the democratic activist Allard Lowenstein who persuaded columnist William Buckley that events in Portugal were not as dire as his brother, Senator James Buckley, claimed. Senator Edward Brooke of Massachusetts publicly extolled Carlucci's views when, during a three-day trip to Portugal in early April, he said, "I don't think there is an irretrievable slide to the left in Portugal." Brooke added that he was deeply concerned that the US "might overreact" to events in that country.[74]

Pressure on Kissinger was also directed from Europe. Not only did Willy Brandt make his views on Portugal known to Kissinger, but Helmut Schmidt continued the lobbying after Brandt resigned as prime minister in May 1974. On several occasions, Georg Leber, Schmidt's minister of defense, discussed with his American counterpart, James Schlesinger, the importance of the United States supporting the moderates in Portugal.[75] The Portuguese, as well, helped their own cause. Prior to the elections, Carlucci arranged for two ministers of the Portugese government to visit Washington. Although Jorge Correira Jesuino, Minister of Information, and Jose da Costa Martins, the Labor

Minister, identified with the left in Portugal's military–civilian government, they enthusiastically spoke of the need for "pluralism" in Portuguese politics. When asked about NATO's exclusion of Portugal from secret nuclear strategy meetings, Jesuino commented, "For the time being we are just ignoring not being invited."[76] Such remarks softened the menacing and adversarial image that the Portuguese government had gained in Washington.

This network helped Carlucci persuade Kissinger that his course of action was correct and that the American embassy was capable of managing it. It also helped to counter the views of the CIA officers within the embassy that predicted the Communist influence would increase. Even though CIA Station Chief David Whipple supported Carlucci's broad strategy, he thought his ambassador should have been more engaged with Sá Caneiro and other more conservative groups. Although Carlucci encouraged all the moderate political groups to work together, it was apparent to him that the Socialists were the largest and most influential of the democratic political parties.

At the conclusion of the policy review, Carlucci won Kissinger's agreement that there would be no "end-runs" around the embassy, the United States would not encourage Azorean separatism, pursue the coup option, or "flirt" with Spínola and the discredited Portuguese right. Carlucci in effect was now in control of American policy toward Portugal. He had the authority to deal with Soares, the Melo Antunes group, and other factions, and assure them that, at minimum, the United States would not undermine or destabilize their efforts to establish democracy in Portugal. Carlucci could also say that the American government was prepared to assist materially in the struggle against the communists in Portugal. For the first time since the beginning of the revolution, there was an agreed-upon policy that the United States would work with the Lisbon government as long as the appearance of democracy remained in Portugal.[77]

The Trojan Horse in NATO

Even though Carlucci and other European leaders expressed their support for democracy in Portugal, the moderate forces were still faced with the specter of Western isolation and communist destabilization. West Germany, Belgium, Holland, Denmark, Italy, and Sweden voiced their concern to Lisbon about the leftward trend symbolized by the make-up of the Fourth Provisional Government. On 17 July 1975, the

French President, Valery Giscard d'Estaing, vetoed an EEC loan "for fear of subsidizing a Socialist–Communist alliance." A month earlier, the EEC Commission had asked for "spectacular" and "immediate" aid "to strengthen Portuguese democracy." Instead, the EEC Council of Heads of State and Government gave Portugal a virtual ultimatum. The Council said that "the EEC, because of its political and historical tradition, can grant support only to a pluralist democracy," which was a not-so-subtle reference to a government run by communists and MFA. To President Costa Gomes, the EEC's attitude was "hostile" political pressure. It would not be until 7 October, after the sixth provisional government had been in office for three weeks, that the EEC granted Portugal significant economic support.[78]

Despite Carlucci's apparent bureaucratic success, Washington continued to criticize the Portuguese government. On 24 May in a meeting with five West European newsmen on the eve of departing for Brussels to attend a meeting of leaders of the Atlantic alliance, President Ford said that he did not understand how there could be communists in an alliance that was formed to oppose communism. The following day, Henry Kissinger said that he was "not surprised" at what Ford had said and added, "I share the President's view on this matter." Kissinger said that Ford had not meant to imply that the Lisbon government was under communist control but was referring to "trends" in the country's political development. In an effort to further "clarify" Ford's remarks, the Secretary of State added that Ford "was not saying that the Portuguese Government is now Communist dominated. (In fact) we wish Portugal well. We hope Portugal will have a democratic revolution. We are not going to Brussels with the intention of producing a confrontation with Portugal."[79]

What occurred, however, was just short of a confrontation. On 29 May, a day after he arrived in Brussels, Ford met with Portuguese President Costa Gomes and Prime Minister Vasco Gonçalves and told him that Portugal was a "trojan horse" in NATO. In explaining this to reporters the next day, Ford said that he had "pointed out the contradiction that would arise if Communist elements came to dominate the political life of Portugal."[80] It came as no surprise when Costa Gomes said, at the conclusion of the meeting, that he had found Ford and Kissinger's view of his country "very distorted and very unjust." This distortion was accentuated by the fact that Gonçalves came across as an unreconstructed Lenninist to Ford and Kissinger.[81]

In anticipation of Washington's hostile attitude, and in an effort to influence it, the foreign ministers of the EEC announced a "Common Market rescue operation" for Portugal's nearly bankrupt economy prior to the opening of the NATO Heads of State meeting. The foreign ministers also proposed improving the EEC's free trade accord with Portugal that had been in effect since January 1973. Still, conditions were attached to the proposal. Irish Foreign Minister, Garret Fitzgerald, president of the EEC Council of Ministers, said he would go to Portugal and make it clear to the Portuguese military regime that help from the Common Market was dependent "on continued decent democratic respect for the rights of the political parties that contested and won the elections."[82]

In a subsequent effort to moderate the distrust between the Portuguese and American governments, West Germany's Foreign Minister, Hans-Dietrich Genscher, arranged for Kissinger and Melo Antunes to meet in Bonn on 20 May. At the end of the forty-minute session, a spokesman for the American secretary said that it had been "a good introductory session."[83]

Melo Antunes, however, found it to be otherwise. The Portuguese foreign minister told the secretary of state that it was essential for the United States to help Angola become an independent and nonaligned nation. To accomplish this, Antunes said that Washington should help the MPLA gain control over the country. This would neutralize the influence of the Soviet Union and reduce the need for the MPLA to rely on external assistance, such as from Cuba. The Portuguese foreign minister found Kissinger to be "cold," "unbelieving," and fatalistic in his conviction that Angola was already lost.[84]

In spite of the "chilly" face-to-face encounters, and in response to Carlucci's efforts and European pressures, the American government did increase its covert funding of non-Communist political groups after the NATO Heads of State meeting in May 1975. In the summer of 1974, the CIA maintained extensive contacts with right-of-center political parties, especially in northern Portugal where Communist Party headquarters were repeatedly burned and demolished by angry crowds. The CIA reportedly infiltrated conservative organizations in the north, working directly through the Roman Catholic Church. By mid-1975, after the military government banned the right-of-center political parties, the Ford administration "revived dormant but traditional connections" between the CIA and anticommunist West European Socialist parties and labor movements. The CIA channeled funds to these groups to keep the "non-communist parties intact, in the streets, and in the business of competing with the Communists for the support of military leaders and soldiers."[85]

Wrapping Up the Rebellion

Although he remained deeply pessimistic about the Communist influence in Portugal, Kissinger went out of his way not to allow the apparent leftward drift to impact on detente. Not until after the Helsinki Accords were signed at the European Security Council in August 1975, did the Secretary of State publicly caution the Soviet Union against interfering in Portugal. During a speech in Birmingham, Alabama, Kissinger warned, "The Soviet Union should not assume it has the option, either directly or indirectly, to influence events contrary to the right of the Portuguese people to determine their own future." Moreover, in a begrudging acknowledgement of his agreement with Carlucci, Kissinger added, "The Portuguese people should know that we and all the democratic countries of the West are deeply concerned about their future and stand ready to help a democratic Portugal."[86] This public warning came on the heels of President Ford's private comments to Leonid Brezhnev that the US would not be party to the Helsinki Accords if there were a Soviet-backed Communist seizure of power in Lisbon.

The Soviet Union pursued a similarly cautious strategy, despite external appearances. With the Portuguese-speaking Arnold Kallinin, who previously had been the Soviet Union's ambassador in Cuba, Moscow had an effective diplomatic presence in Portugal. Yet beside this and covert financial assistance to the Portuguese Communist Party, the Soviet Union offered the Portuguese government little else, especially none of the economic trade credits it so badly needed. Clearly, the Soviet Union was not prepared to assume the burden of supporting the poorest country in Europe. Moreover, given the likely response from Washington and other Western capitals, Moscow chose not to use the Portuguese Communist Party as a stepping stone to the dismemberment of NATO. Against this background, *Pravda* described the Constituent Assembly elections as an "important phase" in Portugal's "free, independent and democratic development."[87]

Kissinger's threats to the Soviet Union came at a point when, to the embassy in Lisbon, it appeared—despite the continuing social and political chaos—"that everything was going to turn out alright."

Another turning point occurred when the Socialist newspaper, *Republica*, was seized by its pro-Communist printers. A week later, the workers at *Radio Renasçenca* threw out their management and declared that the station had also been "liberated." In an effort to capitalize on the situation, the Communists began demanding that foreign newspapers be censored, telex wires and cables be monitored, and Western reporters be expelled from the country.[88]

In Western Europe and the United States, articles and editorials bemoaned the demise of Portugal's free press and the onset of Communism and anarchy. In fact, however, these two events helped to cement the unlikely alliance between Mário Soares and the Catholic Church. Not only did Vasco Gonçalves seem impotent to restore order, but crowds of fifty thousand and more began appearing at rallies held by the Catholics and Socialists. Soares traveled all over the country warning that a Communist dictatorship was at hand and claiming that the takeovers of *Renasçenca* and *Republica* had been a plot hatched by MFA radicals. On 11 July, in an effort to accentuate the government's inability to restore order, Soares, with the encouragement of Carlucci and Okun, resigned from cabinet and withdrew the Socialist Party from the provisional government. A few days later, the Popular Democratic Party also withdrew, effectively bringing down the fourth provisional government that had been formed in the wake of Spínola's failed coup attempt.[89]

The critical moment in Portugal's "hot summer" occurred on 7 August when a letter, which came to be known as the "Document of Nine," was sent to President Costa Gomes, and simultaneously was released to the press. The letter protested attempts to mold Portugal into "the Bulgaria of the West," and insisted that Portugal remain a full member of Western Europe. The document, sent by Melo Antunes, other moderate leaders of the MFA, and military commanders from other parts of the country, reflected the concerns of the majority of the country's military officers. Ironically, the COPCON commander, Otelo de Carvalho, who had recently returned from a week in Cuba, and Carlos Fabião, the country's most powerful general after Carvalho, implicitly supported this protest of Portugal's lack of direction.[90]

Three weeks after swearing in the fifth provisional government, which the Lisbon weekly *Expresso* correctly predicted would be the most provisional of provisional governments, President Costa Gomes fired the leftist Prime Minister Vasco Gonçalves. Gonçalves, who by this point had been abandoned by Portugal's Communists, was replaced as prime minister by Admiral Pinheiro de Azevedo, forming the sixth provisional government on 19 September. Azevedo had been a member of Spínola's original junta and although a leftist, he was more pragmatic than his predecessor and not allied to the Communist Party. Although Azevedo was a member of the Communist Party, the sixth provisional government was dominated by moderate MFA leaders, socialists, and members of the PPD.

In spite of the continuing political upheavals, the embassy concluded that, due to the lack of significant Soviet support and the consolidation of a strong political, military, and religious leadership, it would only be a matter of time before the Communist influence would be neutralized in Portugal.[91] Other governments apparently shared this perception. On 7 October, the EEC's European Investment Bank announced that it would loan the Portuguese government $287 million that had been held in abeyance because of the Communist threat. Several days later, following a visit by Melo Antunes to the White House, the Ford administration announced an $85 million emergency economic aid package. The US also pledged to increase its support of the refugee "air bridge" for the Portuguese fleeing the growing turmoil in Angola.

Throughout the fall strikes, political violence and exaggerated rhetoric continued to dominate the country. Coup rumors were still so prevalent that Herbert Okun began to monitor what he referred to as a "coup coup clock." In a 21 November 1975 briefing memorandum prepared for Kissinger, the acting assistant secretary for European affairs, James C. Lowenstein, contended that "Portugal had become ungovernable" and the moderates were dealing from a position "more of frustration than strength." Moreover, in an effort to provoke President Costa Gomes into "some kind of action," especially as it concerned military indiscipline, the Cabinet on 20 November suspended all ministerial activities. Although "risky," Lowenstein concluded that the suspension of governmental activities was "a step in the right direction," even though, as he noted, "the Communist challenge to the moderates is growing stronger while the government's position is weakening."[92]

Lowenstein's gloomy analysis proved correct when at 11:33 A.M. on 25 November, Carlucci flashed the State Department with the news that a group of mutinous paratroopers had occupied the Monte Real Air Base in northern Portugal, the Montijo Air Base across the river from Lisbon, the Air Force Regional Headquarters in Lisbon, and the Air

Force Communications Command Center in Lisbon. The embassy told Washington the action was probably an "isolated move," but that it "could easily spark further uprisings." Four hours later, the embassy concluded that even if its aims were limited originally, the mutiny "is now playing a commanding role in the Portuguese political crisis."[93]

At 4:30 P.M. the Armed Force General Staff declared a "state of emergency," curtailing freedom of expression and assembly, and said that the mutinous paratroopers "were naively allowing themselves to be dragged into provoking a civil war." At 6:00 P.M., two rebellious paratroopers read a statement on Portuguese National Television (RTP) demanding the removal of Air Force Chief Morais da Silva and three other commanding officers. The embassy reported that "it is clear that RTP is now in hands of the radicals." More encouragingly, however, the enigmatic President Costa Gomes took direct command of the Lisbon military region and called on the paratroopers to end their "counter-revolutionary action."[94]

At 7:30 P.M. Army Captain Duran Clemente, former spokesman of the MFA Assembly, appeared on Lisbon television in "battle dress" and "nervously" read a communiqué from the Metal Workers Union appealing for everyone to take to the streets, and "violently" attacked the state of emergency that had been decreed several hours before. After Clemente finished talking, the MFA symbol appeared on the screen followed by a "Soviet-style ballet."[95]

At 9:30 P.M. on 25 November, in a television message broadcast from Oporto, President Costa Gomes announced that after consulting the Revolutionary Council he had declared a partial "state of siege." Arrayed behind Costa Gomes were Revolutionary Council members who were "uniformly sober looking." At about the same moment, Carlucci suggested to Washington that if the radical mutineers were not brought under control in Lisbon the moderates will move north imposing a de facto split in the country. An hour later, Carlucci had good news for Washington and reported that loyalist commandos had retaken the Air Force Regional Headquarters and the Monte Real Air Base. According to the Ambassador, "It looks like the mutiny is being brought under control."[96]

By noon on 26 November, the situation had largely normalized and the government was fully in control. Key rebel leftist military leaders, including Captain Duran Clemente, had been captured and the two most "dangerous radical units" in Lisbon, Ralis and the military police, had surrendered. Most significant was that COPCON was dissolved early on the morning of 26 November, and, according to the embassy's information, Otelo de Carvalho was "reportedly in tears." Carlucci concluded that these actions "should just about wrap up the rebellion."

The government's decisive responsive to the leftist challenge was exactly what Washington had been seeking. Carlucci reported that the "moderates have just . . . won a striking victory militarily. Progovernment forces . . . are on top and have the momentum bred by success. Politically we expect [the moderates] to take a tougher stance on Communist role in government."[97] Indeed, on 27 November, Army Chief Carlos Fabião and COPCON Commander Otelo de Carvalho were dismissed from their positions. Lieutenant Colonel Ramalho Eanes, who had led the counter-offensive against the mutineers, was named as Fabião 's replacement. "Government forces are moving with speed and decisiveness to consolidate their position," Carlucci noted to Washington. It was apparent that a new political resolve existed in Lisbon and Communist efforts to overthrow the government would no longer be tolerated.[98] In essence, the Communist effort to topple Pinheiro de Azevedo's government and establish an "authentic" left-wing regime had failed and was crushed in a matter of hours.

In the days after the failed coup, Costa Gomes and Pinheiro de Azevedo purged the military, the media, and government of those who were Communists or sympathetic to the ultra-left. The government's effective response to the coup attempt broke the back of the Communist threat to Portugal.

More than any other event since the Constituent Assembly elections, the failed coup created an environment for the emergence of a democratic government in Portugal. The communist left was completely fragmented and the military was no longer subject to the pervasive influence of the Portuguese Communist Party. As for the PCP, it lost the legitimacy that it derived from its identification with these key MFA leaders. At the same time, the decisive response of moderate MFA leaders under the direction of Eanes to the coup attempt demonstrated to all segments of Portuguese society that there was not only a government in name but one in fact as well.

Portugal's democracy, however, was still very fragile. The country's economy was on the brink of bankruptcy, and a democratic president would not be elected until 28 June, 1976, when the forty-one-year-old Ramalho Eanes received sixty-one percent of the vote to the runner-up, Otelo de Carvalho, who received sixteen percent.

From Washington's perspective, however, events in Lisbon no longer represented a threat to western security interests as the political situation in Portugal had stabilized sufficiently. Along with his colleagues in the embassy, Frank Carlucci showed that American policy could influence positively the outcome of the revolutionary forces recasting Portugal's political identity. The key to Carlucci's success was his acute understanding of political realities in Washington and Portugal and the implication of these realities for East-West relations. Carlucci's brand of statesmanship led to the emergence of an American role in Portugal that was consistent with both the aspirations of the vast majority of the Portuguese people and US objectives globally during one of the most confrontational periods of the Cold War.

Chapter 5

Angola's Transition to Independence

The Scramble for Africa—Again

The Soviet-American rivalry that intruded on Africa in the early 1960s was overtaken a decade later by an equally intense competition between the Soviet Union and the People's Republic of China. During the first wave of African independence, the Soviets failed to establish strong bilateral relations with any country, except Somalia in the Horn of Africa, where it had a military base, and Congo-Brazzaville in central Africa. Soviet diplomacy in Africa was haunted by the lingering memory of its futile efforts in Zaire in the early 1960s, its frustrations at trying to develop a stable relationship with Ghana's Kwame Nkrumah before he was deposed in 1966, sharp setbacks with the failure of a communist-led coup in the Sudan in 1971; the erosion of their close relations with Egypt in 1972; and the uncertainty of their ties with Guinea and Mali, two other countries that were nominally aligned with Moscow.[1]

The Chinese, on the other hand, learned from their earlier mistakes in Africa, and now refrained from trying to subvert African governments. Moreover, the end of the Cultural Revolution and the opening of relations with the United States in 1971–1972, as well as the consolidation of Soviet ties with Congo-Brazzaville, however unstable, precipitated a reorientation of China's policy toward southern Africa. The new Chinese approach underscored the importance of government-to-government relations, whereas support for liberation movements was confined to those groups opposing white minority and colonial rule. This policy allowed Beijing to maintain its revolutionary ideology without jeopardizing relations with African governments.[2]

A key element of China's new look in Africa was an aggressive aid strategy that Beijing promoted as being politically disinterested but socially and commercially relevant. China's showcase project was the $400 million, eleven hundred mile "Freedom Railroad," which ran from the port of Dar es Salaam to central Zambia. By providing an alternative to the ports and infrastructure of white minority-ruled Rhodesia and South Africa and Portuguese-controlled Mozambique, Beijing won an important measure of ideological influence with the governments of Tanzania and Zambia as well as the liberation movements headquartered in Dar es Salaam and Lusaka. Indeed, Western governments declined repeated requests to fund the project on the grounds that it was not economically viable.[3]

China's emergent influence in Africa was boosted in the early 1970s when Zambia's President, Kenneth Kaunda, persuaded President Mobutu of Zaire to reassess his strong antipathy toward Beijing. The growing Soviet presence in neighboring Congo-Brazzaville, China's new "legitimacy" following President Nixon's visit in 1972, and the prospect of new sources of development assistance featured prominently in Mobutu's decision to recognize the Beijing government in November and then visit in January 1973. While there he received a thirty-year interest-free loan.

Mobutu's opening to China set the stage for a new dimension of the ongoing rivalry between China and the Soviet Union that focused increasingly on Angola. Beijing took a major step into the Angolan political arena in December 1973, when Holden Roberto led an FNLA delegation on an eighteen-day "working trip" to China. The FNLA leader returned to Kinshasa with a promise of substantial military aid. Two weeks after his return to Zaire, Roberto flew to Bucharest for talks with President Nicolae Ceaucescu of Romania, China's closest ally in Eastern Europe. In a joint declaration of "cooperation and friendship" between the Rumanian Communist Party and the FNLA signed on 21 January 1974, the Rumanians followed the Chinese in promising military assistance to what previously had been considered Angola's predominant anticommunist liberation movement.[4] Beijing briefly considered opening a channel to the MPLA but, following a July 1971 visit by Agostinho Neto to China, decided that the MPLA was too wedded to Moscow and declined to offer any support.

On 29 May 1974 the first contingent of one hundred twelve Chinese military advisers, led by a major general of the Chinese army, arrived in Zaire to train FNLA forces at the organization's base at

Kinkuzu. On 28 August the Kinshasa press reported that the Rumanian Communist Party had presented a large quantity of military equipment to the FNLA. On 10 September, the FNLA publicly acknowledged the receipt of 450 tons of supplies from China. China also had ties to UNITA that dated back to 1964 when Savimbi first met Mao Tse-Tung in Beijing. Given the Chinese position with the FNLA, UNITA, and the government of Zaire, "the cards were heavily stacked in the Chinese favor at the end of 1974"[5] in terms of asserting influence in Angola. Ultimately, however, the Chinese would choose not to play these cards.

To counter China's in-roads, the Soviets in 1972–1973 reinvigorated their policy in black Africa by becoming the main arms supplier to General Idi Amin of Uganda. Support for Amin gave Moscow an apparent "gain" in East and Central Africa as they perceived both Tanzania and Zambia as being "under Chinese influence." Moreover, their close relationship with President Marian Ngouabi of Congo-Brazzaville, provided the Soviets with a base from which to respond to China's moves in the region. Moscow also reassessed its difficult relationship with the MPLA by suspending support to Agostinho Neto and offering it to the MPLA faction led by Daniel Chipenda. During the same month that President Mobutu visited China, however, the Soviets invited Neto to Moscow. Following a meeting with Boris Ponomarev, a Central Committee secretary and candidate member of the Politburo, Neto was assured that "the USSR would continue to support the MPLA against the Portuguese." According to a former Soviet diplomat, "Moscow chose the recipients of its support less and less for their authenticity as liberators-to-be and more and more for their willingness to oppose Peking."[6] Indeed, Soviet military intelligence viewed China's strategy in Africa aimed at exerting its influence over large parts of Africa in a loose coalition with the United States.

The Soviet Union decided to resume military aid to the MPLA, which had been terminated due to the paralyzing fissures within the organization, because of China's maneuvering in the region and to shore up its long-term investment in Angola. Arms and assistance would not start flowing again until August 1974, about the same time that significant Chinese support reached the FNLA.

While Moscow and Beijing probed for diplomatic leverage in Africa, Washington's attention was fixed on its geostrategic diplomacy and, principally, managing relations with the Soviet Union. As Henry Kissinger noted in his memoirs, in Jordan and Cienfuegos in

1970, in the India-Pakistan war of 1971, and in the full-scale military alert at the end of the October 1973 war in the Middle East, "the Nixon Administration vigorously opposed geopolitical challenges by the Soviet Union and its allies." At the same time, by early spring 1973, Washington had achieved a number of agreements in arms control, East-West trade and technical cooperation with Moscow and, of course, had established a dialogue with Beijing. Thus, the "pillars of resistance to Soviet expansion and a willingness to negotiate on concrete issues" with Moscow had reached a workable and unprecedented equilibrium in the Administration's view.[7]

Nevertheless, the decade-long bitter divisions over Vietnam and the pervasive distrust of the Nixon White House generated by the Watergate investigation had had a corrosive effect on détente's domestic support. Most significant, was Congress's growing influence over the formulation and conduct of American foreign policy. This was initially apparent in 1972 when the Senate opposed administration efforts to treat the Azores and Bahrain base treaties as executive agreements—which did not require Congressional approval. The passage of the War Powers Act in October 1973 was a more dramatic move by Congress to exert control over Presidential discretion to commit American military force, and the executive branch's constitutional purview to make foreign policy. Most significant to the administration's policy toward Moscow, however, was the effort made during the summer of 1973 by the Senator from Washington, Henry Jackson, to tie the issue of Jewish emigration from the Soviet Union to the granting of Most Favored Nation (MFN) status. As Kissinger acidly reflected, "Jackson was not a man to welcome debate over firmly held convictions; he proceeded to implement his by erecting a series of legislative hurdles that gradually paralyzed our East-West policy."[8]

The Jackson-Vanik amendment to the trade bill—which had the effect of denying more liberal terms of trade to the Soviet Union—passed the House Ways and Means Committee on 26 September 1973. It was subsequently approved in the Senate, "an even more difficult forum for the administration," in Kissinger's perspective. Capitalizing on their success, the Jackson forces then persuaded the Senate to limit Presidential authority to use the facilities of the Export-Import Bank when presidential authorization came up for renewal on 30 June 1974 as it did biannually. Twenty Senators led by Jackson and Adlai Stevenson of Illinois cajoled Congress into granting them authority to review any Export-Import Bank loan to the Soviet Union in excess of fifty million dollars, and placed a tight ceiling of $300 million on all loans to Russia. To Kissinger, American foreign policy at the end of Nixon's presidency was "stalemated," and "trapped between [an] undifferentiating moralism and [an] overemphasis on geopolitics."[9] In short, the administration's "structure of peace" was on the verge of collapse.

Angola Slips Away

While the Chinese stimulated a revived Soviet interest in central Africa, Washington paid no special attention to the prospect of Portugal disengaging from Africa. After all, Portugal had been a generally reliable ally for years and the conventional wisdom in Washington was that European governments were better prepared to control events in their former colonies than was the United States. Moreover, the fact that Portugal would soon be withdrawing from Angola and Mozambique "was not particularly disturbing to the United States." Indeed, the "new policy of independence . . . was welcomed in Washington because it gave the United States a chance to side with the black majorities in the Portuguese colonies and thus shore up American policy generally."[10]

Against this backdrop, Richard Nixon met for two hours with President Spínola on 19 June 1974 in the Officers Mess at the Lajes air base in the Azores during a stopover on Nixon's return trip from the Middle East. Spínola was alarmed at Soviet efforts to expand its influence in central Africa, particularly Angola. In an effort to counter this activity, Spínola told Nixon that Portugal would abide by the United Nations declarations for self-determination in Africa but added that those living in the territories had a right to determine their own destinies. The General added that there was "great flexibility," or a variety of paths, to independence that each territory might adopt.[11]

In essence, Spínola was seeking American support for his plan to hold a referendum in each of the territories to ensure that a Portuguese-dominated federation or commonwealth would emerge from the decolonization process. As the Portuguese president envisioned it, Angola might not be independent until October 1976. The politically inexperienced Portuguese president was under intense pressure, however, from the MFA, the Socialists and Communists in his government, to grant immediate and unilateral self-determination. Apparently making no reference to his domestic political difficulties,

Spínola pointed out to Nixon that immediate independence in Angola and Mozambique could only benefit the Soviet Union.[12]

Nixon promised to back Spínola's strategy for self-determination. The two leaders also agreed that President Mobutu of Zaire "could be helpful" in Angola's decolonization. In general, however, Spínola found the American president uninformed about Africa and preoccupied solely with stopping the spread of Communism in both the Iberian peninsula and Africa.[13]

Spínola's own political fate worsened as rapidly as Nixon's. In July, his government collapsed, and the MFA's control of the reins of government expanded dramatically with the creation of the second provisional government. Spínola was forced to accept as prime minister, Vasco Gonçalves, a fifty-three-year-old former professor at the Portuguese military academy who had served in both Angola and Mozambique. On 24 July, Lisbon announced the creation of a transitional government, to be led by the leftist-MFA officer, Vice Admiral Rosa Coutinho, that would oversee Angola's decolonization. Three days later Gonçalvez and his hard-line allies in government forced Spínola to announce the immediate and unconditional independence in the territories, thus abandoning his strategy for a slow and orderly disengagement from Africa. The MFA, after all, had made the coup to end the war in Africa, not to prolong it.

Spínola was not, however, finished with trying to control Angola's destiny. In mid-September, he met with Zairian President Mobutu on the Cape Verde Island of Sal. Accompanied by Roberto and Savimbi, the Zairian leader and Spínola agreed that Agostinho Neto and the Marxist factions within the MPLA "could and should" be eliminated from the Angolan political scene during a democratic transition to independence. Spínola, who was unhappy with the course of events in Mozambique, where FRELIMO was being given a free hand to install a Marxist government, concluded that he could achieve this in the context of the plan for Angola's decolonization that had been promulgated by the MFA on 13 August 1974. One of Spínola's key objectives was to ensure that the MPLA would be represented in this government by Daniel Chipenda and the movement's "honorary president," Joaquim Pinto de Andrade, both of whom had led break away factions from the Neto wing of the MPLA.[14]

Spínola's plan was overturned at the end of September when younger, more radical military officers forced him to resign the presidency. Portugal's new government immediately revoked the arrangement that Spínola had worked out with Mobutu that would have eliminated Agostinho Neto's faction of the MPLA from a future Angolan government. Neto thus benefited from his prestige among the leftists that now dominated Portugal's governing military and political coalition.[15] Nevertheless, for the first time in five hundred years, the Portuguese were no longer directly in control of Angola's internal affairs.

Mr. Guinea-Bissau

On the surface, Donald Easum easily fit into the intelligent, outspoken, and aggressive team that Kissinger brought to the State Department following his appointment as Secretary of State. Easum, a career foreign service officer, had come to Kissinger's attention while directing a special National Security Council group study on Latin America during the first two years of the Nixon administration. In September 1973, when Kissinger was filling key positions in the State Department, he sent Easum a telegram in Ougadougou, Burkina Faso's capital, where Easum was ambassador, requesting his presence at the Hotel Pierre in New York forty-eight hours later. When they met, the two diplomats focused their attention on the numerous positions that needed to be filled. Easum expressed his interest in becoming assistant secretary of state for African affairs and, a month later, was offered the position.

Easum's swearing in as assistant secretary was a "warm" occasion, with Kissinger joking that Easum would be the first assistant secretary who wore a beard. The relationship between the secretary and assistant secretary deteriorated "instantaneously," however, as Kissinger had nothing but contempt for the "governing ethos" of the Africa Bureau. In his view, foreign service officers who served in Europe, Asia, and the Middle East were compelled to look at issues from a global outlook as each of these regions contained major powers. In contrast, the "backwaters" of the policy process, "Africa in very large measure," encouraged a parochial and regional perspective that did not adequately account for larger geopolitical realities. In his experience, the foreign service officers who served in Africa "tended to promulgate a rather inflexible version of Wilsonianism." Moreover, as the Bureau was not in the mainstream of policymaking, "many officers in the bureau evolved a kind of siege mentality in which they transmuted their isolation into a claim of moral superiority . . . ."[16]

Easum's first clash with his boss came soon after he assumed his position in early 1974. Kissinger was eager to develop a position paper on Portugal in preparation for the renegotiation of the Azores agreement and to make good on his promise of a reward for their support during the October War. At daily staff meetings, Kissinger constantly reminded Easum and others that Nixon wanted to be "forthcoming" with the Portuguese. Not fully aware of the promises that Kissinger had made to the Portuguese, Easum was subsequently informed by William DuPree, who was on Winston Lord's policy planning staff, of the closer relationship that the Administration was adopting toward Portugal. Easum was also told that Kissinger wanted to make this public by modifying the arms embargo in Congress so as to strengthen his bargaining position with the Portuguese. Apparently, Kissinger had already approved the sale to Lisbon of Hawk and Sea Sparrow missiles, C-130 aircraft, and small vessels suitable for river and coastal patrol work. The only thing lacking was Congressional approval.[17]

From the outset, Easum tried to alert Kissinger to the "devastating" impact that this new policy would have on US interests in Africa. Frustrated in his effort to communicate this to the Secretary, Easum finally received a telephone call from Deputy Undersecretary of State Lawrence Eagleburger, who told him that he had the secretary's permission to prepare a memo on his view of the negative consequences of this policy. Eagleburger further instructed Easum that the memo was to remain highly confidential and that he should not consult with anyone else in the Africa Bureau. Easum, who had been working on drought problems in Burkina Faso for the previous three years, was stunned. When he presented his briefing in a staff meeting several days later, Kissinger remained unmoved by his assistant secretary's arguments.

Even though the coup of 25 April preempted Kissinger's efforts to assist the Portuguese to obtain sophisticated arms, it did not end the rancor between Easum and Kissinger. In fact, it was accentuated, especially during the summer of 1974, as Kissinger resisted Easum's repeated recommendations that the US not veto Guinea-Bissau's application to join the United Nations. Easum was also adamant that the US not align itself with any of the Angolan liberation movements, a position that was vigorously opposed by the CIA.

This conflict over policy was fueled by a profound difference in personalities and outlooks. Easum found Kissinger to be arrogant, sardonic, and belittling, and one who enjoyed placing pressure on people to see how they responded. The assistant secretary was a self-admitted "softie," who resented the secretary's pressures. Therefore, when Kissinger referred to Easum in staff meetings as "Mr. Guinea-Bissau," Easum felt unjustly ridiculed and criticized. More fundamentally, Easum found Kissinger to be "ignorant" on Africa and a firm believer in NSSM 39's premise that "the whites are here to stay." To Easum, Kissinger had no appreciation of what it meant to be a freedom fighter or a black nationalist and therefore could not understand fundamental aspects of African politics. Easum thought it was imperative to declare American support for majority rule in these countries and actively work toward that end. Kissinger, on the other hand, found Easum "naïve" and a "passionate apostle" of a "mystical African skill" predicated on nonalignment and over-reliance on economic aid.[18]

While the personality differences eroded the working relationship between Kissinger and Easum, their philosophical differences led to a decisive policy conflict that occurred in late 1974. Following Portugal's decision to decolonize and the coup that toppled the long-time American ally, Ethiopian President Haile Selassie, in September 1974, Easum decided to make an extensive tour of Africa. A primary purpose of this trip was to reestablish a viable relationship with FRELIMO that was poised to assume governmental power in Mozambique.

On 30 October in Dar es Salaam, Tanzanian president Julius Nyerere arranged for the American assistant secretary to talk with FRELIMO leader Samora Machel. The meeting, which lasted for several hours, was held at the Mozambique Institute. Easum did not ask the State Department for permission to meet with Machel, the first meeting between high level FRELIMO and American officials since Eduardo Mondlane's death in 1969, as it seemed a "logical thing" to do. As Easum subsequently cabled the State Department, the United States was being presented with an opportunity to set the basis for a mutually beneficial relationship with an independent Mozambique.

Easum found Machel conciliatory and willing to "forget the past." Easum expressed an interest in visiting Mozambique to which the President of FRELIMO agreed. Easum was told that even though the Portuguese were a part of the transitional government, FRELIMO was in effect in charge and he was therefore to contact FRELIMO officials and not the Portuguese.

Before their meeting ended, Machel said that Mozambique needed economic assistance from the United States. Easum replied that the two hundred million dollars that Machel had requested exceeded the total amount of aid that the United States gave all of Africa. The assistant secretary then gave Machel "a bit of a lesson" about the complexities of the foreign policy bureaucracy and Congress. Easum concluded the discussion by promising Machel that while he was in Mozambique, he would try to identify specific projects on which the United States could be helpful.[19]

While in Mozambique, Easum met with numerous FRELIMO officials including the interim prime minister, Joaquim Chissano. Chissano emphasized to Easum, the first high-level representative of a Western government to visit Mozambique, his country's most immediate needs were for labor-intensive development projects. Easum responded with a promise to an economic study team from AID to Mozambique by mid-January, 1975.

Immediately upon his return to Washington on 24 November, however, Easum's colleagues told the assistant secretary that the "long knives" were out for him. If his unauthorized visit to Mozambique did not annoy the secretary, certainly some of his public comments contradicted Kissinger's view of American policy toward Africa. In Dar es Salaam, on 2 November, Easum said, "We are using our influence to foster change in South Africa—not to preserve the status quo." Later that day in Lusaka, Easum said that the United States would keep its options open regarding South Africa's membership in the United Nations. For Kissinger, American support for South Africa's membership in the United Nations was not open to question.

At virtually the same time that Carlucci's appointment was being announced and Kissinger was "thawing" on aid to Portugal, he issued instructions for Easum to be fired. On 25 November, Deputy Secretary of State Robert Ingersoll notified Easum that, after only nine months in office, he was being sent to Nigeria as ambassador. As a result, Easum's recommendations to send a study team to Mozambique stalled and the United States lost an early opportunity to establish a working relationship with the new FRELIMO government. Easum's departure also laid the basis for a change in policy toward Angola.

Alvor: The Portuguese Want Out

The decolonization of Angola got underway slowly, yet disagreement and conflict over the process started immediately. Within a week of the creation of the Angolan transitional government, the FNLA issued a communiqué protesting it as "inconsistent with the spirit and letter of the rights of Angolans to self-determination."[20] As the FNLA saw it, the Angolan junta was a reassertion of Portuguese influence in the colony only this time headed by an individual, Rosa Coutinho, who was a known sympathizer with the Portuguese Communist Party and, more significantly, the MPLA.

The creation of the junta preceded the announcement by Lisbon on 13 August of a "timetable for the decolonization" of Angola. After a cease-fire was in place, Lisbon said it would form a provisional coalition government in which all liberation movements would be represented as well as the "most significant ethnic groups." This was a reference to the nearly fifty political and ethnic organizations that had sprung up since the Lisbon coup, including several parties representing Angola's white population. The coalition government was to have responsibility for drafting an electoral law and conducting an electoral census on a one-man, one-vote basis. Constituent assembly elections were to be held within two years to draw up a new constitution, to be followed by another set of elections for a legislative assembly that would form the first independent government.[21]

By the end of October, the Portuguese had reached cease-fire agreements with the MPLA, UNITA, and the FNLA. Also during this period UNITA's Jonas Savimbi undertook a diplomatic drive to forge a UNITA-FNLA-MPLA coalition to negotiate independence with Portugal's military government. On 25 November in Kinshasa, Savimbi and Holden Roberto signed a reconciliation agreement, and on 18 December in Luso, the capital of Moxico province in Angola, Agostinho Neto and Savimbi signed an agreement binding them to a common front that would also include the FNLA. To establish the common front and to respond to pressures from the OAU, Roberto agreed to meet with Savimbi and Neto in Mombasa, Kenya. At the end of the talks on 3–5 January, chaired by Kenyan president, Jomo Kenyatta, the three nationalist leaders signed a trilateral accord that recognized each other as independent parties with equal rights and responsibilities. They also agreed that an unspecified period of transition was necessary before they would be prepared to take over from the Portuguese.[22]

The Mombasa Accord set the scene for a summit meeting between the Portuguese and the three Angolan liberation movements on Angola's future. Held at the luxurious Penina Golfe Hotel at Alvor, on Portugal's Algarve coast, the talks opened on 10 January 1975. Holden Roberto, Agostinho Neto, and Jonas Savimbi led their respective organizations at the talks, and the Portuguese delegation included President Costa Gomes, Foreign Minister Mário Soares, Minister without Portfolio Melo Antunes and the High Commissioner for Angola, Rosa Coutinho.

Amid numerous mini-conferences and intensive caucuses in side rooms and hotel corridors, progress was immediate—or so it appeared. A joint communiqué issued on 12 January by the MPLA, UNITA, and FNLA said that "no obstacle" would impede a "united liberation front" from preparing for independence. A second communiqué on the same date claimed that there had been "substantial progress" made in a joint plan for decolonization submitted by the liberation groups to the Portuguese delegation. Most significantly, Costa Gomes announced in an evening television interview that "Angola will be independent in 1975." The conference culminated on 15 January with the signing of the Alvor Accord and establishment of 11 November 1975 as the date for independence.

In spite of Savimbi's reconciliation diplomacy and the brave gestures of cooperation made by the nationalists during the Alvor negotiations, the embassy in Lisbon saw through the façade of unanimity that both the liberation movements and the Portuguese were trying to create. The joint communiqué notwithstanding, the embassy reported, "Old divisions have probably surfaced on [the] African side and both the Government of Portugal and [the] liberation groups are going to great length to paper them over."[23]

The initial reaction in Angola to the signing of Alvor nevertheless was positive. Most Angolans were optimistic that the bitter conflict over Portuguese colonialism was over and that a formula for independence had been agreed upon. For the liberation movements, it appeared that a decade and a half of life in exile and guerrilla warfare was nearly at an end. As the American Consul General Tom Killoran in Luanda cabled, "The predominant feeling among blacks now is one of relief." For the whites in Angola who numbered nearly one half million, the Alvor Accord signaled a further stripping away of their formerly privileged position. Their personal and economic future was more uncertain than ever before and it was unclear what would happen to them once the Portuguese military began to withdraw.[24]

Most satisfied by the signing of the Accords were the Portuguese military officials in Angola. As Killoran informed Washington, the military felt that it had "brought the colony through an extremely difficult period." Referring to the role of the Angolan High Commissioner both during the transition and in the Alvor negotiations, Killoran reported that the long-suffering Portuguese army was "proud of the job done by Admiral Rosa Coutinho." Indeed, continued Killoran, "He did remarkably well, knocked a lot of heads together and effectively staunched any mischief white extremists may have had in mind." Softening the praise slightly, Killoran allowed that Coutinho "certainly seems to have infringed the civil rights of some whites and suit may well be brought against him in the courts. But he is a remarkably tough and resilient old bird and will not worry about such details."[25]

Although it escaped Killoran, Coutinho's infringement on the civil rights of whites was a telling sign of Alvor's problems. In fact, the Accord accelerated Angola's collapse into anarchy. The Deputy Chief of Mission in Lisbon, Herbert Okun, accurately summarized the situation when he cabled Washington saying that "on paper at least, the Portuguese have managed to negotiate themselves out of a very tricky colonial situation . . . . Above all, the Portuguese wanted out." Lisbon "saw Angola as a political and economic liability and, even worse, as a source of political and economic support for those [conservative white] forces in Portugal that might be plotting a return to the pre-April 25 era."[26]

As designed, Alvor never could have led to the creation of an effective transitional government or served as a blueprint for elections. For one, elections for a constituent assembly were to be held within nine months of the day that the transitional government was to take over. For liberation movements whose entire existence had been predicated on warfare, nine months were insufficient for making the transition to political parties capable of waging a democratic election. Moreover, instead of the two years that Angola was initially to have to prepare for independence, it was now scheduled to receive its freedom within eleven months, on 11 November. During five hundred years of colonial domination, the Portuguese had done nothing to prepare the

Angolans for self-determination. It was now about to be granted independence essentially overnight.

As significant, Alvor ensured that there would be a virtual paralysis in executive authority as the Portuguese prepared for a quick retreat from their colony. The transitional government, for example, was to be led by a three-man presidential college consisting of a member each from the MPLA, FNLA, and UNITA with a rotating presidency. A two-thirds majority was necessary to reach a decision on any issue. Control of the twelve ministries was to be divided evenly between the three nationalist organizations and the Portuguese. In an analysis of the Alvor Agreement, the Bureau of Intelligence and Research noted that "the attempt to balance the administrative authority of the three groups may ultimately paralyze the transitional government."[27]

The Consulate in Luanda correctly, but with significant understatement, commented that "the transitional system . . . is not a formula for speedy and decisive executive action." The Consul General nevertheless misread the depth of antipathy among the liberation movements when he concluded that the arrangement "does seem well suited to Angola's political situation" because "it will give the groups experience in working together, and time to overcome old hostilities and prejudices."[28]

A main objective of the Portuguese going into the Alvor negotiations was to obtain sufficient guarantees to prevent a panicked exodus from Angola by the whites. Their flight from Angola was virtually assured, however, by the fact that only the three liberation groups were allowed to put forward candidates for the constituent assembly elections. The Portuguese government and the liberation groups reasoned that black-white animosities would have been exacerbated if whites had been able to contest the elections. Moreover, the negotiators at Alvor hoped that "forcing whites to function through one of the movements [would] bring about a sense of identification between the two races and to enlarge the scope of concern of each movement."[29] The whites, therefore, as well as the Cabindans and the approximately 750,000 Bakongo refugees in Zaire, were effectively shut out of the process of Angola's transition to independence, in spite of what the Portuguese government had promised four months earlier.

Another source of division was the "integrated" army of twenty-four thousand Portuguese soldiers and eight thousand soldiers from each liberation movement that was to be created on an "accelerated basis" over an eight-month period. The parties in Alvor agreed that the new military would be mixed down to the patrol level but that each liberation movement would be allowed to maintain separate barracks and installations. Furthermore, all operational decisions were to be cleared by the three movements represented in the joint military command as well as their respective headquarters. This cumbersome decision-making process was complicated by the widely divergent size of liberation groups' military force.[30]

Thus with all political groups except for the liberation movements essentially frozen out of the constituent assembly process, the flight of whites as well as Angola's economic and administrative demise was virtually assured. Moreover, the fact that political authority was evenly spread among the three liberation movements—who had a profound and violent distrust of each other—was further evidence that the Portuguese were more concerned about creating a face-saving means for leaving Angola than ensuring that the difficult questions of postcolonial political control were effectively resolved. Success was further jeopardized by the Accord's stipulation that a transitional army was to be molded quickly from an exhausted, demoralized, and ill-equipped Portuguese military as well as with poorly trained blacks from the nationalist organizations who only months before had been engaged in mortal conflict.

Another problem was that no arrangement had been made to channel or assuage the personal ambitions of the leaders of three movements, all of whom coveted the presidency of an independent Angola. In the view of INR, "the major source of antagonism . . . has been the personal ambitions of [the] three leaders, all of whom aspire to be president."[31] In fact, Portuguese actions intensified the competition between the movements. It was an open secret, for example, that Rosa Coutinho was supporting the MPLA by giving it military equipment from the retreating Portuguese forces.[32]

At the same time, there were pervasive rumors of Portuguese support for Jonas Savimbi that emanated from the early 1970s. In fact, in a memorandum for the Secretary of State Kissinger on the Alvor Accord, the Bureau of Intelligence and Research surmised that the Portuguese were relying on Savimbi, "whom they consider to be the ablest politician among the three leaders, to serve as mediator and keep the government from breaking up."[33]

In spite of the evident problems that the Alvor agreement exacerbated, if not created, the State Department took a low key, "hands-off" approach toward its publication. Acting Assistant Secretary of State for African Affairs Edward Mulcahy instructed Killoran to approach the presidential college as a group to express congratulations on successfully concluding the negotiations and to convey US hopes for establishing "close and mutually beneficial relations" with Angola at independence. Killoran also was instructed to see the Portuguese High Commissioner, Rosa Coutinho, and to commend Potugal's "untiring and protracted efforts in bringing about the Angolan agreement."[34]

A Favorable Situation

Angola, like Mozambique, "drifted" within the bureaucracy in the months after the coup as it received little attention from senior American decision-makers. The CIA unsuccessfully spent much of the summer of 1974 trying to get the 40 Committee, which authorized all covert operations, to consider a more active American involvement in Angola. With Watergate having paralyzed the US government, however, the United States extracting itself from Vietnam, and Kissinger's preoccupation with other issues, there was little incentive to commit new American resources to another prospective Third World trouble spot. Furthermore, Assistant Secretary Easum was strongly opposed to covert intervention in Angola.

Without 40 Committee approval, the CIA could only increase its disbursements to Holden Roberto by a small amount, from $10,000 to about $25,000. This decision was made in July 1974 without informing Tom Killoran, the Consul General in Luanda. Although still a relatively small amount, it was "enough for word to get around that the CIA was dealing itself into the race" for influence in Angola. Killoran seemed to reflect this when he subsequently reported that "the belief that Roberto and Mobutu are agents of the US is just about universal in Angola."[35] Nonetheless, by August 1974, the US, the Soviet Union, and China had all increased their stakes in Angola, although not irretrievably, setting the stage for a showdown of superpower political and military strength.

The "drift" on Angola policy ended when Edward Mulcahy, who had been Easum's principal deputy, became the interim assistant secretary of state for African affairs on 1 January 1975. Mulcahy "had no doubt" that events in Angola would soon "crescendo," and he felt it necessary to give the issue higher visibility within the government. Supported by Jim Potts, CIA Africa Division Chief; Jack Foley, the State Department's director of Southern African affairs, Walter Cutler, director of Central African affairs, and Mulcahy, the issue was finally placed on the 40 Committee's agenda at a meeting scheduled for 22 January 1975.[36]

Their proposal to extend significant American assistance to Roberto and Savimbi came up last, at the end of what had been a "crowded" agenda and as participants were gathering their papers. Jim Potts made the case that the Agency had received "some very disturbing intelligence" that the Soviet Union had begun shipping weapons to the MPLA through Congo-Brazzaville. Potts argued that "it was clear that Neto wasn't our man," and that CIA support for Roberto and Savimbi would be "a token" that would give the United States "some capital in the bank" with one of Angola's future leaders. Potts' emphasis on Angola's strategic importance was underscored by the "distress signals" being sent to Washington by Zaire's President Joseph Mobutu over Angola's deteriorating security situation. Indeed, there were signals that Mobutu might expel Dean Hinton, the US ambassador in Kinshasa, in an effort to capture Washington's attention.[37]

Initially, Kissinger was not convinced that the United States should become more involved in Angola. Nevertheless, he did not want "to shake the confidence" of an ally as important as Mobutu. Support for Roberto would also be consistent with the strategy devised by Nixon and Spínola in their Azores conversation and at the subsequent meeting between Spínola and Mobutu on the Isla da Sal in September 1974. Moreover, with Easum gone, an influential bureaucratic coalition led by Potts and Mulcahy had formed to provide strong support for the initiative. Their position was implicitly endorsed at the 40 Committee meeting by Under Secretary of State Joseph Sisco, who decided not to raise the reservations he had expressed earlier in State Department discussions.[38]

Based on these considerations, the 40 Committee approved $300,000 for Holden Roberto but vetoed a $100,000 grant "to open a window to Jonas Savimbi." The financial support for Roberto was to be used for political organizing and to buy "rubber bands, paper clips, etc.," as Kissinger later remarked, with no intention that it would be used for military equipment. The disbursement was seen as an end in itself and not as a first installment. It was intended to help Roberto establish his presence in Luanda. It was also designed "to make him look like a leader" in preparation for the elections that had been agreed to the week before by the Portuguese government and the three Angolan liberation movements. There was no debate within the 40 Committee as to the effect that increased American support for Roberto would have on the Alvor Accord. Moreover, as one intelligence official commented, Kissinger did not know who Holden Roberto was in January 1975.[39]

What was a "token" amount to Washington was a virtual windfall to the FNLA. With the American support, Roberto purchased the leading Angolan newspaper, *A Provincia de Angola*, a television station, and several vehicles. He also established a political office in Luanda. As Roberto's military abilities were "distrusted" by those in the Africa Bureau who had met him, Washington hoped that he could be installed in Luanda without resort to violence. The Consul General in Luanda endorsed this cautious optimism when he reported to the State Department: "The FNLA is no longer seen here as a ragtag handful of murderers but as a serious political organization that espouses a moderate platform and shows signs of being amenable to compromise."[40]

As a safeguard against Roberto falling short of American expectations, William Hyland, director of the Bureau of Intelligence and Research, and Mulcahy sent Kissinger a memorandum on 25 February that endorsed establishing ties to Jonas Savimbi so as to ensure "maximum information on the unfolding drama of Angola." Although the Africa Bureau welcomed the 20 February decision by Daniel Chipenda to merge his faction with the FNLA, there was concern that this might encourage Roberto to attack the MPLA because of his "lopsided" advantage in military strength. Indeed, the view of the Africa Bureau and INR was borne out a month later when the FNLA killed forty-nine MPLA soldiers at a roadblock on the road between Luanda and Caxito.[41]

The perception in the State Department, however, was that the Soviet Union would not significantly help the MPLA overcome its difficulties. Even though the Soviet Union had resumed support to the MPLA the previous fall, Washington viewed the MPLA as the weakest faction in the coalition government. The MPLA had a narrow base of support in Angolan society, was crippled by internal political divisions, and was weak militarily. American policy makers were also operating under the assumption that the Soviet Union intended to observe the Alvor Accord. Therefore, increased covert assistance to Roberto, to help him strengthen his organization politically, seemed to improve a situation that Washington viewed as already favorable to the United States.[42]

Moscow's "End-Run" Around Détente

By the end of March 1975, Kissinger's perceptions of an American advantage in Angola had changed. For one, there was mounting evidence that leftist Portuguese military officials in Angola were violating the Alvor Accord by turning over their weapons to the MPLA and allowing Soviet weapons into the country from Congo-Brazzaville.[43] Moscow transferred its second shipment of arms to Angola at a time when the FNLA, emboldened by the support of Congolese troops and the "token" American assistance, openly attacked the MPLA headquarters in Luanda and killed nearly sixty people at an MPLA training camp in Caxito. To Kissinger, it appeared that the Soviets were escalating their involvement and support for the MPLA at a rate that was "alarming."

Furthermore, Angola was increasingly convulsed by factional conflict. By the beginning of May, more than one thousand people were killed in open fighting between the MPLA and FNLA. It was apparent to the Embassy in Lisbon that the Portuguese had neither the "will nor the capability of major military intervention to save the precarious peace" in the colony.[44]

In early April, Kissinger ordered the new Assistant Secretary of State for African Affairs, Nathaniel Davis, to prepare a staff study on the developing situation in Angola. The memorandum, jointly authored by the Africa Bureau, the Bureau of Intelligence and Research and the Policy Planning staff, pressed for a decision: "We must decide . . . at what level, if any, should we covertly support FNLA's Holden Roberto or other Angolan leaders."[45] The momentum was mounting, in large part driven by the CIA, to increase substantially support for the FNLA and extend material assistance to Jonas Savimbi. Indeed, on 12 May, the Consul General in Luanda was approached directly by Jorge Valentim, head of UNITA in Lobito, who requested "USG support . . . specifically arms, as soon as possible."[46]

Although Davis did not oppose support for Roberto, he warned Kissinger against assisting Savimbi. He acknowledged that Angola was moving toward a "violent denouement," but contended that the US would probably find itself drawn into an escalating conflict "very fast." As he argued in a 1 May 1975 memorandum to Kissinger, the "political price we might pay . . . would, I believe, exceed the possibility of accomplishment." Davis in fact did not think that the administration could undertake a major covert paramilitary operation in Angola, keep it secret, and maintain Congressional support.[47]

Kissinger rejected Davis's recommendations, which put him at odds with his new assistant secretary of state for African affairs. Criticizing the Africa Bureau's "willingness to go its own way," Kissinger later wrote that "Davis turned out to be willing, indeed eager, to implement conventional wisdom, which meant nonintervention." According to the Secretary, Davis lacked the "stomach" for covert operations and for the battle Congress for resources for such operations.[48]

The Secretary, however, had concluded that the Soviet Union had "exceeded the rules of the game" in Angola and that Moscow had caught the United States "off guard."[49] Kissinger's most abiding concern was not events in Angola per se, but that the United States be able to demonstrate the national will to behave as a great power. Indeed, as one State Department document summarized the situation, "The strategic significance to the USSR of a presence in Angola could be important, and the psychological impact would be profound. It would enhance the image of the Soviet Union as a global power with both the will and the means to influence events throughout the world."[50]

An imperative for Kissinger was supporting American allies in a region where it appeared to Washingon that Moscow had no legitimate or traditional interests. Indeed, the emotive Zambian President Kaunda applied pressure on Washington. During a visit to the White House on 19 April, according to Kissinger, Kaunda encouraged President Ford to respond militarily to the Soviet intervention, laying the groundwork for a "new policy [that] grew quite unexpectedly out of the meeting." Kaunda also lobbied for support for Jonas Savimbi, whom he described "as a man of humility and good qualities." Two months later, on 18 June 1975, in a more dramatic gesture, President Mobutu expelled Dean Hinton, the American ambassador in Kinshasa, to underscore his concern over Washington's lack of response to Soviet and MPLA advances. Mobutu's move had its desired effect, especially as Hinton was widely perceived to have been close to the Congolese president and a supporter of his plan to install the FNLA in power in Angola.[51]

On 12 May, Edward Mulcahy, who was acting assistant secretary for Davis (who was traveling), developed an options paper for Kissinger on Angola. Mulcahy noted that it was in the US interests to contain the conflict in Angola and to keep foreign involvement to a minimum. "In the event that anti-US forces appear to be gaining the upper hand," the US should reexamine its options. Mulcahy's first option was "neutrality," which he distinguished between "honest neutrality," defined as "noninvolvement with any faction," and "public" neutrality, which would enable the US to continue its "public protestations of noninvolvement." The second option was to "urge restraint," and listed seven ways of doing that, including approaching Moscow and Beijing directly. The third option was to "actively support one or more of the liberation groups." The only firm recommendation that Mulcahy made was against direct intervention in support of one or more of the contending liberation movements. According to Kissinger, the paper amounted to "homilies irrelevant to our problems."[52]

Four days later, Mulcahy sent Kissinger an action memorandum informing him that Jonas Savimbi was planning to visit the US in late June and recommending that he be received at the assistant secretary level. After all, Mulcahy noted, "While UNITA is militarily weak, it is probably the most popular of three groups with both black and white elements of the population."[53]

On 13 June, an interagency NSC Task Force, chaired by Nathaniel Davis, that was monitoring the escalating crisis in Angola submitted another briefing memorandum to Kissinger. It consisted of three options. On the one hand, the CIA supported Kissinger's view of a Soviet "end-run around détente" into Angola and called for an active American involvement. They recommended a significant increase in support to Roberto and an extension of aid to Savimbi. These moves, it was reasoned, would "discourage further resort to arms and civil war" and restore a "balance" among the movements.

The majority opinion of the task force, which included the Africa Bureau, the Bureau of Intelligence and Research, and the Policy Planning Staff, favored using diplomatic and political means to resolve the Angolan conflict. They argued that a military intervention would commit US resources and prestige in a situation in which the outcome was in doubt and in which the United States would have, at best, limited influence. Therefore, in an effort to avoid a superpower confrontation as well as the risk of adverse domestic consequences, the task force urged the administration to approach the Soviet Union through diplomatic channels and support UN or OAU mediation efforts. The task force also favored working in concert with Tanzania, Zaire, and Zambia in an effort to reduce the arms flow into Angola. A third option, "studied indifference," drew little support.[54]

After submitting this report, Davis left for a two-week trip to Africa. When he returned on 29 June, it was evident that the Angola issue "was moving toward decision." In fact, the outcome was influenced by a visit made to Kinshasa by Sheldon Vance, who had been US ambassador to Zaire during the "good days," from 1969 to 1974, and was personally close to African autocrat. Dispatched to mend fences with Mobutu and assure him that he was not being forgotten at this time of crisis, Vance cabled Kissinger from Kinshasa that "the situation seemed to be paralleling that of earlier disruptive days in the Zaire when Soviets again played a major role in fomenting strife and civil war." Vance also met with Holden Roberto, who told the American diplomat that the situation in Angola had become "grave," and made a "strong plea for support" from the US.[55]

Changing Objectives in Angola

During the first two weeks of July, Nathaniel Davis sent several memoranda to Kissinger and Joseph Sisco arguing that covert intervention would not serve larger American interests, that it could not be kept secret, and that the Soviets "can escalate the level of aid more readily than we." As for "concrete interests," there were virtually none, Gulf Oil's $300 million stake in Cabinda being the principal one. Davis also argued that the CIA was concerned only with the risks of disclosure in Washington and had "grossly" underestimated the repercussions abroad should the program be revealed. He argued, therefore, that "the Secretary is right in his conviction . . . that if we go in, we must go in massively and decisively" to avoid a Vietnam-style buildup. Davis warned, however, that the worst possible outcome "would be a test of wills and strength which we lose." Noting that the CIA had concluded that "in the best of circumstances we won't be able to win" in Angola, Davis recommended that "if we are to have a test of strength with the Soviets, we should find a more advantageous place."[56]

Ironically, none of the bureaucratic combatants appeared to raise the prospect of a massive Cuban military intervention in support of the MPLA. Nor did they anticipate the degree to which American interests in the region would be damaged if the US and South Africa became entangled in a de facto military and political alliance in Angola. As the 4 April 1975 staff study pointed out, "Civil disorder . . . will tend to draw in outsiders, although the extent and effect of such involvement is not foreseeable at this point."

By July Kissinger had changed his view of events in Angola from what they had been six months before. It was precipitated by his perception of a shifting balance of power, symbolized by the projection of Soviet force in Angola, and the need for the United States to assert itself in response. This more forceful tone was conveyed to the Soviets on 15 July 1975, when Kissinger referred to détente as the means to regulate a "competitive relationship."[57] There were other domestic pressures, as well, to which Kissinger was compelled to respond, especially the Secretary's rivalry with Secretary of Defense James Schlesinger. In early June, Schlesinger appeared before a closed hearing of the Senate Armed Services Committee, where he disclosed aerial photographs that seemed to reveal the emplacement of Soviet missile sites in Berbera, Somalia. Schlesinger's testimony was quickly leaked amidst rumors that Schlesinger, dissatisfied with Kissinger's reluctance to contest Soviet encroachment, was mustering support among the Joint Chiefs of Staff and the Republican right for a stronger policy toward the Soviets.

At the same time, there had been strong congressional and public support for the administration's use of military force to secure the release of the *Mayaguez* from the Cambodians in mid-May. The administration interpreted this as a "win," especially in light of Congress's refusal to authorize aid to Saigon in its last hours, and Gerald Ford's approval rating shot up eleven points.

On 18 July, three days after Kissinger committed the United States to a "competitive relationship" with the Soviet Union, President Ford approved the 40 Committee's recommendation for six million dollars in financial aid and arms shipments for the FNLA. Ford's decision authorized the CIA to intervene militarily in Angola under a program called IAFEATURE. Nine days later, on 27 July, Ford authorized an additional eight million dollars for arms and aircraft. Kissinger realized that the decision would lead to Davis' resignation but that it would also afford him the opportunity to "clean out" the Africa Bureau.[58]

As far as Kissinger and his advisers were concerned, this exercise in "controlled escalation" was intended to signal to Moscow that the United States had the resolve to prevent "the quick and cheap installation" of the MPLA in Angola. The "no-win" option was designed "to allow" the Soviet Union "to scale down their intervention without open confrontation," as Assistant Secretary of State for African Affairs William Schaufele would later testify.[59] Yet in tying this strategy to Holden Roberto and the FNLA, Kissinger was ignoring ten years of Africa Bureau experience with Roberto that, as early as 1964, concluded that he was an inept and effectual leader. Indeed, John Stockwell, who visited the FNLA camps in August 1975, and filed a report that encouraged the US to rush arms to the FNLA, nevertheless reflected accurately in his memoir that "I might have served my nation better if I had attempted to discourage them by emphasizing the frailty of the FNLA army to which the US was offering its prestige."[60]

Contrary to its purpose, the decision to increase American involvement escalated the conflict in Angola. In mid-July, the Chinese authorized Zaire to release to the FNLA large stocks of Chinese weapons. North Korea dispatched military instructors to the Chinese army to train MPLA troops, and Mobutu deployed Zairian paracommandos in combat in Angola. The FNLA also began receiving arms from Romania at this time. South Africa, encouraged by "winks and nods" from Washington, began providing clandestine assistance to the FNLA and UNITA. The British and French, as well, initiated their own covert assistance programs at this time.[61]

Fidel Castro had also made the fateful decision, based on the urgings of the MPLA and largely independent of Moscow, to dispatch combat troops to Angola, the first of which appeared in Luanda in mid-September. By the middle of December, more than three thousand Cuban combat troops had been transported to Angola with Soviet assistance.[62] Moscow had transferred approximately $500 million worth of arms by this time and had about two hundred advisers stationed in the country.

Despite this new infusion of external support to the FNLA, the MPLA had established control in eleven of fifteen Angolan provinces and the oil-rich province of Cabinda by late July. The MPLA also expelled the FNLA and UNITA from Luanda, which signaled the formal collapse of the transitional government established by the Alvor Accord.

The decision to intervene accentuated divisions in the State Department. Frustrated in his efforts to dissuade Kissinger, Nathaniel Davis quietly submitted his resignation as Assistant Secretary for African Affairs. Davis accepted a new assignment as ambassador to Switzerland and quickly left Washington on vacation to avoid having to testify before the Senate Foreign Relations African Subcommittee. At the same time, Kissinger, who was traveling, received press guidance that if asked about American military support for the FNLA, he should respond that "no US military equipment has been provided to [the]

FNLA, directly or through Zaire. Nor have US armored vehicles been provided to Zaire."[63]

Indeed, Kissinger seemed indifferent to the entire situation in Angola. When Acting Assistant Secretary for Africa Edward Mulcahy sent a memo to the Secretary informing him of a Portuguese request for humanitarian assistance in Angola, Kissinger replied flaccidly, "We'll help if [the] Portuguese don't back [the] MPLA." Despite Lisbon's flagrant assistance to the MPLA, Washington nevertheless contributed four commercial aircraft to a six million dollar Red Cross program that evacuated approximately 300,000 Portuguese Angolan refugees in September and October 1975.[64]

Neto's "Cheap" Victory

The months between July and October 1975 were the most critical for Angola and the evolution of Ford administration's strategy of preventing the Soviet Union from achieving a "cheap Neto Victory." The Alvor Accord had fallen by the wayside, and a subsequent attempt to revive it, in June 1975 in Nakuru, Kenya under President Kenyatta's auspices, failed. By the end of August, the FNLA and UNITA had withdrawn from the transitional government, leaving Luanda in control of the MPLA supported by the Portuguese High Commissioner. Washington also decided to deepen its involvement as President Ford on 20 August approved an additional $10.7 million for arms and ammunition for the FNLA and, for the first time, for UNITA. The view of the task force was that if the United States showed its resolve to support FNLA and UNITA through elections and independence on 11 November, the Soviets and the MPLA would compromise and seek a negotiated settlement.

Chief among Washington's miscalculations, however, was the underestimation of the South African factor and the paralyzing influence that Pretoria's involvement in Angola would have on American diplomacy.

Until this point, the South African government had been watching warily as events unfolded in the north. The South African government had had contacts with Savimbi earlier in the year in Europe and had held secret talks in May 1975 in Windhoek with Daniel Chipenda, who had defected to the FNLA. Ever cautious to commit South African troops to a hostile environment, Pretoria nevertheless entered the Angolan conflict on 11 August 1975 by stationing troops to protect the hydroelectric damn on the Cunene River at Calueque. Indeed, the deployment of South African troops gave Pretoria a base from which to expand deeper into Angola and coincided with an increase of American support. Although there was no formal agreement, the South Africans and the US, primarily through the CIA stations in Pretoria and Kinshasa, closely coordinated the escalation of their involvement. As Prime Minister John Vorster repeatedly told his ambassador in Washington, Pik Botha, Pretoria had assurances from "the highest levels of the US government," that Washington would stand by South Africa in Angola.[65]

By mid-October, the war in Angola was raging, and it appeared to be swinging in Washington's favor. A consolidated task force of Zairian, FNLA, and Portuguese troops, supported by American armaments, retook the town of Caxito and began a cautious advance on Luanda. At the same time, a South African armored column crossed the border into southern Angola in support of UNITA troops, and pressed on to take Benguela and Lobito. A second South African column drove the Katanganese out of Luso and moved toward Teixeira da Sousa on the eastern border, the last railroad post held by the MPLA. On 11 November, as the MPLA declared independence for Angola, a FNLA/Zairian column was advancing on Luanda, supported by South African supplied and manned artillery. Outside Luanda, the MPLA controlled only three of fifteen provinces. Despite the fact that Washington closed its consulate and CIA station in Luanda, Kissinger's strategy of preventing a cheap MPLA victory looked good.[66]

The Chinese, however, reached a different conclusion and decided to end their involvement in the unfolding war in Angola. In an elliptical but pointed farewell speech at the FNLA camp in DRC, the military group's leader, Li Tung, said that unity between Congolese, Angolans, and Chinese would be "eternal despite the distance separating them."[67]

Holding the Line on Angola

With Angola's independence, claimed on 11 November by the Soviet and Cuban-backed MPLA, Washington launched a new diplomatic offensive designed to deny international recognition to the government in Luanda. Predictably, Africa was the first battlefield in this diplomatic campaign, and Washington saw the government of Zaire as its key ally in this effort. Indeed, when the administration requested Congress to authorize a $79 million aid package in early November (the military portion increased from $3.8 million the year before to $39.4 million), the State Department issued guidance to American diplomats that contended that the support would help Zaire modernize its forces and meet legitimate defense needs. The guidance also made the point that $20 million of the aid request was to help Zaire through a "severe but temporary" balance of payments crisis brought on by a sharp fall in copper prices. As Washington instructed its diplomats in Africa, Zaire's"longer-range prospects are bright, but it has a serious short-term problem."[68]

The lack of agreement among African governments about whom to support in Angola nevertheless complicated the design of a diplomatic strategy to win African support for American objectives. At its July 1975 summit meeting in Kampala, Uganda the OAU, for example, issued a resolution that called for a government of national unity comprising all three liberation movements. In fact, there was no unanimity among African governments. To Moscow's chagrin, Uganda's General Idi Amin, who became chairman of the OAU at the Kampala meeting, explicitly allied himself with President Mobutu of Zaire in support of the FNLA.

More significant than Amin's partisan and mercurial leadership of the OAU was the uncertainty of Africa's key leaders over how to respond to the crisis in Angola. A meeting of the presidents of Zambia, Tanzania, and Botswana in April 1975, arrived at a decision to support Savimbi as the leader of Angola's government of national unity. Kaunda conveyed that decision to President Ford during his official visit to Washington in late April. Savimbi also won substantial backing from the Francophone African countries, especially the Ivory Coast, Senegal, and Cameroon, and was promised support by Nigeria and Ghana in the middle of 1975.[69]

The Ford Administration's campaign was further complicated in late November when it became apparent that Nigeria was about to recognize the MPLA government in Angola. This was especially troubling to Washington because on 8 November, three days before Angolan independence, the Nigerian foreign minister, Joseph Garba, denounced the Soviet Union for its intervention in Angola and suggested that independence be delayed for three weeks to allow more time for a solution to be found.[70]

Kissinger's former antagonist and now ambassador to Nigeria, Donald Easum, received instructions on 22 November to seek a meeting with "the highest official available" in the Nigerian government to head off recognition of the Angolan government. He was to remind the Nigerians of American support for the principle of territorial integrity in Africa, underscore Washington's "heightened concern" at the magnitude of Soviet and Cuban intervention on behalf of the MPLA, and remind the Nigerians that the US supported the OAU's effort to mediate an end to the Angolan conflict.[71]

Easum delivered Washington's demarché to Garba on the evening of 23 November. The Nigerian government, however, had just learned that South African troops had advanced from the Cunene River and were moving rapidly toward Luanda. After Easum delivered his message, Garba protested to the American ambassador South Africa's "invasion" of Angola and asked the American government to prevail on Pretoria to withdraw its invading forces. Twenty-four hours later, due in large part to what Garba referred to as a "tepid, noncommittal reply" from Washington, Nigeria announced its recognition of the MPLA-led Angolan government.

Two weeks later in New York, the newly appointed Assistant Secretary for African Affairs, William Schaufele, met with the Nigerian foreign minister to underscore that Angola was Washington's "principal preoccupation" and to enlist Nigeria's help to "make the MPLA more amenable" to negotiations with the other movements in Angola. Garba responded by telling Schaufele that the US failure to condemn South Africa's intervention in Angola, while openly criticizing the USSR, was the "critical factor" that had led Nigeria to recognize the MPLA. As the foreign minister put it, South Africa's intervention could be ignored when it was modest in strength, but "no self-respecting African state could stand by" when Pretoria invaded with substantial forces.

Schaufele responded to Garba that Angola did not present an "ideological problem" for Washington. Given the currrent state of US–Soviet relations, however, Moscow's presence in Angola threatened to undermine the diplomatic balance that had been so carefully negotiated in the détente process. Schaufele added that the Soviet role in Angola might adversely affect the "freedom from superpower involvement which exists in Africa and which is [a] fundamental tenet of US policy there." The meeting ended in a desultory fashion with Garba asking whether Secretary Kissinger intended to visit Nigeria in January, as the Secretary of State had earlier told Garba he would. Schaufele replied that Kissinger was giving "careful consideration" to a visit to Nigeria but could not name a date.[72]

Washington's effort to deny the MPLA international credibility was faltering. Indeed, in early December the Ford administration sent a cable to all diplomatic posts in Africa expressing its concern "over [the] possible unraveling of [the] African wait-and-see stance on Angolan recognition." In an effort to prevent the recognition by other governments, the American ambassadors in Dakar, Bangui, Libreville, Kinshasa, Abidjan, Monrovia, and Tunis, received instructions from Washington to "immediately request" a meeting with their host governments, who were known to be anti-MPLA, to ask "whether and how" Washington could help other African governments to "hold the line" against recognizing the MPLA, at least through the OAU summit meeting that had been scheduled for mid-January.[73]

To Donald Easum, watching from Lagos, the prospect of American diplomacy asserting influence on the Angolan situation was bleak. He cabled the State Department that "in [the] absence of any US expression of disapproval of South African intervention," the US position on Angola will continue to lose credibility especially as Washington continues to vigorously condemn Soviet and Cuban intervention. As Easum pointed out, Washington seemed "strangely reluctant" to criticize South African intervention, which was a "neuralgic issue" overriding all other concerns of most African governments.[74]

Easum was right. As Bernard Gwertzman of the *New York Times* commented at a State Department press briefing on Angola on 11 December 1975, "as far as details go . . . it has become a case of a lot of details about the Soviets and Cubans but nothing about the American involvement."[75]

Nevertheless, for Kissinger, at stake in Angola was America's credibility for supporting its allies. As he railed at a senior staff meeting on 18 December, "Our concern is not the economic wealth or the naval base. It has to do with the USSR operating eight thousand miles from home when all the surrounding states are asking for our help . . . . I don't care about the oil or the base, but I do care about the African reaction when they see the Soviets pull it off and we don't do anything. If the Europeans then say to themselves, 'If they can't hold Luanda, how can they defend Europe?' the Chinese will say we're a country that was run out of Indochina for 50,000 men and is now being run out of Angola for less than $50 million."[76]

Whereas Easum was concerned about the United States being stigmatized by an association with South Africa in Angola, Daniel Patrick Moynihan was trying to make the UN, to which he was the US ambassador, the primary arena for dealing with Angola. Like many Republicans, he was opposed to American intervention in Angola but felt that the Soviets should be vigorously denounced for violating the spirit of détente. He made the argument to Kissinger that "we should take the issue to the General Assembly and to the Security Council and never let the argument fade until the last Cuban was out of Africa."

Kissinger refused Moynihan's requests, but the Ambassador at the UN nonetheless increased the rhetoric by publicly attacking the Soviet Union as "a new colonial, imperialist power," that wanted to "recolonize" Africa. Pushing further, Moynihan, on 8 December, went to the rostrum at the General Assembly and charged that if only South Africa and not the Soviet Union were condemned, then "the General Assembly would be on record as having found that invasion of African countries by *some* white armies was perfectly acceptable." On 10 December, African states withdrew a proposed General Assembly resolution condemning only South Africa's intervention in Angola. For the first time in at least a decade, the United States had managed to deprive the Soviets of a General Assembly majority on an issue of colonialism and imperialism. As Washington put it, "The withdrawal of the amendment by the Africans was indeed a political setback for the communists."[77]

By mid-December, fourteen African states had recognized the MPLA. Washington nevertheless redoubled its efforts to prevent the MPLA from being acknowledged by the OAU as the legitimate government of Angola. As the State Department framed the issue for its NATO allies, OAU recognition of the MPLA would "so harden" the MPLA's position that it would make a negotiated settlement impossible and "would encourage more intervention and bloodshed." Washington's objective was to maintain a military "stalemate," to bring about negotiations among the FNLA, UNITA, and the MPLA. True, Washington acknowledged to its diplomats at NATO and in Europe, South African intervention had "shaken some key African states that had originally planned to sit on the fence [notably Nigeria and Ghana]," and added, "There is worrisome slippage here, and we are concerned." Still, the State Department professed to understand the embarrassment caused by South Africa's support for UNITA but insisted that the "need for some kind of military balance seems to us [the] overriding [concern] for the moment."[78]

In an ultimately clumsy effort to shore up the diplomatic "slippage" in Africa, President Ford sent a letter on 3 January to a number of

African heads of state underscoring the administration's support for an end to foreign intervention and the creation of a government of national unity in Angola. Ford also emphasized that United States policy was intended to "counter efforts by the Soviet Union to impose one faction as the government of Angola." The letter concluded by pointing out that the mid-January OAU meeting would be important in promoting a "quick finish" to the Angolan civil war and urged the African leaders to insist on an end to foreign intervention in Angola and bring about negotiations between the rival groups.

The stratagem backfired, however, when the Nigerian government released the letter to local newspapers, who criticized it as overbearing, insulting, and patronizing. Indeed, the letter and its public release inflamed anti-American sentiment in Nigeria and led to violent demonstrations outside the US consulates in Kaduna and Ibadan and the embassy in Lagos.[79]

Endgame on Angola

Despite Moynihan's success at the UN, the administration's strategy of trying to deny the MPLA-controlled government recognition by the OAU, while simultaneously strengthening the FNLA and UNITA militarily, proved to be unworkable. The public mood was against any covert paramilitary operation in Africa or anywhere else. Although details of the program had begun to leak into the press, the full scope of the program was published on 13 December in the *New York Times* in an article by Seymour Hersh. Daniel Patrick Moynihan, however, provoked a firestorm of controversy when he admitted on a Sunday talk show on 14 December that "we have given arms, as I understand, to the Government of Zaire and the Government of Zambia, which have passed them on" to the FNLA and UNITA. With these comments, Moynihan inadvertently became the first American official to confirm Washington's secret involvement in the Angolan conflict. Moynihan also helped to send alarms when he warned on the program that if the Soviet Union was successful in Angola, it would then control a "large chunk of Africa" and pose a military threat to Brazil. "The world will be different in the aftermath, if they succeed," the ambassador said.

The administration's most significant problem, however, was in Congress. In the wake of Watergate, the fall of Vietnam, and ongoing Congressional investigations into past CIA covert activities, Congress had no interest in supporting what appeared to be another dubious covert operation in Angola. Republicans in particular were increasingly strident in their criticism of the Ford Administration's foreign policy, especially détente.[80] On the issue of Angola, they contended that the administration should have suspended grain sales to the Soviet Union or broken off talks on strategic arms limitations until Moscow stopped transferring arms and Cuba had withdrawn its forces. The mood was reflected in a comment that the conservative senator from Arizona, Barry Goldwater, made to Pik Botha, South Africa's ambassador to the US, when he said, "This goddamn Kissinger declares wars all over the world that he doesn't want to win." To the administration, the Congress seemed to be a "rogue elephant," lacking political leadership. As President Ford put it, "Congress simply was more rebellious, more assertive of its rights and privileges—and also more irresponsible—than it had been for years." Stating it more forcefully, Kissinger subsequently wrote, "The Congress elected in the McGovernite landslide [of 1974] represented the high point of the radical protest. It was violently opposed to intervention abroad, especially in the developing world, ever suspicious of the CIA, deeply hostile to covert operations, and distrustful of the veracity of the executive branch."[81]

The antagonisms between the administration and Congress came to a head in late November when the White House requested that twenty-eight million dollars in defense funds be reprogrammed for additional covert assistance to the FNLA and UNITA. In response to the request, Senator Dick Clark of Iowa sponsored an amendment to the Foreign Assistance Act that prohibited the transfer of the funds, which President Ford vetoed. Not to be out-maneuvered, on 19 December, Senator John Tunney (D-CA) offered an amendment to the Defense Appropriations Bill that would terminate all funds for covert military assistance to anti-Soviet factions in Angola. This amendment passed, effectively ending American military support for the FNLA and UNITA.

The administration nevertheless gamely pressed on. The day after the Tunney amendment passed, US ambassadors in Libreville, Dakar, Monrovia, Abidjan, and Bangui received instructions to tell their host governments and colleagues in the diplomatic corps that "despite recent Congressional discussions, [the] US still has sufficient funds to continue our program of resistance to Soviet intervention over the immediate period ahead." The ambassadors were urged to tell their African interlocutors that they must "keep steady [the] course," and that the administration had the opportunity to go back to the Congress for more funds in January.[82]

A 24 December message from Kissinger to US ambassadors in Europe instructed the American diplomats to tell their counterparts that the Senate decision to cut off funds "has in no way weakened our determination to proceed with our program of assisting FNLA and UNITA . . . . There are significant funds remaining at our disposal to support current endeavors in Angola and we will use them." In an effort to regain the diplomatic initiative, Kissinger, on the same day, held a press conference in which he called on South Africa along with Cuba to withdraw their forces from Angola.[83]

Trying to maintain the upbeat tone at the 24 December ceremony in Kinshasa where he presented his credentials, the new American ambassador to Zaire, Walter Cutler, told President Mobutu that there had been positive developments on Angola. President Ford had taken a firm line publicly on Soviet military movements in Africa, Gulf Oil refused to make payments to the Luanda regime, and Barbados and Trinidad had denied transit facilities to Cuban flights bound for Angola. To Cutler, Mobutu was encouraged by these developments and expressed confidence that MPLA would not be recognized at the OAU meeting in January.[84]

On 14 January, the OAU met in Addis Ababa to vote on a Nigerian-sponsored resolution calling for the recognition of the MPLA as the only rightful Angolan government. The outcome was a deadlock, with twenty-two of the forty-six member states voting for immediate recognition of the MPLA as the legal government of Angola, while another twenty-two insisted on the need for creating a Government of National Unity. Ethiopia, the host nation, abstained, as did Uganda, the OAU chairman's country. The members also divided evenly between those who wanted to condemn all forms of external intervention and those who wanted to endorse the "positive" role of Russia and Cuba. The OAU did not even agree on whether to condemn South Africa for its intervention in Angola, which Pretoria interpreted as an important diplomatic victory.

Whatever encouragement the US took from this stalemate was undone on 11 February 1976, when the OAU Council of Ministers decided by a simple majority to recognize the MPLA as the legal government of Angola.

American policy toward Angola, conceptually flawed and thwarted in Congress, was equally unsuccessful with Moscow. On 9 December, the White House summoned Soviet ambassador Anatoly Dobrynin to meet with President Ford. According to Dobrynin, Ford said that the

US had no significant strategic interests in Angola but that the events there increasingly were being perceived in the US as a test of the policy of détente. Ford asked whether it was necessary for both "countries to challenge each other in such a faraway place which was of no particular value to either of them?" The American president then proposed that Washington and Moscow jointly appeal to the factions in Angola to stop the war and agree to a peaceful settlement, and call on "all interested states to stop interfering in Angola by sending arms there."[85]

At virtually the same time that Dobrynin was meeting with Ford, Moscow indicated to President Mobutu that it wanted to improve relations between the USSR and Zaire. Moscow proposed that the two countries issue a joint condemnation of South African and mercenary intervention in Angola and announce that the USSR is ready to support Zairean peace initiatives. Assessing the overture, Acting Assistant Secretary for Africa Edward Mulcahy suggested to Kissinger that the Congolese should "play along" to see whether the Soviets were prepared to disengage from Angola.[86]

Not surprisingly, Moscow's move did not go anywhere. Unfortunately for the Ford Administration, neither did the President's conversation with Ambassador Dobrynin. In response to that meeting, Moscow sent an informal note to Washington in which they characterized the FNLA and UNITA as "separatist groups" that could not be equated with the "lawful" MPLA government. Invoking their long-held views about "just wars of liberation," Moscow made the further point that foreign military intervention in Angola should be halted—except for Soviet support to the MPLA. In analyzing the note, William Schaufele, Assistant Secretary for Africa, concluded that Moscow was not serious about negotiating on Angola, "but would be concerned if the US determination to resist the Soviet encroachment would have an unfavorable effect on détente."[87]

Angola increasingly was being perceived as the crucial test of détente, and the policy was failing badly. On 23 December, Kissinger suggested to Dobrynin that the OAU mediate an end to Angola's civil war. Moscow, however, rejected this proposal and accused Washington of "wrecking the normal functioning of the transitional government in Angola." Indeed, in the Kremlin's view, the US was engaged in many conflicts around the world, was consolidating its influence in the Middle East, and had overthrown the democratically elected socialist government in Chile. Therefore, Moscow did not feel compelled to accept Soviet support for the MPLA as a violation of détente.[88]

Toward the end of January, Kissinger went to Moscow on a trip that had originally been scheduled for December but that had to be postponed because of the controversy in Congress over Angola. Kissinger's primary objective was to explore whether it would be possible to conclude a new Strategic Arms Limitation Treaty (SALT) with the Soviet Union in 1976. As President Ford saw it, "Success with SALT . . . would go a long way to ensuring" his election in November 1976.[89] Another objective, although clearly secondary, was to persuade Moscow to reduce its involvement in Angola.

In fact, Kissinger's visit to Moscow was the administration's last chance to show Congress and the American public that the administration could assert influence on Soviet activities. In an effort to prepare the way, in a speech in St. Louis on 5 January 1976, President Ford struck a challenging tone. He warned the Soviet Union that its attempt "to take unilateral advantage of the Angolan problem is inconsistent with the basic principles of US-Soviet relations. If it continues, damage to our broader relations will be unavoidable." The president then undercut his message by announcing a new grain deal with the Soviet Union that would enable Moscow to buy six to eight million metric tons per year for five years. As Ford put it, suspension of the agreement would "produce no immediate gain in diplomatic leverage."[90]

On the plane to Moscow with Kissinger, the Secretary and his advisers told reporters that diplomatic retaliation against Soviet activity in Angola would take several forms. The administration would continue to oppose a Palestinian presence in the Geneva talks on the Middle East that the Soviet Union was chairing, and there could be further delay of a visit to Washington by Soviet leader Brezhnev for the fourth US-Soviet summit of the Nixon-Ford era. Yet in the negotiations in Moscow, Brezhnev was unmoved by Kissinger's pressures on Angola. The Soviet leader refused to engage the issue when it was raised, insisting that the fighting in Angola was "a war of national liberation" and was therefore not relevant to détente.

On 27 January 1976, the House of Representatives ignored a last minute plea from President Ford to House Speaker Carl Albert and voted overwhelmingly (323–99) to block an amendment to the defense appropriations bill that would have restored funding for American support to the FNLA and UNITA. In a letter to Albert, Ford told the Speaker that "resistance to Soviet expansion by military means must be a fundamental element of US foreign policy . . . . There must be no question in Angola or elsewhere in the world of American resolve in this regard." Yet on the floor of the House, Albert spoke forcefully in favor of the cutoff. "This is a typical Ford operation: wave your hand, make a gesture, and that's the end of it." Albert said aid should be blocked because the US was not prepared to match Soviet and Cuban support for its Angolan faction.[91]

The Ford Administration's strategy for responding to the crisis in Angola never would have succeeded, even though Kissinger claimed in his memoirs that he was on the brink of success only to be undermined by the "McGovernite" Congress that "exploded" his policy.[92] The Secretary's inability to read accurately the national and Congressional lack of support for covert operations in foreign lands in the wake of the US experience in Vietnam was only part of the problem.

Kissinger's Angola policy suffered from even deeper flaws. The fact that NSSM 39 "consigned" Africa to the bottom of the US foreign policy agenda ensured that Kissinger had no understanding of the complexities of an area in which he had no interest and no previous experience. His contempt for most of the professionals serving in the Africa Bureau and for its governing "ethos" ensured that he would ignore more than a decade of intelligence and diplomatic analyses that warned against tying American prestige to Holden Roberto, a nationalist leader who was "rigidly uncompromising." Kissinger also disregarded those who contended that American interests in Angola were best served by maintaining a balance among the country's three nationalist organizations instead of siding with one or more groups. Moreover, to fire two assistant secretaries within fifteen months because of their opposition to covert military operations in Angola effectively ended all policy debate within the Administration and ensured that Kissinger's Soviet-focused policy would prevail, with all of its consequences.

It is with some interest, therefore, that Piero Gleijeses, in his important and comprehensive study of the Angolan civil war, contended that it is "fair . . . to conclude that IAFEATURE could have succeeded and the cost for the United States—at least in the short and medium term—would have been low."[93] The reason that US policy in Angola failed, according to Gleijeses, is that IAFEATURE did not take into account the role of the Cubans and the impact Cuban forces would have on the balance of military power in the country. Of course, IAFEATURE also did not take into account how the South African intervention would undermine American efforts to persuade the OAU not to recognize the legitimacy of the MPLA government, handing Washington a significant diplomatic defeat.

More significant than either the impact of the Cubans or South Africans on US policy in Angola was Kissinger's inability to come terms with the fact that, in the wake of Vietnam, Congress, and by extension, the American public, would not support another covert military operation in a far-off land where US interests appeared minimal.

Chapter 6

Conclusion

The story of American foreign policy toward Portugal and its colonial empire is among the most tragic of the decolonization process that began in Sub-Saharan Africa in Ghana in 1957 and concluded in Namibia in 1990. For Portugal, shedding its colonial empire enabled the country to embark on a new era of democratization, growth, and development. In Africa, Portuguese colonialism, combined with the impact of the Cold War, ensured that the people of Angola, Mozambique, and Guinea-Bissau would begin the independence era in poverty and conflict. In fact, the superpower struggle for influence in Africa during the Cold War is among the most defining characteristics of the first generation of Africa's era of independence.

From an American perspective, the effort to induce Portugal to grant independence to its territories was a worthy one. At least two questions emerge, however: why was the effort not successful and why was it not sustained over the course of the Kennedy, Johnson, and Nixon administrations?

Prime Minister Antonio Salazar, for his part, had no intention of changing Portugal's relationship with its colonies. Angola, Mozambique, and Guinea-Bissau, in addition to their colonies in Asia, were an integral part of Portugal's national character and economy. The fact that the fledgling nationalist organizations in these colonies were able to mount sporadic but sustained military campaigns only deepened Salazar's determination to retain control of the colonies. Pressure from the United States added to his resolve.

The movement toward self-determination in Africa and in the Portuguese colonies, nevertheless, put unwelcome pressure on officials in Lisbon. These pressures encouraged "reformist" elements in the

Portuguese government to take action to avoid a protracted and ultimately humiliating military engagement in Africa, such as the effort in April 1961 by Defense Minister Botelho Moniz to depose Salazar. Moniz's frustrations were later reflected in General Spínola's equally unsuccessful effort to convince Salazar's successor, Marcello Caetano, to negotiate a solution to the war with PAIGC leader Amilcar Cabral and President Leopold Senghor of Senegal. The coup of 25 April 1974 was fuelled by these frustrations.

Initially, the United States tried to exploit the turmoil within the Portuguese government. Signals of support by Ambassador Elbrick for General Moniz, the imposition of an arms embargo on the use of American arms in Angola, and maneuverings at the United Nations, among other pressures, generated no sustained movement toward the fundamental objective of independence for the colonies. Although at the time, the extension of financial support to nationalist leaders Eduardo Mondlane and Holden Roberto was a bold signal of American support for African aspirations, the gesture did little to further American efforts. Without a sustained engagement in these issues, Washington found itself at a distinct disadvantage when change occurred.

Portugal's threats to deny Washington access to the Azores was only part of the reason that the United States could not facilitate self-determination in Angola and Mozambique. Indeed, when the Johnson administration tried a different tact by restricting Roberto's access to American diplomats and selling Portugal twenty B-26 aircraft in 1965 in the context of the "Anderson Plan," Lisbon was still not willing to accommodate pressures for self-determination in Africa. In fact, the United States was not prepared to devote the political and diplomatic resources required to pressure Portugal into a different stance on its colonial possessions. Adlai Stevenson's votes against Portuguese colonialism in the Security Council in 1961 sent a signal that the United States was ultimately unable to transform into a sustainable policy. President Kennedy's decision on 19 July 1963 to "seek the best of both worlds" and more significantly to focus pressure on South Africa instead of Portugal to shore up American influence in Africa, put the United States on a new, less confrontational course with respect to the decolonization of Portugal's colonies.

This new course was defined by ensuring that the United States would not lose access to the Azores while at the same time focusing on other issues in Africa, Vietnam, and elsewhere. Indeed, President Johnson's Africa Day speech on 26 May 1966, not only failed to mention Portugal and its colonies in Africa but it was one more signal to Lisbon that there was no cost for trying to maintain its ever-weakening policy in Africa.

Richard Nixon's comment to Franco Nogueira on 6 April 1969 that he would "never do . . . what Kennedy did" to Portugal, was not so much an about-face for American policy toward Portugal as it was a sharp acceleration of the emerging approach. National Security Study Memorandum 39 (NSSM 39), however, broke new ground in American policy toward Portugal, Angola, and Mozambique by rejecting the Kennedy-Johnson assumption of the inevitability of self-determination in Africa in favor of a strategy that would encourage incremental reforms by working through the colonial and white minority governments in the region. This strategy laid the groundwork for normalization of relations with Lisbon, although not to the degree that the increasingly desperate Salazar-Caetano governments needed to sustain their faltering military efforts. The shift also ensured that the US would not be well positioned to respond to the vacuum of power created by the revolution of 25 April 1974.

As a result of the State Department's lack of engagement in Portugal, the Nixon administration was unaware of General Spínola's furious reaction to his stymied efforts to find a political solution to the costly and unsustainable war effort in Guinea-Bissau. Senior officials in the Nixon administration were also unaware that the US intelligence community was reporting that the insurgencies in Angola and Mozambique were getting stronger and not weaker. In fact there was a remarkable consistency to American intelligence reporting for over a decade, from the early 1960s through the early 1970s, that concluded that Portugal could not sustain control of its African colonies. In many reports, analysts also predicted a costly outcome to Portugal's efforts to maintain its African empire.

This intelligence was ignored by NSC Adviser Henry Kissinger and his subordinates who guided NSSM 39 through the bureaucratic process. In their view, "constructive change" could only come through the colonial and white minority regimes. The insurgencies of the nationalist organizations offered no hope for political change. The White House, in the early 1970s, was much more interested in the management of relations with the largest military powers, the Soviet Union and China, and other regional issues such as the Middle East. The battle against the spread of Communism in Africa was fought not only through the policy of détente with the Soviet Union and the opening of relations with the People's Republic of China, but by relying on smaller powers, such as Portugal and South Africa, to contain the spread of Soviet and, to a lesser degree, Chinese influence in Southern Africa. In the case of Portugal, Washington's focus on other priorities obscured the inherent weakness of the Caetano government and the insufficiency of this containment strategy.

Transitioning to the Opposition

One of the underlying themes of the American experience in Angola and Mozambique was the degree to which US policy sought to reach out to opposition leaders who had the potential to be in power at some undetermined point in the future. The challenge was stated succinctly in 1962 by Walt W. Rostow, then director of the Policy Planning Staff, when he identified in a draft policy document a central problem in American foreign policy as one "of developing *rapport* and understanding with the next government while dealing effectively with the current one."[1] Initially, in Portugal, Ambassador Elbrick cultivated quiet contacts with General Moniz. Under Ambassador Bennett there were surreptitious meetings with Mário Soares, head of the Portuguese Socialist Party. Beyond that, successive ambassadors and embassy personnel, especially military attaches, did little to cultivate relations with a broad array of individuals from across the political spectrum, especially those on the far left. Moreover, there is no evidence that the CIA was any more effective in this respect. In this instance, Washington provided little encouragement for American officials to deviate from normal diplomatic practice, or the "rules of propriety."

The broad network of contacts that Ambassador Carlucci and his team in Portugal established in the wake of the revolution underscored the importance of maintaining relations with representatives of all military, political, and social factions, and at various levels. Equally important to Carlucci's success was the credibility and influence he was able to yield in Washington. Without that, the value of his embassy's in-depth reporting and understanding of Portugal's rapidly shifting political terrain would have not generated the diplomatic results that it did.

The US experience in Angola and Mozambique underscores a different dimension to the challenge of protecting US interests in a situation of prospective change, or as Dean Rusk articulated it, "When you know . . . that a regime is not viable."[2] President Kennedy, Robert F. Kennedy, G. Mennen Williams, and Wayne Fredericks, among others, understood that individuals such as Holden Roberto and

Eduardo Mondlane represented Africa's future leaders. In that respect, it made sense to develop relations with them and, to a certain degree, to put the prestige of the United States behind them even though relations with the nationalists came at a cost, albeit a manageable cost. Kissinger never embraced this view, and went as far as firing his assistant secretary of state, Donald Easum, for contacting FRELIMO leader eight months after the coup and only six months before Mozambique's independence.

In the case of Angola, American support became locked on Roberto and the FNLA even when his leadership was determined to be ineffective and mercurial, at best. Secretary Kissinger's reliance on the FNLA to represent American interests during Angola's transition to independence was a serious error in judgment. It also reflected his unwillingness to accept analyses and information that ran counter to his strongly held views, even when it came from his top regional advisers, in this case, the Assistant Secretaries of State for Africa, Donald Easum and Nathaniel Davis. The more appropriate strategy would have been for the United States to have avoided engagement in a conflict in Angola, especially when there was no support in Congress for such an undertaking and when Washington had no effective allies in the country or region.

American policymakers were unable to develop contacts with other opposition groups in Portuguese Africa, especially the PAIGC and, after the death of Eduardo Mondlane, FRELIMO. In these instances, as well as the Senghor-Spínola effort to persuade Lisbon of the need for negotiations with the PAIGC, there was no bureaucratic incentive for engagement, largely because the administration's priorities were elsewhere and the prospects for success seemingly minimal.

The Postcolonial Legacy

Nearly thirty years after Mozambique achieved its independence, the country has established an enduring reputation for good governance and sound economic management. It is also one of the poorest countries in the world. Its poverty stems not only from the impact of Portuguese colonialism, but from the Marxist policies FRELIMO pursued when it assumed control of the country and more recently, like many countries in Africa, the HIV/AIDS pandemic. Mozambique's poverty was deepened by the shadowy organization, subsequently known as the Mozambican National Resistance (RENAMO), that the white-minority government in Rhodesia established in 1976 to harass the government of Samora Machel. When Zimbabwe became independent in 1980, South Africa's military intelligence assumed a supporting role for the insurgency. By 1990, the civil war in Mozambique had cost the country an estimated $15 billion, rendered about two million homeless, and had taken nearly one million lives.[3]

The war came to an end in 1992, after negotiations facilitated by the Sant Egidio Community, a Catholic lay organization closely associated with the Vatican. Successful national elections, in which RENAMO participated, were held in October 1994. At the same time, under the leadership of President Joaquim Chissano, FRELIMO jettisoned its statist economic policies and began working closely with the World Bank and the International Monetary Fund (IMF). After more than a decade, the Mozambican economy is growing as fast as any in Africa and foreign direct investment has begun to enter the country. The country still faces tremendous capacity, infrastructure, and capital challenges that will not be easily resolved. Nevertheless, Mozambique has established itself as one of Africa's more successful democracies and has maintained cordial relations with the United States throughout this period.

Peace, on the other hand, only came to Angola on 4 April 2002, when the government and UNITA signed a comprehensive agreement to end the fighting in the wake of the death of Jonas Savimbi. For twenty-seven years, from 1975 until 2002, Angola had been in a virtual state of war, except for the aftermath of the signing of the Bicesse Accords and the elections of 1992. The reconstruction of Angola could not be a more challenging prospect, with nearly one-quarter of its population internally displaced, an estimated ten million land mines spread throughout the country, and a leadership that has governed without interruption during the postcolonial era.

The challenge to Angola is the degree to which the government can deploy the wealth from its natural resources, especially oil, on behalf of the development of the Angolan people. Clearly, this requires a new degree of commitment to transparency and accountability, and a willingness to work with institutions such as the World Bank and the IMF. Angola needs to diversify its economy beyond the oil sector, especially in the light manufacturing and agricultural sectors. Regular national elections also will be vital to embarking on a truly democratic postconflict era.

In certain respects, Portugal was the biggest beneficiary of the loss of its empire as it fully integrated into Europe. In the aftermath of the revolution, Portugal placed an emphasis on its relations with Western

Europe to stimulate economic development in the country and stabilize its fragile democracy. On 1 January 1986, the country gained formal admission to the European Economic Commission, and in its first five years gained $1.7 billion in grants alone.

Five hundred years of colonial rule, however, left Portugal looking for a new relationship with its former colonies in Africa. With no federal or commonwealth structure to build on, as General Spínola had desired, Portugal found it most difficult to redefine its role in Africa, especially given its lack of economic strength. The country did establish a positive relationship with Guinea-Bissau. In 1984, Lisbon played a constructive role in the Nkomati Accords between South Africa and Mozambique in which Pretoria agreed to cease support for RENAMO and Maputo agreed not to allow its territory to be used as a base from which guerrilla attacks by the African National Congress could be launched against South Africa. In Angola, Portugal, along with the United States and Russia, formed the "troika" that helped to negotiate the Bicesse Accords and the implementation of the Lusaka Accords in the mid-1990s.[4] Nevertheless, Portugal has faced a significant challenge in trying to redefine and reestablish its relations with its former African colonies.

American policy toward Angola and Mozambique was guided by the dictates of the Cold War through the fall of the Berlin Wall in 1989. The ongoing presence of Cuban troops in Angola ensured that the Carter Administration would pay attention to the country, although that administration's top priority in Africa was facilitating Zimbabwe's transition to independence and trying to induce South Africa to grant independence to Namibia. In pursuing its policy of Constructive Engagement, the Reagan administration gave military support to UNITA in an effort to prevent an outright Soviet/Cuban victory. At the same time, it developed a diplomatic architecture that, combined with the decision by Soviet President Mikhail Gorbachev to seek a political solution to Southern Africa's wars, enabled troops from South Africa and Cuba to leave Angolan soil and contributed to Namibia's transition to independence.

Washington would not formally recognize the Angolan government until 1993, when President Bill Clinton normalized relations. The Clinton administration subsequently established the US-Angola Bilateral Consultative Commission to strengthen and deepen a relationship that is one of the most important that the US has in Sub-Saharan Africa. The improvement in relations has continued during the presidency of George W. Bush. Luanda's increasingly pragmatic pursuit of its national interests and its need to obtain resources to rehabilitate the country, combined with America's growing reliance on Angola's oil, suggests that the bilateral relationship will continue to grow in significance to both countries, the colonial past notwithstanding.

Appendix

Author's Interviews

Aniceto Afonso • Vitor Alves • George W. Anderson • Manuel Antonio • Melo Antunes • William Attwood • Mario Azvedo • Stan Baldwin • Francisco Pinto Balsemão • George Ball • Mario Begonha • W. Tapley Bennett, Jr. • William Blue • William Brubeck • McGeorge Bundy • Senator Dick Clark • Jorge Campinos • Palma Carlos • Frank Carlucci • Fritz Caspari • Daniel Chipenda • Vitor Crespo • Silva Cunha • Walter Cutler • Will Dupree • Donald Easum • Carlos Fabião • Luis Esteves Fernandes • Rita Ferreira • Jack Foley • José Manuel Fragoso • Wayne Fredericks • Ed Fuget • João Godinho • Arthur Goldberg • U. Alexis Johnson • Edward K. Hamilton • Nicholas Katzenbach • William Kelly • Colin Legum • Wingate Lloyd • Alan Lukens • Calvet de Magalhães • Marcello Mathias • Donald McHenry • Robert McCloskey • Adriano Moreira • Roger Morris • Bill Moyers • Edward Mulcahy • Lordes Texeira de Mota • Mario Neves • David Newsom • Albino Nogueira • Franco Nogueira • Herbert Okun • Barbosa Pereira • Vasco Futsher Pereira • Don Peterson • Richard St. F. Post • Jim Potts • Manes Preto • Silvestre Martins Rodriguez • E. M. Rabenold, Jr. • F. R. Rarig • Donald Rumsfeld • Dean Rusk • Jorge Sampaião • Mike Samuels • William Schaufele • James Schlesinger • Stuart Nash Scott • Helmut Sonnenfeldt • Ted Sorenson • António de Spinola • Walter Stoessel • James Symington • João Hall Themido • Sheldon Vance • Vernon Walters • Salgado Zenha

Acronyms

AID	Agency for International Development
ALC	African Liberation Committee
CDS	Social Democratic Center
CEUD	Electoral Committee of Democratic Unity
CIA	Central Intelligence Agency
COPCON	Continental Operations
DDRS	Declassified Documents Reference System
DRC	Democratic Republic of the Congo
FES	Frederich Ebert Foundation
FNLA	Front for the National Liberation of Angola
FRELIMO	Front for the Liberation of Mozambique
GNP	Gross National Product
GPRA	Provisional Government of the Algerian Revolution
GRAE	Revolutionary Government of Angola in Exile
ILO	International Labor Organization
IMF	International Monetary Fund
INR	Bureau of Intelligence and Research
JSN	Junta of National Salvation
MAAG	Military Assistance Advisory Group
MDP	Portunguese Democratic Movement
MFA	Armed Forces Movement
MFN	Most Favored Nation
MPLA	Popular Movement for the Liberation of Angola
NASA	National Aeronautics and Space Administration
NATO	North Atlantic Treaty Organization
NBC	National Broadcasting Corporation
NEC	National Electoral Commission
NIO	National Intelligence Officer
NSC	National Security Council
NSSM	National Security Study Memorandum
OAU	Organization of African Unity

PAIGC	African Party of Independence of Guinea and Cape Verde
PCP	Portuguese Communist Party
PDA	Democratic Party of Angola
PFIAB	President's Foreign Intelligence Advisory Board
PIDE	International Police for State Defense
PPP	Popular Democratic Party
PPP	Progressive Party
PSP	Portuguese Socialist Party
RENAMO	Mozambican National Resistance
RTP	Portuguese National Television
SALT	Strategic Arms Limitations Treaty
UK	United Kingdom
UN	United Nations
UNITA	National Union for the Total Independence of Angola
UPA	United Peoples of Angola
US	United States
USC	University of Southern California
USIA	United States Information Agency
USSR	United Soviet Socialist Republics

Notes

[1]*Keesing Contemporary Record*, "Facts on File." (22–28 September 1960), XX: 1039, 325. *Time* (3 October 1960), 20.
[2]Note that the Congo was called The Democratic Republic of the Congo (CDR) starting at independence in 1960. In 1970, President Mobutu renamed the country Zaire. The name was changed back to the Congo or CDR in 1999. For the sake of continuity, this text refers to it as the Congo or CDR throughout.
[3]*New York Times*, 15 December 1960, p. 1. Telephone interview, Dr. Zelma Watson George, 12 February 1984.
[4]Waldemar A. Nielsen, *The Great Powers and Africa* (New York: Praeger Publishers, 1969), 277–278; Dean Rusk, *As I Saw It* (New York: Penguin Books, 1990), p. 272.
[5]Nikita S. Khrushchev, "For New Victories for the World Communist Movement," *World Marxist Review: Problems of Peace and Socialism* 4, no. 1 (January 1961): 13–17.
[6]Arthur M. Schlesinger, Jr., *A Thousand Days* (Boston: Houghton Mifflin Company, 1965), p. 302.
[7]John F. Kennedy, *Public Papers, 1961* (Washington, DC: Government Printing Office, GPO, 1962), p. 1. For an interesting comment on Kennedy's inaugural speech, see Robert Dallek, *The American Style of Foreign Policy* (New York: Alfred A. Knopf, 1983), pp. 223–224.
[8]Walt W. Rostow, Guerrilla Warfare in the Underdeveloped Areas. *The Dept. of State Bulletin,* Vol. XIV, no. 1154, 7 August 1961, p. 235.
[9]Circular Instruction, Joint State/AID/Defense message for the Ambassador, PRC53595, 16 April 1962; A Summary of US Military Counterinsurgency Accomplishments since 1 January 1961, DDRS(75)242C; Interview, U. Alexis Johnson, 13 May 1984, Washington, DC.
[10]Arthur M. Schlesinger, Jr. *Robert Kennedy and His Times* (Boston: Houghton Mifflin, 1978), p. 461.
[11]"National Security Policy" (S/P, Draft, 26 March 1962), DDRS(77)338A.
[12]NSC 2/1: "Base Rights in Greenland, Iceland and the Azores," 25 November 1947, UPA: Documents of the National Security Council, 1947–1977, Reel 1, 0037; Quote of Dean Acheson found in William Minter, *Portuguese Africa and the West,* p. 88. (London: Penguin Books, 1972); Untitled, Undated, DDRS(77)207A, pp. 9–10.
[13]Embtel, 1611 (Section one of two), Delhi, 6 December 1961, NSF, JFKL.
[14]Douglas L. Wheeler, "Nightmare Republic: Portugal, 1910–1926," *History Today* (September 1981), pp. 5–10.
[15]Franco Nogueira, *Salazar, Vol. I* (Coimbra: Atlantida Editora, 1976), p. 281.

[15]Franco Nogueira, *Salazar, Vol. I* (Coimbra: Atlantida Editora, 1976), p. 281.
[16]Embtel, Lisbon, 124, 23 July 1961.
[17]Tom Gallagher, *Portugal: A Twentieth Century Interpretation* (Manchester: Manchester University Press, 1983), pp. 66–73; Antonio de Figueiredo, *Portugal: Fifty Years of Dictatorship* (New York: Holmes and Meier Publishers, Inc., 1975), pp. 68–72.
[18]Douglas L. Wheeler, "In the Service of Order: The Portuguese Political Police and the British, German and Spanish Intelligence, 1932–1945," *Journal of Contemporary History,* Vol. 18 (1983), pp. 3, 18–19.
[19]Hugh Kay, *Salazar and Modern Portugal* (New York: Hawthorn Books, Inc., 1970), p. 87; Gallagher, *Portugal: A Twentieth Century Interpretation*, p.74; Manuel De Lucena, "The Evolution of Portuguese Corporatism Under Salazar and Caetano," in *Contemporary Portugal: The Revolution and its Antecedents*, edited by Lawrence S. Graham and Harry M. Makler (Austin: University of Texas Press, 1979), p. 64.
[20]Antonio de Figueiredo, *Portugal: Fifty Years of Dictatorship,* pp. 36, 204.
[21]Gilberto Freyre, *Um Brasileiro em Terras Portuguesas* (Lisboa: Edicao Livros do Brasil, 1952); see also Marvin Harris, *Portugal's African "Wards,"* Africa Today Pamphlets: 2 (New York: American Committee on Africa, 1958), p. 3, and ibid, *passim*.
[22]Gerald J. Bender, *Angola under the Portuguese* (Los Angeles: University of California Press, 1978), pp. 3–9.
[23]George Ball, *Discipline of Power*, p. 277. Hugh Kay, *Salazar and Modern Portugal*, pp. 16, 19.
[24]"Do Senhor George Kennan ao Doutor Oliveira Salazar," no. 1: 297, Lisbon, 25 October 1943, in *Documentos* (Lisboa: Ministerios dos Negocios Estrangeiros, 1946), p. 30.
[25]Airgram A-524, Lisbon, 15 April 1963, NSF, Box 155, JFKL, in John Seiler, "The Azores as an Issue in US-Portuguese Relations, 1961–1963," paper delivered at the International Conference Group on Modern Portugal, The University of New Hampshire, 21–24 June 1979, p. 3.
[26]Memorandum, Subject: Discussion at the 365th Meeting of the National Security Council, 8 May 1958, DDRS(80)385A.
[27]Memorandum of a conversation with the President, 9 November 1960, 9:30 A.M. Others present: Ambassador Elbrick, Colonel Eisenhower, DDRS(75)452C.
[28]Hugh Kay, *Salazar and Modern Portugal*, pp. 185–186; For a full exposition of Portugal's argument in the United Nations, see Franco Nogueira, *The United Nations and Portugal* (London: Sedgwick and Jackson, 1963).
[29]David Eccles, *By Safe Hand: Letters of Sybil and David Eccles, 1939–1942* (London, The Bodley Head, 1983), pp. 98, 292.

[30]Embtel, Lisbon, 51, 11 July 1961; Interview: Franco Nogueira, Lisbon, 24 July 1983.
[31]Edited draft of report on trip to Middle East and Far East, 3 November 1951, PPP, JFKL, found in Richard D. Mahoney, *JFK: Ordeal in Africa*, (New York: Oxford University Press, 1983), p. 248; Schlesinger, *Robert F. Kennedy and His Times*, pp. 92–93; Herbert S. Parmet, *JFK: The Presidency of John F. Kennedy* (New York: The Dial Press, 1983), p. 352; Richard Reeves, *President Kennedy: Profiles of Power* (New York: Simon and Schuster, 1993), p. 254.
[32]Mahoney, *JFK: Ordeal in Africa*, pp. 20–23; *Congressional Record*, 2 July 1957, p. 10788.
[33]*New York Times*, 18 July 1958; Dean Acheson, *Power and Diplomacy* (Cambridge: Harvard University Press, 1958), p. 123; Theodore C. Sorenson, *Kennedy* (New York: Harper and Row, 1965), p. 65.
[34]Mahoney, *JFK: Ordeal in Africa*, p. 28.
[35]Ibid., p. 29.
[36]Interview, Theodore Sorenson, 17 April 1984, New York City.
[37]Kay, *Salazar and Modern Portugal*, p. 215.
[38]Henrique Galvão, *Santa Maria: My Crusade for Portugal* (New York: The World Publishing Company, 1961), p. 46.
[39]Warren Rogers, Jr., *The Floating Revolution* (New York: McGraw-Hill, 1962), pp. 116–117.
[40]Embtel, Lisbon, 403, 28 January 1961, 7:23 P.M., FOIA; Embtel, Lisbon, 405, 28 January 1961, 7:39 P.M., FOIA; To: The Secretary, From: EUR-Mr. Kohler, Subject: Santa Maria, 28 January 1961, FOIA.
[41]John Marcum, *The Angolan Revolution, Vol. I* (Cambridge: The MIT Press), pp. 126–130; Duffy, *Portugal in Africa* (Baltimore: Penguin Books, Inc., 1962), p. 215; *Time*, *24* February 1961, p. 54.
[42]John F. Kennedy, *Public Papers, 1961*, pp. 22–23.
[43]Mahoney, *JFK: Ordeal in Africa*, p. 188.
[44]Deptel, 1703 to Lisbon, 3 March 1961, NSF, Box 154, JFKL.
[45] Appendix A, Chronology of US Actions, PPK, Box 4–5, JFKL; Status Report on Portuguese Africa, undated, NSF, Box 154, JFKL.
[46]*New York Times*, 16 March 1961; *Yearbook of the United Nations, 1961* (New York: Office of Public Information, United Nations, 1961), p. 137–138.
[47]*New York Times*, 21 April 1961.
[48]Marcum, *The Angolan Revolution, Vol. 1*, pp. 135–147.
[49]Interview: Adriano Moreira, Lisbon, 27 September 1983.
[50]Viana de Lemos, *Duas Crises, 1961 e 1974* (Lisbon: Edicoes Nova Gente, 1977), p. 29.
[51]Embtel, Lisbon, 558, 4 March 1961, DDRS(77)241B; Deptel, 472, 4 March 1961, NSF, Box 154, JFKL.

[52]Embtel, Lisbon, 564, 6 March 1961, NSF, Box 154, JFKL.

[53]Embtel, Lisbon, 684, 28 March 1961, NSF, Box 154, JFKL; Copy of a Communication presumably addressed to Prime Minister Salazar by Former Defense Minister General Botelho Moniz, Undated, NSF, Box 154, JFKL; *Ano*, Vol. 1, no. 31, 25 November–2 December, 1976 (Lisbon) pp. 58–61; Viana de Lemos, *Duas Crises, 1961 e 1974*, p. 31.

[54]Embtel, Lisbon, 684, 28 March 1961, NSF, Box 154, JFKL; Viana de Lemos, *Duas Crises, 1961 e 1974*, p. 44; "Portugal," *Atlantic*, *208*, no. 4, (October, 1961), p. 34.

[55]Embtel, Lisbon, 729, 9 April 1961, DDRS(77)241C; Viana de Lemos, *Duas Crises, 1961 e 1974*, p. 44; Mahoney, *JFK: Ordeal in Africa*, 191–192.

[56]Embtel, Lisbon, 748, 13 April 1961, DDRS(77)241C; Insight Team of the (London) *Sunday Times Insight on Portugal: The Year of the Captains* (London: Andre Deutsch, 1975), p. 23; Gallagher, *Portugal: A Twentieth Century Interpretation*, pp. 151–153.

[57]Embtel, Lisbon, 758, 14 April 1961, DDRS(77)241E; Viana de Lemos, *Duas Crises, 1961 e 1974*, p. 46.

[58]*Diário de Notícias*, 23 March 1961; *Diário de Notícias* 28 March 1961; at the beginning of July, Elbrick cabled Washington, "There is no question that US is now identified as public enemy number one . . ."; Embtel, Lisbon, 38, 7 July 1961, NSF, Box 154, JFKL.

[59]Deptel, Lisbon, 1136, 4 June 1962, NSF, JFKL; *New York Times*, 16 April 1961; Mahoney, *JFK: Ordeal in Africa*, p. 193.

[60]Mahoney, *JFK: Ordeal in Africa*, p. 190.

[61]Kennedy's overstated emphasis on the importance of Williams' appointment was as much to indicate his desire for a new direction in policy toward Africa as it was to assuage liberal democrats who were still embittered with the choice of Lyndon Johnson as vice-presidential running mate. Schlesinger, *A Thousand Days*, p. 556; Interview: Theodore Sorenson, 17 April 1984, NYC.

[62]Warren Cohen, *Dean Rusk*, (Trenton, New Jersey: Cooper Square Publishers, 1980), pp. 7–9, 15, 111.

[63]Interview: William Brubeck, 3 May 1984, Lexington, MA; Waldemar Nielson, *The Great Powers and Africa* (New York: Council on Foreign Relations, 1969), p. 285.

[64]Report of the Chairman of the Task Force on Portuguese Territories in Africa, 4 July 1961, DDRS(79)281C.

[65]To: Wayne Fredericks, From: G. Mennen Williams, Subject: Angola Task Force: Meetings with Henry Fowler, Treasury; Paul Nitze, Defense; McGeorge Bundy, White House, GMWC, NARS; Memorandum for Mr. Bundy, Subject: Angola, 29 June 1961, NSF, JFKL.

[66]Mahoney, *JFK: Ordeal in Africa*, p. 202.

[67]*Guidelines for Policy and Operations: Africa*, Department of State, March 1962, DDRS(78)392B, pp. 2, 6; Kennedy echoed similar sentiments in a meeting with Julius Nyerere, Prime Minister of Tanzania, when he said that the United States had "a moral obligation to help the new and poor nations," while emphasizing that "it was in the America's own security interest to encourage the development of stable and independent states in Africa." Memorandum of Conversation, Subject: Visit of Prime Minister of Tanganyika, Participants: The President, Prime Minister of Tanganyika Julius Nyerere, et al., 17 July 1961, NSF, Box 162, JFKL.

[68]Letter to William H. Taft, III, Consul General, Lourenco Marques (later called Maputo), from G. Mennen Williams, April 5, 1962 GMWC, NARS; To: Mr. Battle, From: G. Mennen Williams, Subject: Renewal of Lincoln University Grant, June 22, 1962, GMWC, NARS. *Memorandum Concerning Recent Actions on African Students*, from Philip H. Coombs, Assistant Secretary for Educational and Cultural Affairs, August 4, 1961, NSF, Box 1-2, JFKL.

[69]*A Report on a Journey Through Rebel Angola*, by George M. Houser, (New York: American Committee on Africa, undated); Embtel, Lisbon, 969, 7 April 1962, NSF, Box 154, JFKL; Interview: Wayne Fredericks, 20 February 1979, NYC.

[70]Memorandum for the President, Subject: Angolese Students in France and Switzerland, From: Maxwell D. Taylor, 21 July 1961, NSF, JFKL; Embtel, Geneva, 5881, 11 July 1961, NSF, JFKL.

[71]Memorandum for the President, Subject Angolese Students in France and Switzerland, From: Maxwell D. Taylor, 21 July 1962, NSF, JFKL.

[72]Letter to William Leonhart, Ambassador, Dar es Salaam, From: G. Mennen Williams, 8 November 1962, GMWC, NARS; To: The Secretary, From: G. Mennen Williams, Subject: Review of AAI Program, Dar es Salaam, for Mozambican Students—Approval Requested, 3 October 1962, GMWC, NARS.

[73]John Bartlow Martin, *Adlai Stevenson and the World*, (New York: Doubleday and Company, Inc., 1977), p. 618. Mahoney, *JFK: Ordeal in Africa*, p. 204.

[74]Mahoney, *JFK: Ordeal in Africa*, p. 204; Confidential Interviews 50 and 54.

[75]Deptel, Circular, 92, July 16, 1963, FOIA.

[76]Embtel, Lisbon, 820, 1 May 1961; Embtel, Lisbon, 820, 1 May 1961, PPK, Box 4-5, JFKL; Embtel, Lisbon, 454, 10 October 1961; Telephone interview, George Ball, 14 June 1984.

[77]Deptel 1590, 23 May 1961, NSF, JFKL; Confidential Interviews 39 and 50.

[78]Embtel, Lisbon, 825, 17 February 1962, FOIA; Interview: Franco Nogueira, Lisbon, 16 June 1983, Lisbon.

[79]Embtel, Lisbon, 840, 21 February 1962; Franco Nogueira, *Diálogos Interditos, Vol. I* (Lisbon: Intervenção, 1979) pp. 83–84.

[80]Embtel, Lisbon, 1036, 27 April 1962, FOIA.

[81]Embtel. Lisbon, 935, 24 May 1961, NSF, Box 154, JFKL; Airgram, Lisbon. A-378, 29 February 1964 FOIA; Mahoney, *JFK: Ordeal in Africa,* p. 196. The value of the aid program was slashed from just over one million dollars to less than twenty thousand dollars. S. J. Bosgra and Chr. van Krimpen, *Portugal and NATO* (Amsterdam: Angola Comite, 1969), p. 26.
[82]Deptel, 06892, 11 August 1961, NSF, PPK, Box 4–5, JFKL.
[83]Embtel, Lisbon 935, 24 May 1961, FOIA; Embtel, Lisbon 1068, 21 June 1961, FOIA.
[84]Embtel, Lisbon 240, 16 August 1961.
[85]Memorandum for the President, Subject: Restriction of Arms Shipments to Portugal and Its Territories, from Dean Rusk, 29 August 1961; Memorandum for the President, Subject: Portuguese Use of US Military Equipment in Angola, from McGeorge Bundy, 31 August 1961, NSF, PPK, Box 4–5, JFKL.
[86]Memorandum for Mr. Bundy, From: Samuel E. Belk, Subject: Updating of Portuguese-US Relations, 24 August 1961, NSF, Box 154, JFKL; Memorandum for the President, From: WWR, Subject: Your Meeting with the New Portuguese Ambassador Pedro Pereira, September 14, 1961, NSF, Box 154, JFKL.
[87]*The New Republic, 146,* no. 2, 2 April 1962, pp. 9–12.
[88]William Minter, *Portuguese Africa and the West* (London: Penguin Books, 1972), pp. 83–86; *The New Republic, 146,* no. 2, 2 April 1962, p. 10.
[89]Embtel, Lisbon 310, 31 August 1961, NSF, Box 4–5, JFKL; de Figueiredo, António, *Portugal: Fifty Years of Dictatorship,* pp. 213–214; Franco Nogueira, *Salazar: A Resistancia, Vol. V, 1958–1964 (Porto: Livraria Civilização, 1984*), p. 325.
[90]Interview: Franco Nogueira, Lisbon, 16 June 1983.
[91]CIA, Information Report, Portugal, TDCS 3/648,988, 28 December 1961; Deptel, Lisbon 789, 29 January 1962, NSF, Box 154, JFKL; CIA, Information Report, Portugal, TDCS 3/3469, 284, 2 February 1962, NSF, Box 154, JFKL; Confidential Interview: 33.
[92]William Minter, *Portuguese Africa and the West,* p. 88; Mahoney, *JFK: Ordeal in Africa,* p. 209; Interview: Theodore Sorenson, 17 April 1984, New York City. Sorenson wrote in his memoir on Kennedy, "The President finally felt that, if necessary, he was prepared to forego the base entirely rather than permit Portugal to dictate his Africa policy." *Kennedy,* p. 538.
[93]Embtel, Lisbon 822, 13 February 1962, NSF, Box 154, JFKL.
[94]Telcon: Bundy/Ball, 16 April 1962; Mahoney, *JFK: Ordeal in Africa,* p. 210.
[95]To: Wayne Fredericks, From: G. Mennen Williams, Subject: Angola and Rhodesia, 16 April 1962, GMWC, NARS; Mahoney, *JFK: Ordeal in Africa,* p. 210; Interview: Wayne Fredericks, 11 April 1984, New York City.
[96]John Bartlow Martin, *Adlai Stevenson and the World,* (Nw York: Doubleday and Company, Inc., 1977), p. 703; David Halberstam, *The Best and the Brightest*

(New York: Random House, Inc., 1969), p. 28–34; Franco Nogueira, *Salazar, Vol. 5: O Ataque* (Coimbra: Atlantida Editora, 1980) p. 253.
[97]From: Mr. Bundy, To: Captain Shepard for the President, Cite: CAP5222-62, NSF, Box 154, JFKL; For the Secretary of State, 25 April 1962, NSF, Box 154, JFKL.
[98]*Dear Mr. President*, from Adlai E. Stevenson, 26 April 1962, NSF, Box 155, JFKL; *Dear Mr. President*, Subject: "Suggested Steps for Azores and Concurrent Policy towards Portuguese Colonies," from Adlai E. Stevenson, 10 May 1962, NSF, Box 154, JFKL.
[99]Memorandum for the Assistant Secretary of State for African Affairs, The Deputy Assistant Secretary of State for European Affairs, Subject: Angola and Brazil, 5 April 1962, FOIA: Rusk expressed to Dantas his concern that Roberto "was losing influence to the de Andrade extremist group tied to Moscow . . . and it would be disastrous to have another Congo in Angola or Mozambique or to have either become a base in Africa for forces hostile to the West.: Subject: Angola, Participants: His Excellency Francisco Clementino San Tiago Dantas, Minister of Foreign Relations, The Honorable Dean Rusk, Secretary of State, et al., 3 April 1962, FOIA.
[100]Memorandum to the President, From: Theodore C. Sorenson, Subject: Azores-Angola, 4 June 1962, NSF, Box 155, JFKL.
[101]Memorandum to the President, From: Chester Bowles, Subject: The Azores, 4 June 1962, FOIA.
[102]Memorandum for Mr. McGeorge Bundy, Subject: the Azores, 6 June 1962, NSF, Box 155, JFKL.
[103]To: Wayne Fredericks, From: G. Mennen Williams, Subject: Angola and Rhodesia, 16 April 1962, FOIA; Memorandum for the President, Subject: The Azores, 23 May 1962, NSF, Box 155, JFKL; To: S/S-RO, From: G. Mennen Williams, Subject: Holden Roberto, 23 May 1962, GMW, NARS.
[104]Franco Nogueira, *Diálogos Interditos, Vol. I*, pp. 102–109.
[105]Embtel, Lisbon, 1165, 12 June 1965; *US News and World Report*, 9 July 1962; Warren Cohen, *Dean Rusk*, p. 125.
[106]Meeting memorandum: "Bilateral Matters," The Ambassador of Portugal, Pedro Theotonio Pereira, The Secretary 18 July 1962, FOIA; Airgram, Lisbon, A-39, 21 July 1962, NSF, Box 154, JFKL; Interview: Dean Rusk, 22 March 1984, Athens, Georgia. Rusk described Salazar as "like a ghost," and the meetings as "almost like a seance;" Dean Rusk, *As I Saw It* (New York: Penguin Books, 1990), p. 275.
[107]From: Lisbon, To: Secretary of State, No: 140, 17 August 1962, NSF, Box 154, JFKL; Franco Nogueira, *Salazar: A Resistancia, Vol. V*, p. 416.

[108]Airgram, Washington, CA-4145, 19 October 1962. Rusk had previously given instructions to ignore the nationalist leader in Guinea-Bissau, Amilcar Cabral. Embtel, Conakry, 579, 26 April 1962, NSF, Box 154, JFKL.
[109]Memorandum to the President, Subject: Meeting with Portuguese Foreign Minister, from: Dean Rusk, 24 October 1962; Nogueira, *Diálogos Interditos, Vol. I,* p. 434.
[110]*Ibid.*, p. 176–180.
[111]Memorandum of Conversation, Subject: US-Portuguese Relations, Participants: The President, Alberto Franco Nogueira, Foreign Minister of Portugal, et al.; Franco Nogueira, *Diálogos Interditos, Vol. I,* pp. 180–181.
[112]Telegraph Branch, Work Copy, INFO: USUN, Re: Angola, 25 January 1962, FOIA.
[113]John Bartlow Martin, *Adlai Stevenson and the World*, pp. 702–703.
[114]*Ibid.*, pp. 585-590.
[115]*Harper's, 224*, no. 1342 (March 1962), p. 115.
[116]John Bartlow Martin, *Adlai Stevenson and the World,* p. 697; Richard D. Mahoney, *JFK: Ordeal in Africa*, pp. 212–213.
[117]To: S-Secretary, U-Mr. Ball, M-Mr. McGhee, From: AF-G. Mennen Williams, Subject: Porter Hardy Committee Inquiry into Angola Policy, GMW, NARS; Telcon: Congressman Hardy, Ball, 26 January 1962, 11:20 A.M.; Mahoney, *JFK: Ordeal in Africa,* p. 214.
[118]Embtel, Lisbon 124, 22 July 1961, NSF, Box 154, JFKL; Airgram, Lisbon A-39, 21 July 1962, NSF, Box 154, JFKL.
[119]Deptel, 3949, 11 November 1962, NSF, Box 154, JFKL; Deptel, 01587, 26 July 1962, NSF, Box 4–5, JFKL; Deptel, 10210, 13 September 1962; Mahoney, *JFK: The Ordeal in Africa,* p. 217.
[120]Embtel, New York 806, 18 September 1962, NSF, Box 4–5, JFKL.
[121]Embtel, New York 2408, 18 December 1962; W. Scott Thompson, *Ghana's Foreign Policy* (Princeton, NJ: Princeton University Press, 1969), p. 223–224; John Marcum, *The Angolan Revolution, Vol. I,* pp. 255–263.
[122]Memorandum of Conversation, Paris, France, 15 December 1962, Participants: The Secretary of State, Foreign Minister Nogueira, et al.; Deptel, 01587, 2 August 1962, NSF, Box 4–5, JFKL; Embtel, New York 797, 17 September 1962; Embtel, Lisbon 377, 27 November 1962, NSF, Box 154, JFKL.
[123]*Yearbook of the United Nations, 1962* (New York: Office of Public Information, United Nations, 1963), p. 93.
[124]Holden Roberto to John F. Kennedy, 18 December 1962, NSF, Box 4–5, JFKL; Mr. Bromley Smith, The White House, from William H. Brubeck, 31 January 1962, NSF, Box 4–5, JFKL.

[125]Current Intelligence Memorandum, OCI No. 0391/62, 3 January 1962, NSF, Box 154, JFKL; Franco Nogueira, *Salazar: A Resistancia, Vol. V*, pp. 303–304, 321.

[126]Hugh Kay, *Salazar and Modern Portugal*, p. 354.

[127]Central Intelligence Agency, OCI No. 1269/62, Subject: The Situation in Portugal, DDRS(77)274A; John Marcum, *The Angolan Revolution, Vol. II* (Cambridge, MA: The MIT Press, 1978) pp. 12. When asked about these rumors, Adriano Moreira replied, "I never took part in any conspiracy against the government." Lisbon, 17 September 1983.

[128]To: The Secretary, From: INR-Roger Hilsman, Intelligence Note: Portuguese Cabinet reshuffle, 3 December 1962, NSF, Box 154, JFKL; CIA Information Report, No. TDCS-3/514,496, Country-Portugal, June 1962, DDRS(77)274C; CIA Information Report, No. TDCS-3/650,876, County-Portugal, 26 July 1962, DDRRS(77)274D; Airgram, Lisbon A-288, 7 December 1962, NSF, Box 154, JFKL.

[129]Embtel, Lisbon 469, 12 October; Eduardo Mondlane, *The Struggle for Mozambique* (Baltimore: Penguin Books, 1969), pp. 118–126; To: The Secretary, from: INR-Roger Hilsman, Subject: Recent Developments in the Angolan Situation, research memorandum, RAF-39, 18 May 1962, DDRS(77)312D.

[130]To: M-Mr. W. Averell Harriman, from: AF-G. Mennen Williams, Subject: Program for Portuguese Africa, 2 May 1963, FOIA.

[131]Interview: Wayne Fredericks, 20 February 1979, New York City; Arthur M. Schlesinger, Jr., *Robert F. Kennedy and His Times*, p. 562; Mahoney, *JFK: Ordeal in Africa*, p. 237.

[132]Memorandum, May 2, 1963, found in John Marcum, "The Politics of Indifference: Portugal in Africa, a Case Study in American Foreign Policy," *Issue 2*, no. 3 (Fall 1972), p. 11.

[133]Interview: F. J. Rarig, 18 May 1984, Gardenville, PA.

[134]Interview: Wayne Fredericks, 20 February 1979, New York City.

[135]Confidential Interview: 39: Telephone Interview, George Ball, 14 June 1984.

[136]Interview: Adam Walinsky, 18 April 1979, New York City.

[137]Robert F. Kennedy to G. Mennen Williams, 25 February 1963; Memorandum to the Attorney General, 21 February 1963, RFK Papers, Box 39, JFKL; Memorandum to the Attorney General, 11 April 1963, RFK Papers, Box 39, JFKL; John Nolan, re: Eduardo Mondlane, 30 April 1963, RFK Papers, Box 39, JFKL; Telcon: Kaysen, Ball, 9 May 1963.

[138]F. J. Rarig to Robert F. Kennedy, 17 April 1963, RFK Papers, Box 39, JFKL.

[139]Confidential Interview: 77; See also Arthur M. Schlesinger, Jr., *Robert F. Kennedy and His Times*, p. 564.

[140]Letter from Francis X. Sutton, Deputy Vice President, The Ford Foundation, to the author, 17 April 1979.

[141]Eduardo Mondlane was very sensitive about the need to diversify FRELIMO's sources of external support. In a trip to China in late 1963, he stopped in Germany "to . . . balance our contacts in that part of Europe. Until then our contacts had been exclusively with East Germany." Moreover, when the Chinese offered to send "technicians" to Africa to train FRELIMO combatants, Mondlane refused because he thought "it might overcompromise *[sic]*our [FRELIMO's] position in relation to the various forces in the cold war . . . ." FRELIMO did accept to send its own troops to China for training. "My Visit to Peking, Nov. 26–Dec.7, 1963, Confidential Notes on China," by Eduardo Chivambo Mondlane.
[142]Subject: US Policy Toward Portugal, 17 January 1962, by Paul Sakwa, NSF, JFKL.
[143]Memorandum for the Secretary, from: Chester Bowles, Subject: Proposal for a Breakthrough in US-Portuguese Relations in Regard to Africa, 10 January 1963, DDRS(79)445A.
[144]Interview: Franco Nogueira, 24 July 1983, Lisbon.
[145]Airgram, Lisbon A-465, 6 March 1963, FOIA.
[146]"The Economic Effects on Portugal of the Angolan Military Operations," 25 October 1963, DDRS(77)209G; Embtel, Lisbon 75, 18 July 1963, FOIA.
[147]Airgram, Lourenco Marques, A-32, 16 September 1963, DDRS(76)103E.
[148]Central Intelligence Agency, OCI No. 0274/63B, "The Angolan Rebellion and White Unrest," 5 April 1963, DDRS(77)85A.
[149]To: The Secretary, From: INR-Thomas L. Hughes, Subject: Prospects for Angolan Nationalist Movement, 5 November 1963.
[150]Colin Legum, *Pan Africanism*: *A Short Political Guide* (New York: F. A. Praeger, 1965), p. 136; *New York Times*, 25 May 1963; *Washington Post*, 24 May 1963; *New York Times*, 26 May 1963; John Marcum, *The Angolan Revolution, Vol. II*, pp. 78–79.
[151]Deptel, 02588, 4 July 1963, NSF, Box 4–5, JFKL.
[152]*New York Times*, 4 January 1964, in Marcum, *Angolan Revolution, Vol. II*, p. 80.
[153]Antánio de Oliveira Salazar, *Declaration on Overseas Policy* (Lisbon: Secretario Nacional de Informação, 1963), pp. 31–32, found in John Marcum, *The Angolan Revolution*, p. 78–79.
[154]Deptel, 02588, 4 July 1963, NSF, Box 4–5, JFKL.
[155]To: The Secretary, From: INR-Thomas L. Hughes, Subject: Prospects for Angolan Nationalist Movement, 5 November 1963, FOIA.
[156]John Marcum, *The Angolan Revolution, Vol. II*, pp. 14–16.
[157]"Unity in Angola?", *West Africa*, 14 December 1963, p. 1399.
[158] *New York Times*, 7 June 1963.
[159]Letter from Adlai E. Stevenson to John F. Kennedy, 26 June 1963, NSF, Box 3, JFKL. Emphasis in original.

[160]Franco Nogueira, *Diálogos Interditos, Vol. I*, p. 246–247.
[161]Waldemar Nielsen, *The Great Powers and Africa*, p. 277–298.
[162]Arthur M. Schlesinger, Jr., *A Thousand Days* (Boston: Houghton Mifflin Company, 1965), p. 582; John Bartlow Martin, *Adlai Stevenson and the World*, pp. 766–768; See also Mahoney, *JFK: Ordeal in Africa*, p. 238–240.
[163]Schlesinger, *A Thousand Days*, p. 582.
[164]Telcon: Ball, Ormsby-Gore, 26 July 1963; Martin, *Adlai Stevenson and the World*, p. 766; Mahoney, *JFK: Ordeal in Africa*, p. 239–240.
[165]To Mr. Bundy, Message from the President, 7 July 1963; Memorandum for the President, from Robert S. McNamara, 14 August 1963, NSF, Box 155, JFKL.
[166]Martin, *Adlai Stevenson and the World*, p. 768; Mahoney, *JFK: Ordeal in Africa*, p. 240; United Nations, Security Council, *Official Records, 1049th Meeting*, 31 July 1963 (S/PV.1049), pp. 6–7.
[167]Telcon: Cleveland, Ball, 31 July 1963; Embtel, Lisbon, 150, 10 August 1963, NSF, Box 155, JFKL; Embtel, New York, 309, 31 July 1963 DDRS(75)733C; Confidential Interview 13, Lisbon 12 October 1983.
[168]Telcon: Ball, Harriman, 31 July 1963.
[169]*New York Times*, 17 August 1963; Franco Nogueira, *Salazar: A Resistência, Vol. V* (Porto: Livraria Civilação Editora, 1984), pp. 503, 510–511.
[170]*New York Times*, 17 August 1963.
[171]Franco Nogueira, *Diálogos Interditos, Vol. I*, pp. 246–247; Telcon: Bundy, Ball, 5 July 1963.
[172]Embtel, Paris 985, 31 August 1963 (Section three of five), NSF, Box 155, JFKL; George Ball, *The Discipline of Power*, pp. 274–281, emphasis in original; Mahoney, *JFK: The Ordeal in Africa*, p. 198, 240; Telephone Interview: George Ball, 14 June 1984.
[173]Memcon, The Prime Minister, Ambassador Caldeira Coelho, The Under Secretary, et al., 7 September 1963, NSF, Box 155, JFKL; Ball, *The Discipline of Power*, pp. 274–281.
[174]"To all Chiefs of Mission," from G. Mennen Williams, 31 December 1963, GMWC, NARS.
[175]Dean Rusk, *As I Saw It* (New York: Penguin Books, 1990), p. 274; Ronald Steel, *Walter Lippmann and the American Century* (Boston: Little, Brown and Co., 1980), p. 540.
[176]Dean Rusk, *As I Saw It* (New York: Penguin Books, 1990), p. 274
[177]Deptel, 01923, 3 August 1963, NSF, Box 4–5, JFKL; Embtel, Lisbon, 104, 26 July 1963.
[178]Embtel, New York, 1964, 29 October 1963, NSF, Box 4–5, JFKL; Communiqué of UN African Group, undated; *The Washington Post*, 31 October 1963.
[179]Memorandum for the President, 7 November 1963, NSF, Box 123, JFKL.

[180]Franco Nogueira, *Diálogos Interditos, Vol. I*, p. 281–283; Ball to Salazar, 21 October 1963, found in Mahoney, *JFK: Ordeal in Africa*, p. 248.

Chapter 2: Lyndon Johnson and Africa: The Right Policy for the Wrong Reasons

[1]Larkin, Bruce D. *China and Africa, 1974–1970.* Berkeley: University of California Press, 1971, pp. 65–70; Cohen, Warren I. *Dean Rusk.* Totowa, New Jersey: Copper Square Publishers, 1980, p. 297.
[2]To: The Secretary. From: INR-Thomas L. Hughes. Subject: An Outline Guide to Communist Activities in Africa, 15 May 1964, p. 9, NSF, Africa, Box 76, LBJL.
[3]*New York Times*, 14 January 1964.
[4]Memorandum for the President, from William H. Brubeck. Subject: Chicom Activity in Africa. 29 January 1964. NSF, Box 77, LBJL.
[5]*New York Times*, 24 February 1964 and 16 January 1965; *Los Angeles Times* 9 April 1975.
[6]*New York Times*, 4 January 1964.
[7]Confidential interviews: 47 and 50; Nielsen, Waldemar. *The Great Powers in Africa*. New York: Praeger Publishers, 1969, p. 293.
[8]See transcript of an interview with W. Averell Harriman (n. d.), NSF, International Meetings and Travel File, Box 30-34, LBJL.
[9]Cohen, Warren. *Dean Rusk.* Totowa, New Jersey: Cooper Square Publishers, 1980, p. 229.
[10]Embtel, 105, Cape Town, 16 March 1964, NSF: Africa, Box 78–80, LBJL.
[11]*New York Times*, 17 January 1964.
[12]Embtel, 575, 21 January 1964, FOIA.
[13] Nogueira said that Portugal had been "perhaps weeks away" from recognizing China. In a difference from his book, he said that Salazar realized he could not persuade his closest supporters of the wisdom of the move no matter how much of an embarrassment it would have been to the United States. Interview, Franco Nogueira, 3 July 1983, Lisbon; Nogueira, Franco. *Salazar, A Resistência, Vol. V.* (Porto: Livraria Civilizção Editora, 1984), pp. 550–553.
[14]Embtel, 1897, Leopoldville, March 27, 1964, NSF, International Meetings and Travel File, Box 30-34, LBJL.
[15]Embtel, Leopoldville, 1292, Dec. 30, 1963, NSF, Portugal, Box 78-79, LBJL; Embtel, Leopoldville, 1897, March 28, 1964, NSF, International Meetings and Travel File, Box 30-34, LBJL; Embtel, 160, Leopoldville, March 28, 1964, DDRS(76)58A.
[16]John Marcum, *The Angolan Revolution, Vol. II* (Cambridge, The MIT Press, 1978), pp. 132-133.

[17]Talk by McGeorge Bundy to the Overseas Press Writers, 26 February 1964, NSF, Aides File, Box 1, LBJL.
[18]Memorandum of Information for the Secretary of the Navy, from the Office of the Chief of Naval Operations, Subject: Portugal, 1964, DDRS(76)39F.
[19]Franco Nogueira, *Diálogos Interditos, Vol. II* (Lisbon: Intervenção, 1979), p. 24; Letter to Governor Williams from Thomas K. Wright, 6 April 1964, Box 28, GMWP, NARS.
[20]Embtel, 591, Lisbon, 24 January 1964 (section 2 of 2), NSC, LBJL.
[21]Airgram, A-378, Lisbon, 29 February 1964, NSF, Portugal, Box 302, LBJL.
[22]Deptel, 654, 3 May 1964, NSF, Portugal, Box 203, LBJL.
[23]Memorandum of Conversation, Subject: Portuguese Africa, Participants: Prime Minister Antonio de Oliveira Salazar, American Ambassador George W. Anderson, et al., 17 April 1964, FOIA, emphasis in the original; Embtel, 15499, Lisbon, 18 April 1964, section two of two, FOIA.
[24]Malyn Newitt, *Portugal in Africa* (Essex, UK: Longman, 1981), p. 230.
[25]"Portuguese Economic Outlook and Its Political Implications," Office of Current Intelligence, Central Intelligence Agency, 22 May 1964, DDRS(77)24A.
[26]Portuguese African Territories: Assessment of Present Situation, handwritten: "Used at NSC/SG Mtg, 2/18/64," NSF, Box 76, LBJL.
[27]To: The Secretary, Through: G-Mr. Johnson, From: AF-G. Mennen Williams, Subject: Portuguese African Territories: Action Memorandum, 29 April 1964.
[28]Confidential Interviews: 54 and 77.
[29]Memorandum for the President, Subject: Some comments on Post-election Problems, from McB., 2 November 1964, NSF, Aides File, Box 15, 16.
[30]Interview, Dean Rusk, 22 March 1984, Athens, Georgia.
[31]Franco Nogueira, *Diálogos Interditos, Vol. II* (Lisbon: Intervenção, 1979), pp. 29–33.
[32]Memorandum of Conversation, Participants: The Secretary, Foreign Minister Nogueira, et al., 13 September 1964, NSF, International Meetings and Travel File, Box 30–34, LBJL.
[33]"Roswell Gilpatricks's Trip," undated, found in Michael Samuels and Steven Haykin, "The Anderson Plan: An American Attempt to Seduce Portugal Out of Africa," *Orbis* 23, no. 3, (Fall 1979), p. 660–661.
[34]David Welsh, "Flyboys of the CIA," *Ramparts*, no. 5 (December 1966), p. 16; See also William Minter, *Portuguese Africa and the West* (London: Penguin Books, 1972), pp. 110–112.
[35]Interview: Ed Hamilton, 5 March 1984, Los Angeles; Telephone Interview: George Ball, 14 June 1984.
[36]To: G/PM-Mr. Kitchen, From: AF-G. Mennen Williams, Subject: Sale of the B-26 Aircraft to Portugal, 17 September 1965.

[37]David Welsh, "Flyboys of the CIA," *Ramparts*, no. 5, (December 1966) pp. 13-14.
[38]Samuels and Haykin, "The Anderson Plan: an Attempt to Seduce Portugal Out of Africa," *Orbis*, *23*, No. 3, (Fall 1979), pp. 665–666; "Portugal," undated, untitled, NSF, LBJL, pp. 2–3.
[39]Portuguese complaints on this subject led the Ford Motor Company to instruct the Ford Foundation to terminate its grant to Janet Mondlane and the Mozambique Institute. It was also reported that the Ford Foundation assured the Salazar government that it would be consulted before any future grants were made to African areas where Portugal had special interests. *New York Times*, 13 September 1964; *New York Times*, 19 December 1964.
[40]Franco Nogueira, *Diálogos Interditos, Vol. II*, pp. 102–106.
[41]"Portugal," (n.d.), untitled, pp. 4–5, NSF, LBJL.
[42]"Portugal," (n.d.), untitled, pp. 4–5, NSF, LBJL; *US Participation in the UN*, Department of State Publication 8137 (Washington: GPO, 1967), pp. 312–325.
[43]"Portugal as a US Ally," (n.d., n.p.), pp. 1–2; Samuels and Haykin, "The Anderson Plan: an Attempt to Seduce Portugal Out of Africa," *Orbis*, *23*, No. 3, (Fall 1979), , p. 666; Franco Nogueira, *Diálogos Interditos, Vol. II*, p. 108.
[44]Enclosure 1 to airgram, Lisbon A-328, 14 March 1966 (emphasis in the original), found in Samuels and Haykin, "The Anderson Plan: an Attempt to Seduce Portugal Out of Africa," *Orbis*, *23*, no. 3, (Fall 1979), pp. 666–667.
[45]CIA, Special Memorandum No. 964, Subject: Salazar's Current Prospects, 8 June 1964.
[46]Philip Geyelin, *LBJ and the World* (New York: Frederick A. Praeger, 1966), p. 16.
[47]Quoted in Geylin, *ibid.*, p. 16.
[48]Confidential Interview: 92.
[49]Interview: Bill Moyers, 25 April 1984, New York City; Interview: Edward Hamilton, 20 February 1984, Los Angeles.
[50]Memorandum for the Record, from Rick Haynes, 5 April 1965, NSF: Name File, LBJL.
[51]Eric F. Goldman, *The Tragedy of Lyndon Johnson* (New York: Knopf, 1974), pp. 488–490; Robert Dallek, *The American Style of Foreign Policy* (New York: Alfred A. Knopf, 1983), pp. 237–238.
[52]McGB from Rick Haynes, 4 March 1965, NSF, Africa, Box 76, LBJL.
[53]Memorandum for Mr. McGeorge Bundy, from Clifford L. Alexander, Jr., NSF, Africa, Box 76, LBJL.
[54]McGB, from R. W. Komer and Rick Haynes, March 30, 1965, NSF, Africa, Box 76, LBJL.
[55]Note for Mr. Bundy, from Rick Haynes, March 4, 1965, NSF, Africa, Box 76, LBJL.

[56]Waldemar Nielsen, *The Great Powers and Africa*, pp. 309–310.
[57]Letter from G. Mennen Williams to Robert F. Kennedy, 26 January 1965, GMWC, NARS.
[58]Memorandum for the President, Subject: Improving US Relations with Africa, from McGeorge Bundy, 8 March 1965, NSF, Africa, Box 76, LBJL. Nikita Khrushchev visited Egypt in May 1964, Chou En-Lai toured ten African countries in December 1963 and January 1964, and Leonid Brezhnev visited four African countries in February 1961.
[59]Memorandum to the President, Thru: Mr. Jack Valenti, Subject: Two requests for brief meetings, 12 February 1965, NSF, Aides File, Box 2, LBJL.
[60]Memorandum to the President from R. W. Komer and McGeorge Bundy, 9 January 1965, NSF, Aides File, Box 2, LBJL.
[61]Report to the President, From: Jack Valenti, February 6, 1965, Papers of LBJ, 1963-1969, Box 6, LBJL; Memorandum for the President, Subject: Improving US Relations with Africa, March 8, 1965, NSF, Africa, Box 76, LBJL; Memorandum for the President, from R. W. Komer and McGeorge Bundy, January 9, 1965, NSF, Aides File, Box 2, LBJL.
[62]Robert A. Caro, *The Years of Lyndon Johnson: The Path to Power* (New York: Random House, Inc., 1982), p. 335.
[63]Draft, Action: Circular to all AF Diplomatic Posts and Luanda, Lourenço Marques, and Salisbury, 28 April 1965, NSF, Africa, Box 76, LBJL; See also Deptel. Circular, 2156, from Rusk, 6 May 1965, DDRS(77)110D.
[64]Embtel, 046, Nairobi, 8 May 1965, DDRS(77)110E.
[65]McGB, Subject: "New Program for Africa," from Rick Haynes, 13 May 1965, NSF, Africa, Box 76, LBJL; Memorandum for Secretary Rusk from McGeorge Bundy, 1 December 1965, NSF Aides File, Box 15, 16, LBJL.
[66]Summary of Discussions and Conclusions, Addis Ababa Conference, 22–26 May 1965, DDRS(77)45A.
[67]McGB, Subject: AF Chiefs of Mission Conferences-""New Policy for Africa," from Rick Haynes, 5 June 1965, NSF, Africa, Box 76, LBJL.
[68]Memorandum for the President, From: Bill Moyers, 14 June 1965, Papers of LBJL, 1963–1969, Box 6, LBJL.
[69]Memorandum for the President from R. W. Komer, 16 June 1965, NSF, Africa, Box 76, LBJL.
[70]Mário Soares, *Portugal's Struggle for Liberty* (London: George Allen and Unwin, Ltd., 1975), translated by Mary Gawsworth, pp. 17922–26200.
[71]Herminio Martins, "Opposition in Portugal," *Government and Opposition*, (n.p.). (Spring 1969), pp. 260–261.
[72]Mário Soares, *Portugal's Struggle for Liberty* , p. 294.
[73]Herminio Martins, "Opposition in Portugal," *Government and Opposition*, p. 261.

[74]Letter from Marvine Howe to Bill Moyers, 15 October 1965, Aides File, LBJL.
[75]Eduardo Mondlane, *The Struggle for Mozambique* (Great Britain: Penguin Books, 1969), p. 139. When asked at a press conference in Dar es Salaam in July 1964 how long it would take until the "liberation" of Mozambique, Mondlane estimated five years after hostilities began. Letter from William Leonhart to Wayne Fredericks, Da es Salaam, 27 July 1964.
[76]Witney W. Schneidman, "The Socio-Economic Development of FRELIMO's Foreign Policy," Master's Thesis, University of Dar es Salaam, 1977, p. 58.
[77]Memorandum to Mr. McGeorge Bundy, the White House, from Benjamin Read, Executive Secretary, 8 October 1965, LBJL.
[78]Ironically, Franco Nogueira, who had enjoyed access to John F. Kennedy, never met with Johnson. Though he twice asked Rusk to arrange a meeting, Nogueira "fell out of the bottom of the bag" because of the President's lack of interest in Portugal and Portuguese Africa. Furthermore, the Azores weren't the critical issue they had been previously and the Portuguese foreign minister was perceived by the White House to be increasingly friendly with the Franco regime in Spain. Interview: Edward Hamilton, 5 March 1984, Los Angeles.
[79]John Marcum, *The Angola Revolution, Vol. II*, pp. 135–136. To Savimbi, Roberto was tribalist because he consistently favored those of the Bakongo region and a racist for his opposition to whites and mestizos.
[80]Marcum, ibid., p. 149.
[81]Marcum, ibid., p. 171.
[82]Marcum, ibid., p. 172; William M. LeoGrande, "Cuba's Policy in Africa, 1979–1980," Policy Papers in International Affairs (Berkeley: Institute of International Studies, 1980), p. 13; for the most comprehensive account of Cuba's activities in Africa, see Piero Gleijeses, *Conflicting Missions: Havana, Washington and Africa, 1959–1976* (Chapel Hill: The University of North Carolina Press, 2002), pp. 174–178.
[83]Philip Geyelin, *LBJ and the World*, p. 126–128. "The Treatment" could be anything from having LBJ grab one's lapel to spending a weekend in Texas on the Johnson ranch.
[84]Memorandum for McGB from Rick Haynes, 20 October 1965, NSF, National Security Council History, Box 14, LBJL.
[85]US-UK Talks, Washington, 28–29 June 1965, "Committee of 24," NSF, United Nations, Box 288, LBJL; US-UK Talks, Washington, 28–29 June 1965, "Portuguese Territories," NSF, United Nations, Box 288, LBJL.
[86]Memorandum for Mr. Bundy, Subject: Security Council-Kashmir, Portuguese Territories and Apartheid, from Gordon Chase, 2 November 1965, NSF, United Nations, Box 288, LBJL.
[87]"Dear Mr. President," from Arthur J. Goldberg, 12 November 1965, NSF, United Nations, Box 288, LBJL.

[88]Airgram, A-144, 18 October 1965, NSF, United Nations, Box 288, LBJL.
[89]To: The Secretary, From: AF-G. Mennen Williams, Subject: Strengthened African Program-Action Memorandum, 17 September 1965, DDRS(80)392B.
[90]Letter from G. Mennen Williams to Bill Lang, 3 September 1965, GMWC, NARS.
[91]Memorandum for the President from R. W. Komer, 16 June 1965, NSF, Africa, Box 76, LBJL.
[92]Memorandum for the President, from Dean Rusk, Subject: Strengthened African Program, 14 October 1965, NSF, National Security Council History, Box 14, LBJL; Interview: Edward Hamilton, 20 February 1984, Los Angeles.
[93]Memorandum for the President from R. W. Komer and hand signed by McGeorge Bundy, 23 November 1965, NSF, National Security Council History, Box 14, LBJL. Emphasis in original.
[94]Memorandum for Secretary Rusk, from Lyndon Johnson, Subject: Strengthened African Program, NSF, National Security Council History, Box 14, LBJL.
[95]Waldemar Nielsen, *The Great Powers and Africa*, pp. 312–314.
[96]Memorandum to: The Secretary, From: AF-G. Mennen Williams, Subject: Strengthened African Program-Action Memorandum, 9 March 1966, DDRS(80)392C; Dear "Soapy," from Lyndon B. Johnson, 2 March 1966, Papers of LBJL, Box 6, LBJL; Waldemar A. Nielsen, *The Great Powers and Africa*, p. 293.
[97]Confidential Interviews: 50 and 90. As Tony Lake wrote, Fredericks "gained a reputation for committing one of the most terrible bureaucratic gaffes; he made no secret of his beliefs, and treated foreign policy problems as something more than technical issues." *The "Tar Baby" Option*, (New York: Columbia University Press, 1976), p. 56.
[98]Franco Nogueira, *Diálogos Interditos, Vol. II*, p. 191; Interview: W. Tapley Bennett, 1 June 1984, Washington, DC.
[99]Dear Mr. President, from Arthur J. Goldberg, 23 April 1966, DDRS(80)393A.
[100]Dear Mr. President, from Arthur J. Goldberg, 23 April 1966, DDRS(80)393A.
[101]To: AF-Ambassador Palmer, From: Benjamin H. Read, Executive Secretary, 23 April 1966, NSF, National Security Council History, Box, 14, LBJL.
[102]Telephone Interview: Arthur Goldberg, 10 May 1984.
[103]Lyndon Baines Johnson, *The Vantage Point* (New York: Holt, Rinehart and Winston, 1971), p. 353.
[104]Interview: Edward Hamilton, 20 February 1984, Los Angeles; Philip Geyelin, *Lyndon B. Johnson and the World*, pp. 277–278.
[105]Special Memorandum No. 8-66, Subject: The Current Political Situation and Prospects in Tropical Africa, 20 May 1965, Central Intelligence Agency, DDRS(75)10C.

[106]Memorandum for the Honorable Jack Valenti, from Joseph Palmer, 24 March 1966, General Country Papers, Box 6, LBJL; *The Economist*, 19 March 1966, Papers of LBJ, 1963–1969, Box 6, LBJL. This optimism was based in part on the fact that within nine months, two Third World leaders most hostile to the West, Ben Bella of Algeria and Kwame Nkrumah of Ghana, had been deposed, and it appeared that President Sukarno of Indonesia, another critic of the US, was on his way out of power.
[107]Memorandum for the President, Subject: Reception for African Ambassadors from OAU States, from Dean Rusk, LBJL; Memorandum for the President, from W. W. Rostow, 4 May 1966; Confidential Memorandum for the President, from Burke Marshall (handwritten) 21 May 1966; all documents found in WHCF-CF, Box 58, LBJL.
[108]Mr. President, from Bill Moyers, 26 May 1966, NSF, National Security Council History, Box 14, LBJL; The animosity between the two politicians had been exacerbated by the fact that weeks before Kennedy had publicly criticized Johnson's policies in Vietnam. In South Africa, at the University of Cape Town, Robert Kennedy would deliver what the *London Daily Telegraph* referred to as "the most stirring and memorable address ever to come from a foreigner in South Africa." Following his visit to South Africa, Kennedy traveled to Tanzania where he met with Eduardo Mondlane in Dar es Salaam. See Arthur M. Schlesinger, Jr., *Robert Kennedy and his Times*, pp. 743–749.
[109]Interview: Edward Hamilton, 20 February 1984, Los Angeles. In the view of the White House, it had been an extremely delicate process guiding civil rights legislation through Congress. They were concerned that new demands from civil rights activists might upset the political coalition. Some in the White House saw the Africa speech as a way to buy time with these activists and to take pressure off the White House. Interview: Bill Moyers, 25 April 1984, New York City.
[110]*New York Times*, 27 May 1966; "Papers on Presidential Decisions in Foreign Policy," President Johnson's Speech of 26 May 1966 on African Policy, NSF, National Security Council History, Box 14, LBJL.
[111]*New York Times, ibid.*, 27 May 1966.
[112]*New York Times, ibid.*, 27 May 1966.
[113]"Press and Diplomatic Reaction to the President's 26 May Speech on Africa, 7 June 1966, DDRS(80)394C.
[114]Memorandum to Bob Hardestay, et al., from Robert E. Kintner, 28 October 1966, LBJL.
[115]*New York Times*, 27 May 1966. When asked whether Johnson's speech was an explicit criticism of South Africa and Rhodesia, an administration official responded to the *New York Times*, "I would say that the President is not trying to be undisturbing."
[116]Memorandum for the President, from W. W. Rostow, 7 June 1966, LBJL.

[117]Franco Nogueira, *Historia de Portugal, 1933–1974, Vol. 11*, Supplement (Porto: Livraria Civilizaçáo, 1981) pp. 350–351; Interview: Franco Nogueira, 3 July 1983, Lisbon; Interview: W. Tapley Bennett, 1 June 1984, Washington, DC.
[118]To: The Secretary, From: I.R.-Thomas L. Hughes, Subject: Implications of the UK Disengagement from Southern Africa, Intelligence Note, 26 July 1966, DDRS(78)257B.
[119]NATO Ministerial Meeting, Paris, 14–16 December 1966, 3 December 1966, DDRS(78)425A. Interview: Franco Nogueira, 16 June 1983 and 3 July 1983, Lisbon.
[120]Memorandum for Mr. Walt Rostow from Benjamin H. Read, 22 April 1966, NSF, LBJL; *New York Times*, 24 March 1966. According to an interview with Adriano Moreira, 27 September 1983, in Lisbon, to Salazar, it was "half a responsibility," and "irrational," that NATO restricted itself only to the north Atlantic. A properly constituted NATO from Salazar's viewpoint would have included the south Atlantic in its defense area.
[121]William Minter, *Portuguese Africa and the West*, (London: Penguin Books, 1972), pp. 104, 108; Mohamed A. El-Khawas, "US Foreign Policy Towards Angola and Mozambique, 1960–1974," *A Current Bibliography on African Affairs*, *8*, no. 3 (1975), p. 130; Robert A. Diamond and David Foquet, "Portugal and the United States," *Africa Report, 15,* no. 5 (May 1970), p. 17; Lyndon Baines Johnson, *The Vantage Point* pp. 305–306.
[122]Mohamed A. El-Khawas, "U.S. Foreign Policy Towards Angola and Mozambique, 1960–1974." *A Current Bibliography on African Affairs, 8*, no. 3 (1975), p. 190–191.
[123]Barry Munslow, *Mozambique: the Revolution and its Origins* (New York: Longman, 1983), pp. 48, 114–115.
[124]Malyn Newitt, *Portugal in Africa* (London: Longman, 1981), p. 235.
[125]Embtel 12282, Lisbon, 13 May 1966.
[126]Summary Notes of the 572nd NSC Meeting, 13 July 1967, NSC, NSC Meeting File, Vols. 3–5, Box 2, LBJL. Katzenbach was even more pessimistic about Namibia's future. As Katzenbach told the meeting, "There is no solution for the Southwest African problem."
[127]Memorandum for Marvin Watson from Francis M. Bator, 30 May 1967, NSF Name File, Box 1, 2, LBJL.
[128]Hugh Kay, *Salazar and Modern Portugal* (New York: Hawthorne Books, 1970), pp. 415–416.
[129]*New York Times*, 23 February 1967, p. 10; New York Times, 20 November 1968, p. 15.
[130]*New York Times,* 6 October 1968, p. 14.
[131]Untitled official policy study "Portugal," p. 6, Case # NLJ 83–135, (n.d.) LBJL.

[132]Confidential Interview 91 with a White House adviser to the President on Africa.
[133]Barry Munslow, *Mozambique and Its Origins*, pp. 102–113.
[134]Interview: Wayne Fredericks, New York, February 20, 1979.
[135]In a January 1966 interview, Mondlane expressed his frustration by saying that "In view of the attitude of the American government toward my people dying, if I were to continue to admire the United States for its democratic ideals the way I used to, I would have to be judged mentally deranged." "Another 'Vietnam' in Africa?," *War/Peace Report* (January 1966), p. 7.
[136]Munslow, *Mozambique and Its Origins*, p. 111.
[137]John Marcum, *The Angolan Revolution, Vol. II*, pp. 183–186.
[138]*Ibid.*, pp. 191–196.
[139]*New York Times*, 6 January 1968.

Chapter 3: Nixon, Caetano, and Spínola: Partners in Uncertainty

[1]Henry A. Kissinger, *Diplomacy* (New York: Simon and Shuster: 1994), p. 704.
[2]Richard Nixon, *The Memoirs of Richard Nixon, Vol. I* (New York: Warner Books, 1978), p. 425.
[3]Henry A. Kissinger, *Diplomacy*, pp. 707–708.
[4]*Ibid.*, p. 707.
[5]Henry A. Kissinger, *The White House Years* (Boston: Little, Brown and Company, 1979), p. 1136; "News Conference of Dr. Kissinger," Moscow, 29 May 1972, *Department of State Bulletin, 66*, no. 1722, 26 June 1972, p. 885.
[6]Alexander George, *Managing US–Soviet Rivalry: Problems of Crisis Prevention* (Boulder, CO: Westview Press, 1983) pp. 107–110; Interview: Walter Stoessel, 1 June 1984, Washington, DC.
[7]Kissinger, *Diplomacy*, pp. 729–730.
[8]Eric N. Baklanoff, "The Political Economy of Portugal's Old Regime: Growth and Change Preceding the 1974 Revolution," *World Development, Vol. 7*, pp. 799–811; Manuel de Lucena, "The Evolution of Portuguese Corporatism under Salazar and Caetano," in Lawrence S. Graham and Harry Makler, (Eds.), *Contemporary Portugal* (Austin: University of Texas Press, 1979), p. 77.
[9]António de Figueiredo, *Portugal: Fifty Years of Dictatorship* (New York: Holmes and Meier Publishers, Inc., 1975), p. 226–227; Manuel de Lucena, *Portuguese Corporatism,* p. 79; *New York Times*, 22 November 1970.
[10]Kenneth Maxwell, "Portugal: A Neat Revolution," *The New York Review of Books, 21*, no. 10 (13 June 1974), p. 6.
[11]Howard J. Wiarda, "The Corporatist Tradition and the Corporative System in Portugal," in *Contemporary Portugal: The Revolution and Its Antecedents,* edited

by Lawrence S. Graham and Harry M. Makler (Austin: University of Texas, 1979), pp. 106–110.

[12]Richard Robinson, *Contemporary Portugal* (London: George Allen and Unwin, 1979), pp. 168–169.

[13]António de Figueiredo, *Portugal: Fifty Years of Dictatorship*, (New York: Holmes and Meier Publishers, Inc., 1975), p. 225.

[14]Marcello Caetano, *Depoimento*, (Rio de Janeiro: Distribuidora Record, 1974), p. 15.

[15]*Ibid.*, p. 17.

[16]Marcello Caetano, *Portugal Belongs to Us All*, (Lisbon: Secretariat of Information and Tourism, 1970), p. 15.

[17]Marvine Howe, "Portugal at War: Hawks, Doves and Owls," *Africa Report 14*, no. 7 (November 1969), p. 17–18; Interview: Wingate Lloyd, 21 May 1983, Bryn Mawr, PA.

[18]Embtel, Lisbon 2157, 2 October 1969, National Archives, Washington, DC.

[19]Confidential Interview: 95, A senior intelligence official; *New York Times*, 25 September 1975.

[20]Franco Nogueira, *Diálogos Interditos, Vol. II* (Lisbon: Intervencao, 1979), pp. 249–252; Richard D. Mahoney, *JFK: Ordeal in Africa* (New York: Oxford University Press, 1984), p. 243; Confidential Interview: 58 a State Department official.

[21]A-642 from Lisbon, Memorandum of Conversation, Participants: Alberto Franco Nogueira, Richard M. Nixon, William L. Blue, 15 June 1963, found in Mahoney, *JFK: Ordeal in Africa* (New York: Oxford University Press, 1983), p. 237–238.

[22]*New York Times*, 7 April 1957; *Chicago Sun-Times*, 29 March 1957.

[23]Richard Nixon, *The Memoirs of Richard Nixon, Vol. I* (New York: Warner Books, 1978), pp. 349–350.

[24]Roger Morris, *Uncertain Greatness* (New York: Harper and Row, 1977), p. 131; Seymour M. Hersh, *The Price of Power* (New York: Summit Books, 1983), p. 110–111.

[25]National Security Study Memorandum 39, 10 April 1969, DDRS(78)187A; Roger Morris, *Uncertain Greatness* (New York: Harper and Row, 1977), p. 113; Henry Kissinger, *Years of Renewal* (New York: Simon & Schuster, 1999), p. 903.

[26] Roger Morris, *Uncertain Greatness*, p. 81; Anthony Lake, *The "Tar Baby" Option: American Policy Toward Southern Rhodesia* (New York: Columbia University Press, 1976), p. 126; Telephone Interview, Roger Morris, 30 August 1985.

[27]Anthony Lake, *The "Tar Baby" Option: American Policy Toward Southern Rhodesia*, p. 125.

[28]Interview: David Newsom, 21 May 1984, Washington, DC.

[29]"Study in Response to National Security Memorandum 39: Southern Africa," National Security Council, Interdepartmental Group for Africa, AF/NSC-IG, 69-8, Rev. A, 9 December 1969, DDRS(78)187A. This document also lists a sixth option: "increased US measures of coercion, short of armed force, bilaterally and on an international basis, to induce constructive change in white regime policies;" Lake, *The "Tar Baby" Option: American Policy Toward Southern Rhodesia*, p. 128.

[30]Roger Morris, *Uncertain Greatness,* p. 115.

[31]Roger Morris, *Uncertain Greatness*, p. 114–115; Telephone interview: Winston Lord, 3 September 1985.

[32]Donald McHenry, *Background on US Policy*, 16 September 1976.

[33]Telephone interview, Roger Morris, 30 August 1985.

[34]Embtel, Luanda, 16 October 1970.

[35]*Angola: An Assessment of an Insurgency*, 16 September 1970, Bureau of Intelligence and Research, Department of State. FOIA.

[36]To: The Secretary, Through S/S, From: INR-George C. Denney, Jr., Subject: Mozambique: Insurgency Increases in Tete District, 3 October 1969. FOIA.

[37]"Study in Response to National Security Memorandum 39: Southern Africa," National Security Council, Interdepartmental Group for Africa, AF/NSC-IG, 69.8, Rev. A, 9 December 1969, DDRS(78)187A.

[38]Hudson Institute Report, HI-1278-RRI, p. 29.

[39]David Abshire and Michael Samuels (eds.), *Portuguese Africa: A Handbook* (New York: Praeger Publications, 1969), p. 464; Dean Acheson, *Grapes from Thorns*, p. 182.

[40]Telephone Interview: Roger Morris, 30 August 1985; Roger Morris, "*Background on US Policy*, 1969–1970, 16 September 1976.

[41]Memorandum for the President, From Henry A. Kissinger, Subject: Policy Issues Regarding South Africa and the Portuguese Territories, p. 2, 15 January 1970, FOIA.

[42]National Security Decision Memorandum 81, To: The Vice President, et al., Subject: Implementation of the Arms Embargo on South Africa and the Portuguese Territories." Emphasis in the original.

[43]*Diário de Notícias*, 10 June 1969.

[44]US Congress, House Committee on Foreign Affairs, "Policy Toward Africa for the Seventies," Hearings before the Subcommittee on Africa, 91st Congress, 2nd Session, 1970, p. 307; "US Arms Embargo," hearings before the Subcommittee on Africa, 93rd Congress, 1st Session, 1973, p. 145. See Mohammed El-Khawas, "US Foreign Policy towards Portugal and Mozambique, 1960–1974," *A Current Bibliography on African Affairs* 8, no. 3 (1975). US Congress, House Committee on Foreign Affairs, hearings before the

Subcommittee on Africa, "The Complex of United States-Portuguese Relations: Before and After the Coup," 14 March; 8, 9, 22, October 1974, p. 157.
[45]Henry A. Kissinger, *Years of Upheaval*, p. 149.
[46]Interview: Wingate Lloyd, 30 May 1984, Washington, D.C.; Tad Szulc, "Letter from the Azores," *The New Yorker, 47*, no. 46, 1 January 1972, pp. 54–55.
[47]John Marcum, "The Politics of Indifference: Portugal and Africa, A Case Study in American Foreign Policy," *Issue, 11*, no. 3 (Fall 1972), pp. 13–14; See also Basil Davidson, "Nixon Underwrites Portugal's Empire," *The New Statesman 83*, no. 2132 (28 January 1972), p. 103.
[48]*Department of State Bulletin, LXVI*, no. 1699, 1972, pp. 55–56; *New York Times*, 18 December 1971; *New York Times*, 7 February 1972.
[49]Confidential Interviews: 19 and 28, Lisbon. Both interviewees were high-level Portuguese diplomats during this period.
[50]Interview, Wingate Lloyd, 30 May 1984, Washington, D.C.
[51]Kenneth W. Grundy, *Confrontation and Accommodation in Southern Africa*, p. 315–323.
[52]"US Foreign Policy for the 1970s, A Report to the Congress," by Richard M. Nixon, 18 February 1970 (Washington: GPO), p. 89; "The United States and Africa in the Seventies," Policy Statement by William P. Rogers, *Department of State Bulletin, 62*, no. 1608, 20 April 1970, p. 521; *New York Times*, 1 June 1970.
[53]*Yearbook of the United Nations*, 1970, p. 191; "United States Foreign Policy, A Report of the Secretary of State," Department of State Publication 8575, p. 142.
[54]Embtel, 18 January 1971, FOIA.
[55]José Freire Antunes, *Os Americanos e Portugal (Lisbon: Publicações Dom Quixote, 1986)*, p. 137.
[56]"Briefing on the Military Situation in Angola," 16 October 1970, Department of State, FOIA; Angola: An Assessment of the Insurgency, 16 September 1970, Bureau of Intelligence and Research, FOIA; Interview: Major Aniceto Afonso, 11 September 1983, Lisbon.
[57]*Angola: An Assessment of the Insurgency*, 16 September 1970, Bureau of Intelligence and Research, FOIA.
[58]Colonel Sivestre Martins Rodriguez, 5 July 1983, Lisbon.
[59]Paul M. Whitaker, "Arms and the Nationalists," *Africa Report, 15*, no. 5, May 1970, pp. 12–14.
[60]Angola: An Assessment of the Insurgency, 16 September 1970, Bureau of Intelligence and Research, FOIA; Aquino de Braganca, "Savimbi: The Career of a counter-revolutionary," *Mozambican Studies*, no. 2, 1981, p. 90.
[61]Patrick Chabal, *Amílcar Cabral: Revolutionary Leadership and People's War*, (Cambridge: Cambridge University Press, 1983), p. 68; Interview: Tapley Bennett, 1 June 1983, Washington, D.C.
[62]Interview: Donald Easum, New York, 10 April 1984.

[63]Bruce Oudes, "Clark McGregor's Vacation,"*Africa Report, 18*, no. 1 (January–February, 1973), p. 9. *Angola: An Assessment of an Insurgency*, Bureau of Intelligence and Research, 16 September 1970, FOIA; Edgar Lockwood, "National Security Study 39 and the Future of United States Policy to Southern Africa, *Issue, IV,* no. 3 (Fall 1974), p. 66; In Rhodesia, MacGregor publicly mentioned that Nixon might be willing to recognize the Smith regime "in two to four years."

[64]"US Foreign Policy for the 1970s," *A Report to Congress by Richard Nixon, President of the United States*, 3 May 1973 (Washington, DC: GPO), p. 159.

[65]Piero Gleijeses, *Conflicting Mission: Havana, Washington and Africa, 195-1976* (Chapel Hill: The University of North Carolina Press, 2002), p. 210. See also United Nations General Assembly, "Report of the Special Mission Established by the Special Committee at its 840th meeting on 14 March 1972," UN document A/AC.109/L.804, 3 July 1972, p. 19, found in Gleijeses, fn. 128, p. 453. George Bush, American Ambassador to the United Nations, cabled Washington in August 1972 about the findings of the UN delegation that had visited liberated areas of Guinea-Bissau in March–April 1972. He reported that Sevilla-Sacasa, the Nicaraguan leader of the delegation, had found Cabral to be a "formidable opponent," and that the Portuguese inevitably would have to concede the right of self-determination to Guinea-Bissau. USUN 2132, American Mission at the United Nations to Department of State, 6 August 1972, Subject: Security Council Mission to Casamance-Chairman's comments." National Archives, found in Antunes, *Os Americanos e Portugal*, p. 190.

[66]Mário Soares, *Portugal's Struggle for Liberty* (London: George Allen and Unwin, Ltd., 1975 translated by Mary Gawsworth), p. 271; *Le Monde*, 15 June 1970.

[67]According to António de Spínola, although he never met directly with Cabral, the leader of the PAIGC had accepted Spínola's proposal to create a federation of Portuguese states made up of the independent colonies. Spínola also said that Senghor was an important influence for him and that Spínola's notion of "a better Guinea," (or Guiné Melhor), to make colonial rule more "beneficial" in Guinea's cities and towns, had been Senghor's. Interview: António de Spínola, 31 October 1983, Lisbon. Mário António de Oliveira, et al., *A Descolonização Portuguesa, I* (Lisbon: Instituto Democracia e Liberdade, 1979), pp. 244–247; Marcello Caetano, *Depoimento*, pp. 189–192. See also, Patrick Chabal, *Amílcar Cabral: Revolutionary Leadership and People's War*, (Cambridge: Cambridge University Press, 1983), pp. 133–134. Chabal made reference to the "secret negotiations" between Spínola and the PAIGC mediated by President Senghor but contended that the Portuguese had a parallel strategy in development to encourage Cabral's assassination.

[68]Marcello Caetano, *Depoimento*, p. 191.

[69]Silva Cunha, *O Ultramar, a Naçãao e o "25 de Abril,"* (Coimbra: Atlântida Editora, 1977), pp. 51–52.
[70]Richard Robinson, *Contemporary Portugal*, p. 179.
[71]US Congress, House Committee on Foreign Affairs, *Implementation of the US Arms Embargo*, Hearings before the Subcommittee on Africa, 93rd Congress, 1st Session, 1973, pp. 141–143.
[72]Telephone interview: David Newsom, 4 June 1984; *Expresso*, 20 January 1973; Patrick Chabal, *Amílcar Cabral* (Cambridge: Cambridge University Press, 1983), p. 96.
[73]Charles C. Diggs, "We are on the wrong side," *Africa Report* (September–October, 1973), pp. 7–13; Confidential Interview: 26.
[74]Michael Degnan, "The Three Wars of Mozambique," *Africa Report* (September–October, 1973) pp. 7–13; *Expresso*, 21 July 1973, p. 13. The vote in the House of Commons was 299 to 271.
[75]Insight Team: *Insight on Portugal: The Year of the Captains*, (London: Andre Deutsch, 1975), p. 33.
[76]For a copy of the letter see Manuel Barão Da Cunha, *Radiografia Militar* (Lisbon: O Seculo, 1975), pp. xv–xvii. See also Otelo Saraiva de Carvalho, *Alvarado em Abril* (Lisbon: Livraria Bertrand, 1977), pp. 140, 148–149.
[77]Insight team, *Insight on Portugal: The Year of the Captainsl*, p. 38.
[78]Thomas Gallagher, *Portugal: A Twentieth Century Interpretation* (Manchester, England: Manchester University Press, 1983), p. 170; Silva Cunha, *O Ultramar, A Nação e o 25 de Abril*, p. 289.
[79]Richard Robinson, *Contemporary Portugal*, p. 179.
[80]*Expresso*, 2 February 1974; Confidential Interview: 19.
[81]Ministry of Foreign Affairs 433, From the Embassy of Portugal in Washington, Translation Division, 12 October 1973, General Number 13387, found in Jose Freire Antunes, *Os Americanos e Portugal*, p. 252–254. The Tunney-Young amendment was aimed at tightening the loopholes in the exiting legislation that enabled the administration to sell Portugal such "gray area" materials as herbicides and Boeing long-range aircraft.
[82]Ministry of Foreign Affairs 240, From the Embassy of Portugal in Washington, Translation Division, 13 October 1973, general Number 11859, found in Antunes, *Os Americanos e Portugal*, p. 256–258.
[83]Ministry of Foreign Affairs 241, from the Embassy of Portugal in Washington, Translation Division, 13 October 1973, general Number 11879, found in Atunes, *Os Americanos e o Portugal*, p. 256–258.
[84]*Ibid*, p. 257.
[85]Henry A. Kissinger, *Years of Upheaval*, p. 520.
[86]Confidential interviews: 19 and 73.
[87]Henry A. Kissinger, *Years of Upheaval*, p. 792.

[88]Interview: João Hall Themido, September 1983, Lisbon.
[89]Confidential interviews: 28, 75, and 81. See also Henry M. Jackson, *From the Congo to Soweto*, pp. 62–63. Gerald J. Bender, "Kissinger in Angola: Anatomy of a Failure," in Rene Lemarchand, *American Policy in Southern Africa* (Washington, DC: University Press of America, 1978), p. 70–71; and Bruce Oudes, "In the wake of the Middle East War," *Africa Report 19*, no. 1 (January–February 1974), p. 13. See also Piero Gleijeses, Conflicting Missions: Havana, Washington, and Africa, 1959–1976, pp. 230–232. Gleijeses cited a declassified transcript that quoted Kissinger at a 28 January 1974 staff meeting saying that he was "willing to explore the possibility of using 'a plausible third country supplier' for the weapons the Portuguese wanted . . . ."
[90]Leslie Gelb, "Nixon Role in Foreign Policy is Altered; Some Assert Kissinger is Now in Charge," *New York Times*, 23 December 1973, p. 1.
[91]Interview: Wingate Lloyd, 21 May 1983, Bryn Mawr, PA.
[92]Confidential interview: 46.
[93]Caetano, *Depoimento*, p. 196.
[94]Kenneth Maxwell, *New York Review of Books, 21,* no. 10 (13 June 1974), p. 16; Insight Team, *Insight on Portugal: The Year of the Captains*, pp. 25–26.
[95]António de Spínola, *Portugal e o Futuro* (Lisbon: Arcadia, 1974); See also Kenneth Maxwell, "Portugal: A Neat Revolution," *New York Review of Books, 21*, no. 10 (13 June 1974), p. 16; David B. Ottaway, "Revolt Triggered by Book," *Washington Post*, 26 April 1974, p. 12.
[96]*Diário de Notícias*, 15 March 1974.
[97]Avelino Rodrigues, *O Movimento dos Capitães eo 25 de Abril* (Lisbon: Morães Editores, 1975), pp. 90–92; M. Manuela de S. Rama and Carlos Plantier, *Melo Antunes: Tempo De Ser Firme* (Lisbon: Liber, 1976), pp. 143–147; Insight Team, *Insight on Portugal: The Year of the Captains*, pp. 44–45.
[98]*New York Times*, 17 March 1974.
[99]*The Guardian*, 30 March 1974.
[100]"The Complex of United States-Portuguese Relations: Before and After the Coup," Hearings Before the Subcommittee on Africa of the Committee on Foreign Affairs, 93rd Congress, 2nd Session, 14 March; 8, 9, and 22 October 1974 (Washington, DC: GPO), p. 460.
[101]Interview: Stuart Nash Scott, 18 April 1984, New York.
[102]"Portugal: The US Caught Napping," "The Pike Papers: House Select Committee on Intelligence," CIA Report, *The Village Voice*, 16 February 1976, p. 21.
[103]US House of Representatives, Select Committee on Intelligence, "US Intelligence Agencies and Activities: The Performance of the Intelligence Community," Part 2, 11, 12, 18, 25, 30 September and 7, 30, and 31 October 1975 (Washington, DC: GPO), p. 785.

[104]*Ibid.*, p. 787.
[105]Interview: Wingate Lloyd, 30 May 1984, Washington, DC..
[106]Embtel, Lisbon, Flash, 9452, 25 April 1974, FOIA; Deptel 086231, 25 April 1974, FOIA.
[107]*New York Times*, 26 April 1974.
[108]Embtel, Lisbon, 1608, 26 April 1974, FOIA; Embtel, Lisbon, 1636, 27 April 1974, FOIA.
[109]Avelino Rodrigues, *O Movimento dos Capitães e o 25 de Abril*, pp. 19–21.
[110]Lawrence S. Graham, "The Military in Politics: The Politization of the Portuguese Armed Forces," in *Contemporary Portugal* p. 243.
[111]*Expresso*, 15 June 1974; *O Seculo*, 23 May 1975; Henrique Barrilaro Ruas, *A Revolução das Flores*: O Governo de Palma Carlos (Lisbon: Editorial Aster), p. 210.
[112]*Ibid.*
[113]*Expresso*, 1 June 1974.
[114]*A Revoluçãao das Flores: O Governo de Palma Carlos*, p. 223; Interview: Jorge Campinos, 21 September 1983, Lisbon.
[115]Kenneth Maxwell, "The Transition in Portugal," No. 81, Woodrow Wilson International Center for Scholars, p. 2; Alex Macleod, "The French and Italian Communist Parties and the Portuguese Revolution," in *In Search of Modern Portugal*, edited by Lawrence S. Graham and Douglas Wheeler. (Madison: The University of Wisconsin Press, 1983), p. 297=–320.
[116]Henry A. Kissinger, *Years of Renewal*, p. 627.
[117]Interview: Helmut Sonnenfeldt, 6 June 1984, Washington, DC; Telephone Interview: William Kelly, 9 October 1984. *Washington Post*, 19 November 1974.
[118]Interview: António de Spínola, 31 October 1983, Lisbon; Interview: Palma Carlos, 22 September 1983, Lisbon.
[119]Interview: António de Spínola , 31 October 1983, Lisbon; António de Spínola, *País Sem Rumo (Lisbon: Editorial Sicre, 1978)*, p. 1577, 30, and 31163; Tad Szulc, "Lisbon and Washington: Behind the Portuguese Revolution," *Foreign Policy*, 21 (Winter 1975–76), p. 24–25.
[120]Interviews: Wingate Lloyd, 30 May 1984, Washington, D.C.; Interview: Tapley Bennett, 1 June 1984.
[121]Embtel, 2372, 11 June 1974, FOIA.
[122]Interview: Richard Post, 30 May 1984, Washington, DC; Interview: William Kelly, 9 October 1984, Washington, DC.
[123]Interview: Stuart Nash Scott, 18 April 1984, New York City.
[124]Interview: Stuart Nash Scott, 18 April 1984, New York City.

Chapter 4: Kissinger, Carlucci, and Portugal's Revolution

[1]John C. Campbell, "The Mediterranean Crisis," *Foreign Affairs, 53*, no. 4 (July 1975), p. 606; *Washington Post*, 11 November 1975; "Notes on my tour as Ambassador to Portugal," by Stuart Nash Scott, unpublished manuscript, undated, p. 13; Henry Kissinger, *Years of Renewal* (Boston: Little, Brown and Company, 1982), p. 627.
[2]Confidential Interview: 46; Kenneth Maxwell, "The Transition in Portugal," Latin American Program, Working Papers, no. 81, The Wilson Center, Washington, DC, p. 23–24.
[3]Insight Team, *Insight on Portugal* (London: Andre Deutsch Ltd., 1975), p. 168.
[4]For a detailed account of these events see *Insight on Portugal*, pp. 166–178; For Spínola's embittered resignation speech, see António de Spínola, *País Sem Rumo* (Portugal: Scire, 1978), pp. 238–242. Interview: António de Spínola, 31 October 1983, Lisbon.
[5]"Notes on My Tour as Ambassador to Portugal," by Stuart Nash Scott, unpublished manuscript, (n.d.), pp. 17–18.
[6]Interview: Richard St. F. Post, 23 May 1984, Washington, DC; Interview: Admiral George Anderson, 24 May 1984, Washington, DC; Tad Szulc, "Lisbon and Washington: Behind the Portuguese Revolution," *Foreign Policy, 21* (Winter 1975–1976), p. 33–34.
[7]Interview: Michael Samuels, 26 May 1984, Washington, DC; *Washington Post*, 27 November 1974.
[8]Interview: William Kelly, 9 October 1984; Interview: Michael Samuels, 26 May 1984; Telephone Interview: Alan Lukens, 14 June 1984.
[9]Tad Szulc, "Lisbon and Washington: Behind the Portuguese Revolution," *Foreign Policy, 21* (Winter 1975–1976), p. 33–34; In his memoirs, Kissinger would describe his comments to Soares as "not so tactful" but nevertheless reflective of his concern over the Leninist tendencies in the Portuguese government. Henry Kissinger, *Years of Renewal*, p. 630.
[10]Ibid., p. 3, 28.
[11]*New York Times*, 24 February 1964; *Los Angeles Times*, 3 December 1986.
[12]Szulc, Tad Szulc, "Lisbon and Washington: Behind the Portuguese Revolution," *Foreign Policy, 21* (Winter 1975–1976), p. 33–34, p. 34.
[13]*New York Times*, 14 December 1974.
[14]*Washington Post*, 14 December 1974.
[15]Interview: Alan Lukens, 21 May 1984; Interview: William Kelly, 9 October 1984, Washington, DC; Confidential Interview: 35.

[16]Interview: Frank Carlucci, 4 June 1984, Washington, DC; Interview: Herb Okun, 22 May 1984, Washington, DC; Henry Kissinger, *Years of Renewal*, p. 631.

[17]Interview: Frank Carlucci, 4 June 4, Washington, DC.

[18]Department of State, Briefing Memorandum, 6 January 1975, To: The Secretary, From: EUA-Arthur A. Hartman, Your Meeting with Ambassador Frank C. Carlucci, Tuesday, 7 January–4:30 P.M., FOIA.

[19]Jane Kramer, "The Portuguese Revolution," *The New Yorker*, *51*, no. 43, 15 December 1975, p. 62; Thomas Gallagher, *Portugal: A Twentieth Century Interpretation* (Manchester, England: Manchester University Press, 1983), p. 208–209; Douglas Porch, *The Portuguese Armed Forces and the Revolution* (Stanford, CA: Hoover Institution Press, 1977), p. 135; *Expresso*, 18 January 1975, no. 107. The conflict was decided when the MFA accepted a document supporting a single trade union but included provisions that weakened PCP dominance. In his account of the *Intersindical* incident for the *New York Times*, Henry Giniger concluded, perhaps prematurely, that the issue became "a debate over the whole future of Portuguese democracy." *New York Times*, 21 January 1974.

[20]*New York Times*, 2 February 1975.

[21]Confidential Interview: 80; Interview: Frank Carlucci, 4 June 1984, Washington, DC. As an example of the sensitivity of the issue, a meeting of the NATO Nuclear Planning Group which was to have taken place in the second week of November 1974 in Rome, was postponed indefinitely. Because of the rotating membership, this would have been the first meeting of the group in which the Portuguese would have participated since the revolution.. *Washington Post*, 11 November 1974, p. 3. A precedent for handling this type of problem had been established on a previous occasion when Communists joined the Iceland government. In this instance NATO responded in a "low key" manner to avoid exacerbating the problem.

[22]Telephone Interview: William Kelly, 9 October 1984, Washington, DC; Interview: Herbert Okun, 22 May 1984, Washington, DC.

[23]Embtel, Lisbon 00380, 22 January 1975, FOIA.

[24]Embtel, Lisbon 00565, 31 January 1975, "Subject: Consultation on Portugal," FOIA.

[25]Embtel, Lisbon 00698, 5 February 1975, FOIA.

[26]Embtel, Lisbon 01238, 6 March 1975, Subj: Pre-Election Assessment, Section I of 2, FOIA. The issue of "institutionalization" consumed the Armed Forces and the public throughout the winter of 1974–975. It centered on the degree to which the political parties were capable of governing, and the "guiding" role that the MFA should play in the Portuguese political system.

[27]Embtel, Lisbon 00764, 8 February 1975, FOIA.

[28]Embtel, Lisbon 01238, 6 March 1975, Subj: Pre-Election Assessment, Section 1 of 2, FOIA.
[29]Embtel, Lisbon 01238, 6 March 1975, Subj: Pre-Election Assessment, Section 2 of 2, FOIA.
[30]Confidential Interview: 51.
[31]Jane Kramer, "The Portuguese Revolution," *The New Yorker, 51*, no. 43, 15 December, 1975, p. 64.
[32]Embtel, Lisbon 01238, 6 March 1975, Section 2 of 2, FOIA.
[33]Confidential Interview: 81.
[34]"Portugal leans to Non-Alignment," *Christian Science Monitor*, 31 March 1975. Even Francisco Pinto Balsemao, a leader of the PPD, proclaimed that "Third Worldism" was a "realistic means" through which Portugal could "disentangle itself from American and Soviet imperialism"; Embtel, 02106, 8 April 1975, FOIA; As Carlucci commented of those who held this position, "Curiously, they see no conflict between Third Worldism and membership in NATO." Embtel, Lisbon 01631, 22 March 1975, FOIA.
[35]Interview: Vitor Alves, New York, 19 May 1984; *Washington Star-News*, 23 August 1974.
[36]As part of its strategy to prevent this from occurring, the American government announced that it would provide Cape Verde with three million dollars for its agricultural sector and additional loans and grants of two million dollars. This announcement was made three days before Cape Verde became independent on 5 July 1975. "U.S. Provides Assistance to Cape Verde," USAID Press Release, 2 July 1975, *Department of State Bulletin, 73, no. 1885*, 11 August 1975, p. 215.
[37]Embtel, Lisbon 01306, 11 March 1975, Subj: Troop Clash at the Airport, (Sitrep, no. 1), FOIA.
[38]Embtel, Lisbon 01318, 11 March 1975 (Sitrep no. 5), FOIA; Emtel, Lisbon 01323, 11 March 1975, (Sitrep, no. 8), FOIA.
[39]Embtel, Lisbon 01150, 10 March 1975 Section 2 of 2, FOIA.
[40]Embtel, Lisbon 01333, 11 March 1975, Subject: Preliminary Assessment of March 11 Coup Attempt, (Sitrep no. 15), FOIA.
[41]Embtel, Lisbon 01347, 12 March 1975, FOIA.
[42]Embtel, Lisbon 01398, 13 March 1975, Subject: Portuguese Coup: Assessment and Implications, FOIA.
[43]*Ibid.*
[44]Not only had the embassy warned political moderates of coup possibilities from the left, but it had failed to warn them of an actual approach from the Portuguese right. On 30 January 1975, the embassy reported that it had been asked by an individual on the right for assistance in staging a coup. Carlucci reported that the individual was "responsible and competent. Key question is what following he can command hence, what are his chances of success. We will try to find out.

Unless instructed to the contrary, I am directing . . . to tell his contact that US equipment not available . . . next meeting with him scheduled for February 1 at 0930 local." Embtel, Lisbon 00552, 30 January 1975, Subj: Possible Rightist Coup: Request for US Equipment, FOIA.

[45]Embtel, Lisbon 01398, 13 March 1975, Subject: Portuguese Coup: Assessment and Implications, FOIA.

[46]The Supreme Revolutionary Council absorbed all elements of the previous institutions of state that contained military representatives—the Junta, certain military officials, the MFA Coordinating Committee and eight members moniated by the MFA. Insight Team, *Insight on Portugal*, p. 227; Embetl, Lisbon 01422, 14 March 1975, Subj: Coup Aftermath: Political Developments, FOIA; Embtel, Lisbon 01545, 19 March 1975, Subj: Political Roundup, FOIA.

[47]Incarceration of Salazar and Caetano sympathizers began following Spínola's resignation as president in September 1974. By the following March, Otelo de Carvalho said the number of political prisoners being held was 1,331. Journalists put the figure at more than 3000, which exceeded the number ever held at one time by Salazar. *New York Times*, 27 April 1975; Embtel, Lisbon 01470, 17 March 1975, Subj: Political and Electoral Roundup, FOIA.

[48]Embtel, Lisbon 01632, 22 March 1975, FOIA.

[49]Embtel, Lisbon 01631, 22 March 1975, FOIA; Embtel, Lisbon 01632, 22 March 1975, FOIA. Carlucci also noted that PCP leader Cunhal "has repeatedly made it clear" that he would not raise NATO and Lajes issue "at thie time." "Curiously," Carlucci commented, "they see no conflict between Third Worldism and membership in NATO."

[50]*New York Times*, 27 March 1975.

[51]*New York Times*, 27 March 1975.

[52]*The Washington Post*, 10 April 1975. The next day the State Department described the Post's story as a "vicious fabrication." The leak was subsequently attributed to Alan Lukens who was then reassigned from his position as Director of Iberian Affairs to the embassy in Stockholm, Sweden.

[53]Confidential Interviews: 58 and 59.

[54]*The Washington Star*, 24 November 1975; Confidential Interview: 58; As Tad Szulc noted, intelligence ties existed through individuals in the large Portuguese–American community in New England who had familial and numerous other ties in the Azores and metropolitan Portugal. Tad Szulc, "Lisbon and Washington: Behind the Portuguese Revolution," *Foreign Policy*, *21* (Winter 1975–1976), p. 33–34, p. 11.

[55]*The New York Times*, 15 June 1975.

[56]Interview: Frank Carlucci, 4 June 1984, Washington, DC..

[57]*New York Times*, 27 March 1975; *Los Angeles Times*, 9 April 1975.

[58]"Military and Economic Assistance to Portugal," Hearing before the Subcommittee on Foreign Assistance of the Committee on Foreign Relations, US Senate, 95*th* Congress, 25 February 1977 (Washington: GPO, 1977).
[59]Embtel, Lisbon 02067, 11 April 1975, FOIA; Embtel, Lisbon 01984, 7 April 1975, FOIA.
[60]Embtel, Lisbon 02258, 18 April 1975, FOIA.
[61]Embtel, Lisbon 01238, section 2 of 2, 6 March 1975, FOIA.
[62]Embtel, Lisbon 2070, 11 April 1975, FOIA.
[63]Embtel, Lisbon 02203, 17 April 1975, FOIA.
[64]Embtel, Lisbon 02328, 22 April 1975, FOIA.
[65]Embtel, Lisbon 02328, 26 April 1975, FOIA; John L. Hammond, "Electoral Behavior and Political Militancy," edited by Lawrence S. Graham and Harry M. Makler, *Contemporary Portugal: The Revolution and Its Antecedents,* (Austin: University of Texas, 1979), pp. 257–280.
[66]The embassy had predicted the following results: PSP, 32 percent; PPD, 28 percent; PCP, 15 percent; MDP/CDE, 5 percent; PPM, 2 percent; Far Left, 3 percent combined. Embtel, Lisbon 02328, 22 April 1975, FOIA. The final results were: PSP, 37.9 percent; PPD, 26.4 percent; PCP, 12.5 percent; CDS, 7.6 percent; MDP/CDE, 4.1 percent; PPM, 0.6 percent; Far Left, 1.2 percent. Found in Lawrence S. Graham and Douglas L. Wheeler (eds.), *In Search of Modern Portugal*, p. 23.
[67]Confidential Interview: 26.
[68]Rainer Eisfeld, "Outside Influence in the Portuguese Revolution: The Western European Role," paper presented at the III International Meeting on Modern Portugual, University of New Hampshire, 31 May–3 June 1984, p. 6.
[69]Willy Brandt, *People and Politics: The Years 1960–1975*, translated by J. Maxwell Brownjohn (Boston: Little, Brown and Company, 1976), p. 488–490.
[70]*The Washington Post* reported that the Soviet Union was using a shipping concern in Antwerp to transfer funds to the PCP. In early 1975, they sent five million dollars through Belgium to Portugal.
[71]To: George S. Springsteen, From: EUR-Arthur A. Hartman, Subject: Issues Paper on Portugal, 1 May 1975, FOIA.
[72]Interview: Frank Carlucci, 4 June 1984, Washington, DC.
[73]Interview: Frank Carlucci, 4 June 1984, Washington. DC.
[74]*New York Times,* 10 April 1975.
[75]Confidential Interview: 80.
[76]*New York Times*, 18 May 1975.
[77]*New York Times*, 15 June 1975; Interview: Frank Carlucci, 4 June 1984, Washington, DC.

[78]Jonathan Story, "Portugal's Revolution of Carnations: Patterns of Change and Continuity," *International Affairs, 52* (1976), p. 431; *New York Times*, 28 March 1975.
[79]*New York Times*, 25 May 1975. These remarks by Ford did cause considerable concern among those on the center-right who feared that they would be abandoned by the United States and those on the center-left who were working to keep Portugal a part of NATO as opposed to the Communists, who wanted Portugal to withdraw. Interview: Melo Antunes, 14 October 1983, Lisbon.
[80]*New York Times*, 8 June 1975.
[81]*New York Times*, 8 June 1975; Henry Kissinger, *Years of Renewal*, p. 630.
[82]*Los Angeles Times*, 27 May 1975.
[83]*New York Times*, 21 May 1975.
[84]Interview: Melo Antunes, 14 October 1983, Lisbon.
[85]Tad Szulc, "Lisbon and Washington: Behind the Portuguese Revolution," *Foreign Policy* 21 (Winter 1975–976), p. 11–12; *Washington Post*, 9 October 1974.
[86]*Los Angeles Times*, 15 August 1975.
[87]Joan Barth Urban, "Contemporary Soviet Perspectives on Revolution in the West," *Orbis 19*, no. 4, (Winter, 1976), 1373–1374, 1399–1402.
[88]Jane Kramer, "The Portuguese Revolution," *The New Yorker, 51*, no. 43, 15 December 1975, p. 64.
[89]Jane Kramer, "The Portuguese Revolution," *The New Yorker, 51*, no. 43, 15 December 1975, p. 66. Interview: Herbert Okun, 28 April 1984, New York City.
[90]Jane Kramer, "The Portuguese Revolution," *The New Yorker*, 15 December 1975.
[91]Interview: Herbert Okun, 28 April 1984, New York City.
[92]Department of State, Action Memorandum, To: The Secretary, Thru: C-Helmut Sonnenfeldt, From: EUR, James C. Lowenstein, Acting, 21 November 1975 (handwritten), FOIA.
[93]Embtel, Lisbon 6999, (Flash), 25 November 1975, FOIA; Embtel, Lisbon 7015, (Sitrep no. 4), 25 November 1975, FOIA.
[94]Embtel, Lisbon 7022, (Sitrep no.5), 25 November 1975, FOIA.
[95]Embtel, Lisbon 7025 (Sitrep no. 7), 25 November 1975, FOIA.
[96]Embtel, Lisbon 7031 (Sitrep no. 12), 25 November 1975, FOIA.
[97]Embtel, Lisbon 7084, 26 November 1975, FOIA.
[98]Embtel, Lisbon 7104, 28 November 1975, FOIA; Embtel, Lisbon 7133, 29 November 1975, FOIA.

Chapter 5: Angola's Transition to Independence

[1]Colin Legum, "The Soviet Union, China and the West in Southern Africa," *Foreign Affairs, 54*, no. 3 (July 1976), p. 748.
[2]Charles K. Ebinger, "External Intervention in Internal War: The Politics and Diplomacy of the Angolan Civil War," *Orbis, 20* (Fall 1976), p. 680–681.
[3]Kenneth Grundy, *Confrontation and Accommodation in Southern Africa* (Berkeley: University of California Press, 1973), 53–55.
[4]John Marcum, *The Angolan Revolution, Vol. II* (Cambridge: The MIT Press, 1978), p. 230.
[5]Colin Legum, "The Soviet Union, China and the West in Southern Africa," *Foreign Affairs,* p. 748; John Stockwell, *In Search of Enemies* (New York: W. W. Norton and Company, 1978), p. 67. On Savimbi and China, see Fred Bridgland, *Jonas Savimbi: A Key to Africa* (New York: Paragon House Publishers, 1987), pp. 65–66.
[6]*Tass*, 24 January 1973, found in Bruce D. Porter, *The USSR in Third World Conflicts*(Cambridge: Cambridge University Press, 1984), p. 156; Anatoly Dobrynin, *In Confidence* (New York: Times Books, 1995), p. 362; Arkady N. Shevchenko, *Breaking with Moscow* (New York: Alfred A. Knopf, 1985), p. 271; Odd Arne Westad, "Moscow and the Angolan Crisis, 1974–1976: A New Pattern of Intervention," *Cold War International History Project*, nos. 8–9, Woodrow Wilson International Center for Scholars, Washington, DC, Winter, 1996/1997, p. 22.
[7]Henry Kissinger, *Years of Upheaval* (Boston: Little, Brown and Company, 1982), p. 982.
[8]*Ibid.*, p. 985; Henry Kissinger, *Diplomacy* (New York: Simon and Shuster: 1994), p. 751.
[9]Henry Kissinger, *Diplomacy*, p. 757.
[10]William G. Hyland, *Mortal Rivals: Superpower Relations from Nixon to Reagan* (New York: Random House, 1987), pp. 132–133.
[11]António de Spínola, *Píis Sem Rumo* (Lisbon: Editorial Scire, 1978), p. 161.
[12]*Ibid.*
[13]Interview: António de Spínola, 31 October 1983, Lisbon.
[14]John Marcum, *The Angolan Revolution, Vol. II*, pp. 250–251; 24 July 1974, Lisbon 0081, FOIA; 13 August 1974, Lisbon 03454, FOIA.
[15]John Marcum, "Lessons from Angola," *Foreign Affairs, 54*, no. 3 (April 1976), p. 412.
[16]Interview: Steve McDonald, 21 August 1991, Washington, DC.; Interview: Donald Easum, 10 April 1984, New York; Henry Kissinger, *Years of Renewal*, pp. 799–801.

[17]Interviews: Donald Easum, 10 April 1984, New York City; Interview: William DuPree, 8 June 1975, Washington, DC; Bruce Oudes, "The United States' Year in Africa: Postscript to the Nixon Years," in *Africa Contemporary Record,* edited by Colin Legum (New York: Africana Publishing Company, 1976), p. A123; Piero Gleijses, *Conflicting Missions: Havana, Washington, and Africa, 1959–1976* (Chapel Hill: University of North Carolina Press, 2002), pp. 230–232.
[18]Interview: Donald Easum, 10 April 1984, New York City ; Bruce Oudes, "The Sacking of the Secretary," *Africa Report, 20,* no. 1 (January–February 1975), p. 17; Kissinger, *Years of Renewal*, p. 801.
[19]Interview: Donald Easum, 26 April 1984, New York City; John A. Marcum, "Southern Africa After the Collapse of Portuguese Rule," in *Africa: From Mystery to Maze, Critical Choices for Americans, Vol. XI,* edited by Helen Kitchen (Lexington, Massachusetts: Lexington Books, 1976), p. 81.
[20]Embtel Kinshasa 6611, 30 July 1974, FOIA.
[21]Embtel, Lisbon 03454, 13 August 1974, FOIA.
[22]Fred Bridgland, *Jonas Savimbi: A Key to Africa* (New York: Paragon House Publishers, 1987), p. 112–114; Colin Legum, *Africa Contemporary Record, 1975–76*, pp. A6–A8.
[23]Embtel Lisbon 175, 13 January 1975, FOIA.
[24]Embtel, Luanda 0048, 16 January 1975, FOIA.
[25]*Ibid.*
[26]Embtel, Lisbon 271, 16 January 1975, FOIA.
[27]Intelligence Note, Bureau of Intelligence and Research, 23 January 1975, "The Angola Agreement," FOIA.
[28]Embtel, Luanda 0058, 17 January 1975, FOIA.
[29]Embtel, Luanda 00062, 17 January 1975; See also John Marcum, *The Angolan Revolution, Vol. II,* pp. 255–256.
[30]The Portuguese military reported to the American Consulate in Luanda that the FNLA had a force of 21,000, the MPLA under Agostinho Neto had 10,000, and UNITA had 8,700. Embtel, Luanda 0050, 16 January 1975, FOIA. For an excellent analysis of the military balance of forces in Angola during this period, see William G. Thom, "Angola's 1975–76 Civil War: A Militray Analysis," *Low Intensity Conflict and Law Enforcement,* 7, no. 2 (Autumn 1998), pp. 1–44.
[31]Intelligence Note, Bureau of Intelligence and Research, 23 January 1975, "The Angola Agreement," FOIA.
[32]Coutinho deepened these suspicions when he told the Belgian weekly, *Le Soir*, on 9 May 1975 that Holden Roberto was "an agent of international imperialism," and flatly declared that his sentiments were with the MPLA, which he considered to be the most "progressive" and representative of all nationalist organizations; Embtel, Brussels 4136, 9 May 1975, FOIA; Killoran obliquely referred to this in a cable in which he commented that criticism in Angola has been "directed at the

Admiral for his supposed favoritism toward one group or another;" (Embtel, Luanda 0048, 16 January 1975). Piero Gleijeses, on the other hand, argued that Portugal's help to the MPLA was minimal. See, Piero Gleijses, *Conflicting Missions: Havana, Washington, and Africa, 1959–1976* (Chapel Hill: University of North Carolina Press, 2002), p. 272, and William Thom, "Angola's 1975–76 Civil War," *Low Intensity Conflict and Law Enforcement, 7,* no. 2, (Autumn 1998), pp. 1–44.

[33]"Intelligence Note," Bureau of Intelligence and Research, "The Angola Agreement," 23 January 1975, FOIA. See also William Minter, *Operation Timber: Pages from the Savimbi Diary*, (Trenton, New Jersey: Africa World Press, 1988). In July 1974, the Paris-based journal *Afrique-Asie* published four documents that purported to be letters between Savimbi and the Portuguese military and that proved that at least since the early 1970s, Savimbi had been an "agent" of the Portuguese. *Afrique-Asie,* no. 61, 8 July 1974. See Bridgland, *Jonas Savimbi: A Key to Africa*, pp. 105–107; As Bridgland concluded, "Some degree of Portuguese-UNITA collaboration against the MPLA cannot be ruled out." More recently, the South African historian, W. S. Van Der Waals, noted that "it is obvious," as confirmed by the South African vice consul in Luanda, that "a special relationship did exist between UNITA and the Portuguese." W. S. Van Der Waals, *Portugal's War in Angola, 1961–1974*, (Rivonia, South Africa: Ashanti Publishing, 1993), pp. 174–175. See also Piero Gleijeses, *Conflicting Missions: Havana, Washington, and Africa, 1959–1976*, pp. 240–241.

[34]Embtel, State 020882, 29 January 1975.

[35]Embtel, Luanda 893, 18 October 1974, FOIA; See also Odd Arne Westad, "Moscow and the Angolan Crisis, 1974–1976: A New Pattern of Intervention," *Cold War International History Project*, nos. 8–9, Woodrow Wilson International Center for Scholars, Washington, DC, Winter, 1996/1997, p. 24.

[36]Interview: Edward Mulcahy, Washington, DC, 24 May 1984.

[37]Interview: Edward Mulcahy, May 24, 1984, Washington, DC.; *The Washington Post*, 6 January 1976. Bruce Oudes; "The United States Year in Africa: Postcript to the Nixon Years," in *Africa Contemporary Record,* edited by Colin Legum (New York: Africana Publishing Company, 1976), p. A124; Interview: Walter Cutler, 11 June 1997, Washington, DC.

[38]Bruce Oudes, "The United States Year in Africa.," in *Africa Contemporary Record*, p. A123.

[39]Colin Legum and Tony Hodges, *After Angola: The War Over Southern Africa* (London: Rex Collings, 1976), p. 47; Interviews: Edward Mulcahy, 24 May 1984, Washington, DC; Interview: Jack Foley, 7 June 1984, Washington, DC; Confidential Interview: 95.

[40]Embtel, Luanda 887, 16 October 1974, FOIA. Killoran would report a month later that the reporting in *A Provincia* had become "so slanted as to be painfully embarrassing." Embtel Luanda 0321, 25 March 1975.
[41]"Assessment of the Angolan Situation," To: The Secretary, Through: P-Mr. Sisco, From: INR-William G. Hyland, AF-Edward Mulcahy, 25 February 1975, FOIA; Embtel, Luanda 0326, 27 March 1975, FOIA.
[42]Interview: Edward Mulcahy, 24 May 1984, Washington, DC; Gerald J. Bender, "Kissinger in Angola: Aanatomy of a Failure," in *American Policy in Southern Africa*, edited by Rene Lemarchand (Washington, DC: University Press of America, 1981), p. 73; US Congress, Senate, Committee on Foreign Relations, Subcommittee on African Affairs, *Hearings on Angola* (Washington, DC, GPO, 1976), p. 193, found in Alexander George, Managing U.S.-Soviet Rivalry: Problems of Crisis Prevention (Boulder: Westview Press, 1983), p. 203.
[43]William G. Hyland, *Soviet-American Relations: A New Cold War?* (1981), p. 43.
[44]Embtel, Lisbon 01782, 18 March 1975, FOIA.
[45]"Angola," To: The Secretary, Through: P-Mr. Sisco. From: AF-Nathaniel Davis, INR-William G. Hyland, S/P-Winston Lord, 4 April 1975, FOIA. The appointment of Nathaniel Davis to replace Easum was controversial in Africa. Davis had no African experience and, more importantly to his critics, had been ambassador to Chile at the time of the CIA-backed coup against Salvador Allende. The OAU Council of Ministers passed a resolution in which it "noted with concern" Davis' appointment as assistant secretary of state for Africa. Roger Morris, "A Rare Resignation in Protest: Nat Davis and Angola," *The Washington Monthly, 7*, no. 12 (February 1976), p. 26; Bruce Oudes, "Kissinger confronts Africa," *Africa Report, 20*, no. 2 (March–April 1975), pp. 45–46.
[46]Embtel, Luanda 0699, 16 May 1975. Killoran had been approached by a UNITA representative for arms several weeks before.
[47]"Jonas Savimbi," To: The Secertary, Through: P-Mr. Sisco, From: AF-Nathaniel Davis, 1 May 1975, FOIA; Nathaniel Davis, "The Angola Decision of 1975: A Personal Memoir," *Foreign Affairs*, *57*, no.1 (Fall 1978), p. 111; Interview: Walter Cutler, 11 June 1997, Washington, DC.
[48]Henry Kissinger, *Years of Renewal*, p. 801.
[49]Interview: Edward Mulcahy, 24 May 1984, Washington, DC; Interview: Helmut Sonnenfeldt, 16 June 1984, Washington, DC.
[50]Untitled document, in section entitled, "Effect of MPLA Victory," June 1975, FOIA. In his memoirs, Kissinger wrote, "The issue, in short, was not the intrinsic importance of Angola, but the implications for Soviet foreign policy and longer-term East-West policies." Henry Kissinger, *Years of Renewal*, pp. 797, 810.

[51]Colin Legum, "Foreign Intervention in Angola," *Africa Contemporary Record, 1975–1976*, (London: Rex Collings, 1976), p. A7. Stockwell, *In Search of Enemies*, p.44. Kissinger, *Years of Renewal*, p. 791.

[52]"Options on Angola," To: The Secretary, Through: P-Mr. Sisco, From: AF-Edward W. Mulcahy, Acting, 12 May 1975, FOIA; Kissinger, *Years of Renewal*, p. 803.

[53]"US Visit of Jonas Savimbi," To: The Secretary, Through: P-Mr. Sisco, From, AF-Edward W. Mulcahy, Acting, 16 May 1975, FOIA.

[54]Nathaniel Davis, "The Angola Decision of 1975: A Personal Memoir," *Foreign Affairs, 57*, no. 1 (Fall 1978) p. 111; Interview: Jack Foley, 7 June 1984, Washington, DC; Alexander George, *Managing U.S.-Soviet Rivalry: Problems of Crisis Prevention* (Boulder: Westview Press, 1983, p. 207; Piero Gleijeses, *Conflicting Missions: Havana, Washington, and Africa, 1959–1976*, p. 286.

[55]Embtel, Kinshasa 85278, 25 June 1975.

[56]Memorandum to: Under Secretary Sisco, From: AF-Nathaniel Davis, RE: Angola, 12 July 1975, FOIA.

[57]William Hyland, *Soviet-American Relations: A New Cold War?* (1981), pp. 31–32.

[58]John Stockwell, *In Search of Enemies*, p. 54; Kissinger, *Years of Renewal*, p. 808; Piero Gleijeses, *Conflicting Missions: Havana, Washington, and Africa, 1959–1976*, pp. 292-293.

[59]US Congress, Senate, Committee on Foreign Relations, Subcommittee on African Affairs, *Hearing on Angola* (Washington, DC: GPO, 1976), p. 52.

[60]John Stockwell, *In Search of Enemies*, p. 135.

[61]Chester A. Crocker, *High Noon in Southern Africa: Making Peace in a Rough Neighborhood* (New York: W. W. Norton, 1992), pp. 48–49.

[62]For a comprehensive and insightful account of the Cuban role in the Angolan civil war, see Piero Gleijeses, *Conflicting Missions: Havana, Washington, and Africa, 1959–1976*, especially chapters 14–15.

[63]State, 180337 3 July 1975, FOIA.

[64]To: The Secretary, Through: P-Mr. Sisco, From: AF-Edward W. Mulcahy, RE: "Angola," 19 August 1975, FOIA; Memorandum For: AF-Mr. Mulcahy, Subject: Angola, 21 August 1975, FOIA; John Stockwell, *In Search of Enemies*, p. 165.

[65]Interview: Pik Botha, Pretoria, South Africa, 7 March 1997. On this critical point, Kissinger wrote: "South Africa had opted for intervention without prior consultation with the United states. We learned of it no later than the CIA report of October 31, and local CIA personnel may well have known about it earlier." *Years of Renewal*, p. 820; See also Gleijeses, *Conflicting Missions*, pp. 294–299, for a detailed analysis of US-South African interaction on the decision to intervene in Angola.

[66]John Stockwell, *In Search of Enemies*, p. 163–165.

[67]Colin Legum, "Foreign Intervention in Angola," *Africa Contemporary Record*, (London: Rex Collings, 1976), p. A15.
[68]Deptel, FM SecState, WASHDC 265162, 8 November 1975, FOIA.
[69]Colin Legum, "Foreign Intervention in Angola," *Africa Contemporary Record*, p. A 7.
[70]*Ibid.*, p. A23.
[71]Deptel, State, 277367, 22 November 1975, FOIA.
[72]Deptel, State 292791, to USDEL Secretary NIACT Immediate, 15 December 1975, FOIA. When Garba and Kissinger met for the first time in late January 1976, Garba said to Kissinger, "You have a good man in Lagos," referring to Easum. Ever critical of Easum, the Secretary shot back, "Good for whom, you or us?" Joseph Garba, *Diplomatic Soldiering: Nigerian Foreign Policy, 1975–1979 (Ibadan, Nigeria: Spectrum Books, 1987)*, p. 28.
[73]Deptel, State 286319, 4 December 1975, FOIA.
[74]Embtel, Lagos 11986, 3 December 1975, FOIA.
[75]Deptel, Washington 292619, 11 December 1975, FOIA.
[76]Walter Isaacson, *Kissinger: A Biography* (New York: Simon and Shuster, 1992), pp. 682–683.
[77]Daniel Patrick Moynihan, *A Dangerous Place* (Boston: Little, Brown and Company, 1978), pp. 248–251; Deptel, State 292619, 11 December 1975, FOIA.
[78]Deptel, State 302573, 24 December 1975, FOIA.
[79]*New York Times*, 8 January 1976; *New York Times*, 9 January 1976.
[80]The governor of California, Ronald Reagan, who was positioning himself to challenge Ford for the Republican presidential nomination, was very critical of the President. In New Hampshire, on 12 January 1976, Ronald Reagan said, "It's time to straighten up and eyeball it with Russia, and the time to start is in Angola." *Newsweek*, 19 January 1976.
[81]Interview: Pik Botha, Pretoria, South Africa, 7 March 1997; Gerald R. Ford, *A Time to Heal* (New York: Harper and Row, 1979), p. 355; Kissinger, *Years of Renewal*, p. 826.
[82]Deptel, State 299944, Subject: Angola: Holding the Line, December 20, 1975.
[83]Deptel, State 302573, December 24, 1975; *Financial Times* (London), December 24, 1975; William G. Thom, op. cit., p. 34.
[84]Embtel, Kinshasa 10976, 24 December 1975. In December 1975, the Ford Administration requested Gulf to suspend its operations in Cabinda and put the $125 million in taxes and royalties it owed the Angolan government into escrow. The payments were released on 9 March 1976 and Gulf resumed operations in Cabinda a month later. See Gleijeses, *Conflicting Missions* p. 312, 343.
[85]Anatoly Dobrynin, *In Confidence* (New York: Times Book, 1992), p. 361. Following the meeting Ford and Kissinger departed on a two-week trip to Asia. The day after they left Indonesia, that country invaded the small neighboring

nation of East Timor, another colony recently freed by the Portuguese that was being threatened by left-wing rebels. According to Walter Isaacson, Kissinger and Ford knew of the plans by the Indonesian government and gave their tacit approval for the rebellion on Timor to be suppressed using American-supplied weapons—in contravention of American law. Walter Isaacson, *Kissinger*, p. 680.

[86]To: The Secretary, Through: C-Mr. Sonnenfeldt, From: AF-Edward W. Mulcahy, Acting, "Angola: A Soviet Overture?" 14 December 1975, FOIA.

[87]To: The Secretary, Through: P. Mr. Sisco, C-Mr. Sonnenfeldt, From: AF-William E. Schaufele, Jr., "Soviet Note on Angola of 18 December," 19 December 1975, FOIA.

[88]Dobrynin, *In Confidence*, pp 362–363.

[89]Gerald R. Ford, *A Time to Heal* (New York: Harper & Row Publishers, 1979), p. 345.

[90]*Los Angeles Times*, 6 January 1976.

[91]Gerald R. Ford, *A Time to Heal*, p. 346; *Los Angeles Times*, 28 January 1976.

[92]Henry Kissinger, *Years of Renewal*, p. 825.

[93]Piero Gleijeses, *Conflicting Missions*, p. 358.

Chapter 6: Conclusion

[1]*National Security Policy* (S/P, Draft, 26 March 1962) DDRS(77)338A. Emphasis in original.

[2]Warren Cohen, *Dean Rusk* (Towtowa, New Jersey: Cooper Square Publishers, 1980) p. 111.

[3]Witney W. Schneidman, "Conflict Resolution in Mozambique," in *Making War and Making Peace: Foreign Intervention in Africa*, edited by David R. Smock (Washington, DC: United States Institute of Peace, 1993) p. 219.

[4]Paul Hare, *Angola's Last Best Chance for Peace* (Washington, DC: United States Institute of Peace, 1998) pp. 35–36.

৷ Acknowledgments

I owe tremendous gratitude and appreciation to many people who made this book possible.

Jim Humphrey, of Ladner, British Columbia and I traveled after graduating from high school, not only in East Africa but through India, Pakistan, Afghanistan, Iran, and Turkey, forging a friendship I have valued greatly ever since. Ed Hawley, editor of *Africa Today*, was my first professor of African Studies at the University of Denver and encouraged me to pursue an independent study of the transition to independence of Kenya, Tanzania, and Uganda, and the liberation movements of Angola, Mozambique, and Guinea-Bissau. He also introduced me to George Houser of the American Committee on Africa and pointed me toward the University of Dar es Salaam. At Temple University, Professor L. D. Reddick was an extraordinary teacher of African-American history and the American experience.

At the University of Dar es Salaam, Yash Tandon, Ibrahim Mahiga, and Nathan Shamuyarira guided my course of study, especially my master's thesis on FRELIMO's foreign policy as a liberation movement. While in Dar es Salaam, I encountered for the first time Ambassador Don McHenry, who has since become a most valued friend.

Following the completion of a masters degree in Dar es Salaam, I lived in New York City and worked with *Southern Africa Magazine*, edited by Jennifer Davis and Stephanie Urdang. At this time, George Houser put me in touch with Herb Shore, who was assembling an archive on the life of FRELIMO's first president, Eduardo Mondlane, one of Africa's great leaders whose life was cut short by the Portuguese secret police. In the course of this work I began an enduring friendship with Wayne Fredericks, who understood the significance of African nationalism and was the true architect of US policy in the Kennedy Administration during the critical years of Africa's transition to independence.

The work on the Mondlane Archive took me to Los Angeles, California where I enrolled at UCLA and had the good fortune to study under Richard Sklar, an Africanist of great intellect and integrity. I then transferred to the School of International Relations at the University of Southern California and studied under the tutelage of Professor Jerry Bender, to whom I owe a significant debt of gratitude. Jerry Bender not only was committee chair for my doctoral dissertation, *American Foreign Policy Towards Portugal, Angola, and Mozambique, 1961–1976*, but he also gave new definition to the concept of a mentor. Indeed, his commitment to Africa, his honesty of judgment, and his keen insight into many issues beyond Africa has formed the basis for a most unique and valuable friendship. This book, including the cover, which he and Tammy Bender helped to develop, would not have been possible without his constant support and commentary.

I am appreciative to the Calouste Gulbenkian Foundation, which provided a grant that enabled me to live in Lisbon for half a year. The research from that period shaped a vital aspect of this manuscript. I would also like to thank the Lyndon Baines Johnson Foundation for a grant to conduct research at the Johnson Presidential Library. The staff at the Kennedy Presidential Library was also most helpful to my research.

Following the completion of my Ph.D., I was offered a job as the South African analyst in the State Department's Bureau of Intelligence and Research by Martin Lowenkopf, then director of the Office of African Analysis. Under his guidance, and with the supervision of the late Joan Seasword and Dick Ristano, I was exposed to a level of analysis and writing I am still trying to match. Also during that period, I benefited from watching closely Chester Crocker and his team in the Africa Bureau, led by his principal deputy, Chas Freeman, and then Jeffrey Davidow, conclude the negotiations that led to the withdrawal of Cuba's military force from Angola thus setting the stage for Namibia's independence.

For nearly a decade the manuscript lay dormant until I received a telephone call from Piero Glejesies, a Professor of American Foreign policy at the School of Advanced International Studies, Johns Hopkins University. Professor Glejesies had read my dissertation in the course of his own unsurpassed research on Cuba's role in Angola's civil war. I am most grateful to him for reawakening my desire to transform my academic thesis into a study of American diplomatic history. The extraordinary and pioneering work of John Marcum, as well as his encouragement, was also an invaluable source on which to build.

In bringing this book this book to life I would like to thank several others who have provided essential support, friendship, and not the least, accommodations, along the way. This includes Ronald Steel, Harold and Roberta Schneidman, Becky and Woo Toland, Rich King, Louise Richardson, David Anderson, Tad Daley, Shawn McCormick, and Jim Rosenau. Without the lifelong friendship of Jane Lea and Joe Atterbury, this book would not have been written. Rick Ehrenreich, Terry Lyons, Paul Hare, Charlie Perkins, José Freire Antunes, Ken Maxwell, Don McHenry, Jerry Bender, Dick Mahoney, Michele Peters, and Mike Samuels read parts or all of this manuscript. Frank Carlucci, who during the Portuguese revolution set a standard for the conduct of American diplomacy, not only read the entire manuscript but graciously wrote the Foreword. Marcy Thorner, the Grammar Guru, not only edited the manuscript with great skill and an equal measure of patience and good humor, but made it camera ready as well. Ambassador Nicholas Veliotes and Judy Rothman of the University Press of America played a significant role in the publication of this book.

To all, I would like to say thank you, while also recognizing that any mistakes in this book are solely my own.

This diplomatic history is based principally on declassified documents obtained from the Kennedy and Johnson Presidential Libraries, the National Archives, the Declassified Documents Reference System, and through the Freedom of Information Act. The interviews that I conducted were intended to add perspective to information obtained from the declassified documents and secondary sources. In certain instances, the individuals whom I interviewed requested anonymity while conveying specific information. A list of all of the interviews that I conducted is provided in the appendix.

In important aspects, this book has benefited from my own experience in government, where I served as Deputy Assistant Secretary of State for African affairs in the Clinton administration. For that, I would like to thank my colleagues Susan Rice, Johnnie Carson, Howard Jeter, Nancy Powell, Gayle Smith, Joe Wilson, John Prendegast, Nora Dempsey, Cathy Byrne, and Sandy Thurman for working to make the relationship between process and policy so substantive and meaningful. I would also like to acknowledge the two US ambassadors to Angola, Don Steinberg and Joe Sullivan, with whom I worked closely and most productively.

Throughout the long life of this project, and many trips to Africa, I have had the unstinting love and support of my wife Priscilla and our two wonderful children, Sam and Ellie. My mother, Peggy Tilghman, has been unwavering in her support of my interests in Africa and, at every turn, I have been inspired by the memory of my father, Milton Schneidman. To them, I give my deepest and most heartfelt gratitude.

About the Author

Witney W. Schneidman is president of Schneidman & Associates International, an Africa-focused trade and investment consulting firm in Washington, D.C. Prior to starting his company, he served as Deputy Assistant Secretary of State for African affairs in the Clinton administration. His professional career has been largely centered on Africa, where he has worked with several other consulting firms and the World Bank. Dr. Schneidman received his B.A. from Temple University, his master's degree from the University of Dar es Salaam in Tanzania, and his Ph.D. from the School of International Relations at the University of Southern California. He lives in Alexandria, Virginia with his wife and two children.

Index